# Arthurian Narrative in the Latin Tradition

Arthurian literature is a popular field, but most of the published work focuses on the vernacular tradition. This book, uniquely, looks at Latin Arthurian works. Geoffrey of Monmouth is treated at length and this is the first book to put him in a context which includes other Latin histories, monastic chronicles, saints' lives, and other Latin prose Arthurian narratives. Like Geoffrey's works, most can be associated with the Angevin court of Henry II and by placing these works against the court background, this book both introduces a new set of texts into the Arthurian canon and suggests a way to understand their place in that tradition. The unfamiliar works are summarized for the reader, and there are extensive quotations, with translations, throughout. The result is a thorough exploration of Latin Arthurian narrative in the foundational period for the Arthurian tradition.

SIÂN ECHARD is Assistant Professor in the Department of English at the University of British Columbia. She is author, with Claire Fanger, of *The Latin Verses in the "Confessio Amantis": An Annotated Translation* (1991).

# CAMBRIDGE STUDIES IN MEDIEVAL LITERATURE

*General editor*
Alastair Minnis *University of York*

*Editorial board*
Patrick Boyde, *University of Cambridge*
John Burrow, *University of Bristol*
Rita Copeland, *University of Minnesota*
Alan Deyermond, *University of London*
Peter Dronke, *University of Cambridge*
Nigel Palmer, *University of Oxford*
Winthrop Wetherbee, *Cornell University*

This series of critical books seeks to cover the whole area of literature written in the major medieval languages – the main European vernaculars, and medieval Latin and Greek – during the period c. 1100–1500. Its chief aim is to publish and stimulate fresh scholarship and criticism on medieval literature, special emphasis being placed on understanding major works of poetry, prose, and drama in relation to the contemporary culture and learning which fostered them.

A complete list of titles in the series can be found at the back of the book

# Arthurian Narrative
# in the Latin Tradition

SIÂN ECHARD

PUBLISHED BY THE PRESS SYNDICATE OF THE UNIVERSITY OF CAMBRIDGE
The Pitt Building, Trumpington Street, Cambridge CB2 1RP, United Kingdom

CAMBRIDGE UNIVERSITY PRESS
The Edinburgh Building, Cambridge CB2 2RU, United Kingdom
40 West 20th Street, New York, NY10011–4211, USA
10 Stamford Road, Oakleigh, Melbourne 3166, Australia

© Siân Echard 1998

First published 1998

Printed in the United Kingdom at the University Press, Cambridge

Typeset in Garamond 11/13pt {CE}

*A catalogue record for this book is available from the British Library*

*Library of Congress cataloguing in publication data*
Echard, Siân.
Arthurian narrative in the Latin tradition / Siân Echard.
p.   cm. (Cambridge studies in medieval literature; 36)
Includes bibliographical references and index.
ISBN 0 521 62126 7 hardback
1. Latin literature, Medieval and modern – Great Britain – History and criticism.
2. Romances, Latin (Medieval and modern) – History and criticism.
3. Geoffrey, of Monmouth, Bishop of St. Asaph, 1100?–1154. Historia
regum Britanniae.   4. Arthurian romances – History and criticism.
5. Great Britain – History – Henry II, 1154–1189.
6. Britons – Historiography.   7. Narration (Rhetoric).
8. Rhetoric, Medieval.   9. Twelfth century.
I. Title.   II. Series.
PA8045.G7E25   1998
870.9′351–dc21   97–42206   CIP

ISBN 0 521 62126 7 hardback

FOR MY PARENTS

# Contents

# Acknowledgments

My first thanks must go to A.G. Rigg and David Klausner; while they may scarcely recognize the result, this project began when they introduced me to Latin romance. A.G. Rigg, David Townsend, and Claire Fanger have offered constant help with thorny Latin questions and Gernot Wieland meticulously checked the entire manuscript; needless to say, any errors of translation that remain are my own. Friends and colleagues at the University of British Columbia have graciously endured the effects of years of revision: Judy Segal and Patricia Badir have been particularly stalwart. Thanks also to Alastair Minnis for his support from the first, and to Kate Brett and then Victoria Sellar for seeing the project through to the end. Finally and always, heartfelt thanks to Eric, Patrick, and Catherine, for their stoic acceptance of the demands made by this cuckoo in our nest.

# Note on translations

All translations of Latin, French, Welsh, and German texts are my own, with two exceptions; I have followed D.W. Robertson Jr.'s familiar translation of Augustine's *On Christian Doctrine*, and I have quoted Winthrop Wetherbee's splendid new translation of the *Architrenius*.

# Introduction: Latin Arthurian narrative
# and the Angevin court

The *Queste del Saint Graal* ends with an account of its own redaction:
the romance has been drawn from records in the library at Salisbury
by "Master Walter Map," working "for the love of King Henry, his
lord."[1] *La Mort le Roi Artu* later repeats the attribution:

> After Master Walter Map had put down in writing what seemed
> enough to him about the *Adventures of the Holy Grail*, his lord
> King Henry was of the opinion that what he had done would not
> suffice, were he not to recount the end of those of whom he had
> made mention before, and how those whose prowess he had
> mentioned in his book had died. And for this reason he began this
> last part.[2]

Although these attributions are not taken at face value today, they
form a useful point of departure for this study of Latin Arthurian
narrative. While Map did not write these vernacular romances, it is
nevertheless probable that someone *like* him did. The attributions
contain in germ all the important material for this study. The
supposed author of a seminal vernacular cycle of Arthurian romance
is figured to be a Latinate courtier-cleric, university educated, and a

---

[1] *La Queste del Saint Graal*, ed. Albert Pauphilet (Paris: Champion, 1949), pp. 279–80:

> Et quant Boorz ot contees les aventures del Seint Graal telles come il les avoit veues,
> si furent mises en escrit et gardees en l'almiere de Salebieres, dont Mestre Gautier
> Map les trest a fere son livre del Seint Graal por l'amor del roi Henri son seignor, qui
> fist l'estoire translater de latin en françois.

> And when Bors had recounted the adventures of the Holy Grail just as he had seen
> them, they were set down in writing and kept in the library at Salisbury, whence
> Master Walter Map drew them out in order to make his book of the Holy Grail, for
> the love of King Henry, his lord, who had the story translated from Latin into
> French.

[2] *La Mort le Roi Artu*, ed. Jean Frappier (Geneva: Droz, 1954), p. 1:

> Aprés ce que mestres Gautiers Map ot mis en escrit des *Aventures del Seint Graal*
> assez soufisanment si com li sembloit, si fu avis au roi Henri son seigeur que ce qu'il
> avoit fet ne devoit pas soufire, s'il ne ramentevoit la fin de ceus dont il avoit fet devant
> mention et conment cil morurent dont il avoit ameteües les proesces en son livre; et
> por ce commença il ceste derrienne partie.

member of the circle of Henry II, the Angevin king widely praised as *litteratus*. Map's lord is the patron credited with the impulse for the creation ("translation") of the work. Even though it is probably spurious, the attribution is in another sense perfect. By placing romance in the Angevin court and more particularly in the hands of the courtier who is also archdeacon of Oxford, it matches much of what we know or imagine about literary activity, vernacular and Latin, in the twelfth century.

This study is more narrowly concerned with the relatively few examples of Arthurian narrative in Latin rather than in the vernacular. Several of the writers discussed are anonymous, but enough of them can be identified to allow us to speak with some confidence about their backgrounds and preoccupations. The roster of names includes Geoffrey of Monmouth, Gerald of Wales, Etienne de Rouen, Johannes de Hauvilla, Andreas Capellanus, and Walter Map himself. Robert of Torigny, tentatively suggested in chapters 4 and 5 as the author of the two most complete Latin Arthurian narratives which survive, is like these men in many ways. In each case, we are dealing with an educated cleric,[3] and in most, that cleric is associated in some way with the most glittering court of the day, that of Henry II. These men are writers of chronicle history, satire both religious and political, political theory, legal works, travelogues, anecdotes, and conduct-books. They are figures of the twelfth-century renaissance, participating in that literary explosion in the context of the courts. Historians speak of the spirit of the twelfth century as one of renewal, of new interest in the intellectual and creative powers of humankind:

> . . . we must regard the renaissance as the totality of that culture: its
> restless searching after ancient – and new – authorities; its tireless
> quest for new knowledge, and its insistence on restructuring knowl-
> edge new and old alike; its astonishing creativity in the arts and
> literature; its profoundly innovative spirituality, balanced in part by

---

[3] Geoffrey of Monmouth is recorded as *magister* and clearly spent time at Oxford. Gerald of Wales studied in Paris, eventually lecturing on canon law; by 1184 he had become a royal clerk. Johannes de Hauvilla was a *magister* at the cathedral school at Rouen, and his link to the court may be seen in the flattering comments he makes about Walter of Coutances, a royal clerk about to become archbishop of Rouen. Walter Map, another *magister*, studied at Paris and was a royal clerk from the 1170s. Etienne de Rouen's background is less clear; we do know that at Bec he had a rich library from which to draw his models and citations. Andreas Capellanus is conventionally associated with the court of Marie de Champagne, daughter of Eleanor of Aquitaine; his clerical connections are clear enough, but there is doubt about the depth of his learning. William of Rennes is largely unknown to us, although the form of his work suggests a classicizing habit; his work is dedicated to an ecclesiastical patron.

its occasional secularity, sometimes earnest and sometimes laughing; its sense of renewal, reform, rebirth; its freshly positive assessment of nature, man, and the world; its heightened consciousness of the self and of society, of past and future . . . [4]

Nowhere are these features of the renaissance seen more clearly than in the realm of creative literature. The vernacular explosion of writing about Arthur in the twelfth and thirteenth centuries is in many ways the direct result of the work of one of the courtier-clerics on whom this study focuses. Geoffrey of Monmouth's *Historia regum Britannie* may not be the very first Arthurian narrative, but it is clearly one of the most influential. The vernacular romance tradition, too, originates with writers such as Chrétien de Troyes and Gottfried von Strassburg, also men of the sort just described.[5]

The role of Latin writers in the production of vernacular romance is variously explained. For C. Stephen Jaeger, the courtly romance is the pedagogic tool by which the courtier civilizes the warrior,[6] while for Michael Clanchy the schoolmen were also the pioneers of writing in the vernaculars because "the basic training of the schools was in the use of language, and the techniques learned there could be applied from Latin to the more difficult task of creating styles for writing vernaculars. Often perhaps it was the most sophisticated and not the most primitive authors who experimented with vernaculars."[7] Yet the schoolmen seem to have partitioned their literary activities, so that, with the notable exception of Geoffrey, one finds relatively little *Latin* Arthurian material. While Latin chroniclers do follow Geoffrey in adding Arthur to their accounts, the process of creative adaptation and metamorphosis from chronicle towards romance is left to vernacular translator-adaptors like Wace. The initial impulse for this book, then, lay in a perceived gap, in a scarcity of texts rather than a wealth of them.

---

[4] Robert L. Benson and Giles Constable, eds., *Renaissance and Renewal in the Twelfth Century* (Oxford: Clarendon Press, 1982), p. xxx.

[5] Notable exceptions are Hartmann von Aue and Wolfram von Eschenbach, but Joachim Bumke argues that Hartmann's self-definition as a knight who could read would be pointless were these attributes not unusual; *Courtly Culture: Literature and Society in the High Middle Ages*, trans. Thomas Dunlap (Berkeley: University of California Press, 1991), pp. 493–94.

[6] "The architects of chivalry were clerics functioning in their capacity as educators; their most effective pedagogic instrument was the courtly romance"; C. Stephen Jaeger, *The Origins of Courtliness: Civilizing Trends and the Formation of Courtly Ideals 939–1210* (Philadelphia: University of Pennsylvania Press, 1985), p. 213. Later Jaeger remarks that courtly romance is the creation exclusively of clerical authors, p. 233.

[7] M.T. Clanchy, *From Memory to Written Record: England 1066–1307*, 2nd edn. (Oxford: Blackwell, 1993), p. 215.

I soon discovered, however, that while it is true that the number of connected, extensive Latin narratives about Arthur can be counted on the fingers of one hand, the picture becomes considerably more complex when one examines episodes embedded in chronicle responses and the appearances of Arthurian episodes or motifs in narratives whose primary thrust is not Arthurian. Furthermore, while it is true that the vast majority of the material to be examined here can be dated to the twelfth century, Latin Arthurian narrative continues to make sporadic appearances well into the fourteenth. There is more material than one might originally have thought, then, but it remains true that while the birth of Arthurian narrative, the explosion of writing in the twelfth century, and the characteristics of courtly production, have all been well examined, the confluence of these features in the texts in this study remains largely neglected.

The chapters which follow aim to remedy this situation. Here I wish to sketch out some necessary background for the understanding of the texts to follow. Most of the works in this study are Angevin and, even more narrowly, British texts, and they need to be understood against their own particular cultural backdrop. By placing these texts in the context of the courts of the twelfth century, I hope to create a framework which will have explanatory force even for those few of my texts which fall outside these geographical and temporal boundaries. Latin Arthurian narratives, I argue, share more than simply a common language and a common subject, and their shared themes and methods have their genesis in the cultural world of the Angevin empire.

## THE ANGEVIN COURT

The union of Eleanor of Aquitaine with Henry II is seen by Reto Bezzola as uniting the two most vital centers in Europe of literary, spiritual, and artistic activity.[8] Egbert Türk describes the result when he says that "To the political and material power of the English court, then, corresponded an intellectual explosion without parallel in Europe, and one would have to wait until the end of the Middle Ages before another prince would be able to assemble around himself a group of men as astonishing as that which Henry II succeeded in

[8] Reto Bezzola, *Les Origines et la formation de la littérature courtoise en occident (500–1200): Troisième partie: La société courtoise: Littérature de cour et littérature courtoise* (Paris: Champion, 1963), p. 2.

assembling."[9] These comments are borne out by the astonishing amount of writing produced by this court, but they also tend to gloss over one of the most difficult problems in discussing this phenomenon. Where, exactly, was this "court?" Who were the courtiers? What did it mean to be a courtier? It is notoriously difficult to determine who was actually "at" court at any given time, and the whole notion of the court as a place is itself problematic. In the most general sense, a court consists of a lord and his household, but when the lord is the king of a collection of lands such as those which made up what we now call the Angevin empire,[10] then the household in question divides into several groups: the king himself and his closest *familiares*, who travel with this most peripatetic of rulers; the households of the great lords, clerical and lay, who have the king's ear; and the administrative machinery, the increasingly specialized officers, clerks, and scribes who are most likely to remain at Westminster. Richard Mortimer summarizes this potentially confusing situation: "The king's moving household, with the people it met in the places it travelled through, constituted the royal court. It may seem difficult to reconcile the centre of literary and intellectual patronage of some historians with the dry administrative machine of others, and to fit them both into this unfamiliar world of packhorses and muddy roads."[11] The Angevin court, in other words, is neither fixed nor single. Nevertheless, historians are willing to describe some of the qualities of the court and of the man who made it. We begin, then, with the king.

The Angevin empire was "a highly personal entity, owing much to the personality of its ruler."[12] With Henry II's political and dynastic ambitions and accomplishments we will have little to do, although certain specific moments in Angevin rule are reflected in the texts to follow: Henry's Breton campaign clearly in the *Draco Normannicus*,

---

[9] Egbert Türk, *Nugae curialium: Le règne d'Henri II Plantagenêt (1145–1189) et l'éthique politique* (Geneva: Droz, 1977), pp. xvii–xviii: "A la puissance politique et matérielle de la cour anglaise correspondait donc un rayonnement intellectuel sans pareil en Europe et il faudra attendre la fin du moyen âge avant qu'un autre prince rassemble un groupe d'hommes aussi étonnant que celui qu'Henri II avait réussi à rassembler."

[10] The term is an anachronism; W.L. Warren points out that there were separate administrations for each of the main provinces of Henry II's domains (England, Normandy, greater Anjou, Brittany, and Aquitaine), and that "so far as the 'empire' can be said to have had any unity at all, it was a unity which rested solely in Henry's peripatetic court and household"; *Henry II* (London: Eyre Methuen, 1973), p. 229.

[11] Richard Mortimer, *Angevin England 1154–1228* (Oxford: Blackwell, 1994), p. 21.

[12] Mortimer, *Angevin England*, p. 6.

and perhaps the forest laws and the protest they engendered, in the *Historia Meriadoci*. But for now, we are concerned with court writers and thus with Henry chiefly in his role as the inspiration for some of that writing. Henry's part in the actual commissioning of literary works is unclear.[13] Eleanor, too, is frequently the dedicatee of literary works – in her case usually in the vernacular – but her degree of involvement also remains a matter of dispute, as does the very existence of the famous, or infamous, courts of love said to have been held by Eleanor and her daughter Marie. Yet whether Henry master-minded them or not, it is clear that certain literary documents contributed to the support of Angevin ambitions,[14] suggesting at least a pragmatic reason for the Angevins to cultivate literate men at court. In addition, we can speak with some confidence about Henry's own education and about his tastes. John of Salisbury made literacy a requirement for a good ruler:

> From these things it is clear that it is necessary for princes, who are commanded to reflect daily in their reading upon the law of God, to be skilled in letters . . . since an illiterate king is like a crowned ass . . . If nevertheless, through a dispensation by the merit of excellent virtue a prince should happen to be illiterate, it is necessary for him to get the counsel of literate persons, so that matters might proceed properly.[15]

The Angevins appear to have met this requirement. From the time of Henry I (nicknamed Beauclerk), Angevin rulers were trained in Latin, the only kind of literacy indicated by that term in the twelfth century and later.[16] As Clanchy has pointed out, the ubiquity of the pairings *illiteratus/ laicus* and *litteratus/ clericus* may mislead us as to the actual level of literacy, vernacular and Latin, in lay society. Upper-class boys

---

[13] Mortimer argues that passages naming the king or queen are not evidence of patronage, and adds that there is no work which can be securely thought to have been commissioned by Eleanor and Henry; Wace, commissioned by Henry to write the *Roman de Rou*, he regards as an exception; *Angevin England*, pp. 212–13. Nevertheless the Angevin courts were fertile ground for literary activity, and it is this literary atmosphere which I am studying.

[14] Türk, *Nugae curialium*, argues that for Henry, letters were part of his policy of reinforcing the monarchy, p. xvii.

[15] John of Salisbury, *Policraticus*, in *Joannis Saresberiensis Opera Omnia*, ed. J.-P. Migne, *Patrologia Latina* 199 (1855), IV.6:

> Ex quibus liquido constat, quam necessaria sit principibus peritia litterarum, qui legem Domini quotidie revolvere lectione jubentur . . . quia rex illitteratus est quasi asinus coronatus. Si tamen ex dispensatione ob egregiae virtutis meritum, principem contingat esse illitteratum, eumdem agi litteratorum consiliis, ut ei res recte procedat, necesse est.

[16] Clanchy, *From Memory to Written Record*, p. 235.

had both knightly and clerical masters, and "Though boys were destined for careers at an early age, they did not begin to specialize in knightly or clerical education until the middle to late teens, by which time they had acquired a range of skills including in many cases basic literacy. Hence there were both literate laymen and hunting and fighting clerics."[17] The situation is no different for the very top of the social pyramid. Henry II's education, like that of other aristocrats, would not have been the same as that of the university men he increasingly favored as part of his circle, but it could well have been delivered by them. John of Salisbury was closely associated with Henry for some years, and Thomas Becket was tutor to the Young King. Peter of Blois's famous remark, that there was school every day for the king of England,[18] may reflect a real taste as well as a courtier's flattery. Walter Map's description of Henry suggests an acceptable level of competence, if not of specifically literary focus: ". . . he was *litteratus* as far as was suitable and useful, and he knew every language from the French sea to the Jordan, although he made use of only Latin and French. He was careful and wise in the making of laws and in every aspect of governing, and he was a subtle maker of judgments in difficult cases . . ."[19] The stress on Henry's involvement in the making of law and rules for governing is important in suggesting just how much Latin would be "suitable and useful." Henry's interactions with his household and their (shifting) duties, as well as with the documentary side of his growing bureaucracy, would of necessity impose a high level of accomplishment. Clanchy suggests that Henry relished the tests to which the increasingly documentary character of Angevin administration put his skills. Henry

> showed his mastery of written instruments in a series of judgements concerning the charters of the abbeys of St Albans in 1155, Battle in 1157 and 1175, and Bury St Edmunds in 1187. He evidently enjoyed presiding over legal wrangles between abbots and bishops in his court, as it gave him an opportunity to scrutinize their

---

[17] Clanchy, *From Memory to Written Record*, p. 195.

[18] Quoted in Clanchy, *From Memory to Written Record*; Clanchy explains that this remark refers to "a circle of learned schoolmen discussing questiones as they did at Paris or Oxford," p. 235.

[19] Walter Map, *De nugis curialium*, ed. and trans. M.R. James, rev. C.N.L. Brooke and R.A.B. Mynors (Oxford: Clarendon Press, 1983), V.vi: ". . . litteratus ad omnem decenciam et utilitatem, linguarum omnium que sunt a mari Gallico usque ad Iordanem habens scienciam, Latina tantum utens et Gallica. In legibus constituendis et omni regimine corrigendo discretus, inusitati occulte iudicii subtilis inuentor . . ."

charters and demonstrate that he was their master in intellect and legal wisdom as well as in material power.[20]

As the word becomes a tool – and a weapon – of policy, it becomes increasingly appropriate and necessary that the king be able to wield it.

Henry II is the center of a highly personal realm, but the texts to be examined here do not seem so much generated *for* him as *around* him. It is not necessary to enter the argument about the degree of direct literary patronage at the courts of Henry and Eleanor to recognize that these Latin texts would have as their most probable audience the most Latinate part of the court, those courtier-clerics with whom Henry increasingly surrounded himself. From the king, then, we move to consider his household: who they were, where they came from, and how they spent their time.

Just how large was the circle around the king? Bumke's general description of the courtly audience suggests it is unlikely that there would be more than twenty to twenty-five people who "could have participated continuously in the literary life at the courts";[21] in considering the courts of Henry II we must both expand and contract that number. The number of the *familiares*, those closest to the king, might be as small as twelve,[22] but there are several thousand names which appear on the Pipe Rolls for the thirty-five years of Henry's administration.[23] The discrepancy reflects both the difficulty of assessing the status of those called *curiales* and the turnover in the king's immediate circle. But the king's circle alone is not "the court"; many royal clerks were in fact attached to the entourages of the *familiares*. It is difficult to decide how much involvement a person designated *curialis* actually had with any of these courts; people like Map and Gerald appear to have had long-term associations, while others seem to have spent only a short time at court. The status of an individual outside the immediate world of the court may provide some clues as to his status within that world, because positions such

---

[20] Clanchy, *From Memory to Written Record*, p. 235.

[21] Bumke, *Courtly Culture*, p. 508.

[22] Ralph Turner, *Men Raised from the Dust: Administrative Service and Upward Mobility in Angevin England* (Philadelphia: University of Pennsylvania Press, 1988), p. 14. The term is a difficult one to understand, as Warren admits: "*Familiares* is a word which defies adequate translation: a familiares [*sic*] was an intimate, a familiar resident or visitor in the household, a member of the *familia*, that wider family which embraces servants, confidants, and close associates"; *Henry II*, pp. 204–5.

[23] Discussed in Türk, *Nugae curialium*, pp. 6–7.

as Map's archdeaconry or Gerald's bishopric are generally seen as rewards to valued servants of the king. Perhaps we may begin with the social origins of those servants.

It is a notable peculiarity of the Angevin administration that it made considerably more use of *magistri*, university-educated clerics, than did other European administrations. Even though France produced many of the men who worked at Henry's courts, both in England and on the continent, the Angevin kings used more French-educated scholars than did French rulers. John Baldwin's study of the employment of *magistri* in English and French administration in the twelfth and thirteenth centuries offers some statistics. Royal charters suggest that the Angevin king was frequently in the company of two or three masters; a high proportion of both episcopal administrators and canons are also recorded as masters.[24] The concentration of schoolmen at the court of Henry II seems to increase as the years of his reign go by. In his study of Angevin kingship, J.E.A. Jolliffe suggests that this increase was related to the king's growing maturity:

> As Henry's mind developed in the experience of his civil reign the preoccupations of his middle years began to diversify his Court and enrich it with the rising men of the clerical administrations and the law. From about the seventies – before then by exception – the king's clerks, the justices, the civilian members of the Household offices, begin to bulk larger in Exchequer Roll and Charter.[25]

If the preceding discussion about Henry's education and tastes is correct, it may be the case that he simply enjoyed, more and more, having around him people who could test his intellectual mettle. It is also true that the increasingly complex administration of the Angevin lands required a large number of literate men to run it. The specialization of the thirteenth century is still to come; in the time of Henry II, much of the governing is in the hands of the members of the king's household, along with *their* households.[26] Turner traces the change in

---

[24] John W. Baldwin, "*Studium et regnum*: The Penetration of University Personnel into French and English Administration at the Turn of the Twelfth and Thirteenth Centuries," *Revue des Etudes Islamiques* 44 (1976), 205–9. The masters in the king's company include Walter of Coutances, Roscelin, and Richard Marsh (205). Among thirteen English sees sampled, all but one have between four and eight masters in their administration, and while from 1180–1223 only 19 percent of the canons of Laon are masters, in the same period in London the figure is 46 percent and in York, also 46 percent (207–9).

[25] J.E.A. Jolliffe, *Angevin Kingship* (London: Adam and Charles Black, 1955), p. 144.

[26] ". . . much of the government must have consisted of the households of its leading members"; Mortimer, *Angevin England*, p. 71. Turner, too, notes that for both the men who accompanied Henry and those who remained at Westminster, there were few specific duties;

the social composition of Henry's household to the growth of administration:

> The magnates were more likely to offer their monarch the older feudal virtues of loyalty to sworn lord, good counsel, and military prowess than they were proficiency with letters and numbers. More and more, the kings required intimates who were numerate and literate, masters of skills needed for administration ... By Henry II's early years, secular government was becoming a subject for reasoned analysis ... Recent works by several scholars assert the significance of this connection between reason, learning, and a new ministerial class.[27]

Turner goes on to argue that, despite the complaints of court writers about men of the lower orders rising to (undeserved) influence at court, the Angevin administrators came from the lower or middle levels of the knightly class,[28] a social origin which I believe may help to explain the role of Latin writers in the creation of Arthurian narrative. A route to career advancement for such men would be a stint at Paris or Bologna, followed by attachment to the household of one of the king's close advisors.[29]

The growing bureaucracy may well have extended both opportunities and Latin literacy further down the social scale than we might imagine. Clanchy argues that "It is possible that the great majority of clerks and accountants, however lowly their occupations and abilities may seem when viewed through twentieth-century eyes, were trained at universities."[30] This group of men constitutes a new class, and the fact that its particular skills are those of the word points the way to rich new developments in literature as well as in government. In the

---

"the only meaningful definition of *curialis*, then, depends upon one's relations with the king, one's presence at court" (*Men Raised from the Dust*, p. 14).

[27] Turner, *Men Raised from the Dust*, p. 9.

[28] Turner, *Men Raised from the Dust*, p. 2.

[29] So significant were the qualifications that such study conferred that "Ambitious men aped the style of Bologna even when they lacked its substance"; M.T. Clanchy, "*Moderni* in Education and Government in England," *Speculum* 50 (1975), 683.

[30] Clanchy, "*Moderni* in Education and Government," 685. Mortimer is cautious, however, about the appearance of literacy among administrators, arguing that many of the so-called *magistri* were not masters in the technical sense of the term; *Angevin England*, p. 74. Baldwin notes that the title "was used by any cleric who was granted the right to teach ... by the ecclesiastical authority of the region" ("*Studium et regnum*," 201); while it is possible that such assessments varied in rigor, the considerable prestige associated with the title, also noted by Baldwin, suggests to me that the temptation to misrepresentation might be offset by the eagerness of others to check the status of a marker of such potential value. And as Clanchy (681) points out, Nigel Wireker's *Speculum Stultorum* satirizes the employment of schoolmen in administration; such satire would presumably have reflected a real situation.

twelfth century, Winthrop Wetherbee writes, "The intellectual had emerged as a social type, a professional class increasingly defined by its role in a secular society, alert to the opportunities for advancement that education made possible, and possessed of the artistic skill to express its new social awareness in a range of new literary forms."[31] Nowhere is this type of writer and this range of material more evident than at the court of Henry II.

## WRITING AT COURT: AUTHORS, AUDIENCES, AND THEMES

Joachim Bumke begins his massive study of courtly culture with an assertion of the intimate link between literary and historical circumstances:

> The architectural layout of the Hohenstaufen castles and palaces, with the great hall as the center of social life, created the setting that allowed the representative forms of court life to unfold in grand style. Literature also benefited from this development, since it was in the great halls that the poets reached their audience . . . Only the establishment of separate chanceries at the court of the secular princes at the end of the twelfth century created a written administration on a regular basis, and this guaranteed the poets stable work. These are only a few examples of the link between literary and social culture . . . [32]

Bumke's stress here on the aristocratic serves best to situate vernacular courtly texts, but his focus on the formative role of court culture in the literary discourse of the period is central to my subject too. Jaeger's vision of court culture is one in which literate statesmen set about deliberately transforming the values of the ruling and warrior classes; the courtly romance is the vehicle for a "transference of values" which "crested in the great vernacular literature of France and Germany in the twelfth and early thirteenth centuries."[33] The Latin Arthurian narratives to be studied here are positioned precisely on the axis of that transference; on the one hand they show many of the characteristics which mark Latin writing at court in this period; on the other, they begin, and in some cases complete, the movement of those concerns from the realms of historical, political, and satirical

---

[31] *Johannes de Hauvilla: Architrenius*, ed. and trans. Winthrop Wetherbee (Cambridge: Cambridge University Press, 1994), p. x.
[32] Bumke, *Courtly Culture*, pp. 16–17.
[33] Jaeger, *The Origins of Courtliness*, p. 14.

writing into the realm of imaginative fiction. To understand the beginnings of that movement toward the vernacular Arthurian tradition in both Latin and the vernacular, we must examine the characteristics of the Latin court culture which planted its seeds.

It is tempting to characterize the court (particularly for a study placed chronologically and geographically as this one is) through the proliferation of satire, which is one of the most characteristic features of court writing in the twelfth century. John of Salisbury, Peter of Blois, Gerald of Wales, Nigel Wireker, and Map himself all criticize life at the Angevin court, even as some of them at least live it.[34] Frequent complaints are that the court is chaotic, that its intrigues distract one from the pursuit of real philosophy, that courtiers are liars and flatterers, that those worthy of advancement, whether because of skills or because of noble birth, are shoved aside by ambitious upstarts. Map may have praised Henry II, but he seems to have thought little of his court:

> If, with reference to the court, we may say what Boethius most truly asserted about Fortune, it is indeed true, that the court is stable only in its instability. The court pleases only those who obtain her grace. For she does give grace: she does not, indeed, love the lovable or those worthy of being loved, but rather she gives her grace to those who are unfit to live. Indeed, this is a grace which comes without reason, which alights without desert, which presents itself to the ignoble for hidden reasons . . . Cupidity, the lady of the court, exhorts us with so many prickings, that laughter is erased by care.[35]

---

[34] Bumke calls John of Salisbury the founder of the tradition of court criticism; *Courtly Culture*, p. 415. John is another courtier-cleric: educated at Paris, he entered the service of Archbishop Theobald of Canterbury in 1147 as secretary, and thenceforth had much to do with the court of Henry II: "John seems to have been a member of a small circle of learned bureaucrats whose members included Thomas Becket . . . It was this circle of like-minded men that constituted the immediate audience for much of John's writing"; Cary J. Nederman, ed., *Policraticus. Of the Frivolities of Courtiers and the Footprints of Philosophers* (Cambridge: Cambridge University Press, 1990), p. xvi. Important documents of court criticism include John's *Policraticus*, Peter of Blois's *Epistle 14*, Johannes de Hauvilla's *Architrenius*, and Nigel Wireker's *Tractatus contra curiales et officiales clericos*.

[35] *De nugis curialium*, I.i:
> Si quod Boecius de fortuna ueraciter asserit de curia dixerimus, recte quidem et hoc, ut sola sit mobilitate stabilis. Solis illis curia placet qui graciam eius consecuntur. Nam et ipsa gracias dat: non enim amabiles aut merentes amari diligit, sed indignos uita gracia sua donat. Hec est enim gracia que sine racione uenit, que sine merito considet, que causis occultis adest ignobili . . . Tot nos hortatur aculeis dominatrix curie cupiditatis, quod pre sollicitudine risus eliminatur.

For John of Salisbury, if Cupidity is the lady of the court, then flattery is her product and the court's chief vice:

> The flatterer is inimical to every virtue, and like a mote in the eye he fixes himself with his words to the one with whom he entwines himself. And he is the more to be avoided, because he does not hesitate to harm under the appearance of love, until he blunts the keenness of reason and extinguishes the modicum of light which seems to be present . . . This plague [of flatterers] has increased to the extent that, despite God's indignation, if it should happen that there should be a conflict, I fear that good and modest men would be more easily expelled than able to expel.[36]

Jaeger argues that to take the familiar motifs here epitomized by Map and John merely as literary *topoi* is to miss what they have to tell us about the reality of court culture. The values and ideals of the court are here "treated from a negative perspective," but "writers do not polemicize against literary fictions or conventional ideal schemata."[37] Thus, he writes, there is an underlying "reality" to court life, a situation which can be described positively as well as negatively. We may follow Jaeger's lead by seeing, for example, that the granting of favors to the unworthy is the underside of the court's role as source of support and prestige. Perhaps most relevant for a discussion of the literary products of the court are the aspects of verbal behavior reflected negatively in the accusations against flatterers. Flattery is a particular kind of lying, deceptive speech; but there is another kind of speech, equally artificial perhaps, also associated with courtly behavior. Jaeger reviews the Latin vocabulary of courtesy, a vocabulary which appeared in court literature from the early Middle Ages, and isolates certain qualities, among them *urbanitas* and *decorum*. Urbane, civilized behavior includes a mode of speech in which jesting (*jocus*) and wit (*facetia*) are prized.[38] To these characteristics of court speech

---

[36] *Policraticus*, III.iv, III.vi:

    Adulator enim omnis virtutis inimicus est, et quasi clavum figit in oculo illius, cum quo sermonem conserit, eoque magis cavendus est, quo sub amantis specie, nocere non desinit, donec rationis obtundat acumen, et modicum id luminis, quod adesse videbatur, exstinguat.

    Haec tamen pestis, jam in tantum, Domino indignante, invaluit, ut si ventum forte fuerit ad conflictum, vereor ne modestos et bonos viros possint facilius expellere, quam expelli.

[37] Jaeger, *The Origins of Courtliness*, p. 55.

[38] Jaeger, *The Origins of Courtliness*, pp. 115–17. The ultimate source for these concepts, Jaeger argues, is Cicero's *De officiis*: it was a school text in the Middle Ages, and St. Ambrose adapted it in his own *De officiis ministrorum ecclesiae*. Both texts were widely available in cathedral and monastic schools (pp. 118–19).

I would link the growth in the use of the term *modernus* in the twelfth century, and the consistent linking of *modernitas* with *subtilitas*.[39] The term *modernus* was often used to characterize those schoolmen who challenged the *status quo* in the schools. Clanchy draws a distinction between these "new" men and their approach to Latin and the older, purely religious *litterati*:

> . . . this new Latin was associated not so much with the monks and prelates who had been the transmitters of the Romano-Christian heritage, as with the secular *moderni* of the schools. The schoolmen, the 'masters' of Paris and Bologna and then of Oxford, were a novel phenomenon of the twelfth century. Latin was their primary language, whether they were lawyers, academics, or royal officials. They were responsible for ensuring that Latin could cope with the new demands made on it by the schools, city communes, religious orders, and royal lordships which took shape in the twelfth century and produced documents in unprecedented numbers.[40]

While Clanchy is dealing with the creation of Latin as the language of business and government, the "new" Latin of the new men may also be understood in the context of courtiers and their speech. Map defends his modernity against what he characterizes as an unreasonable prejudice for the past: "My only crime is that I live; nevertheless, I do not plan to correct this situation with my death . . . Every age has disliked its own modernity, and every age, from the first, has preferred its past to itself."[41] Johannes de Hauvilla sounds a similar note: "Accept the fact that modern times have produced me, and do not, because you have seen the author, value the book more lightly or deny it whatever honor it may deserve."[42] John of Salisbury's *Metalogicon*, on the other hand, attacked the new masters while also praising the difficulty of ancient writers: in the ancients, one finds *subtilitas* with substance. Subtlety, whether positively presented as the conscious ambiguity of the ancients or more negatively as the pretense

---

[39] Clanchy discusses the linking of *modernitas* with *subtilitas* in "*Moderni* in Education and Government"; see in particular his comments on John of Salisbury, 675, and on the mistrust for *subtilitas* when associated with the new men, 677–78.

[40] Clanchy, *From Memory to Written Record*, p. 215.

[41] *De nugis curialium*, IV.v: "Hoc solum deliqui, quod uiuo. Verumptamen hoc morte mea corrigere consilium non habeo . . . Omnibus seculis sua displicuit modernitas, et queuis etas a prima preteritam sibi pretulit . . ."

[42] *Architrenius*, I.3. The translation is Wetherbee's, p. 9.
Sustineas quod me dederint hec tempora nec, si
Videris auctorem, precio leviore libellum
Argue nec, si quem meruit, deperdat honorem. (78–80)

to learning without the substance, was associated with the new men. And these men, as we have seen, inhabited the courts as well as the schools, moving in a realm where irony becomes a dominant mode of speech.

*Jocus, facetia, subtilitas*: these approaches to speech at court offer the courtier a way of delivering a potentially unpalatable truth in relative safety. Jaeger argues that "Jesting was one form of legitimized criticism, of telling the truth to the ruler without offending him."[43] It is necessarily ironic in the broadest sense of saying one thing while meaning another. Walter Map, for his part, suggests that there is more to his *nugae* than meets the eye. He concludes his romance of *Sadius and Galo* in this way:

> Perhaps this story will seem foolish and frivolous, but only to the foolish and frivolous, to whom we offer nothing; there may be a word about such people when the time is right, but not to such people. We spend what we can do and what we know on the good-hearted and the clever [*argutis*], knowing that the exemplary bee tastes wormwood and thyme in order to bring together into the treasure-house of wisdom the honeycomb from bitter and sweet, from these frivolous things . . . [44]

John of Salisbury allows that there might be occasions when a true philosopher might wish to refresh himself with frivolities: "I do not judge it to be inappropriate for the wise man to engage in sensual pleasure now and then, if indeed moderation is displayed . . . not so that the practice of virtue may fade, but rather so that it may flourish and he may be somewhat revived."[45] Thus far John's distinction appears to be between the proper work of the philosopher and his necessary recreation, but elsewhere John seems to echo Map in the suggestion that narrative, even fictional, frivolous narrative, may serve the serious purposes of philosophy: "I do not promise that all the things which are written here are true, but, whether they be true or

---

[43] Jaeger, *The Origins of Courtliness*, p. 163. Jaeger suggests that the irony characteristic of medieval romance has to do with the atmosphere of the court.

[44] *De nugis curialium*, III.ii:
> Fatua forsitan hec uidebitur et friuola narracio, sed fatuis et friuolis, quibus nichil proponimus; de talibus forte nobis erit sermo cum inciderit, at non talibus. Quod possumus et scimus benignis <et> argutis inpendimus, scientes quod abscinthium et thimum argumentosa degustet apis, ut electos/ ex amaris et dulcibus conferat in thesaurum sapiencie fauos, ex friuolis his . . .

[45] *Policraticus*, VIII.xii: "Verum si moderatio adhibeatur, in his interdum sensuum voluptamen versari, sapienti non arbitror indecorum . . . non tamen ut virtutis exercitium evanescat, sed quo magis vigeat, et quoddammodo recreetur."

false, they will be of use to the reader";[46] "For frivolous things are mixed with serious ones, and false things with the true, so that all may be turned to the cultivation of truth."[47] John and Map in fact have quite different notions of frivolity, as the very different tone of the two works makes clear, but each appeals to the biblical notion that all that is written, is for our doctrine. Each accepts that fiction may serve truth, and each imagines a select audience, Map's *arguti*, for whom this material will have worth.

The audience imagined by John and Map may include like-minded courtier-clerics, but at the Angevin court one must also consider the king who held school every day. The need to tell the truth, however disguised, to the ruler points to another feature of court writing in the twelfth century. John of Salisbury is credited with raising the importance of the genre of the mirror for princes.[48] Gerald of Wales's *De Instructione principum* is another example of the genre, and like John's *Policraticus* combines court satire with a description of the ideal prince. Model kings are offered, including Solomon, David, Augustus, Trajan, Alexander, Constantine, Charlemagne.[49] When one remembers the nature of Angevin kingship, this preoccupation with the molding of a ruler is hardly surprising. As Jolliffe points out, the twelfth century "is still an age when the reign is largely determined by the personal qualities of the King ... The King may act *juste* or *injuste, per legem aut per voluntatem*, and those two contraries sum up the notions of legitimate and illegitimate kingship for the age."[50] John of Salisbury draws a distinction between the tyrant and the good king on the basis of the law: "And this therefore is the difference between the tyrant and the prince, that the latter observes the law, and rules his people by its will, whose servant he believes himself to be, and all the business and duties which must be undertaken he performs with the support of the law . . ."[51] John had required that a prince be *litteratus* in order to be able to study (God's) law, and Gerald of

---

[46] *Policraticus*, Prol.: " . . . qui non omnia, quae hic scribuntur, vera esse promitto; sed sive vera, seu falsa sunt, legentium usibus inservire."

[47] *Policraticus*, VII.prol.: "Sic enim nugis seria immiscentur, et falsa veris, ut ad summae veritatis cultum, omnia ex proposito referantur."

[48] Bumke, for example, traces the new importance of the genre in the twelfth century to John's images of just and unjust rulers; see *Courtly Culture*, pp. 277–80.

[49] The list is from Bumke, *Courtly Culture*, pp. 279–80.

[50] Jolliffe, *Angevin Kingship*, p. 55.

[51] *Policraticus* IV.i: "Est ergo tyranni et principis haec differentia sola, quod hic legi obtemperat, et ejus arbitrio populum regit, cujus se credit ministrum, et in reipublicae muneribus exercendis, et oneribus subeundis, legis beneficio sibi primum vindicat . . ."

Wales, too, was at pains to argue that literacy and prowess in war go hand in hand, pointing to Alexander, Julius Caesar and Charlemagne.[52] While the *rex litteratus* would have the tools necessary to acquaint himself with the law, John, Gerald, and others also clearly imagine a group of advisors to keep him on the right path. The interest in legal matters found in many of the works in this study may reflect, then, both the training and the daily preoccupations of courtiers in their interactions with rulers.

It is the duty of the true courtier, revealed in both the mirrors for princes and in the manuals for courtiers, to advise the prince (rather than to flatter him). The central focus of the mirror for princes is education, an emphasis inherited from the classical models upon which the genre was based. Claus Uhlig, for example, links the moral-philosophical collections of late antiquity to the mirror for princes. Twelfth-century humanism's focus on issues of education and politics, he argues, "Owes its origins not least to the need to give an ethical basis to the business of governing."[53] In a time when kingship is still largely a personal thing, then, it is through the education of the ruler that one has the best chance of creating the basis for ethical government.[54] The philosopher at the court of a king like Henry II may offer such education and advice directly, or in the more indirect mode of the exemplary narrative. The latter allows one to displace criticism, and it also fulfills the ancient dictum to please as well as to teach. I will suggest later that the preoccupation in the Latin texts in this study with Arthur as both ideal king and the less familiar *tyrannus* figure has a great deal to do with this renewed interest in kingship and rule. The pairing of good and bad kings, a feature of many of the texts in this study from Geoffrey on, also has its counterpart in the similar strategy of the mirror for princes.[55] The ironic, sometimes parodic stance of many of the Latin Arthurian texts

---

[52] See Bezzola, *Les Origines et la formation de la littérature courtoise*, p. 75.

[53] Claus Uhlig, *Hofkritik in England des Mittelalters und der Renaissance. Studien zu einem Gemeinplatz der europäischen Moralistik* (Berlin: Walter de Gruyter, 1973), p. 7: "Probleme der Erziehung und der Politik stehen im Zentrum dieser vom Humanismus des 12. Jahrhunderts begründeten Gattung, die ihre Entstehung nicht zuletzt dem Bedürfnis verdankt, dem Geschäft des Regierens eine ethische Basis zu geben."

[54] Describing Peter of Blois's *Epistle 150*, Jaeger compares the medieval and renaissance ideals of the courtier: Peter "sees the court service of the cleric justified in terms similar to those which Castiglione was to use: at their best they guide the state and the prince along the path of virtue ... the instruction of kings is a major element of this ideal"; *The Origins of Courtliness*, p. 84.

[55] Bumke, *Courtly Culture*, cites the common opposition of just and unjust kings in the mirrors for princes, pp. 277–78.

can also be seen as part of a tradition of court writing, resulting from the twin uses of *facetia* as protective covering for truth-telling and as a kind of habitual wit consistent with life at court. Indeed Jaeger argues that the ironic stance so characteristic of much romance, far from reflecting the outsider status of the clerical writer at an aristocratic court, demonstrates the atmosphere of court life, an atmosphere created in large part precisely by such writers: "Irony and wit were the rule at court, not the response of an outsider to a somewhat foreign sphere on which he looks with ironic disdain."[56]

The reference to romance leads me to a new focus and a new problem, for political philosophy and court satire are not the only sorts of writing one finds at the Angevin court, and indeed, while the texts in this study display characteristics of court writing, in their focus on kingship and in their frequently ironic stance, none of them *is* in fact a political tract, a conduct book, or even a mirror for princes. Some, like Geoffrey of Monmouth's *Historia regum Britannie* and the chronicle adaptations which follow it, look most like what we are accustomed to call chronicle history. Others, like the stories of Gawain and Meriadoc, bear the familiar markers of vernacular romance. Yet none of these terms is an easy fit even for those texts which seem most like one or the other of these poles, and there are in addition many which fit none of the available generic terms. Nevertheless, I believe that the answer to describing, if not defining, these texts lies in the practices of court writing. Let us explore a little further, then, the characteristics of the literary products of the Angevin court.

*Facetia* we have discussed thus far as an ironic covering for truth-telling, but it can also be simple cleverness and even jesting. The root value of *urbanitas*, Jaeger writes, is itself in one refraction "a witty, ironic manner of joking," a manifestation of which is "putting someone on."[57] I will argue later that the *musa jocosa* whom Geoffrey of Monmouth invokes at the outset of his *Vita Merlini* can best be understood as the literary goddess of the court, and I do not believe Geoffrey to be alone in his facetious approach to writing. Walter Map may be his most obvious soul-mate.[58] What John of Salisbury

---

[56] Jaeger, *The Origins of Courtliness*, p. 165.

[57] Jaeger, *The Origins of Courtliness*, pp. 145–46.

[58] Christopher Brooke, describing Map's history of Gado, argues that the work is "a remarkable parody, or imitation, of Geoffrey of Monmouth's fictitious history by a man who evidently knew how Geoffrey had worked"; *The Twelfth Century Renaissance* (London: Thames and Hudson, 1969), p. 171.

dismisses as the frivolities of the court, Map seems often to revel in, and the concentration on *nugae* in Map's work may be seen as a direct reference to John's own *Policraticus*, subtitled *de nugis curialium et vestigiis philosophorum*. Map's jocular tone and self-definition and defense as a *modernus* make a telling contrast to John's work.[59] Richard Mortimer writes that Map's *De nugis* shows us "yet another aspect of the court, its moments of relaxation."[60] For Türk, Map is to be understood precisely as the embodiment of court speech: *urbanitas*, *facetia*, and *dicta* were, he says, the qualities which formed the basis of Map's relationship to the king.[61] Map's modern editors seem to comply with this assessment by calling his work "the commonplace-book of a great after-dinner speaker,"[62] yet I would argue that all of these assessments err precisely in seeming to split Map's product from those other products of the Angevin court with which we have dealt thus far. We have already seen that Map implies there is more to his *nugae* than meets the eye. Cleverness and relaxation – what Map and John both, with differing motives, call *nugae* – may simultaneously serve frivolous and serious purposes. That is, the court at play is not so different, in expression or interest, from the court at work. If Map is indeed, as he has been called, "an indication, a kind of thermometer of the temperature of the age,"[63] we should perhaps scrutinize more closely the stance of his "commonplace-book."

G.T. Shepherd suggests that the real question in Map's *De nugis* is whether it is possible to present *nugae* seriously.[64] The answer is yes, because even *nugae*, or perhaps the telling of *nugae*, are serious.[65] Map suggests the importance of *nugae* in the prologue to the third distinction:

---

[59] There are other parallels between the works of Map and John: both review British history from Cnut to Henry II (omitting William I), and both contain passages on the unruliness of the Welsh and antimatrimonial passages. Some of the parallels suggest deliberate attacks on Map's part; while John usually favors religious orders, Map denounces them, and while John denounces hunting (a common denunciation in court satire, doubtless because of Henry II's passion for the sport), Map characterizes himself as a huntsman.

[60] Mortimer, *Angevin England*, p. 211.

[61] Türk, *Nugae curialium*, p. 166. A.G. Rigg, *A History of Anglo-Latin Literature, 1066–1422* (Cambridge: Cambridge University Press, 1992) observes that *facetus* was one of Map's favorite words, p. 92.

[62] *De nugis curialium*, p. xlv. The editors add that the work is easily misunderstood "if one is entirely sober when one reads it."

[63] Brooke, *The Twelfth Century Renaissance*, p. 172.

[64] G.T. Shepherd, "The Emancipation of Story in the Twelfth Century," in *Medieval Narrative: A Symposium* (Odense, 1979), p. 53.

[65] For a discussion of the metafictional aspect of Map's work, see my "Map's Metafiction: Author, Narrator, and Reader in *De nugis curialium*," *Exemplaria* 8 (1996), 287–314.

You order me to write *exempla* for posterity by which either pleasure may be roused or morals edified. Although this command is impossible for me to fulfill, since "the poor poet does not know the cave of the Muses," it is not difficult to pick out or write something which the goodness of the good may make useful (for all things tend to the good in the good), nor to commit to the good earth seed which may prosper. But who can cultivate a bad and uncultivated mind, when Scripture says, "he who sings songs to an evil heart is vinegar on nitre"?[66]

Beneath the conventions of the modesty *topos*, Map is making serious claims for his work. His stories are not *nugae* here, but the far more praiseworthy category of *exempla*. It is appropriate, then, that the passage contains biblical echoes, both in direct quotation from *Proverbs* and *Romans*,[67] and in the reference to seed which calls to mind the parable of the sower. Author as sower, audience as ground; we are back again with John of Salisbury and the contention that all that is written, is for our doctrine. Map's *nugae* have the same status as John's work, at least in Map's mind, and Map's view of himself as educator stresses again that the material must meet fit and like minds. Map's characteristically witty turn of the traditional modesty *topos* at the end of the second distinction situates his work in the court context and calls upon that audience to turn his work to good in terms that stress the rhythms of court life:

I offer to you a forest and timber, not, I will say, of fables, but of jottings; for I do not aim at the refinement of words, nor would I succeed should I try. Each reader must cut into shape the roughness offered him, so that through his effort it may appear in public with a decent face. I am your huntsman; I bring you game, and you must make dishes out of it.[68]

While Map's use here of *lector* implies that this is a reading audience,

---

[66] *De nugis curialium*, III.i:
   Scribere iubes posteris exempla quibus uel iocunditas excitetur uel edificetur ethica. Licet inpossibile michi sit hoc mandatum, quia "pauper poeta nescit antra Musarum," non difficile legere uel scribere quod bonis sua faciat utile bonitas (cum omnia bonis cooperentur in bonum) nec terre bone mandare semina que proficiant. Sed quis animum nequam et discolum excolat, cum dicat scriptura "Acetum in nitro qui cantat carmina cordi pessimo."

[67] *Proverbs* 25:20 and *Romans* 8:28.

[68] *De nugis curialium*, II.xxxii:
   Siluam uobis et materiam, non dico fabularum sed faminum appono; cultui etenim sermonum non intendo, nec si studeam consequar. Singuli lectores appositam ruditatem exculpant, ut eorum industria bona facie prodeat in publicum. Venator uester sum: feras uobis affero, fercula faciatis.

the images of dining and of going out in public remind us as well of the social context for court writing. Whether one is *lector* or *auditor* – and in fact Map seems elsewhere to use these terms interchangeably – Map's emphasis is on the audience's responsibility for the creation of meaning. This passage draws attention to the idea of writing at court as a social exercise, one in which authors expected lively reaction and participation from their audience.

Yet having said all this, it is also important to stress that Map's collection of supper-table anecdote, antimatrimonial satire, history, comedy, parodic romance, ghost story, and antimonastic satire contains much which does indeed appear to exist primarily for entertainment rather than for edification. If thus far I have stressed the ironic stance of court writing as either a cover for truth-telling or a habitual style promoted by life at court, it is important to add that there is a well-developed taste in court literature for what seems to serve primarily as entertainment – despite the occasionally serious implications of Map's *nugae*. For Bezzola, for example, "A distinctive element of courtly literature in the second half of the twelfth century is the taste for the 'worldly marvellous' which is ubiquitous in narrative literature."[69] He finds this focus particularly in Gerald of Wales.[70] Gerald and Map both produced collections which include a good deal of obviously fantastic narrative, in Gerald's accounts of the superstitions of the Celtic peoples he describes, and in Map's retellings of Celtic ghost- and fairy-stories. Discussions of the marvelous in the rising romance genre often trace this strain in the narrative to its Celtic roots, and there are some who argue that an interest in the fantastic is a peculiarly English phenomenon in this period. I move then to my last contextual thread, the place of Britain in the twelfth-century renaissance. It is here that I hope to offer a generic description for the works which follow.

From the time of Haskins's classic study, historians have sought to delineate England's role in the twelfth-century revival, to balance earlier insistence on the primacy of France and Italy.[71] Such studies

---

[69] Bezzola, *Les Origines et la formation de la littérature courtoise*, p. 61: "Un élément distinctif de la littérature courtoise dans le seconde moitié du XIIe siècle, est le goût du merveilleux profane, qui pénètre partout dans la littérature narrative."

[70] Bezzola, *Les Origines et la formation de la littérature courtoise*, p. 86. Bezzola speaks of Gerald's humanistic interests, but my concern is more for his focus on the fantastic.

[71] In his *Renaissance of the Twelfth Century* (Cambridge, Mass.: Harvard University Press, 1927), Haskins concentrated on France and Italy. R.W. Southern's "The Place of England in the Twelfth-Century Renaissance," *History* 45 (1960), 201–16, was one attempt to right the

have often emphasized both the wealth and the distinctive character of Anglo-Latin literature.[72] Sir Richard Southern calls the England of the twelfth century "a sort of nodal point for the gathering together and rediffusion of legends and marvels of every kind."[73]

Clanchy explains the phenomenon through England's position in medieval Europe:

> Innovation can be easier on the fringes of a culture, where cross-fertilization makes adaptation more necessary and the centre's dominance less secure. Within England itself in the twelfth century, growing-points can be observed on the frontiers: notably in the region of Hereford on the Welsh border and Durham on the Scottish border. From the Welsh border came the most original and influential authors writing Latin for entertainment – Geoffrey of Monmouth, Walter Map, and Gerald of Wales . . .[74]

If we may substitute for "England" the phrase "the Angevin empire," which I believe we often do when we consider the affiliations of the writers who have led modern observers to make such comments as these, then we arrive at last at the phenomenon which I believe to be central to this study of Latin Arthurian narrative.[75]

Meriadoc, whose adventures are discussed in chapter 5, exclaims, after a particularly strange set of events, that he has experienced a *dies fantastica*, a fantastic day. Meriadoc's experiences have turned the world of both knight and audience upside down, while also leading to situations which comment on kingship and knighthood. All the works in this study present a similar atmosphere and similar opportunities. Sometimes the focus is most clearly on the "message"; at other times, the experience of the text itself seems primary. The experimental nature of these works takes their readers on narrative adventures which may be as bewildering as those experienced by Meriadoc and others of his knightly brethren, and the difficulty one finds in

---

balance; the collection of essays edited by Daniel Williams, *England in the Twelfth Century* (Woodbridge, Suffolk: Boydell and Brewer, 1990), is a more recent one.

[72] For a definition and defense of the term "Anglo Latin," see Rigg, *A History of Anglo-Latin Literature*.

[73] Southern, "The Place of England," 212.

[74] Clanchy, *From Memory to Written Record*, p. 16. Elsewhere Clanchy attributes the whole phenomenon of Latin literature in England to the historical circumstances which caused the Norman conquerors to build a bureaucracy whose very existence promoted the growth of Latin literacy, p. 18.

[75] What may appear a rather casual segue from "England" to "Angevin empire" is in fact a fairly common practice; when Clanchy writes that "the experience of literacy in England at this time is quite coherent because of the domination of the royal bureaucracy" (Clanchy, *From Memory to Written Record*, p. 5), he is of course speaking of the Angevin bureaucracy.

classifying these works generically is part of this experience. The histories display elements of the fantastic, elements which we know, from the disapproving comments of men like William of Newburgh and William of Malmesbury, were not accepted as appropriate in serious history. The romances, for their part, seem consistently to parody their own form. And the odd Arthurian episodes which appear in everything from monastic chronicle to verse satire to a manual of courtly love defy categorization, except by their common use of Arthurian motifs and episodes in the context of what I have called the court style of ironic writing and the court themes of kingship and rule, of subjects or of self. The vagueness of the classification "Arthurian narrative" is thus explained: although I argue that the court issues of deception and rule are at the center of these works, those themes do not necessarily allow one to move to a narrower classification. While linked by their common language and their common subject, these texts are not, strictly speaking, romances, or histories, or mirrors for princes.

Some vagueness with respect to generic classification remains, then. But just as common themes can be discerned in these texts, so too can a common method be described. A primary feature of most of the Latin narratives discussed here is an aware, critical stance, a stance which often manifests itself in a characteristic handling of the narrative process. The training in rhetoric which was part of every medieval schoolman's background offered excellent preparation for both the serious and the playful manipulation of language and literary form. The tools of this manipulation are drawn from the court writer's standard stock, and include irony, parody, and humor. The resulting stance of the narratives makes generic classification and audience response problematic. Some readers, themselves sophisticated members of the court circle, Map's *arguti*, may read a history like Geoffrey's with full consciousness and appreciation of its parodic elements. Others, necessarily Latinate but not perhaps part of the artificial and stylized world of the court, may be either bewildered, or taken in to the extent that the text functions for them as a perfectly normal example of the subverted genre. Geoffrey's *Historia*, despite its manipulation of conventional historiography, was certainly taken at face value by many readers for a long time. It is also true that *facetia* has a purely playful element, and some of the texts in this study seem to make extensive use of blatant parody and raucous humor purely to produce hearty laughter. The generic elusiveness of the texts in this study is, then, a result of their origins and perhaps even paradoxically a defining feature. I will nevertheless confess to feeling often as Meriadoc does when his own *dies fantastica* leaves him in doubt about all that he has experienced.

The Latin writing of the Angevin court gives one the impression of the Latin of the twelfth century as "a definitely new literature, characterized especially by youthful vigour,"[76] and the wit and subtlety with which Angevin writers employed both the language and the literary heritage it implies suggest that they were not in fact particularly troubled by standing on the shoulders of giants. This period of transition, from Latin to vernacular and from non-literate to literate modes, was one of both anxiety and opportunity. Clanchy stresses the anxiety:

> Unaccustomed to the convention of the fictitious narrator in the modern novel, twelfth-century readers were unsure whether Geoffrey of Monmouth or Walter Map was a historian or a liar. Writing was untrustworthy in itself, and furthermore its use implied distrust, if not chicanery, on the part of the writer. An honest person held to his word and did not demand written proof.[77]

For the writers in this study, the mistrust surrounding the use of language becomes in itself a theme to exploit in their games with its supreme representative, the Latin tongue. Even when they make claims to plain speech, Angevin writers signal their duplicity. John of Salisbury, for example, expresses confidence that his faithful reader ". . . will heed not the sense which the words at first sight signify, but whence they get that sense, or the sense for which they are created"; he goes on to note that he has mingled frivolities with serious things and truth with falsehood.[78] All of this subtlety, for John, is in the service of the greater truth, but the *nugae* and the *falsa* are nevertheless there, and indeed have a role to play. One must always look twice in reading, a theme of much of the Latin narrative to be examined in these pages.

Clanchy argues that "Because England stood on the periphery of

---

[76] Sidney R. Packard, *12th Century Europe: An Interpretive Essay* (Amherst: University of Massachusetts Press, 1973), p. 224.

[77] Clanchy, *From Memory to Written Record*, p. 193.

[78] *Policraticus*, VII.prol.:
　　　. . . et non quem sensum prima facie verba significent, sed ex quo sensa, vel ad quem sensum fiant, fidelis lector, attendes. Sic enim nugis seria immiscentur, et falsa veris, ut ad summae veritatis cultum, omnia ex proposito referantur.

Latin culture, its attitude to it was ambivalent."[79] Such ambivalence could be expressed in the facetious employment of the language and also in the use of the language for novel purposes; John of Salisbury, humanist and opponent of the *moderni*, was nevertheless himself an innovator, and conscious of it, in his use of Latin in the writing of a treatise of government.[80] The same may be said, I will argue, for all the other authors, named and anonymous, of the Latin Arthurian narratives studied here. These texts offer a unique opportunity to see a small group of educated, Latinate writers dealing with the literary issues raised by the general explosion of writing in the twelfth and early thirteenth centuries. These surviving Latin Arthurian texts show a marked interest in narrative issues, in experimenting with the roles of writer and reader and in exploring the nature of their relationship. The particular courtly interest in rule, and the courtly taste for invention and cleverness, mark these products and perhaps also suggest analogous developments in the vernacular proliferation of Arthurian narratives. The self-consciousness with which these Latin writers approach new material in an old tongue is itself a manifestation of the literary inventiveness of the age, something we are perhaps more accustomed to granting to vernacular than to Latin writers.[81]

I would conclude with several *caveats*. First there is the whole question of the propriety of studying, as if they formed a logical object for such study, a group of texts which share subject and language but not national origin (for as will be seen below, even my designation "Angevin" does not encompass absolutely every text here described). Studies of Arthurian material, or of romance material more generally, tend either to range widely across many national literatures to explore the recurrence of certain themes, patterns, or characters on a grand scale, or to limit themselves to specific national manifestations of this international phenomenon. A study such as Susan Crane's *Insular Romance*, which considers Anglo-Norman and Middle English romances as forming a distinct group, separable from

---

[79] Clanchy, *From Memory to Written Record*, p. 18.

[80] Clanchy argues that John and writers like him were "conscious of their originality in using learned Latin to discuss matters as mundane as the regulation of courts"; *From Memory to Written Record*, p. 19.

[81] Martin Stevens, "The Performing Self in Twelfth-Century Culture," *Viator* 9 (1978), 193–212, has argued that fully-developed "performing selves" like the Chaucer-pilgrim find their roots in the twelfth century, and he includes both Chrétien de Troyes and Geoffrey of Monmouth in his examples of twelfth-century self-representation and artistic self-consciousness. He suggests as a reason for the rise of this sort of figure the "human identification with and control over the works of the mind" (208) which is part of twelfth-century humanism.

continental romance, is cross-linguistic but nevertheless creates a new national group. That is, Crane argues that the unique social and political concerns of the Norman baronage of England are reflected in their literature, in both their tongues.[82] But what kind of a classification, exactly, is Latin Arthurian narrative?

While most of the works in this study fit the term Angevin, some do not. Gerald of Wales was clearly associated with the Angevin court, but much of Wales for much of this time period enjoyed a kind of independence. Some of the works studied here fall outside the chronological range of the Angevin empire. And while I argue in the pages that follow for a kind of stylistic unity, I see the facetious stance of these texts and the frequent focus on the thematic element of rule and the stylistic element of play as threads of coherence, but not as necessary preconditions for inclusion in this study. That is, these are Latin Arthurian narratives, and they often, although not always, share characteristics beyond their subject matter. Some readers might feel that these works would be better integrated into that part of the Arthurian corpus to which they belong by virtue of their temporal and geographical affiliations. I have two replies. The first is that, for most of the texts in this study, such integration cannot happen until the texts come to be better known than they now are. Second, there *is* a certain consistency imposed by the Latin language, because of the context in which it tended to be learned and employed. Intellectuals had national affiliations, certainly, but the common characteristics of their education can be traced in their employment of their *lingua franca*. We return then to the discussion of the characteristics of court language above, as well as to the general sense of the ludic possibilities of Latin, possibilities which have not always been explored because of Latin's perceived status as the tongue of the Fathers. Latin Arthurian narrative may lack national affiliations, but its combination of a base of common material and a base level of intellectual culture leads it to share common themes, such as the central role of kingship, and common approaches, such as the use of the marvelous or the subversive or the playful to foreground these themes. Such sharing is not purely fortuitous or haphazard, but it is important, in closing, to insist on some of the differences between these texts. The brief descriptions below indicate some of the lines of argument with

---

[82] Susan Crane, *Insular Romance: Politics, Faith, and Culture in Anglo-Norman and Middle English Literature* (Berkeley: University of California Press, 1986).

respect to both similarity and difference to be pursued in the chapters that follow.

The first and sixth chapters of this study deal with Geoffrey of Monmouth. He is the least neglected of the Latin writers examined here, but the radical nature of his experiment in the writing of what purports to be history has not been universally appreciated. Chapter 1 considers his *Historia regum Britannie*, and chapter 6 the far less familiar *Vita Merlini*. These works represent the grimmest possibility of the critical attitude of Latin Arthurian writers. Undermining the form of Arthurian story, or history, is in Geoffrey's works a pointer to the fundamental uncertainty at their heart about the place of humanity in the cosmos, an uncertainty which at its extreme approaches nihilism. The humanism of the twelfth century was not always, for Geoffrey at least, particularly confident or serene, and the good kings of whom Arthur is a supreme representative offer less refuge than one might hope; Geoffrey's own experience of the Anarchy under King Stephen may have had something to do with the pessimism which colors his exploration of the role of kings in history. Chapter 2 considers chronicle responses to Geoffrey's creation of Arthurian history, and includes the anonymous *Vera historia de morte Arthuri*, which offers an alternate ending to Geoffrey's *Historia*, and the strange and lighthearted transformation of the Breton hope in Etienne de Rouen's *Draco Normannicus*. The chapter also shows how even those writers who criticized Geoffrey were not above a little Arthurian story-telling themselves. An attempt to discuss every use of Geoffrey in Latin chronicle would triple the size of this book, and so I have limited my discussion of the more conventional uses of Geoffrey to William of Rennes's *Gesta regum Britanniae*, an attempt to write an epic Arthurian history on the model of epics about Alexander the Great.

The works discussed in chapter 3, more than any of the others, resist generic classification. They are a Gawain-episode from Johannes de Hauvilla's *Architrenius*; the Sparrowhawk episode from Andreas Capellanus's *De amore*; and what is probably the latest Latin work in this study, an episode from John of Glastonbury's chronicle of his abbey. All but the episode from the *Architrenius* could safely be described as "romantic episodes"; none, including the episode from the *Architrenius*, is truly encapsulated by such a description. Arthurian or romance motifs are, in these works, pressed to ends which push and even exceed the limits of both chronicle history and romance.

Chapters 4 and 5 are concerned with two anonymous prose romances by the same author, the *De Ortu Waluuanii* and the *Historia Meriadoci*. Both co-opt the form and matter of Arthurian story in an unsettling way, and narrative fireworks and sleight-of-hand seem at first to be the sum total of the narrative stance of these works. Yet each has serious issues common in court writing at its core. A concern for appearance and reality and an allied suspicion of the ability of speech to convey truth suggest the negative aspects of court speech, while a focus on flawed rulers, including Arthur, dramatizes the concerns of both court satire and the mirror for princes. These works also represent the court at play, and the fantastic element of their narrative offers amusement even as it unsettles its protagonists and audiences alike.

Chapter 6, in addition to the *Vita Merlini*, includes texts which, like those in chapter 3, are particularly difficult to classify generically, and in this case even the interpretative framework I have been offering based on the characteristics of court writing may not be completely helpful. The Welsh saints' lives and *Arthur and Gorlagon*, a very funny and accomplished parody of Welsh narrative conventions, cannot be clearly identified as Angevin court writing. Yet I am reluctant to exclude them, in part from a desire to be comprehensive, and in part because I recognize in them clear resemblances to the other works in this study. The hagiographers have no hesitation in figuring Arthur as the *rex tyrannus* with whom their saints must contend, and this "hijacking" of Arthurian material fits both the practice of the works discussed in Chapter 3 and the concern with kingship and rule which most of the works in this study share. The court setting for *Arthur and Gorlagon* implies similar authorship and audience to those of other works in this study, and the tale is preserved in manuscript along with the *Historia Meriadoci*. The existence of these Welsh-influenced texts may suggest that the characteristics which I have argued have their roots in Angevin court literature and court culture may be more widely found in Latin court writing in general. Perhaps the true basis of the similarity is the combination of a (necessarily) Latin education with a temporal and geographical location (Clanchy's "fringe") which encouraged an experimentation and a sense of playfulness already well-developed in one kind of Latin at least.

And perhaps there is something in the Arthurian material which intersected most fruitfully with the combination of circumstances just described. This study does not present a linear argument, a view of the development of a trend from an identifiable source over time. I would nevertheless argue that the twelfth-century revival, in the rich encounters it produced between the creative minds of the period and Arthurian story, has produced an unexplored treasure-trove whose echoes are to be seen in the vernacular Arthurian tradition. It has been argued that irony is integral to romance.[83] The peculiar combination of the fantastic with the historic in the Arthurian material produced an unparalleled opportunity for writers who shared a critical interest in issues of narrative and interpretation. Jaeger sees the writing of vernacular romance by courtier-clerics as a salvo in the professional feud at court between singers of tales and clerics, the latter of whom won out because they could co-opt that which was appealing in the oral tales – the fantastic – and amalgamate it with their history.[84] While I am not entirely comfortable with the metaphor of competition, it does seem to me that Latin writers at court performed something similar to what Jaeger describes *in Latin* in the Arthurian narratives of this study. While a full comparison of these works with their vernacular counterparts must await another study, I close here by underlining what Haskins called the "interpenetration" of Latin and vernacular in the twelfth century.[85] This interpenetration and the resulting spread in literacy was a necessary condition for the growth of romance literature. Clanchy identifies this period and this mingling of Latin and vernacular as pivotal in the history of literacy:

> ... the twelfth and thirteenth centuries are crucially important because these are the years in which the traditional division between cleric and lay, literate and illiterate, was broken down. Gradually, by all sorts of avenues, a little literacy, in the sense of minimal Latin or *clergie*, became commonplace until 'benefit of clergy' came to mean the ability to read a few words of Latin. Because literacy had been identified with Latin for a thousand years, it had first to be learned by the laity in this clerical and alien form. Those old rivals,

---

[83] See D.H. Green, *Irony in the Medieval Romance* (Cambridge: Cambridge University Press, 1979).

[84] Jaeger, *The Origins of Courtliness*, p. 229.

[85] Haskins, *The Renaissance of the Twelfth Century*, p. 8.

the *clerici-litterati* and the *laici-illiterati*, had to come to terms and absorb each other's thought processes before literacy could become a common vernacular habit ... Knights absorbed clerical culture and clergy lived alongside knights.[86]

Perhaps we may think of Arthurian narrative as a "habit" which the two groups acquired together. In any event, should this work make some contribution towards encouraging the routine study of Latin Arthurian narrative *with* the vernacular, then its author will be well content.

---

[86] Clanchy, *From Memory to Written Record*, p. 251.

# "The Anger of Saturn shall fall": Geoffrey of Monmouth's *Historia regum Britannie* and the limits of history

The first text to be examined here is in some ways atypical of the works in this study. Unlike the largely unknown and uninfluential works in the chapters to follow, Geoffrey of Monmouth's *Historia regum Britannie* was one of the most widely read of medieval Arthurian texts.[1] I have chosen to begin with it, then, because its familiarity to medieval and modern audiences alike helps to prepare the way for the discussion of those characteristics which it shares with the other works to be discussed later. The *Historia* is arguably the most influential product of British Latin writing in the twelfth century. Its author is a *magister* who was part of the circle of some of the most important men of his day, one who ended his life with the title, if not the possession, of a bishopric, suggesting the sort of recognition to which such educated clerical writers aspired.[2] Most important from my perspective is the posterity of the *Historia*. The arguments about the literary and historical values of the work which began almost immediately after its appearance and which continue to this day, provide a dramatic example of the delight and perplexity provoked by many of the works in this study.

Part of the problem in discussing Geoffrey's *Historia* lies in the

---

[1] Julia Crick's *The Historia regum Britannie of Geoffrey of Monmouth III: A Summary Catalogue of the Manuscripts* (Cambridge: D.S. Brewer, 1989), records 215 manuscripts. Two more have recently been added; see Julia Crick, "Two Newly Located Manuscripts of Geoffrey of Monmouth's *Historia regum Britannie*," *Arthurian Literature* 13 (1995), 151–56.

[2] Geoffrey's name appears on seven charters from the area of Oxford between 1129 and 1151, and in 1139 appears with the title *magister*; it has been suggested that he was a secular canon of the Augustinian Saint George's College in the city. He seems to have been associated with Alexander, bishop of Lincoln, and Walter, archdeacon of Oxford; the *Historia* is dedicated to Robert, earl of Gloucester and Waleran, count of Mallent. By 1150, Geoffrey is signing himself as "bishop-elect" of St. Asaph, a Welsh see which the turmoil of the time apparently prevented him from ever assuming. He died in 1155. For a concise summary of the evidence for Geoffrey's life, see Michael J. Curley, *Geoffrey of Monmouth* (New York: Twayne, 1994), pp. 1–6.

generic terms available to us for that purpose. It is often treated as a history with literary features, or as literature masquerading as history. This implied separation between history and fiction is in part a modern one. While it was recognized in the Middle Ages that the process of narrating history involved the imposing of "the formal organization of stories,"[3] no contradiction between this literary process and the achieving of historical truth was perceived because history was understood as a branch of eloquence.[4] Historical truth, then, was not necessarily a matter of fact, and we have already seen as sober a writer as John of Salisbury defending the notion that the truth of a thing lies more in its moral utility than in its actual relation to "reality." In the Arthurian world, Wace will later defend his own translation of Geoffrey in words which echo John; what he writes is "ne tut mençunge, ne tut veir"; Gabrielle Spiegel understands the phrase to mean that Wace's work "purports to tell the truth about past facts, and thus is a fiction implying that its fiction is not simply a fiction"; she christens the poetic response of the *roman* to the past "fictional factuality."[5] But Spiegel is talking about the shift from Latin to vernacular, and from verse to prose. Geoffrey, writing what appears to be Latin prose history, seems to be carving out a different narrative space for himself, and indeed in chapter 2 we shall see that some of the outraged response to his work derives precisely from his use of Latin, the language of authority, for his "fantasies." If Latin is indeed the language of textuality, the language that establishes "*prima facie* its own authority,"[6] then Geoffrey's use of it for what we would call fictional or literary narrative may be part of his subversive intent. However, understood in the context of the practices of court writing, Geoffrey's use of Latin language and historical form may be seen as an unusually well-developed illustration of the duplicitous possibilities of this, or any, language. Spiegel sees the vernacular Arthurian romance as a break from the demands of textual truth: "No longer at the service of historical or religious truth, Arthurian romance inscribes itself as a

---

[3] Suzanne Fleischman, "On the Representation of History and Fiction in the Middle Ages," *History and Theory* 22 (1983), 280.

[4] For a discussion of this rhetorical understanding of history, see Ruth Morse, "'This Vague Relation': Historical Fiction and Historical Veracity in the Later Middle Ages," *Leeds Studies in English* 13 (1982), 85–103; and Nancy F. Partner, "The New Cornificius: Medieval History and the Artifice of Words," in *Classical Rhetoric and Medieval Historiography*, ed. Ernst Breisach (Kalamazoo, Mich.: Medieval Institute, 1985), pp. 5–59.

[5] Gabrielle M. Spiegel, *Romancing the Past: The Rise of Vernacular Prose Historiography in Thirteenth-Century France* (Berkeley: University of California Press, 1993), p. 62.

[6] Spiegel, *Romancing the Past*, p. 69.

literary game in which the playful artifice of the writer produces in the reader that pleasure in the text which is at the same time the sign of its literary autonomy."[7] I will argue that it is precisely this ludic employment of language which characterizes the practice of both Geoffrey and many of the other writers in this study. If vernacular romance found this narrative space for itself then perhaps it did so because that space was already present or implicit in its origins.

Yet while we may create a new category for Geoffrey's work – *historia fantastica*, perhaps – the question of whether to evaluate Geoffrey according to some vague but "felt" criteria of "literature" or "history" remains, in part because of Geoffrey's apparent determination to be considered an academic historian. He begins and ends his *Historia regum Britannie* with a claim to special knowledge which has been, ever since, a focus for much debate:

> ... Walter, archdeacon of Oxford, ... [gave me] a certain very ancient book in the British language, which continually and in order, in most beautiful language, displays the deeds of all these men, from Brutus, the first king of the Britons, up to Cadwallader, the son of Cadwallo. Thus at Walter's request, I have taken the trouble to translate the book into Latin ...

> The writing of the material concerning their kings, who succeeded from that time in Wales, I concede to my contemporary Caradoc of Llancarfan, while the kings of the Saxons I leave to William of Malmesbury and Henry of Huntingdon. I order these men to keep silent about the kings of the Britons, because they do not have the book in the British language which Walter, archdeacon of Oxford, brought from Wales, which I have made the effort to translate into Latin in this way, for it was composed truly concerning the history of the aforementioned princes and in their honor.[8]

---

[7] Spiegel, *Romancing the Past*, p. 63.
[8] Geoffrey of Monmouth, *The Historia regum Britannie of Geoffrey of Monmouth I, Bern, Burgerbibliothek, MS. 568*, ed. Neil Wright (Cambridge: D.S. Brewer, 1985), cc. 2, 208:

> ... Walterus Oxinefordensis archidiaconus ... quendam Britannici sermonis librum uetustissimum qui a Bruto primo rege Britonum usque ad Cadualadrum filium Caduallonis actus omnium continue et ex ordine perpulcris orationibus proponebat. Rogatu itaque illius ductus, ... codicem illum in Latinum sermonem transferre curaui.

> Reges autem eorum qui ab illo tempore in Gualiis successerunt Karadoco Lancarba-nensi contemporaneo meo in materia scribendi permitto, reges uero Saxonum Willelmo Malmesberiensi et Henrico Huntendonensi; quos de regibus Britonum tacere iubeo cum non habeant librum istum Britannici sermonis quem Gualterus Oxenefordensis archidiaconus ex Britannia aduexit, quem de hystoria eorum ueraciter editum in honore predictorum principum hoc modo in Latinum sermonem tranferre curaui.

In both of these passages, Geoffrey claims to be little more than a translator; the *incipit* also includes the usual apologies for a rude style. This last disclaimer is a *topos*, to be understood in the same way as the similar claims made by John of Salisbury and Walter Map. Geoffrey's own particular touch is the audacious claim to possess a "very ancient book," although here as well Geoffrey can be aligned with the common practice of creating or forging authorities, a practice which Clanchy argues is the source for much of the mistrust of writing in this period.[9] This book is, accordingly, usually assumed to be a fiction.[10] The purpose of this fiction, however, is a question which has yet to be settled.

The ancient book is, first of all, a legitimizing device, a way of giving the *Historia* authority as history. Through an insistence on his role as translator, Geoffrey makes of himself a simple conduit for historical lore, rather than a creator of the kinds of fantasies decried by contemporary historians like William of Malmesbury.[11] The book also provides an explanation for the sudden influx of information in the *Historia* about a past which up until the appearance of that work had been described only fitfully. Geoffrey is careful, too, to insert this new information into the existing *lacunae* in insular history, making accommodation with existing authorities whenever their accounts

---

[9] Clanchy points out that "throughout twelfth-century Europe charters and title-deeds were frequently forged by monks, the experts in writing"; *From Memory to Written Record*, p. 193. Even John of Salisbury invented an authority, the *Instruction of Trajan*, which he claimed had been authored by Plutarch and which he named as a source for his *Policraticus*.

[10] But Geoffrey Ashe defends the book as the source for Arthur's Gallic campaigns; "'A Certain Very Ancient Book': Traces of an Arthurian Source in Geoffrey of Monmouth's *History*," *Speculum* 56 (1981), 301–23. A more modest claim is made by Brynley F. Roberts, "Geoffrey of Monmouth and Welsh Historical Tradition," *Nottingham Medieval Studies* 20 (1976), 29–40, who believes it likely that Geoffrey may have had access to written Welsh genealogies (38). Roberts also notes that the learned classes of Wales had developed a coherent historiography of the Britons, which may have provided a pattern for Geoffrey's work: "Geoffrey of Monmouth, *Historia regum Britanniae*, and *Brut y Brenhinedd*," in Rachel Bromwich, A.O.H. Jarman, Brynley F. Roberts, and Daniel Huws, eds., *The Arthur of the Welsh: The Arthurian Legend in Medieval Welsh Literature* (Cardiff: University of Wales Press, 1991), p. 101. The response of Welsh historians to Geoffrey's version of British history is discussed briefly in chapter 2.

The Variant version of the *Historia* has itself been suggested as Geoffrey's source. But Neil Wright, in his edition of the Variant version, concludes that the Variant was not Geoffrey's source, nor was it written by Geoffrey; it is rather a redaction of the Vulgate version, to be dated to between 1138 and the early 1150s (*The Historia regum Britannie of Geoffrey of Monmouth II, The First Variant Version: a critical edition* [Cambridge: D.S. Brewer, 1988], p. lxx).

[11] William's doubts, along with those of Gerald of Wales and William of Newburgh, are discussed in chapter 2.

impinge on his own.[12] It is often assumed that Geoffrey's purpose is that a work which has been described as "essentially literary"[13] should be read as history. Nevertheless, there seems to be little doubt that Geoffrey is seeking to give his work some kind of particular authority through his insistence on its origins. For J.S.P. Tatlock, Geoffrey wants to be taken seriously because he has a serious message; he writes to hold up a mirror to events of his day, and, out of a sense of "racial patriotism," to exalt the Britons.[14] Martin Shichtman and Laurie Finke make the same argument, substituting merely the focus of the propaganda, when they argue that Geoffrey's goal was to allow the Norman overlords of Britain to refigure themselves as British kings, in the interest of consolidating their hold on the island.[15] I will argue that Geoffrey does indeed show a marked interest in national history and in the role of kingship in that history. There are clear stylistic and thematic affinities between the *Historia regum Britannie* and the mirror for princes, and this concern with kingship may be a defining quality of much Latin Arthurian writing. But the *Historia* is also marked by that other characteristic of court writing, *facetia*, in all its guises. It is this stance, as well as its content, which marks the *Historia* as different from other historical writing of the period.

For some readers, Geoffrey is aping the form of history in order to parody the writing of history. Christopher Brooke argues that Geoffrey displays this tendency in the misuse he makes of authorities, as well as in the reiteration of the translation *topos*; William and Henry cannot have access to the book because it does not exist.[16] Brooke also identifies a specific target for Geoffrey's wit, arguing that the description of Arthur's court at Caerleon is directed at contemporary quarrels over episcopal supremacy.[17] We might note

---

[12] See R. William Leckie, Jr., *The Passage of Dominion: Geoffrey of Monmouth and the Periodization of Insular History in the Twelfth Century* (Toronto: University of Toronto Press, 1981).

[13] Christopher N.L. Brooke, "Geoffrey of Monmouth as a Historian," in *Church and Government in the Middle Ages: Essays Presented to C.R. Cheney on his 70th Birthday*, ed. C.N.L. Brooke *et al.* (Cambridge: Cambridge University Press, 1976), p. 78.

[14] J.S.P. Tatlock, *The Legendary History of Britain: Geoffrey of Monmouth's Historia regum Britanniae and its Early Vernacular Versions* (Berkeley: University of California Press, 1950), pp. 425–27. Leckie and Roberts agree Geoffrey is seeking to teach a lesson; for both, the lesson has to do with the importance of strong central rule, a theme discussed below as a manifestation of the specific concerns of court writing.

[15] Martin B. Shichtman and Laurie A. Finke, "Profiting from the Past: History as Symbolic Capital in the *Historia Regum Britanniae*," *Arthurian Literature* 12 (1993), 4.

[16] Brooke, "Geoffrey of Monmouth," p. 83.

[17] He argues Geoffrey is striking impartially at the claims of Canterbury, St. David's, Llandaff,

here that there seems to be a similar reference to episcopal quarrels in the *Vera historia de morte Arthuri*, discussed in chapter 3. That work seems to function as an alternate ending to the Arthuriad of the *Historia*; its author's inclusion of the episcopal strife may support the notion that Geoffrey had a specific contemporary target for at least some of his work.

Valerie Flint has also explored the idea of Geoffrey as a parodist, arguing that the misuse of sources, and the direct mention of William and Henry, are indications that the targets are monastic historians and monastic values, and she describes his tone as one of "teasing abuse."[18] But what is most striking for me is not Geoffrey's wit, delightful though that is. Instead, I am interested in his subversion of the writing of history through the application of its conventions to material which has been created and arranged towards a completely unconventional final assertion. It is not Geoffrey's creation of (fictive) stories which is subversive, although he does create incident rather more gleefully and thoroughly than do his contemporaries. It is the implication of his stories, what Hayden White would call their underlying mythoi,[19] which sets Geoffrey apart. White has suggested that historical narrative "tells us in what direction to think about the events and charges our thoughts about the events with different emotional valences";[20] I will argue that Geoffrey sets his audience's thoughts in unaccustomed and alarming directions. Behind the portraits of rulers which may have links to the mirror for princes and to the tumultuous events of Geoffrey's own time; behind the facetious use of Latin for anecdote and amusement as well as for instruction; lies a thoroughgoing subversion of conventional historiography, a subversion which has far more serious implications than either Flint or Brooke allow. Geoffrey's manipulation of the traditional form and material of history points to an underlying concern with the traditional message of history. Spiegel describes the ubiquity of anachronism in medieval treatments of the past as the symptom of "an intellectual attitude that refused to acknowledge the past as either irretrievably lost or ethically

---

York and London: "Thus he declared a pox on all their houses, and can have intended nothing but mockery and mischief"; "Geoffrey of Monmouth," p. 82.

[18] See Valerie I.J. Flint, "The *Historia regum Britanniae* of Geoffrey of Monmouth: Parody and its Purpose. A Suggestion," *Speculum* 54 (1979), 463, 454.

[19] For White's discussion of the process by which historical fact is turned into narrative, see his *Tropics of Discourse: Essays in Cultural Criticism* (Baltimore, Md: Johns Hopkins, 1978); especially "Interpretation in History," pp. 51–80; and "The Historical Text as Literary Artifact," pp. 81–100.

[20] White, "The Historical Text," p. 91.

irrelevant."[21] Geoffrey is, I think, far less certain of the status of the past than many of his contemporaries, and consequently, the playfulness of the narrative space he creates gives way to a destruction of narrative and historical certainties which approaches the nihilistic. The *Historia*, however fantastic, however ludic, is indeed what Nancy Partner has called a "serious entertainment."[22]

Chapter 6 of this study discusses the appearance of both formal and sporadic parody in Celtic-inspired Arthurian narrative; these stylistic parodies are usually aligned with less than sympathetic portraits of a ruler, both in Arthurian and non-Arthurian narrative alike. If Geoffrey did make use of Welsh material, he might well have absorbed some of these attitudes. A suggestive resemblance is that between the endings of the *Historia* and the parodic Welsh Arthurian text, *Breudwyt Rhonabwy*. Geoffrey advises Caradoc, William, and Henry not to stray beyond the boundaries he has set for them, because they do not have access to his book. In the *explicit* to the *Breudwyt Rhonabwy*, a *tour de force* demolition of Welsh storytelling technique is followed by these words: "This story is called the Dream of Rhonabwy, and here is the reason: no man, neither bard nor storyteller, knows the dream without a book, because there were so many colors on the horses, and such strange colors of arms and equipment and precious cloaks and powerful stones."[23] This author is flaunting his creative skill; Geoffrey's "book" allows him to flaunt his skill while hiding it, yet the taunt at other, presumably lesser, artists is the same.[24]

The *Historia* is not, of course, simply an account of the reign of Arthur, yet I will restrict discussion to the Arthurian portion of the work, that section which was most influential for the developing

---

[21] Spiegel, *Romancing the Past*, p. 102.

[22] Nancy F. Partner, *Serious Entertainments: The Writing of History in Twelfth-Century England* (Chicago and London: University of Chicago Press, 1977). Partner does not discuss Geoffrey at length, but her recognition that the writing of history in England was often a literary endeavor with the twin goals of the entertainment and education of an audience is important in the understanding of Geoffrey's more radical procedure.

[23] *Breudwyt Rhonabwy, allan o'r Llyfr Coch o Hergest*, ed. Melville Richards (Cardiff: University of Wales Press, 1948), p. 21: "A'r ystorya honn a elwir Breidwyt Ronabwy. (A llyma yr achaws na wyr neb y breidwyt, na bard na chyfarwyd, heb lyuyr, o achaws y geniuer lliw a oed ar y me[i]rch, a hynny o amrauael liw odidawc ac ar yr aruev ac eu kyweirdebeu, ac ar y llenneu gwerthuawr a'r mein rinwedawl)."

[24] *Breudwyt Rhonabwy* is a later text than the *Historia*, but I see here an attitude in Welsh literature which parallels Geoffrey's own. Briton or Breton, Geoffrey seems to have had enough Welsh to make use of Welsh traditions; see T.D. Crawford, "On the Linguistic Competence of Geoffrey of Monmouth," *Medium Aevum* 51 (1982), 152–62. Roberts supports the view that Geoffrey was of Breton origin; see "Geoffrey of Monmouth, *Historia regum Britannie*, and *Brut y Brenhinedd*," p. 98.

romance genre. This influence, in the vernacular realm, appears to be largely a matter of narrative, of incident. The Latin texts in this study, however, share with the *Historia* a characteristic approach to that raw material. Geoffrey's *Vita Merlini*, like the *Historia*, shows moments of broad comedy alternating with moments of despair. The *Vita*, the *De Ortu Waluuanii*, and the *Historia Meriadoci* all mingle serious themes about the importance of strong rule and the difficulty of maintaining it, with narrative experimentation and generic subversion. Such experimentation reaches its full flower as Arthurian parody in *Arthur and Gorlagon*, and Arthur is the specific focus of negative comment in the *Draco Normannicus* and the Welsh saints' lives too. I make no argument here for direct influence of the *Historia*, either on the other Latin works in this study or on those texts of the vernacular tradition whose retelling of Arthurian story focuses particularly on issues of kingship and the rule of law. I would suggest, however, that the complexities of the *Historia* are no isolated phenomenon, but rather a particularly original manifestation of a strain of Latin writing in the Angevin period which had its origins in the concerns and discourse of school and court.

Despite the signals which the opening of the *Historia* may be sending about the unexpected or unpredictable nature of what is to follow, the work is structured around an important and appropriate central theme; that is, the need for strong and legitimate central rule. The *Historia* is, however, pessimistic as to the likelihood of such rule existing and persisting. There may be a contemporary context for such pessimism, for Geoffrey was writing around the time of the Anarchy. The rather bleak view of British history is constant throughout the work, but it is most striking in the Arthuriad, because that period represents one still point when it appears that Britain might achieve peace and stability. The Arthurian story clearly held a particular fascination for Geoffrey; in it we may find expressed all of the major concerns and strategies of the *Historia*. For all that, the Arthuriad cannot be excised from the rest of the *Historia*, and this dependence is in itself significant. The story of Arthur and his court is part of the seamless flow of British history – what the *Gawain*-poet memorably calls a history of "blysse and blunder."[25]

Somewhat arbitrarily, then, an examination of the theme of legit-

---

[25] *Sir Gawain and the Green Knight*, ed. J.R.R. Tolkien and E.V. Gordon, 2nd edn., rev. Norman Davis (Oxford: Oxford University Press, 1967), line 18.

imate rule in the Arthurian portion of the *Historia* may begin with the account of the three sons of King Constantine II, Constans, Aurelius Ambrosius, and Uther Pendragon. Constantine is a shadowy figure who receives little attention, and it is typical of Geoffrey's concern with the forces which inhibit peace that his entire career is granted only a few lines: "Afterwards, when ten years had passed, a certain Pict who had been in his service came to him and, acting as if he had to have a private meeting [with Constantine] in a thicket, killed him with his knife once all the king's men had left."[26] There is no explanation given for the action of the Pict, although the fact that he *is* a Pict may imply that Vortigern is behind the assassination. There is no mourning described for the king whose ten years of rule were, one assumes, a time of peace. There is no narrative pause to respond to this situation either. Instead, the narrative moves on immediately to a picture of civil discord, as various factions supporting the three brothers quarrel over who is to receive the crown. This discord provides an opportunity for the schemer Vortigern to install Constans as his puppet.

The account of Vortigern's machinations is peppered with references to the illegitimacy of the whole enterprise. Constans is crowned "hardly with the people consenting."[27] In the *De Ortu* and the *Historia Meriadoci*, too, there is a strong concern for the role of consultation in government, a concern which may be understood in part by the fact that in the twelfth century the formalization of the giving of counsel to the king has not yet occurred. Kings certainly received counsel from their *familiares*, but custom was not law. The shifting allegiances of the magnates who swore to uphold Matilda and then turned to Stephen might be also reflected here; in any case, Geoffrey's Constans takes the throne without proper legal or moral authority. It is equally important for Geoffrey that Constans is not the right *kind* of person to rule, as he demonstrates when he hands power over to Vortigern:

> Now it was the weakness of his character which made him do this; for in the cloister he had learned things other than how to govern a kingdom. When Vortigern noticed this, he began to plan to himself how he could be raised to the crown; for he had desired this above

---

[26] *Historia regum Britannie*, c. 93: "Postremo, cum .x. anni preterissent, uenit quidam Pictus qui in obsequium suum fuerat et quasi secretum colloquium habiturus in uirgulto quodam semotis cunctis eum cum cultro interfecit."

[27] *Historia regum Britannie*, c. 94: ". . . atque uix annuente populo . . ."

all things from the first. Now it seemed that the time was right for him to be able to bring his desire to fruition easily, for the whole kingdom was committed to his control; nor was Constans, who was said to be king, anything but a shadow of a leader. There was neither severity nor justice in Constans, nor was he feared by his people or by the people of neighbouring areas.[28]

This unflattering picture of Constans may indeed, on one level, represent the kind of antimonastic satire which Valerie Flint argues is the main thrust of the *Historia*. At the same time, it is hardly surprising that a monk would not have learned how to run a kingdom. At any rate, if this is satire, it is placed here in the service of the larger themes of the work. The crucial point is that Constans is a king unduly constituted, entirely inappropriate, and fundamentally unfit for rule; his weakness allows a tyrant to seize the crown. The character of the king is perhaps even more important to Geoffrey than is the issue of kingship, for it is the flaws of her rulers which subject Britain to much, if not all, of the cycle of misery which characterizes her history. The education of the ruler through exemplary history is, then, doubly important.

Vortigern, the paradigm in the Arthuriad of the bad king, receives treatment as full as or fuller than that accorded to the good kings. When, as in the case of Vortigern (or Arthur), Geoffrey lingers over a ruler's career, he often includes anecdotes, dialogue and incidents of a more clearly "literary" coloring, but these all tend to contribute to the central theme. In Vortigern's case, there is some direct characterization. His duplicitous reaction to Constans's death, which he had himself engineered, is described: "When Vortigern had seen this [Constans's head] he burst into tears as if he were terribly saddened, although in fact he had never before experienced such joy."[29] The conflict between appearance and reality is one which recurs in the

---

[28] *Historia regum Britannie*, c. 95:

> Quippe debilitas sensus ipsius id faciebat; nam infra claustra aliud quam regnum tractare didicerat. Quod cum calluisset Uortigernus, cepit apud se deliberare qualiter sullimari potuisset in regem; nam id prius super omnia concupierat. Uidebat etenim congruum tempus instare quod desiderium suum leuiter ad effectum duci poterat. Totum nanque dispositioni eius regnum commissum fuerat; nec Constans qui rex dicebatur nisi pro umbra principis astabat. Nullius enim asperitatis, nullius iusticie fuerat nec a populo suo nec a uicinis gentibus timebatur.

[29] *Historia regum Britannie*, c. 96: "Quod cum inspexisset Uortegirnus, quasi contristatus in fletum erupit nec unquam prius ma<i>ori gaudio fluctuauerat." *Fluctuo*, which normally has the sense of "waver" or "fluctuate," is an odd choice of words here, and may be a further clue to Vortigern's hypocrisy.

*Historia* and which also appears in many of the other texts in this study.

Even more important than direct comment to the characterization of Vortigern, however, are his associates. Besides his alliance with the Picts who kill Constans – the Picts are a notoriously untrustworthy and bloodthirsty people – there is his association with the Saxons. It is a rebellion by the Picts which drives Vortigern into the arms of Hengist and Horsa, and it is the Saxons' shrewd manipulation of his weaknesses which provides Geoffrey's most cutting criticism of Vortigern's character. It is made clear from the outset that the Saxons are pagans, but while Vortigern pays lip-service to his religion by disapproving of theirs, he has no hesitation about accepting their aid. He rationalizes his acceptance in a most interesting way: "I grieve greatly about your belief, which I rather call unbelief, but I rejoice in your arrival, since either God or someone else has provided you in my need at a most opportune time."[30] Vortigern's belief that God or "someone else" has sent him aid shows him to be less than a perfect Christian himself. At the same time, the introduction here of some other power besides God has implications for the whole of the *Historia*. Historians like Gildas argued that it was, in fact, God who sent the Saxons, not to aid Vortigern, but to punish the Britons. Geoffrey, however, by emphasizing the alien nature of the Saxons and by introducing, through the use of *alius*, an ambiguity as to whose agents they are, raises an unsettling and radical possibility about God and His attitude towards His creation. Are malignant fates controlled by God and ultimately in the service of His providential (even when punitive) purpose, or are they either exempt from God's control or an expression of His own malignancy and inconstancy? The latter conclusion would seem remarkable for any medieval writer, but some sort of cooperation between human evil and fate does seem to be a central problem in the *Historia*; and if God is in charge of the process, He is nevertheless rarely mentioned in the text. It may be that Geoffrey is rewriting conventional history because his interpretation of that history is so much at variance with what had gone before.

The implications of the arrival of the Saxons may be radical or merely grim; in any case, their arrival gives Geoffrey an opportunity to craft a narrative episode which both underlines his central concerns

---

[30] *Historia regum Britannie*, c. 98: "De credulitate uestra – potius incredulitas dici potest – uehementer doleo. De aduentu autem uestro gaudeo quia in congruo tempore uos necessitati mee siue Deus siue alius obtulerit."

and functions in a literary context as something approaching comic relief. The passage concerns the meeting between Vortigern and Hengist's daughter Renwein:

> When Vortigern had been replenished by the royal banquet, the girl came out of a chamber, carrying a golden goblet full of wine. Then, coming next to the king, she curtseyed, and said, "Lauerd king, Wasseil!" And he, seeing the girl's face, admired her great beauty and grew hot for her. He asked his interpreter what the girl had said and how he ought to respond to her. The interpreter said to him, "She called you lord king, and honored you with a phrase of greeting. You ought to answer, 'Drincheil'." So Vortigern responded "Drincheil," and ordered the girl to drink, and took the goblet from her hand and kissed it and drank. From that day to this the custom endures in Britain that whoever drinks at a banquet says "Wasseil" to his fellow, who next receives the drink and responds "Drincheil."
>
> Now Vortigern, drunk with a different kind of drink, and with Satan having entered his heart, fell in love with the girl, and sought her hand from her father. I say that Satan entered his heart because he, who was a Christian, desired to mate with a pagan.[31]

This passage is highly revealing of Geoffrey's methods. First, it is simply entertaining, and that on several levels. As pure comedy, it is an admirably deft characterization of the tipsy king who is suddenly swept off his feet by the beautiful girl introduced by her cunning father for precisely this purpose. The audience has little reason to admire Vortigern, and may enjoy seeing him made a fool of in this fashion. Second, there is entertainment of a more educational sort to

---

[31] *Historia regum Britannie*, c. 100:

> Ut ergo regiis epulis refectus fuit, egressa est puella de thalamo aureum ciphum plenum uino ferens. Accedens deinde propius regi flexis genibus dixit: "Lauerd king, Waesseil!" At ille, uisa facie puelle, ammiratus est tantum eius decorem et incaluit. Denique interrogauit interpretem suum quid dixerat puella et quid ei respondere debeat. Cui interpres dixit: "Uocauit te dominum regem et uocabulo salutationis honorauit. Quod autem respondere debes, est 'Drincheil'." Respondens deinde Uortegirnus "Drincheil" iussit puellam potare cepitque ciphum de manu ipsius et osculatus est eam et potauit. Ab illo die usque in hodiernum mansit consuetudo illa in Britannia quia in conuiuiis qui potat ad alium dicit "Waesseil." Qui uero post illum recipit potum, respondet "Drincheil." Uortegirnus autem diuerso genere potus inhebriatus intrante Sathana in corde suo <amauit puellam et postulauit eam a patre suo. Intrauerat, inquam, Sathanas in corde suo> quia, cum Christianus esset, cum pagana coire desiderabat.

The phrase "diuerso genere potus inhebriatus" may mean that Vortigern has been mixing his drinks, or that he has been given some kind of love potion, or that love is itself an intoxicant; in every case, the portrait of the king – or of love – is hardly a flattering one.

be had in the explanation of the drinking custom; Geoffrey shows that he understands the appeal of an interesting and instructive anecdote, and one thinks again of the characterization of Walter Map, who could have written such a scene, as a consummate after-dinner speaker. Finally, the passage is set off nicely from the flow of battles which surrounds it, providing a welcome resting-point, and the refreshment of the new. In this anecdote, then, Geoffrey the historian displays many of the powers and concerns of the storyteller.

Yet this passage is more than just a pleasant interlude from the usual concerns of the *Historia*. It is clearly meant to be seen as historically accurate; the references to Saxon customs, and to the use of translators, give the passage an air of verisimilitude. It was in fact permissible for an historian to create out of whole cloth, provided that the creation exemplify the truth; from one point of view, Geoffrey is simply better at creating such moments than most. Yet his deployment of these moments suggests the storyteller's manipulation of audience reaction. As soon as the audience is relaxed and enjoying the scene, the narrative voice makes a rare, first-person intrusion to note that Satan has entered Vortigern's heart.[32] Immediately, the audience is reminded that the Saxons are pagan, while Vortigern is supposed to be a Christian king. The audience's enjoyment of the tyrant getting his comeuppance is soon replaced by concern for the fate of the country as a result of Vortigern's drunken foolishness; a king can never lose sight of the bigger picture and must never subordinate the interests of the country to his own personal desires. This is a recurring theme throughout the *Historia*; king after king forgets his national responsibilities in pursuit of his own desires, and disaster inevitably follows. From a structural point of view, this particular scene is crucial to an understanding of the start of Arthur's career, since it will be recapitulated in Uther's obsession with Igerna. There is, then, a serious message behind the laughter, and if in passages like this one Geoffrey's storytelling seems to swamp the

---

[32] Part of this passage (indicated by brackets) is omitted from the Bern MS, the basis for Wright's edition. It is possible that the bracketed passage is simply the result of an error in copying; Wright notes the recurrence of "in corde suo" (*Historia regum Britannie*, p. lvi). The absent passage, however, does occur in full in London, British Library, MS Arundel 237, whereas other instances of what seem to be a similar error are absent from the other manuscripts deriving from the Bern MS (*Historia regum Britannie*, ed. Wright, p. lvi, n. 103). The phrase occurs in "Nennius," *Historia Brittonum*, in *Nennius: British History and The Welsh Annals*, ed. and trans. John Morris (London: Phillimore, 1980), c. 37: "Illis autem bibentibus, intravit Satanas in corde Guorthigirni, ut amaret puellam . . ."

apparently historical event contained therein, the lesson to which the event points is nevertheless clear.

Vortigern is a British ruler, but one whose spurious claim can be supported only by foreign influence. There is a suggestive resemblance between Vortigern and John of Salisbury's characterization of Stephen:

> . . . and a foreign man was allowed to rule the kingdom, a disdainer of goodness and equity, one whose counsel was foolish from the beginning, whose cause was founded on iniquity and perfidy, a man negligent with respect to discipline, so that all men were provoked to everything, and the clergy and the people were not so much ruled as beaten down and brought into conflict . . . [33]

I am not suggesting that Geoffrey is betraying specific political allegiances here; the three main forms of the dedication in manuscripts of the *Historia* are to Matilda's stalwart supporter, Robert of Gloucester, to Robert and Waleran of Meulan, or to Stephen and Robert.[34] Instead, Geoffrey's weak usurper and John's undisciplined, alien king may both be seen as manifestations of the concern for rightful kingship in the period in which both men were writing. Geoffrey's good kings, too, suggest John's characterization of the king ruled by law, discussed above. The practices of Arthur and of his immediate, good predecessors contrast those of the *tyranni* of both Geoffrey and John.

When Vortigern is eventually replaced by the admirable Aurelius, the Arthuriad begins to take on an appearance familiar from the rest of the *Historia*; bad kings are often succeeded by good ones, but the good ones are often granted only too brief a tenure. Aurelius is a case in point. He is strong, honest, and pious: " . . . generous in giving, earnest in attending the divine services, modest in all things and above all unwilling to tell a lie. He was strong on foot and stronger on

---

[33] *Policraticus*, VI.xviii:
> . . . et in regno alieno regnare hominem contemptorem boni et aequi, cujus consilium infatuatum est ab inito, cujus causa in iniquitate et perfidia fundata est, negligentem disciplinae, ut eo non tam regnante, quam concutiente et collidente clerum et populum, provocarentur omnes ad omnia.

[34] Exact parallels certainly have been drawn, however. Walter F. Schirmer, *Die frühen Darstellungen des Arthurstoffes* (Cologne: Westdeutscher Verlag, 1958), suggests that Geoffrey wished to write a political treatise about contemporary events, p. 28. More recently, in "Profiting from the Past," Shichtman and Finke note that the frequent appearances of women in Geoffrey's narrative may suggest that he is creating a context for the idea of legitimate female rule, 22–23.

horseback, and skilled in the leading of an army."[35] Aurelius triumphs, and proves his exemplary nature by restoring lost lands to the aristocracy, rebuilding the churches and the church hierarchy, and reestablishing the rule of law. These accomplishments had already been predicted by Merlin, but it is significant that the prediction linked Aurelius's accomplishments with his doom: "He will bring peace to the peoples and restore the churches, but he will die by poison."[36] The result is that it would be almost impossible for an alert reader to relax and appreciate these accomplishments once they are described: "His whole attention was turned to the restoration of the realm, the rebuilding of the churches, the renovation of peace and laws, and the ordering of justice."[37] In these two passages the author's voice is operating at two different levels, delivering two different messages. On the one hand, there is Aurelius's reign, presented in carefully balanced phrases which in their own order echo the order Aurelius is bringing to the realm. Style and content reinforce each other to create an impression of stability and order. On the other hand, there is the echo of the prophet's prediction, a prediction which uses the same events to point to the king's end. It is as if the organizing efforts of men and art are being placed against unknown forces whose mouthpiece, Merlin, functions in part as a bitter representation of an author who is at once omniscient and powerless, despite his foreknowledge and his art.

The reign of Uther, Arthur's father, will be discussed when we come to consider the structural parallels through which Geoffrey makes many of his thematic points. If we continue for a moment to focus, however, on the question of the nature of good rule, then Arthur is properly considered immediately after Aurelius. From the moment he appears on the scene, Arthur is portrayed as an ideal figure:

> Now Arthur was a youth of fifteen years, of outstanding virtue and generosity. His innate goodness gave him such great grace that he was loved by almost all the people . . . Arthur, because his strength was linked with generosity, decided to harass the Saxons so that he

---

[35] *Historia regum Britannie*, c. 120: ". . . largus in dandis, sedulus in diuinis obsequiis, modestus in cunctis et super omnia mendatium uitans, fortis pede, fortior equo, et ad regendum exercitum doctus."

[36] *Historia regum Britannie*, c. 118: "Pacificabit nationes, restaurabit ecclesias, sed ueneno deficiet."

[37] *Historia regum Britannie*, c. 127: "Tota intentio ipsius uersabatur circa regni restitucionem, ecclesiarum reformationem, pacis ac legis renouationem, iusticie compositionem."

could enrich the household which served him with their wealth. Righteousness also moved him, for he ought by hereditary right to have the rule of the whole kingdom.[38]

Like Aurelius, Arthur is shown to be both brave and concerned with what is right. He has other qualities, however, which have not been stressed in the "ideal" kings of the *Historia* discussed thus far; for example, he is eminently practical and shrewd. These qualities, allied with his innate goodness, suggest that he will be less likely to fall prey to the treachery which tends to overtake the good kings, as well as to the vice which tends to overtake the bad.

The Arthuriad is, as we will see, different in formal terms from what has gone before, but its protagonist, if described in greater detail than usual, is nevertheless familiar. Like other good kings before him, Arthur reestablishes the churches, restores the hereditary rights of the aristocracy, and brings the land under the rule of law again. His marriage to Guenevere occurs in a catalogue of such accomplishments, and is presented without embellishment, a deliberate contrast, perhaps, to the ill-considered unions of Vortigern (and Uther). Arthur's marriage is part of setting the realm in order, nothing more. Again there is a suggestive resemblance between Arthur's practice with respect to land rights and the eventual conclusion (after the writing of the *Historia*, but suggestive nevertheless) of the Anarchy. The terms set for peace at Winchester in 1153 included that "the disinherited should be restored to their own lands and enactments made binding on all as they used to be."[39] Arthur is the fulfillment of ideas of kingship which belong to both the political philosophy and even the later political reality of the twelfth century.

Arthur's military career, like his domestic policy, is considered and legitimate. Geoffrey is careful to provide Arthur with justifications for his desire "to bring all of Europe under his rule."[40] Arthur begins by aiding Loth, who should be king of Norway, against a usurper. Arthur's conquest in Gaul is followed by a court in which "he called

---

[38] *Historia regum Britannie*, c. 143:
> Erat autem Arturus .xv. annorum iuuenis, inaudite uirtutis atque largitatis. In quo tantam gratiam innata bonitas prestiterat ut a cunctis fere populis amaretur . . . Arturus ergo, quia in illo probitas largitionem comitabatur, statuit Saxones inquietare ut eorum opibus quae ei famulabatur ditaret familiam. Commonebat etiam id rectitudo, cum totius insule monarchiam debuerat hereditario iure obtinere.

[39] Quoted in Warren, *Henry II*, p. 62.

[40] *Historia regum Britannie*, c. 154: ". . . totam Europam sibi subdere."

all the clergy and the people together, and strengthened the state of the kingdom peacefully and legally."[41] The Roman wars, too, are presented as a just response to previous oppression and as an expression of Arthur's legitimate claim; it is also significant that, in a text which makes remarkably little reference to God or Providence, the victory of the Britons is assigned precisely to the divine plan: "This outcome was established by divine power, for as in former times the ancestors of those Romans had harassed the ancestors of the Britons with invidious iniquities, so now those Britons strove to defend the liberty which the others sought to take away from them, refusing to pay the tribute which had been unjustly demanded of them."[42] Arthur's reign, like that of other British rulers, is marked by warfare, but Geoffrey continually emphasizes that this warfare is righteous, as are its results. For once Britain has a ruler who is strong, shrewd, and just, and the text continues to dwell on the golden results for some time.

Strong, legitimate rule and the difficulty of achieving it are, then, central themes in Geoffrey's history, themes so far presented through the king-portraits with which Geoffrey's narrative is studded. This method appears to be analogous to that of the mirror for princes, and Arthur has simply joined the ranks of David, Augustus, Charlemagne, and the rest. Bumke quotes a popular passage from pseudo-Cyprian which appeared in many works of political philosophy in the twelfth century, and which seems to describe Aurelius and Arthur, as well as to condemn men like Vortigern:

> It is the justice of the king not to oppress anyone by unjust force; to judge people without regard for reputation of a person; to be a defender of strangers, orphans, and widows; to prevent theft; to punish adultery; not to elevate the unjust; not to support the unchaste and minstrels; to destroy the godless; not to permit murderers to live; to protect the churches and feed the poor with alms; to entrust the just with the business of royal government; to have experienced, wise, and prudent advisors; to pay no heed to the superstitious customs of magicians, soothsayers, and sorceresses; to

---

[41] *Historia regum Britannie*, c. 155: ". . . ubi conuocato clero et populo statum regni pace et lege confirmauit."

[42] *Historia regum Britannie*, c. 175: "Quod diuine potentie stabat loco cum et ueteres eorum priscis temporibus auos istorum inuisis inquietationibus infestassent; et isti tunc libertatem quam illi eisdem demere affectabant tueri instarent, abnegantes tributum quod ab ipsis iniuste exigebatur."

suppress rage; to defend the realm bravely and effectively against enemies, and to trust God in all things.[43]

But the *Historia* is more than a string of exemplary portraits. It is in his attention to the overall structure of his work that Geoffrey most clearly distinguishes himself from his contemporaries. His careful manipulation of narrative momentum, his creation of anecdotes whose significance echoes beyond their immediate context and, above all, his radical disruption of the narrative flow with Merlin's *Prophetie*, have no match among twelfth-century historians. These features, as much as the invented story material, explain the modern critic's sense that Geoffrey is an artist who manages to "fuse and confuse historical truth and narrative truth."[44] The impact of these features on the central theme highlights Geoffrey's radical departure from the assumptions of contemporary historiography, even as he shares some of its interests.

The first structural aspect of note is the break which the Arthuriad represents in the overall rhythm of the piece. The *Historia regum Britannie* is composed of a series of king portraits of varying length, linked together by the material which recites how each king came to and lost power; we have already seen a part of this pattern at work in the Constantine/ Vortigern/ Aurelius sequence. The Arthurian story receives disproportionate treatment, occupying about a third of the entire *Historia*. While it is impossible to disentangle the Arthuriad entirely from the narrative fabric into which it is woven, it is nevertheless the case that the sheer bulk of this portion of the text encourages the reader to forget, for a time, the normal pattern of the *Historia*. William of Rennes's thirteenth-century adaptation of the *Historia*, discussed in chapter 2, acknowledges the separateness of Geoffrey's Arthuriad by writing a new invocation for that part of the narrative. Geoffrey's treatment results in a suspension of the work's relentless chronology, a suspension which is heightened by stylistic aspects of the Arthurian episode, and has thematic, as well as artistic, force.

For a long time, the *Historia* dwells on Arthur's successes. If the usual rhythm of the *Historia* encourages pessimism – good kings seem inevitably to be succeeded by bad – then this leisurely treatment of Arthur's reign seems designed to obviate or suspend that pessi-

[43] Quoted in Bumke, *Courtly Culture*, pp. 277–78.
[44] Shichtman and Finke, "Profiting from the Past," 13.

mism. For pages, instead of paragraphs, we are allowed to dwell on the strengths of a king and the glory he brings to his people. In the end, however, the forces of history once more come into play. The effect is that much more devastating because it is delayed, and because the glowing picture of the age of Arthur has permitted, and in fact encouraged, us to forget the constant warnings in everything which leads up to this apparent golden age. Thus Geoffrey's manipulation of narrative momentum and audience reaction hammers home his grim vision of the nature of the historical process much more effectively than would direct statement.

It is immediately clear in the story of Arthur's attempts to gain firm control of his realm that we have moved towards a more detailed form of narrative than has hitherto been Geoffrey's practice. With the exception of the occasional description or anecdote, like that concerning Vortigern's infatuation with Renwein, the body of the *Historia* has been presented in a fairly straightforward fashion. This is not to say that the narrative has been plain; despite his protestations to the contrary, Geoffrey makes free use of various rhetorical techniques to lend interest to his battle sequences, and to the set speeches given to various characters. Nevertheless, all of these passages have a certain sameness about them; the description is that of battles in general rather than in particular, and the various speeches are of historical importance but normally have little in them to particularize the speaker. In the Arthuriad, detail suddenly becomes richer and more individual. It also broadens out beyond the focus on battles and historical set speeches. The treatment of Arthur is a case in point. When Arthur is first introduced in the passage cited above, there is much to recall the portraits of other kings like Aurelius. In this case, however, Geoffrey adds more detail:

> Arthur himself was clothed in a breastplate worthy of so great a king, and he placed on his head a golden helmet sculpted in the likeness of a dragon. On his shoulders was his shield, called Pridwen, on which the image of the blessed Mary, mother of God, was depicted, so that she was continually called to his memory. He was girded with his sword Caliburn, the best of swords, made in the island of Avalon, and a spear called Ron adorned his right hand; this spear was long and broad, well-suited for battle.[45]

---

[45] *Historia regum Britannie*, c. 147:
   Ipse uero Arturus lorica tanto regi digna indutus auream galeam simulachro draconis insculptam capiti adaptat: humeris quoque suis clipeum uocabulo Priduen in quo

49

The arming of the hero is a familiar convention in epic and romance; Geoffrey's use of it here distinguishes Arthur from the kings who have gone before him. The naming of the weapons and the indications of their provenance also suggest the heroic world, perhaps derived from the semi-mythic early Welsh tradition which is so much in evidence in the early part of Geoffrey's other work, the *Vita Merlini*.[46] It is not surprising, with the expectations set up by the heroic overtones of the arming scene, that we should shortly be told that Arthur "killed four hundred and seventy men with his sword Caliburn alone."[47]

The description of Arthur's plenary court at Caerleon at Whitsun is a further opportunity to emphasize the magnificence of the Arthurian court, and the success that such magnificence implies. Again, Geoffrey provides more detail in this passage than has been his custom in earlier parts of the *Historia*. A rhetorical set-piece, the description of the city, is followed by a lengthy list of those in attendance. The number of names emphasizes how far-reaching is Arthur's influence, as figures from all over Europe arrive to attend the court. In the summary of the activities at this gathering, Geoffrey sounds the familiar notes of later romance:

> . . . whatever knight of that country was famous for prowess wore clothing and arms of one color. The women, too, fashionably attired in the same colors, would have nothing of the love of any man, unless he had been proven three times in battle. The women, then, were made chaste and more virtuous, and the soldiers more brave for the love of them.[48]

---

imago sancte Marie Dei genetricis impicta ipsum in memoriam ipsius sepissime reuocabat. Accinctus ergo Caliburno gladio optimo et in insula Auallonis fabricato lancea dextram suam decorat que nomine Ron uocabatur. Hec erat ardua lataque lancea, cladibus apta.

[46] Neil Wright notes that the last line of this description forms an internally rhymed hexameter line (*Historia regum Britannie*, p. 104, n. 1). It is extremely common for Welsh prose texts to make use of verse at significant moments; in the fourth branch of the *Mabinogi*, Gwydion sings a series of *englyn* to lure Lleu, in the form of an eagle, from a tree. In the Arthurian tale of *Culhwch ac Olwen*, Arthur mocks Cei with an *englyn*, an act so significant that from then on there is enmity between them. Geoffrey may be echoing a practice familiar to him from such sources.

[47] *Historia regum Britannie*, c. 147: ". . . quadringentos septuaginta uiros solo Caliburno gladio peremit."

[48] *Historia regum Britannie*, c. 157:

> Quicunque . . . famosus probitate miles in eadem erat unius coloris uestibus atque armis utebatur. Facete etiam mulieres consimilia indumenta habentes nullius amorem habere dignabantur nisi tertio in milicia probatus esset. Efficiebantur ergo caste et meliores et milites pro amore illarum probiores.

Jaeger argues that Geoffrey's references to *facete mulieres* and *facetia incolarum* demonstrate the existence of the cult of love two decades before the first vernacular romances were composed.[49] The passage could certainly be seen as the product of a court writer in his role as didactic civilizer of the aristocracy. But it is also important that the narrative pause for the description of this display of excellence. Elsewhere in the *Historia*, the narrative is halted for occasional informative anecdotes, important speeches, or comic moments of serious import. The leisurely description of peacetime activities here is part of the strategy of the whole Arthuriad, occupying as it does a disproportionate share of the work. It is true that Arthurian history was one of the *lacunae* which Geoffrey was at some liberty to fill. At the same time, the expansion of this section of the *Historia* has the effect of setting it off for a time from the flow of British history, and the static descriptions of the excellence of the Arthurian world contribute to the sense that this period is somehow apart from that flow. This "otherworldliness," the product not of fantastic detail as in later romance narrative but rather of a structural strategy, suggests a tendency common to many of the texts in this study, a tendency, that is, to play with the expectations of the audience. The audience is, through this strategy, encouraged to forget the ominous message of Britain's history of bliss and blunder, exemplified in the murder of both Aurelius and of Arthur's own father Uther. While the result of the (temporary) removal of the Arthuriad from the process of history is for a time simply entertaining, the final effect is quite devastating, as this best of worlds, apparently apart from the world, succumbs to the same forces which seem to lurk everywhere in British history. We are allowed to forget history in order that, ultimately, the lesson of history will be underlined that much more dramatically. This history teaches; but the courtly manners exemplified in the passage above are merely a surface lesson over a much deeper and more problematic one.

The suspension of the normal narrative flow in the Arthuriad tends, I have suggested, to encourage readers to give themselves over to the Arthurian world. Yet the alert audience has also been provided, by Geoffrey, with clues that the apparent immunity of the Arthurian world from the cycles of British history is and will be illusory. One structural strategy, the alteration of king portraits, has been tempora-

---

[49] Jaeger, *The Origins of Courtliness*, p. 166.

rily suspended, but another, the careful use of parallel episodes, is retained. I refer here to Geoffrey's account of Arthur's father Uther, an account which should fill the alert reader with unease for what is to follow.

Uther succeeds Aurelius, and like his brother strengthens and extends the rule of law throughout the land. When he calls his nobles to court at London at Easter, the stage is set for a festive celebration of what is shaping up to be another period of peace and law in Britain. Yet while Aurelius bears no fault for the treachery which cuts short his reign, Uther is about to do as many British kings have done before him; he is going to put his personal interests above those of his country, and the result this time, as well as the usual discord, will be the birth of Arthur.

If Geoffrey intends us to condemn Uther and see a stain on Arthur's birth, he first plays with us by introducing the problem in a scene which is on one level comic. At the banquet are Gorlois, duke of Cornwall, and his wife Igerna. The presence of Igerna throws Uther into confusion:

> Among others, there came Gorlois, duke of Cornwall, and his wife Igerna with him, whose beauty surpassed that of all the women of Britain. And when the king spotted her among the other women, he suddenly burned with love for her, to the extent that, leaving all other things aside, he turned his whole attention towards her. To her alone he directed dishes incessantly, to her he sent his servants with golden goblets. He smiled at her often, and exchanged joking words with her. When her husband took notice of this, he suddenly became angry and left the court without leave.[50]

As was the case with the scene between Renwein and Vortigern, this piece is a lovely comic interlude, with the king-as-buffoon providing the humor. Yet Vortigern was a tyrant, and part of the pleasure of the former passage was in seeing the Saxons make a fool of him. It soon became clear, too, that the comic interlude between Vortigern and Renwein was to have extremely serious repercussions. If anything, the audience is allowed to laugh for even less time here. Uther has

---

[50] *Historia regum Britannie*, c. 137:

Aderat inter ceteros Gorlois dux Cornubie cum Ingerna coniuge sua, cuius pulchritudo omnes mulieres Britannie superabat. Cumque inter alias inspexisset eam rex, subito incaluit amore illius ita ut postpositis ceteris totam intencionem suam circa eam uerteret. Hec sola erat cui fercula incessanter dirigebat, cui aurea pocula familiaribus internuntiis mittebat. Arridebat ei multociens, iocosa uerba interserebat. Quod cum comperisset maritus, confestim iratus ex curia sine licencia recessit.

been shaping up to be a good king like his brother; an ominous note is sounded when we are told that his "whole attention" suddenly turned to Igerna. Aurelius's "whole attention" had been directed to the restoration of religion and justice. Uther's is now directed to the winning of another man's wife, a man who has been presented to us as a loyal soldier. The passage from pseudo-Cyprian quoted above says that the good king does not tolerate adultery; here the king prepares to practice it. It is true that the cuckolded husband is a stock figure of comedy, but even had the positive presentation of Gorlois not undermined this comic possibility, then once Uther moves from seduction to the declaration of war the whole situation begins to take on such serious overtones that laughter becomes an inappropriate response. The echo of the Vortigern episode is troubling enough; the scene also suggests, although the association is never made explicit, David and Bathsheba. As in the *Vita*, the audience's laughter at a familiar situation soon gives way to an uneasy recognition that events are more serious than they seem. The way in which these events catch the audience unprepared is in itself a dramatization of the danger of relaxing one's vigilance, in the *Historia* or in this world, for even a moment.

The ultimate outcome of Uther's infatuation will, of course, be the birth of Arthur; Geoffrey chooses to stress as well several more immediate consequences which underline the serious themes embedded in the episode. First, the language of the scene is unequivocal, stressing deception:

> And thus the king spent the night with Igerna and relieved himself through the sexual relations he desired. He deceived her through the false appearance which he had assumed. He also deceived her with the false words which he carefully composed, for he said that he had come secretly from the besieged camp so that he could see to the thing which was so dear to him, and also to his town. She, believing him, refused him nothing that he asked. Also that night was conceived that most famous of men, Arthur, who afterwards through his wonderful bravery won great renown.[51]

---

[51] *Historia regum Britannie*, c. 137:
Commansit itaque rex ea nocte cum Ingerna et sese desiderata uenere refecit. Deceperat namque eam falsa specie quam assumpserat. Deceperat etiam ficticiis sermonibus quos ornate conponebat. Dicebat enim se egressum esse furtim ab obsesso oppido ut sibi tam dilecte rei atque oppido suo disponeret. Unde ipsa credula nichil quod poscebatur abnegauit. Concepit quoque eadem nocte celeberrimum uirum illum A<r>turum qui postmodum ut celebris foret mira probitate promeruit.

This is not love, but the same lust which motivated Vortigern to betray his people. Like Vortigern at the death of Constans, Uther puts on a false face – literally, in this case – and he is aided and abetted in his deception by Merlin, who is preparing the way for Arthur. It is important that Uther is said to deceive Igerna with his lying words; Aurelius, it will be remembered, above all other things refused to tell a lie. There is no break between the deception and the conception, and so one must wonder if the means used to achieve the desired end are not also sabotaging that end from the first.

Throughout the *Historia*, the Britons are shown to be incapable of achieving a lasting peace; the story of Arthur, at once their greatest king and their most tragic, may indicate that the root of the problem is to be found somewhere in the Britons themselves, or in the fates which take a hand in their history, or in some less than happy alliance between the two. What happens while Uther is with Igerna lays out the problem quite clearly.

Uther's army decides, in the absence of their commander, to attack the fortress where Gorlois is besieged. Gorlois is killed, and the army indulges in looting. Geoffrey makes it perfectly clear that this unacceptable behavior is possible because the leader who should control such excesses is nowhere to be found: "The camp which they had besieged was captured, and the treasure deposited there was divided in an unequal fashion, for each seized with greedy fist as much as fortune and strength permitted."[52] Fortune may not be in control of human affairs all the time, but she certainly is when the attention of authority has been distracted. Here would seem to be the heart of the history of bliss and blunder in Britain; her leaders far too often allow their attention to wander, and this inattention opens the door for the malignant forces which are always waiting in the wings. A king must be ruled by law, and be ruler over his own desires, because if he is not, the forces of destruction will take advantage of his weakness, and his people will suffer.

Geoffrey also refuses to sanitize the union retroactively. Geoffrey is later quite clear as to Arthur's legitimacy; it is the nature of the marriage itself which is more ambiguous. With Gorlois dead, the way is clear for Uther to take Igerna. He does so, but while the text says that he was relieved that she was free from her marital obligations, it

---

[52] *Historia regum Britannie*, c. 138: "Captum est oppidum quod obsederant et opes introposite non equa sorte diuise. Nam ut cuique administrabat fortuna et fortitudo, capaci ungue rapiebat."

is not absolutely clear as to whether Uther and Igerna were in fact married, or happily married: "From then on they lived together equally, joined by no love at all, and they brought forth a daughter and a son."[53] It is possible that this phrase – *cum minimo amore* – is simply an oversight on Geoffrey's part, or a scribal error, but it may also be another intentional ambiguity, further shadowing Arthur's future career.

As I have said, Geoffrey does not allow the stain of *illegitimacy* to affect Arthur's succession, and the curious account cited above of Uther and Igerna's union has a single manuscript witness. The foolish conduct of a father need not necessarily affect his son's ability to rule; Vortigern, for example, has the wholly worthy Vortimer as his son, but Vortimer is murdered by the very Renwein who facilitated the Saxon arrival. Yet the unsettling echoes set up by the Vortigern/Uther parallel is not the only structural feature of the *Historia* which should signal caution before the account of Arthur's reign begins. Even more striking is the effect of the *Prophetie Merlini*. Their strange placement in the *Historia*, as well as the link they make between celestial and apocalyptic imagery, set up a disturbing matrix of associations which reverberates throughout the whole of the *Historia*.

It appears at first as if the story of Merlin will simply be woven into the fabric of the narration, in this case of Vortigern's flight from the Saxons. Yet the search for the blood of a fatherless boy soon gives way to Merlin's explanation of the red and white dragons, and at this point the *Prophetie* begin. These prophecies, which circulated separately from the *Historia*, are introduced almost as a text in their own right, and Geoffrey's prologue to this section sounds several notes we have heard before:

[53] *Historia regum Britannie*, c. 138: "Commanserunt deinde pariter cum minimo amore ligati progenueruntque filium et filiam." The phrase "cum minimo amore" seems to be unique to the Bern MS; the usual reading is "non minimo amore," or "by no little love." The First Variant reading omits the issue of love but is quite clear as to the legitimacy of the marriage: "The king and queen Igerna celebrated their marriage legitimately and magnificently" ("Nuptiis igitur legittime atque magnifice celebratis commanserunt pariter rex et regina Igerna" (Wright, c. 138)). It would of course be dangerous to build an interpretation on a single witness, however authoritative, but the Bern reading seems to be very much in accord with the negative attitude towards love, or lust, as it is expressed in the two "love" interludes which we have examined thus far. It will also be seen that the relationship between Arthur and Guenevere is portrayed solely in terms of its suitability, with no mention of love at all. Given Wright's assertion that the First Variant is a redaction of the Bern MS, it may be that a later reader took the phrase at face value and decided that this unsavory situation needed to be regularized.

> Love of your nobility, Alexander, bishop of Lincoln, compelled me
> to translate from British into Latin the prophecies of Merlin, before
> I had finished the history of the deeds of the British kings which I
> had begun. I had intended first to complete that work, and then to
> write this one, lest while the labor of both pressed upon me, my
> sense might prove too weak for either.[54]

As he did in the prologue to the whole work, Geoffrey is here
minimizing his own role. He is a mere translator, and a rather feeble
and limited one at that. The protestations of inadequacy are an
expected *topos*, yet the disclaimers also allow Geoffrey to shirk
responsibility for the content of the passage to come. This neutral
position can be playful and even mischievous, as the references in the
*explicit* to Henry of Huntingdon and William of Malmesbury may
suggest, but it can also be part of the uncertainty generated by the
*Historia*. The authorial voice admits no responsibility for the material
which follows or even, it is implied, for the way in which it has been
inserted, apparently rather haphazardly, into the fabric of the
*Historia*; this latter oddity is the responsibility of Alexander, bishop
of Lincoln. While it may indeed be unlikely, as Michael Curley
argues, that Geoffrey would have gone so far as to lie about
Alexander's initiation of the project – Geoffrey was, after all, closely
associated with Lincoln and his comments were unlikely to escape the
bishop of Lincoln's attention[55] – I would argue that we are at perfect
liberty to consider the ways in which Geoffrey has chosen to deploy
material apparently requested by his patron. The *Prophetie* contribute
a great deal to the overall theme of the *Historia*, and their placement,
too, can be shown to have great relevance for the subsequent
unfolding of the text. Geoffrey's protestations, then, can be seen as an
attempt to divert attention from what is in fact a clue to the
interpretation of the whole *Historia*. This is a work with various
levels of meaning, not all of them equally available to all in the
audience; indeed, the author seems at pains to hide, as much as to
suggest, the various possibilities. The ability of the *Historia* to

---

[54] *Historia regum Britannie*, c. 110:
> Coegit me, Alexander Lincolinensis presul, nobilitatis tue dilectio prophetias Merlini
> de Britannico in Latinum transferre antequam historiam parassem quam de gestis
> regum Britannicorum inceperam. Proposueram enim <illam> prius perficere istudque
> opus subsequenter explicare ne, dum uterque labor incumberet, sensus meus ad
> singula minor fieret.

[55] Curley, *Geoffrey of Monmouth*, pp. 48–50; Curley remarks on the interest in prophecy
among intellectuals of the day; see chapter 2.

support various levels of interpretation may explain its later popularity, even if that popularity suggests that most of Geoffrey's audience accepted the most superficial reading of the work, and that with the connivance of the author.

Chapter 6 will discuss Geoffrey's use of Merlin's prophetic ability in his *Vita Merlini*; as problematic as that text's reference to a "jocose Muse" might be, there is little doubt that laughter, however dark, is a dominant element in that work. The prophecies of the *Historia*, on the other hand, are revealed through tears rather than through laughter. The *Prophetie* are overwhelmingly concerned with the rise and fall of rulers, and with the social and religious dislocation that this cycle provokes. One senses again both the specific context of the Anarchy and the broader context of national and, ultimately, human history. Even when some of the prophecies may be tied with certainty to events in British history, broader references to disaster in almost biblical cadences are interspersed with them: "A bloody rain shall fall and a dire famine shall afflict mortals"; or "Death will seize the people and empty all the nations, and those who are left will desert the soil of their birth and will sow their seeds in foreign fields."[56] Images of civil and religious unrest predominate.

The last clearly identifiable prophecy states that "The lion's cubs shall be turned into fish of the sea."[57] The reference is to the sinking of the White Ship and the death of the children of Henry I in 1120, the event which ultimately precipitated the contest between Stephen and Matilda. This prophecy, however, occurs quite early on in the list, and what remains is tantalizing because one can never be sure if reference or irreverence is intended. There are several prophecies, for example, which sound like nonsense; "The feet of those that bark shall be cut off," for example, or "Thereafter, from the first to the fourth, from the fourth to the third, from the third to the second shall the thumb be rolled in oil."[58] R.W. Southern has noted that the ambiguity of

---

[56] *Historia regum Britannie*, c. 112, (3); (5): "Pluet sanguineus ymber et dira fames mortales afficiet." "Arripiet mortalitas populum cunctasque nationes euacuabit. Residui natale solum deserent et exteras culturas seminabunt." Tatlock argues that this style bears "a marked resemblance to the Psalms" (*Legendary History*, p. 406).

[57] *Historia regum Britannie*, c. 113, (12): "Catuli leonis in equoreos pisces transformabuntur . . ."

[58] *Historia regum Britannie*, cc. 113, (11); 114 (16): "Pedes latrantum truncabuntur." "Exin de primo in quartum, de quarto in tertium, de tertio in secundum rotabitur pollex in oleo." Tatlock suggests that the first of these may refer to the practice of cutting off dogs' feet in punishment for hunting violations (*Legendary History*, p. 358); the thumb in oil remains a mystery.

prophetic language was often regarded as evidence of genuineness;[59] Geoffrey's ambiguous language may be another legitimating device, or it may be intended to parody prophetic utterance and hence to question the efficacy of prophecy as explanation, as "that which illuminated God's plan."[60] It should be noted that these prophecies were received as genuine by many medieval readers, as chapter 2 makes clear.

Other prophecies seem to belong to the strain of "marvels" literature; passages which focus on marvels occur also in the *Vita*, and in the *De Ortu Waluuanii*. The taste for the marvelous, discussed in the Introduction, seems to be characteristic of much writing associated with the court. The purpose of such passages may be entertainment, or mockery, or some mixture of these; the wit of the writer often seems to be the main focus. In the *Historia*, for example, there is this exotic description of the springs of Winchester:

> Three springs will burst forth in the city of Winchester, whose streams will divide the island into three parts. Whoever drinks from the first will enjoy a long life and will never be oppressed by the coming of any illness. Whoever drinks from the second will die from insatiable hunger, and pallor and horror will sit on his face. Whoever drinks from the third will die a sudden death, nor will it be possible for his body to be buried.[61]

There are also many prophecies in the *Historia* which concern themselves with sexual pratices, perhaps to parallel the sense of social disintegration which comes to dominate, or perhaps merely to provide titillation; for example, "The fetid breath from their nostrils will corrupt wives and make them available to all, and the father will not know his own son because all will copulate as cattle do."[62] Chapter 3 discusses the possibility that Andreas Capellanus is deliberately titillating a clerical courtly audience with his accounts of sexual antics at court; perhaps Geoffrey is here feeding a similar taste.

---

[59] R.W. Southern, "Aspects of the European Tradition of Historical Writing: 3. History as Prophecy," *Transactions of the Royal Historical Society* 22 (1972), 161.

[60] Southern, "Aspects of the European Tradition of Historical Writing: 3," 172.

[61] *Historia regum Britannie*, c. 116, (31):
> Tres fontes in urbe Guintonia erumpent quorum riuuli insulam in tres portiones secabunt. Qui bibet de uno diuturniori uita fruetur nec superuenienti languore grauabitur. Qui bibet de altero indeficienti fame peribit et in facie ipsius pallor et horror sedebit. Qui bibet de tertio subita morte periclitabitur nec corpus ipsius subire poterit sepulch<r>um.

Compare the section on rivers and lakes in the *Vita Merlini*, discussed in chapter 6.

[62] *Historia regum Britannie*, c. 116, (53): "Fetore narium mu<l>ieres corrumpent et proprias communes facient. Nesciet pater filium proprium quia more pecudum lasciuient."

There may well be elements of facetious wit, of a peculiar kind of playfulness, in this section of the *Historia*, and these elements, combined with examples of prophecies whose cryptic quality seems exaggerated to the point of parody, may suggest that this section is not always to be taken seriously. On the other hand, there are constant, serious themes running through the *Prophetie*. The rise and fall of rulers is continually emphasized, and is always coupled with an awareness that the fates of these men have profound effects on the people of their realms. The animal imagery, imagery which grows more dense as the *Prophetie* approach their conclusion, underlines the bestial nature of internal warfare, and emphasizes how far such behavior is from the ideal which might be hoped for from humanity. The *Prophetie* seem designed to show, in fact, that man is a beast, and in this respect their message is much grimmer than that in the *Vita*.

The *Vita*'s prophecies close with a recognition that Christ is the only refuge from the turbulent fortunes of the world. The *Historia* certainly shows the same awareness of the vagaries of fortune, but the conclusion of its prophecies offers no explicit way off the wheel. Instead, the imagery changes once more, from the animal to the celestial, in a picture of a final apocalypse:

> The splendor of the sun will languish in the amber of Mercury, and there will be horror among those who see this. Mercury of Arcady will change its shield, and the helmet of Mars will call to Venus. The helmet of Mars will cast a shadow, and the rage of Mercury will cross over its orbit. Iron Orion will bare its sword, and watery Phoebus will torment the clouds. Jupiter will leave its ordained paths and Venus will desert its appointed lines. The anger of the star Saturn will fall and kill mortals with a curved sickle.[63]

The heavens are out of joint and are showing themselves to be the enemy of humanity. The world is in bondage to the vagaries of Fortune, to the stars, and the stars are both unreliable and ill-disposed. What, then, are we to make of the possibilities of mockery raised earlier in this discussion? If there is parody here, it seems to be tending towards nihilism rather than towards corrective laughter. Prophecy is mocked because of its inefficacy; Merlin can recite the

---

[63] *Historia regum Britannie*, c. 117, (73):
> Splendor solis electro Mercurii languebit et erit horror inspicientibus. Mutabit clipeum Stilbon Archadie, uocabit Uenerem galea Martis. Galea Martis umbram conficiet, transsibit terminos furor Mercurii. Nudabit ensem Orion ferreus, uexabit nubes <Phebus> equoreus. Exibit Iupiter licitas semitas et Uenus deseret statutas lineas. Saturni syderis liuido corruet et falce recurua mortales perimet.

most horrible of futures and yet have no effect whatsoever on the course of fate. His impotence is a matter for bitterness, and if the prophetic voice is in some sense also the author's – the voice of the one who knows what is going to happen, even if his control of events is at best illusory – then the impact of the *Prophetie* may bring the whole endeavor of the *Historia* into question. Geoffrey, like Merlin, can warn, but he seems to have little confidence that he can effect any kind of change in his countrymen, their kings, or their future. Jan Ziolkowski has suggested that in the *Vita*, Merlin's early prophecies "evince a hopelessness that any divine order governs events in the human world."[64] The Merlin of the *Historia* is fixed in such a hopelessness; to conclude the *Prophetie* with apocalypse without redemption suggests history cannot perform its usual medieval functions – to reveal God's plan and to teach good behavior – because human beings can neither understand nor learn. Brynley Roberts suggests that the *Prophetie* demonstrate "the moral principle that a nation reaps what is sown in past ages."[65] What distinguishes Geoffrey's exemplification of that principle from similar lessons in other Latin histories and in the mirror for princes is the pessimism with which he approaches the exemplary aspect of the historian's task.

The *Prophetie* have local as well as cosmic significance; they occur in the middle of the developments leading up to the coming of Arthur. If we do not take seriously Geoffrey's statement that he is simply putting them in here to please his patron, then we may consider the impact which this structure has on the material to follow. For Roberts, the placement of the *Prophetie* is a significant part of their message: "History stands still for a moment while we seek its significance."[66] History's significance is exemplified by the fate of Arthur. Arthur will be a very bright spot in an otherwise somber history, yet the forecasting of doom before he appears on the scene darkens the picture from the outset. The perversion of the stars, too, shadows Arthur's rise, since his coming has been presaged by celestial display; Merlin explains the phenomenon thus to Uther:

[64] Jan Ziolkowski, "The Nature of Prophecy in Geoffrey of Monmouth's *Vita Merlini*," in *Poetry and Prophecy: The Beginnings of a Literary Tradition*, ed. James L. Kugel (Ithaca, New York: Cornell University Press, 1990), p. 160.

[65] Roberts, "Geoffrey of Monmouth, *Historia regum Britannie*, and *Brut y Brenhinedd*," p. 103.

[66] Roberts, "Geoffrey of Monmouth, *Historia regum Britannie*, and *Brut y Brenhinedd*," p. 103.

For that star signifies you, as does the fiery dragon beneath the star. The ray which stretches towards the shores of Gaul portends your future son, who will be most powerful, and whose power will extend over all the kingdoms which he will protect. And the other ray signifies your daughter, whose sons and grandsons will hold the kingship of Britain in turn.[67]

There is no indication here that Uther will die of poison as did his brother, or that Arthur's rule will give way to more civil discord. Yet the celestial imagery has overwhelmingly negative implications because of the apocalyptic ending of the *Prophetie*, and Arthur's rule is thus both predicted and shadowed.

The negative implications of celestial portents continue to reverberate once Arthur has assumed his throne, for the dream which Arthur has on his way to his battle with Lucius suggests aspects of the *Prophetie*:

> As he lay drowsing, in his sleep he saw a bear flying through the air, at whose growling all shores shook; there was also a terrible dragon, flying in from the west, which illuminated the country with the glow of its eyes. When the one met the other, a marvelous battle occurred. The aforementioned dragon attacked the bear over and over again, burning it with its fiery breath and casting it, entirely burned, down to the earth. Arthur, awaking, described what he had dreamed to those standing about. They, interpreting it, said that the dragon signified him, and the bear some giant with which he was to fight; their battle portended the war to come between them, and the victory of the dragon was that which would come to him. But Arthur, thinking otherwise, conjectured that the vision had come about because of himself and the emperor.[68]

---

[67] *Historia regum Britannie*, c. 133:
Te etenim sydus istud significat et igneus draco sub sydere. Radius autem qui uersus Gallicanam plagam porrigitur portendit tibi futurum filium et potentissimum cuius potestas omnia regna que proteget habebit. Alter uero radius significat filiam, cuius filii et nepotes regnum Britannie succedenter habebunt.

[68] *Historia regum Britannie*, c. 164:
Sopitus etiam per somnum uidit ursum quendam in aere uolantem cuius murmure tota litora intremebant; terribilem quoque draconem ab occidenti aduolare, qui splendore oculorum suorum patriam illuminabat. Alterum uero alteri occurrentem miram pugnam committere. Sed prefatum draconem ursum sepius irruentem ignito anhelitu comburere combustumque in terram prosternere. Expergefactus ergo Arturus astantibus quod somniauerat indicauit. Qui exponentes dicebant draconem significare eum, ursum uero aliquem gigantem qui cum ipso congred<e>retur; pugnam autem eorum portendere bellum quod inter ipsos futurum erat; uictoriam uero draconis illam quae ei proueniret. At Arturus aliud coniectabat existimans ob se et imperatorem talem uisionem contigisse.

The beast imagery, the conflict, and the celestial display all recall the end of the *Prophetie,* and the dream, like the *Prophetie,* requires interpretation. The interpretation provided, however, is another feature which serves to undermine any real possibility of understanding, for both those who interpret the dream for Arthur, and Arthur himself, are correct as to its significance. Shortly after the dream, Arthur fights with and defeats the giant of Mont-St.-Michel. Later, after several battles, Lucius too is defeated. However, the dream continues to reverberate through the rest of the narrative. The campaign against the Romans is both the height of the Arthurian period, in which Arthur joins the ranks of Brutus and Belinus, and the beginning of the end, for it is while Arthur is absent on this campaign that Modred seizes the queen and power in Britain, provoking yet another internal war whose final result is the death of Arthur, along with the flower of Britain's warriors. The return to the animal and celestial imagery of the *Prophetie* in this dream points to the dream's negative implications. Arthur is the bear as well as the dragon, the victor and the vanquished in this dream. The dream which signifies his success simultaneously presages his fall; the grim implication is that the seeds of destruction are present even at the moment of victory. The wheel is about to turn again; where does Geoffrey lay the blame?

In later chronicle treatments of the Arthurian story, like William of Rennes's *Gesta regum Britanniae,* blame is laid partly at Arthur's door. Arthur moves from just to unjust conquest, and suffers retribution accordingly. In the vernacular, too, Arthur may be figured as a conqueror in the negative sense. He is clearly called covetous in the *Awntyrs off Arthure,* discussed in chapter 5, and some readers argue that the *Alliterative Morte Arthure* also presents a king whose movement from just to unjust conquest is offered as the reason for his downfall.[69] Geoffrey does not allow this possibility. Wandering attention and self-centeredness on the part of British rulers have been shown to be responsible for some of the disasters of the past, but there is little evidence of these flaws in Arthur. It has already been noted that Geoffrey is at great pains to provide Arthur with legitimate

[69] William Matthews, in *The Tragedy of Arthur: A Study of the Alliterative "Morte Arthure"* (Berkeley: University of California Press, 1960) argues that Arthur is modeled on Alexander and is guilty of lust for conquest. But Elizabeth Porter reads the *Morte* as celebratory: Arthur's actions are understandable in the context of medieval laws of war, and Arthur declares for the Crusade; "Chaucer's Knight, the Alliterative *Morte Arthure,* and Medieval Laws of War: A Reconsideration," *Nottingham Medieval Studies* 27 (1983), 56–78.

reasons for his conquests. Arthur, like Aurelius, is one of the good kings who falls victim, not to his own vices, but rather to human treachery. Sin may indeed provide an explanation for the fall of Arthurian society, but because the sin is not Arthur's, it is that much more difficult to accept the fall as part of some benevolent final plan.

We have seen that providence, rarely referred to in the *Historia*, is made responsible for Arthur's victory over the Romans. It is almost immediately after this victory that Arthur receives word of Modred's treachery. Because divine intervention receives little mention elsewhere in the *Historia*, its introduction here seems particularly pointed. The juxtaposition of divine power in the battle and the treachery of Modred draws that treachery, and the lack of a providential explanation for it, to our attention. It is the central assumption of medieval history that there is a benevolent plan guiding the unrolling of human history. It would be astonishing were any medieval author to *deny* this assumption, but Geoffrey gives it precious little play, and concentrates instead on the fact of treachery rather than on anything which might reconcile us to its results. Instead, he offers only the cycles of history, cycles which by their very nature never benefit the Britons for long.

In this light, Geoffrey's treatment of Modred's treachery is striking:

> Nor will Geoffrey of Monmouth, most noble consul, be silent about this. Instead he will, with his lowly pen and briefly, set forth the battles which that famous king fought with his nephew upon his return to Britain after his famous victory, as he found them in the aforementioned British book, and has also heard them from Walter of Oxford, a man most learned in many histories.[70]

The return to the British book at this bleak moment may be an attempt on Geoffrey's part to evade the implications of his history. The fiction of the British book is a liberating device for Geoffrey throughout the *Historia*, allowing him to invent material and point it towards his desired ends with relative freedom. The reintroduction of the book at this point in the text certainly looks like an evasion of responsibility for the end of the story – a storyteller's apology that things must turn out badly, or a facetious covering of the truth – but

---

[70] *Historia regum Britannie*, c. 177:
Nec hoc quidem, consul auguste, Galfridus Monemutensis tacebit sed, ut in prefato Britannico sermone inuenit et a Gwaltero Oxenefordensi in multis historiis peritissimo uiro audiuit, uili licet stilo breuiter propalabit que prelia inclitus ille rex post uictoriam istam in Britanniam reuersus cum nepote suo commiserit.

it also allows Geoffrey to distance himself from the implications of the way in which he has chosen to present the story, for it does seem that he is doing something quite radical. Hayden White suggests that the desire to "narrativize" experience into history is connected to a desire to moralize that reality;[71] what is astonishing about Geoffrey is that *his* moral – what White would call the underlying mythos to which he conforms his emplotment of events – is so much at odds with the assumptions of his contemporaries.

Several modern historians have understood Geoffrey's treatment of history as radical in terms of medieval historiography. Brooke notes that while his predecessors found divine judgment to be the main foundation for historical events, ". . . human causes, and impersonal Fate, played an increasing part in Geoffrey – partly because, though pretending to be a historian, he wrote fiction and therefore felt freer to play with new ideas."[72] I have already suggested that "fiction" and "history" are rather blunt categories, but Brooke's remarks point to an important distinction between Geoffrey and conventional historians. Geoffrey and many of the other Latin writers in this study have seized the opportunity presented by the confluence of ironic writing, an interest in the marvelous, and the possibilities of Arthurian story, to engage in narrative experiment which in some cases leads to a reevaluation of traditional modes of understanding as well as telling. Antonia Gransden asserts that Geoffrey alone, among the historians of his age, "abandoned the Christian intention of historical writing."[73] Elsewhere she describes the contents of twelfth-century English historical prologues; it is significant that Geoffrey's prologues omit the standard *topoi* of history as revelatory of God's plan and as didactic in intent.[74] Robert Hanning, too, after detailing the development of medieval historical writing, in which history becomes the means by which God reveals His plan for the world, argues that Geoffrey deliberately removed Christian features from his material, in order to construct a narrative in which men have power over history,

---

[71] Hayden White, "The Value of Narrativity in the Representation of Reality," *Critical Inquiry* 7 (1980), 18.

[72] Christopher N.L. Brooke, "Historical Writing in England between 850 and 1150," *La storiografia altomedievale*, 17, pt. 1 (Spoleto, 1970), 224.

[73] Antonia Gransden, *Historical Writing in England c. 550–c. 1307* (London: Routledge and Kegan Paul, 1974), p. 187.

[74] Antonia Gransden, "Prologues in the Historiography of Twelfth-Century England," in *England in the Twelfth Century*, ed. Daniel Williams (Woodbridge, Suffolk: Boydell, 1990), pp. 64–65.

but history also has power over men.[75] Geoffrey's relationship to the romance genre may be located in part in his questioning of the meaning of history. Spiegel argues that "By situating itself between the vaguely demarcated boundaries of history and 'fable,' courtly romance had problematized, by inverting, the traditional relationship between the historical 'truth' of the past and the imaginative 'truth' of fiction, calling into question the moral utility of the former through its implicit validation of the latter."[76] Geoffrey certainly seems to be questioning the utility of historical truth, but what is the nature of his "truth"? Hanning comes closest to appreciating the full implications of Geoffrey's procedure when he writes that Merlin's apocalyptic vision is a statement about the absence of divine providence: "the impersonal universe which has presided over the rise and fall of kingdoms will lose control of itself and history will dissolve into nothingness."[77] This is hardly the vaunted twelfth-century optimism about human nature and human destiny, but one should remember that John of Salisbury and Peter of Blois, famous humanists both, painted a picture almost as grim, if more circumscribed in scope, in their denunciations of the court and its ability to corrupt all that it touched. Geoffrey may simply have extended the pessimism and occasional misanthropy of court satire to the world stage.

The final message of the *Historia*, then, is bleak indeed, and Geoffrey's handling of its dying moments underlines this bleakness. The final battle between Arthur and Modred receives a fair bit of description, but Arthur's death, although its famous ambiguity would generate a great deal in romances to come, is shockingly brief: "But that most famous king Arthur was mortally wounded; Arthur having been taken from there to the island of Avalon for the healing of his wounds, he handed over the crown of Britain to his cousin Constantine, son of Cador, duke of Cornwall, in the year 542 after the incarnation of our Lord. May his soul rest in peace."[78] The bald nature of this death, in contrast to the time spent on Arthur's life, pulls the audience up short. Arthur's reign is followed by a return to

---

[75] Robert W. Hanning, *The Vision of History in Early Britain: From Gildas to Geoffrey of Monmouth* (New York: Columbia University Press, 1966), pp. 138–72.

[76] Spiegel, *Romancing the Past*, p. 64.

[77] Hanning, *The Vision of History in Early Britain*, pp. 171–72.

[78] *Historia regum Britannie*, c. 178: "Set et inclitus ille rex Arturus letaliter uulneratus est; qui illinc ad sananda uulnera sua in insulam Auallonis euectus Constantino cognato suo et filio Cadoris ducis Cornubie diadema Britannie concessit anno ab incarnatione Domini .dxlii.. Anima eius in pace quiescat."

the quick narration of a succession of rulers which characterized much of the earlier part of the *Historia*. This structure emphasizes that, although Arthur seemed to be holding the malignant forces of history at bay, in the end they have overwhelmed even him. The audience moves from the leisurely progression of the exploits of Britain's most famous king, to the shocked recognition that he is in fact no more immune to fate than were any of his predecessors. Geoffrey is certainly playing with history, but not simply, or even mainly, by inventing material and enlivening it with "literary" conventions. Indeed most of Geoffrey's literary moments, I have argued, are easily understood as the rhetorical embellishment expected of and routinely practiced by Latin writers in many genres. It is when Geoffrey removes this mask that he separates himself from traditional historians. His manipulation of traditional historical writing has as its target the central assumption of medieval historiography itself; that is, that history is the unfolding of a providential plan for mankind, whose benefit can be recognized by those with the right clues. Geoffrey, like Merlin the prophet, has all the clues but is powerless to bring about a satisfactory outcome to his *Historia*. This is not to say that the providential plan does not exist, but Geoffrey clearly lacks the confidence of many of his contemporaries that it is easy to discern. Perhaps this is a problem of hermeneutics rather than of faith; yet in the human realm such a problem remains acute. History and prophecy are not in the end revelatory, but rather another *speculum* through which we gaze *in aenigmate*, viewing little of what is on the other side.

Geoffrey's attack on medieval historiography does not seem to have impressed itself upon his contemporaries. Historians concerned themselves with worrying about his sources and the mass of new material which he introduced, while the burgeoning romance genre eagerly adopted and expanded his "stories." Yet we may see his legacy in more than merely the details of the Arthurian story. If later writers either failed to perceive or, perceiving, eschewed the nihilistic implications of the *Historia*, there are nevertheless many, Latin and vernacular alike, who digested and reflected in their own works the use of Arthur as an exemplary British king. In Geoffrey, Arthur is a hero; in some of the works to be examined in the chapters to follow, he is less praiseworthy. The thread of continuity lies in the use of a central, attractive or at least attracting royal figure to illustrate some concerns about kingship and rule. While Geoffrey's pessimism about the end of history may not often recur, his cynical view of the all too human foibles of most kings is found again and again. Few writers will put Arthur in so frightening a cosmic context, but many will use him as their model for good or bad kingship. And there are some post-Galfridian Latin writers who seem to have been inspired to play with conventions and with their audiences, whether for education, entertainment, or some mixture of the two.

# 2

# "This is that Arthur": chronicle responses to Arthur

While Geoffrey of Monmouth may surely be credited with producing the first ordered, sequential, and complete Arthurian story, that story quickly moved from the realm of Latin history (or pseudo-history) into the world of vernacular romance and chronicle adaptation. By the end of the twelfth century, we see the romances of Chrétien de Troyes and the vernacular adaptations of Geoffrey in Wace's *Brut* and in the Welsh *Bruts*[1]; by the thirteenth there are Layamon's translation and adaptation of Wace,[2] the Welsh adaptations of French romances,[3] and the great French prose cycles. The few free-standing Latin Arthurian narratives studied in the chapters that follow seem slight next to this vernacular proliferation. It would however be misleading to suggest that they are the only evidence for the prominence – or lack of it – of the Arthurian story in Latin prose and verse.

[1] The dates of the latter are uncertain; Robert Huntington Fletcher, *The Arthurian Material in the Chronicles, especially those of Great Britain and France* (Cambridge, Mass.: Harvard University Press, 1906), notes only that there is a manuscript of one of the main forms dating to the early thirteenth century (p. 117, n. 8). For a recent discussion of the relationship between the Welsh *Bruts* and Geoffrey see Roberts, "Geoffrey of Monmouth, *Historia regum Britanniae*, and *Brut y Brenhinedd*," pp. 97–116; Roberts notes that these are generally straight translations which add names, patronymics and so on from the store of Welsh genealogical lore, pp. 111–12.

[2] Another difficult date; Layamon's *Brut* makes use of the past tense in reference to Eleanor of Aquitaine as queen of Henry II, suggesting to most readers a date after either Henry's death in 1189 or Eleanor's own death in 1204. The language of the two manuscript copies has been dated to about the second half of the thirteenth century. The presence of elements of the Old English tradition, among other things, leads W.R.J. Barron and S.C. Weinberg to conclude that "the original composition can hardly have been written later than the opening decades of the thirteenth century"; see *Laȝamon's Arthur: The Arthurian Section of Laȝamon's Brut*, ed. W.R.J. Barron and S.C. Weinberg (Harlow, Essex: Longman, 1989), pp. xi–xii.

[3] The degree to which these three "romances" are translations or adaptations of their analogues in the work of Chrétien de Troyes is still at issue; and the dating of these works is uncertain, with many commentators opting for thirteenth-century composition while agreeing that the late twelfth century would also be possible. See the entries for each work in *The Arthur of the Welsh*, ed. Bromwich et al.: Roger Middleton, "*Chwedl Geraint ab Erbin*," pp. 147–57; R.L. Thomson, "*Owain: Chwedl Iarlles y Ffynnon*," pp. 159–69; and Ian Lovecy, "*Historia Peredur ab Efrawg*," pp. 170–82.

There is a wealth of Arthurian reference in Latin chronicles, both before[4] and after Geoffrey.[5] Before Geoffrey, Arthur appears (perhaps) as the unnamed victor of Badon in Gildas,[6] as the *dux bellorum* of "Nennius," with his list of battles,[7] and the Arthur who died at Camlann with Medraut in the *Annales Cambriae*.[8] Also before Geoffrey's *Historia* is the famously disgruntled remark of William of Malmesbury in his *Gesta Regum Anglorum*: "This is that Arthur about whom the foolish tales of the Britons rave even today; one who is clearly worthy to be told about in truthful histories rather than to be dreamed about in deceitful fables, since for a long time he sustained his ailing nation, and sharpened the unbroken minds of his people to war."[9] William's remark is important for its testimony to the pre-Galfridian existence of the Breton hope, discussed below with respect to the *Vera historia de morte Arthuri* and the *Draco Normannicus*. It is also important for the distinction it implies between *veraces historiae* and *fallaces fabulae* and *nugae*. This distinction is one we

---

[4] For a recent overview of the two most important Latin sources, see Thomas Charles-Edwards, "The Arthur of History," in *The Arthur of the Welsh*, ed. Bromwich *et al.*, pp. 15–32.

[5] See Fletcher, *The Arthurian Material in the Chronicles*. Excerpts from many of the Latin works are found in E.K. Chambers, *Arthur of Britain* (London: Sidgwick and Jackson, 1927). Laura Keeler's *Geoffrey of Monmouth and the Late Latin Chroniclers 1300–1500* (Berkeley: University of California Press, 1946), concentrates on the later use of Geoffrey in Latin histories, while Schirmer's *Die frühen Darstellungen des Arthurstoffes* concentrates on Wace and Layamon.

[6] In his *De Excidio et Conquestu Britanniae*. While Gildas does not name the leader of the Britons at Badon (although in a previous chapter he names Aurelius as their leader), it is often argued that the victor at Badon was still in the sixth century so famous as to need no introduction.

[7] The *Historia Brittonum* is probably to be dated to around 800. "Nennius" names Arthur and lists for him twelve major battles, perhaps drawing on a Welsh battle poem. There is also Arthurian material in the "mirabilia" section of the work, which tells of a footprint left by Arthur's dog Cafal and of the burial place of one Amr, identified as Arthur's son. Cafal's footprint is at Carn Cafal in Builth, and the stones from this cairn, if removed, will always return to the cairn. Amr's grave changes its size constantly. *Historia Brittonum* cc. 56, 73.

[8] An annals list dating from the tenth century, which lists Badon and Camlann, with dates of 516 and 537 respectively. The annals note that Arthur and Medraut died at Camlann; the idea that Arthur killed Medraut is a later development. The *Historia Brittonum* and the *Annales Cambriae* are both in *Nennius: British History and The Welsh Annals*, ed. and trans. John Morris.

[9] William of Malmesbury, *Gesta Regum Anglorum*, ed. W. Stubbs, RS 90 (1887), i.II; I.8: "Hic est Artur de quo Britonum nugae hodieque delirant; dignus plane quem non fallaces somniarent fabulae, sed veraces praedicarent historiae, quippe qui labantem patriam diu sustinuerit, infractasque civium mentes ad bellum acuerit." William makes a careful distinction between an historical Arthur and later mythical accretions. It is ironic that William's own *De Antiquitate Glastonie Ecclesie* should later have been heavily edited in order to interpolate a great deal of questionable Arthurian material; see William of Malmesbury, *The Early History of Glastonbury: An Edition, Translation and Study of William of Malmesbury's De Antiquitate Glastonie Ecclesie*, ed. John Scott (Woodbridge, Suffolk: The Boydell Press, 1981), pp. 27–33.

have seen Geoffrey anticipating in the degree to which he builds the *auctoritas* of his version with reference to the *liber vetustissimus*; a parodic joke for the circle of like-minded courtier-historians, it provided a wall of credibility for those outside the charmed circle. The relative paucity of what one might call "imaginative literature" in Latin about Arthur may stem from precisely this sense of what is and is not appropriate for history and, as we will see below in the discussion of William of Newburgh, for its proper language, Latin. There are nevertheless a few chroniclers who respond, in some degree, to the fantastic as well as the exemplary possibilities of the Arthurian story.

After Geoffrey, the Latin chronicles routinely include much Arthurian material. Geoffrey himself becomes a source, used uncritically by many and more judiciously by some. In two famous cases, caution with respect to Geoffrey's narrative becomes outright contempt. Gerald of Wales addresses Arthurian material in several of his works. He twice gives an account of the finding of the king's bones at Glastonbury Abbey in 1190 or 1191,[10] the first of which I excerpt here:

> In our time Arthur's body, which fables had treated mysteriously, claiming it had, at the end, been spirited away to some distant place and had somehow resisted death, was found at Glastonbury hidden deep in the earth in a hollow oak, between two stone pyramids, set up long ago in the cemetery . . . And there was a lead cross fixed

---

[10] The exhumation is also reported by Ralph of Coggeshall in his *Chronicon Anglicanum* (1187–1224) and by Adam of Damerham in his *Historia de Rebus Gestis Glastoniensibus* (c. 1247 for the first section), quoted by Chambers, *Arthur of Britain*, p. 280. Adam includes the epitaph placed on the new tomb constructed for Arthur after the exhumation:

Hic iacet Arturus, flos regum, gloria regni,
Quem mores, probitas, commendant laude perhenni.
Arturi iacet hic coniux tumulata secunda,
Quae meruit coelos virtutum prole fecunda.

This epitaph and later reports of it are discussed in Michelle P. Brown and James P. Carley, "A Fifteenth-Century Revision of the Glastonbury Epitaph to King Arthur," *Arthurian Literature* 12 (1993), 179–92. Brown and Carley describe additions made to the epitaph in London, British Library, MS Royal B.XV, a manuscript owned by John Shirley. The epitaph continues with twelve more lines, some quite garbled, which describe Arthur as "Spes Britonum flos milicie" ("Hope of the Britons, flower of knights"). Brown and Carley argue that the preservation and extension of the epitaph show the renewed fascination in Arthurian material among the sorts of London readers to whom Caxton would appeal in his edition of Malory's *Morte* (190). Such Latinate Arthurian enthusiam is interesting enough, but in "A New Arthurian Epitaph?" *Arthurian Literature* 13 (1995), 145–49, Neil Wright assesses the additions to the epitaph and argues that the new lines are in fact a separate poem, one which could well have been written as early as the twelfth or thirteenth centuries (147). Wright wonders whether there might not once have been an exemplar which preserved these, and perhaps other, Latin Arthurian poems (149).

under . . . a stone slab. I have seen this cross, and have traced the
letters sculpted into it . . . and they said: "Here lies buried the
famous King Arthur with Guenevere his second wife in the island
of Avalon." Several notable things arise from this inscription: that
Arthur had two wives, of whom the second was buried with him,
and indeed her bones were found with the bones of her husband . . .
There a tress of female hair, blond, pristine with its original color,
was found, but a monk snatched it with a greedy hand and it
immediately dissolved into dust . . . [It] was in large part Henry the
Second, king of England, who had told the monks, just as he had
heard from an old British bard [*ab historico cantore Britone*], that
they would find the body deep in the earth, that is to say at least
sixteen feet deep, and not in a stone tomb but rather in a hollow
oak . . .

The place which is now called Glastonbury was in the old time
called Avalon. And it is like an island, completely surrounded by
marshes, whence it is called in the British tongue Inis Avallon, that
is, the island of apples. Apples, indeed, are called aval in the British
tongue, and they abounded in that place. It was here, to this island
which is now called Glastonbury, that Morgan, a noble matron and
the ruler and patron [*dominatrix atque patrona*] of those parts, and
also close in blood to King Arthur, took Arthur after the battle of
Camlann for the healing of his wounds . . . And you should also
know that the bones of Arthur which were found were so large, that
the poet's words seemed to be fulfilled in them: "And they will
wonder at the size of the buried bones they have unearthed." For
indeed one of the tibia, which the abbot showed me, when it was
placed on the ground next to the foot of the tallest man there,
reached a good three fingers above that man's knee. And the skull
was like a prodigy, so wide and so large it was, so that the space
between the eyebrows and the space between the eyes was as wide
as a man's palm . . .[11]

---

[11] Gerald of Wales, *De Instructione Principum*, in *Giraldi Cambrensis Opera*, ed. J.S. Brewer,
J.F. Dimock, and G.F. Warner, RS (1861–91), vol. 8, Distinctio I:

Huius autem corpus, quod quasi phantasticum in fine et tanquam per spiritus ad
longinqua translatum, neque morti obnoxium fabulae confinxerant, his nostris diebus
apud Glastoniam inter lapideas pyramides duas, in coemiterio sacro quondam erectas,
profundius in terra quercu concava reconditum . . . Unde et crux plumbea lapide
supposito . . . quam nos quoque vidimus, namque tractavimus litteras has insculptas
. . . continebat: "Hic jacet sepultus inclitus rex Arthurus cum Wenneveria uxore sua
secunda in insula Avallonia." Occurrunt hic autem notabilia plurima; habuerat enim
uxores duas, quarum ultima simul cum ipso sepulta fuerat, et ossa ipsius cum ossibus
viri simul inventa . . . ubi et trica comae muliebris flava cum integritate pristina et
colore reperta fuit, quam ut monachus quidam avide manu arripuit et sublevavit, tota

This find is generally supposed to have been engineered by the monks themselves, anxious to raise funds after a fire had destroyed their abbey in 1184.[12] The monks of Glastonbury, like those of many other monastic foundations, do seem to have been involved, even before the fire, in the venerable practice of emphasizing their ancient origins and thus their rights: I discuss their use of William of Malmesbury for this purpose in chapter 3. The involvement of Henry II, whose vision directed the monks to search for Arthur between two pyramids, may be connected to a dynastic desire to end any hope of Arthur's return,[13] a hope which, we will see below, was in fact mobilized in rebellions in Brittany against his rule. In the later of his two accounts, the *Speculum Ecclesiae* of c. 1216, Gerald concludes with a specific reference to the death of the Breton hope, sounding much like William of Malmesbury:

> Furthermore, since many things have been reported and fables

> statim in pulverem decidit . . . rex Angliae Henricus secundus, sicut ab historico cantore Britone audierat antiquo, totum monachis indicavit, quod profunde, scilicet in terra per xvi pedes ad minus, corpus invenirent, et non [in] lapideo tumulo sed in quercu cavata . . . Quae nunc autem Glastonia dicitur, antiquitus insula Avallonia dicebatur. Est enim quasi insula tota paludibus obsita, unde dicta est Britannice Inis Avallon, id est, insula pomifera. Pomis enim, quae aval Britannica lingua dicuntur, locus ille quondam abundabat. Unde et Morganis, nobilis matrona et partium illarum dominatrix atque patrona, necnon et Arthuro regi sanguine propinqua, post bellum de Kemelen Arthurum ad sanandum ejusdem vulnera in insulam quae nunc Glastonia dicitur deportavit . . . Sciendum etiam quod ossa reperta corporis Arthuri tam grandia fuerunt, ut et illud poetae completum in his videri posset: "Grandiaque effossis mirabitur ossa sepulchris." Os enim tibiae ipsius appositum [tibiae] longissimi viri loci, quem et nobis abbas ostendit, et juxta pedem illius terrae affixum, large tribus digitis trans genu ipsius se porrexit. Os etiam capitis tanquam ad prodigium vel ostentum capax erat ac grossum, adeo ut intercilium et inter oculos spatium palmalem amplitudinem large contineret.

12  Scott argues that Gerald was part of a plan "to ensure that the story would become widely known"; *The Early History of Glastonbury*, p. 29. But C.A. Ralegh Radford's archaeological work has shown that the monks did dig in the area; see "Glastonbury Abbey" in *The Quest for Arthur's Britain*, ed. G. Ashe (London: Pall Mall Press, 1968), pp. 119–38. Leslie Alcock argues that too little attention has been paid to the cross, which he dates on epigraphic grounds to the tenth or eleventh centuries (based on a 1607 drawing of the cross; the object is now lost); he combines this dating with the excavations of 1954 and 1962 to suggest that Arthur, buried in the mausoleum in the ancient cemetery, was moved when St. Dunstan, abbot of Glastonbury, raised and walled the cemetery some time after 945. The cross was provided at that time; *Arthur's Britain* (Harmondsworth, Middlesex: Penguin, 1971), pp. 76–80. Lesley Abrams and James P. Carley, eds., *The Archaeology and History of Glastonbury Abbey: Essays in Honour of the Ninetieth Birthday of C.A. Ralegh Radford* (Woodbridge, Suffolk: The Boydell Press, 1991) reviews much of this material.

13  Lewis Thorpe, for example, suggests Henry II hoped that "the discovery would . . . put an effective end to Welsh dreams that their hero would come back one day to help them in their resistance to the Norman kings." Henry died in 1189, so the exhumation actually took place under Richard I; Lewis Thorpe, trans., *The Journey through Wales/The Description of Wales*, (Harmondsworth, Middlesex: Penguin, 1978), p. 282, n. 632.

concocted about King Arthur and his doubtful ending, and the stupidities of the Britons thus assert that he is still alive, I have endeavored, now that the truth about all this has been clearly shown, to add a few more things, so that the fables may be snuffed out and the true and certain facts openly shown.[14]

The foolishness of the Britons is compounded by a sort of heresy; like the Jews, they expect the return of a Messiah:

> After this the lying Britons and their singers were accustomed to say that some fantastic goddess, namely that one also called Morgana, took the body of Arthur to the island of Avalon in order that his wounds might be cured. And when they are cured, then the king will return, strong and powerful, to lead the Britons, they say, as he used to; and for this reason, they anticipate his return just as the Jews await their Messiah . . .[15]

There is some professional competition implied here, as Gerald implicitly contrasts the practice of the oral, Welsh storytellers with his own textuality. Like William of Malmesbury, Gerald finds the Britons to be at best credulous fools, and at worst malicious and habitual liars and blasphemers. But while William of Malmesbury was writing before the appearance of the *Historia regum Britannie* and thus addressed only the popular belief in Arthur's return, Gerald's doubts about the Arthurian story include a particular focus on Geoffrey. Here, one courtier-cleric challenges another.

Gerald includes an anti-Galfridian anecdote in his *Itinerarium Kambriae*. He tells of Meilyr, a man who could always tell when someone was lying and could, although illiterate, point out deceptive passages in books thanks, he said, to devils who pointed the places out to him. Once, when Meilyr was being tormented by these spirits, the Gospel of St. John was placed on his lap and the demons fled; but ". . . when it was taken away afterwards, and the History of the

---

[14] Gerald of Wales, *Speculum Ecclesiae*, in *Giraldi Cambrensis Opera*, ed. J.S. Brewer *et al.*, RS (1873), vol. 4, II.9:
> Porro quoniam de rege Arthuro et ejus exitu dubio multa referri solent et fabulae confingi, Britonum populis ipsum adhuc vivere fatue contendentibus, ut fabulosis exsufflatis, et veris ac certis asseveratis, veritas ipsa de caetero circiter haec liquido pateat, quaedam hic adjicere curavimus indubitate veritate comperta.

[15] *Speculum Ecclesiae* II.9:
> Propter hoc enim fabulosi Britones et eorum cantores fingere solebant, quod dea quaedam phantastica, scilicet et Morganis dicta, corpus Arthuri in insulam detulit Avalloniam ad ejus vulnera sanandum. Quae cum sanata fuerint, redibit rex fortis et potens, ad Britones regendum, ut dicunt, sicut solet; propter quod, ipsum expectant adhuc venturum sicut Judaei Messiam suum . . .

Britons by Geoffrey of Monmouth was put in its place, as an experiment, the evil spirits would settle all over his body and over the book too, and would stay there much longer than usual and be even more irksome."[16] A splenetic story, indeed: but while William of Malmesbury's remarks about the "ravings" of the Britons may look like the academic contempt of a serious historian for popular belief in "marvels," it is hard to assign the same motives to Gerald. He himself follows the practice of most historians after Geoffrey by making considerable use of the *Historia* in his own work.[17] His work also includes material which appeals directly to the twelfth-century appetite for marvels; the works on Wales and on Ireland contain anecdotes and local lore which are not really different in kind from, for example, the Nennian *mirabilia*, Arthurian and otherwise. And the accounts of the discovery of Arthur's tomb at Glastonbury include, even if we grant that Gerald speaks with the absolute truth of an eye-witness, details which suggest the skill of the storyteller. In the second account, for example, the action of the monk is moralized as a demonstration that "All things are perishable . . . since, as the philosopher says, 'the glow of beauty is swift and fleeting, and swifter than the mutability of spring flowers.'"[18] While this moralization is firmly in keeping with the practices of "serious," exemplary history, the account also includes some material which could in fact be seen to encourage the very "fairy tales" Gerald professes to despise. Such material includes the visions which preceded the discovery, the "old British bard," the references to Morgan *matrona, dominatrix,* and *patrona,* and the size of Arthur's bones. Even the discussion of Avalon has, despite Gerald's conclusion in the *Speculum Ecclesiae* version, some room for the credulous: Arthur is taken away "for the healing of his wounds." Gerald may not be an Arthurian storyteller, but he is a storyteller who sees the appeal of Arthurian material even as he claims to debunk it; or perhaps one who appreciates the factuality of fiction, in the service of both entertainment and moral utility. One need only compare his version to Ralph of Coggeshall's

---

[16] *Itinerarium Kambriae*: "Quo sublato postmodum, et Historia Britonum a Galfrido Arthuro tractata, experiendi causa, loco ejusdem subrogata, non solum corpori ipsius toti, sed etiam libro superposito, longe solito crebrius et taediosius insederunt."

[17] Thorpe remarks that Gerald's "debt to the *Historia regum Britannie* is considerable" (*The Journey through Wales/ The Description of Wales*, p. 280).

[18] *Speculum Ecclesiae*, in *Opera*, Distinctio ii.8: ". . . namque cunctis praefiguravit esse caduca, . . . Quoniam, ut ait philosophus, 'formae nitor rapidus est, et velox, et vernalium florum mutabilitate fugacior.'"

account to see how Gerald has moved beyond the strictest confines of chronicle record. The 1191 entry for the *Chronicon Anglicanum* is plain and succinct:

> In this year were found at Glastonbury the bones of the most famous Arthur, once king of Britain, in a certain very old, hidden sarcophagus, near which two ancient pyramids had stood upright, on which certain letters had been engraved, but they could not be read because they were extremely outlandish and badly defaced. The bones were found in this way: while they were digging up the earth to bury a certain monk who in his life had chosen this place and most vehemently desired to be buried there, they found a certain sarcophagus, on which a lead cross had been affixed, on which was engraved: "Here lies buried the famous King Arthur, in the island of Avalon." For this place was once surrounded by marshland, and so it was called the island of Avalon (that is, the island of apples).[19]

Clearly Gerald's version is a better story, and this is precisely the point: despite his attack on Geoffrey in the *Itinerarium Kambriae*, Gerald shows himself equally susceptible to the appeal of storytelling in general, and of the Arthurian material in particular. Nor should these "literary" (more properly, rhetorical) skills come as a surprise. Gerald, friend and rival of Walter Map, is another court writer who moves easily between fiction, fact, and *facetia*.

A more direct attack on Geoffrey as an historian is made by William of Newburgh in the *Prooemium* to his *Historia rerum Anglicarum* (1196–98). The twelfth century was the great period of Latin chronicle history, and writers other than Geoffrey had indeed reviewed the British past. William of Malmesbury's reaction to popular lore about that past we have already seen. Another chronicler of the British kings was Henry of Huntingdon, famous as one of the earliest known readers of Geoffrey. Henry, comparing the meager results of his own researches for his *Historia Anglorum* to Geoffrey's

---

[19] Ralph of Coggeshall, *Radulphi de Coggeshall Chronicon Anglicanum*, ed. Joseph Stevenson (RS 36, 1875 [s.a. 1191]):

> Hoc autem anno inventa sunt apud Glastingeberiam ossa famosissimi Arturi, quondam regis Britanniae, in quodam vetustissimo sarcophago recondita, circa quod duae antiquae pyramides stabant erectae, in quibus literae quaedam exaratae erant, sed ob nimiam barbariem et deformationem legi non poterant. Inventa sunt autem hac occasione. Dum enim ibidem terram effoderent ut quemdam monachum sepelirent qui hunc locum sepulturae vehementi desiderio in vita sua praeoptaverat, reperiunt quoddam sarcophagum, cui crux plumbea superposita fuerat, in qua ita exaratum erat; "Hic jacet inclitus rex Arturius, in insula Avallonis sepultus." Locus autem ille olim paludibus inclusus, insula Avallonis (id est insula pomorum), vocitatus est.

book, is content with expressing himself "amazed" (*stupens*) at the detail in the *Historia regum Britannie*.[20] William of Newburgh, on the other hand, takes his own knowledge of the sources available to himself and his predecessors and launches an unprecedented attack on Geoffrey.[21] Geoffrey is a liar, a maker of fables, not fit to be compared with Gildas or with Bede. Gildas, William argues, proves his own reliability by his condemnation of his people. Geoffrey betrays an opposite impulse:

> But in our own days, instead of this practice, a writer has emerged who, in order to expiate the faults of these Britons, weaves the most ridiculous figments of imagination around them, extolling them with the most impudent vanity above the virtues of the Macedonians and the Romans. This man is called Geoffrey, and his other name is Arthur, because he has taken up the fables about Arthur from the old, British figments, has added to them himself, and has cloaked them with the honorable name of history by presenting them with the ornaments of the Latin tongue.[22]

Geoffrey's crime consists in part in cloaking (vernacular) stories in the Latin language and style. William, it seems, sees Latin in Bakhtinian terms as the "authoritative word," cloaked in authenticity and with priority over all others: "The authoritative word is located in a distanced zone, organically connected with a past that is felt to be

[20] In his famous, *Epistola ad Warinum*, Henry explains why his history omitted the deeds of the kings from the time of Brutus to the time of Julius Caesar: "But this very year, I was amazed to find at the Abbey of Bec a book recording these things." ("Hoc tamen anno . . . apud Beccensem abbatiam scripta rerum praedictarum stupens inveni"); the *Chronica* of Robert of Torigny, ed. R. Howlett, *Chronicles of the Reigns of Stephen, Henry II and Richard I* (RS 82, 1889), iv, 64. Henry's decision to put the Galfridian material in an appendix rather than to modify his own history may suggest suspicion, but Henry expands Geoffrey's version of Arthur's death and makes explicit reference to the Breton hope.

[21] Unprecedented, that is, in its severity. As Gransden has pointed out, William is not the only medieval historian to use the technique of comparing sources, and the general test of probability, in his assessment of a source; see "Prologues in the Historiography of Twelfth-Century England," 72–73.

[22] William of Newburgh, *The History of English Affairs*, book I, ed. and trans. P.G. Walsh and M.J. Kennedy (Warminster: Aris and Phillips, 1988), *Prooemium*, p. 28:

> At contra quidam nostris temporibus pro expiandis his Britonum maculis scriptor emersit ridicula de eisdem figmenta contexens, eosque longe supra virtutem Macedonum et Romanorum impudenti vanitate attollens. Gaufridus hic dictus est agnomen habens Arturi, pro eo quod fabulas de Arturo ex priscis Britonum figmentis sumptas et ex proprio auctas per superductum Latini sermonis colorem honesto historiae nomine palliavit.

William is wrong about the reason for Geoffrey's *agnomen*; Geoffrey signs himself Geoffrey Arthur in five of the charters from 1129 on; Curley, *Geoffrey of Monmouth*, p. 2. Roberts points out that the name was a common Breton one, although it was not particularly popular among the Welsh in the twelfth century; "Geoffrey of Monmouth, *Historia Regum Britanniae* and *Brut y Brenhinedd*," p. 98.

hierarchically higher. It is, so to speak, the word of the fathers. Its authority was already *acknowledged* in the past. It is a *prior* discourse."[23] Geoffrey's gall in (mis)using Latin for his fictions is only underlined for William by his ignorance or willful misuse of prior (Latin) *auctores*. William compares Geoffrey to Bede:

> Since these events agree with the historical truth set forth by the Venerable Bede, all the things which that man took care to write about Arthur and either his predecessors after Vortigern or his successors, can be seen to have been partly concocted by himself and partly by others, either because of a frenzied passion for lying or in order to please the Britons, most of whom are known to be so primitive that they are said still to be awaiting the return of Arthur, and will not suffer themselves to hear that he is dead.[24]

Later, William asks why it is that Gildas, Bede and the rest would have been silent about so great a figure as Arthur:

> For how could the old historians, to whom it was a matter of great concern that nothing worthy of memory should be omitted from what was written, who indeed are known to have committed to memory quite unimportant things, how could they have passed over in silence so incomparable a man, whose deeds were notable above all others? How, I ask, could they have suppressed with silence Arthur and his acts, this king of the Britons who was nobler than Alexander the Great . . .[25]

Again, we see the contrast between what it is that historians do, and what it is that Geoffrey did. The old historians carefully examined all the material available to them and incorporated it in their work, work marked by study and care. Geoffrey makes things up out of his own fevered imagination or, with equal culpability,

---

[23] M.M. Bakhtin, *The Dialogic Imagination*, ed. Michael Holquist, trans. Caryl Emerson and Michael Holquist (Austin: University of Texas Press, 1981), p. 342.

[24] *The History of English Affairs*, book I, *Prooemium*, p. 32:
> Haec cum juxta historicam veritatem a venerabili Beda expositam constet esse rata, cuncta quae homo ille de Arturo et ejus vel successoribus vel post Vortigirnum praedecessoribus scribere curavit partim ab ipso, partim et ab aliis constat esse conficta, sive effrenata mentiendi libidine sive etiam gratia placendi Britonibus, quorum plurimi tam bruti esse feruntur ut adhuc Arturum tanquam venturum exspectare dicantur, eumque mortuum nec audire patiantur.

[25] *The History of English Affairs*, book I, *Prooemium*, p. 34:
> quomodo enim historiographi veteres, quibus ingenti curae fuit nihil memorabile scribendo omittere, qui etiam mediocria memoriae mandasse noscuntur, virum incomparabilem ejusque acta supra modum insignia silentio praeterire potuerunt? quomodo, inquam, vel nobiliorem Alexandro Magno Britonum monarcham Arturum ejusque acta . . . silentio suppresserunt?

incorporates with chauvinistic impulse the untrustworthy material of popular culture and superstition. William of Newburgh does not appear to be the sort of historian who will grant that some fiction may point to fact; or at least, he finds Geoffrey's fictions too outrageous to be allowed even under such a concession. Merlin he finds particularly offensive: "With even greater daring he has published the fallacious prophecies of a certain Merlin, to which he has in any event added many things himself, and has translated them into Latin, [thus offering them] as if they were authentic prophecies, resting on immutable truth."[26] Once more, part of Geoffrey's crime is the translation of these lies into Latin. William's resistance to the facetious or jocose use of Latin suggests that not all educated men participated willingly in this particular mode of discourse. William's objections may stem from the seriousness with which twelfth-century intellectuals treated prophecy; one does not lie about such things, perhaps. William later compares Merlin to Isaiah, and there is again the suggestion that the language of Merlin's prophecies might lead the credulous to imagine that Merlin and Isaiah had equal sanction and validity. But William's attitude towards Geoffrey's prophecies is extremely unusual. As early as about 1134 or 1135, Ordericus Vitalis quoted from the *Prophetie Merlini* in his *Historia Ecclesiastica*, saying that he had taken these prophecies from the "little book of Merlin" *(de Merlini libello)* because "they can be seen to coincide with events of our own times."[27] Abbot Suger says that Merlin's prophecies are as true as they are elegant.[28] While Ordericus and perhaps Suger might have read the *Prophetie* before Geoffrey's vogue was fully established through the publication of the *Historia*, it is nevertheless clear that the appearance of that work did not, for most readers, undermine the credibility of the *Prophetie*. There is significant manuscript evidence for the wide and independent circulation of the *Prophetie Merlini*; Julia Crick records some eighty-five

---

[26] *The History of English Affairs*, book I, *Prooemium*, p. 28: "qui etiam majori ausu cujusdam Merlini divinationes fallacissimas, quibus utique de proprio plurimum adjecit, dum eas in Latinum transfunderet, tanquam authenticas et immobili veritate subnixas prophetias vulgavit."

[27] Ordericus Vitalis, *Historia Ecclesiastica*, xii.47, quoted in Chambers, *Arthur of Britain*, p. 258: "Unde libet mihi quaedam huic opusculo inserere, quae temporibus aetatis nostrae videntur competere."

[28] In his *Gesta Ludovici Regis*, quoted in Chambers, *Arthur of Britain*, p. 259, Suger says that Merlin spoke "tam eleganter quam veraciter"; Julia Crick refers to the appeal of the *Prophetie Merlini* in her "Geoffrey of Monmouth, Prophecy and History," *Journal of Medieval History* 18 (1992), 357–71.

copies.[29] Commentaries were written on the *Prophetie*,[30] and R.W. Southern has asserted the importance of prophecy in the medieval understanding of history: "Prophecy was at once a source of information and interpretation, of hope and fear, and of assured truths which needed to be distinguished from the grossest errors and frauds . . . it was the chief inspiration of all historical thinking."[31] William of Newburgh is not, of course, denying the validity or importance of prophecy, but only Merlin's claims to be seen as a prophet. The easy acceptance of the *Prophetie Merlini* may well support William's charge that, by clothing his lies in the language of history, Geoffrey has succeeded in misleading people about the veracity of his work. In her study of the dissemination and reception of the *Historia*, Crick argues that most historians saw Geoffrey as at least partially credible, because his text is often included with the work of more obviously "serious" historians.[32] Yet the criticisms voiced by William of Newburgh, Gerald of Wales, and even William of Malmesbury may suggest why so few Latin writers followed Geoffrey into the realms of clearly fictional history. To step wholeheartedly into the world of romance was something few Latin writers seemed prepared to do. There are however some Latin responses to Geoffrey which develop the Arthurian material with considerable freedom, although towards different ends.

There are three such developments from the Latin chronicle tradition with which I will deal here. The first is the *Vera historia de morte*

---

[29] Crick, "Geoffrey of Monmouth, Prophecy and History," 360, n. 13. See also Caroline D. Eckhardt, "The *Prophetia Merlini* of Geoffrey of Monmouth: Latin Manuscript Copies," *Manuscripta* 26 (1982), 167–76. Crick points to the wide use of Merlin's prophecies to defend various political actions, such as Henry II's intervention in Ireland; Herbert of Bosham complained that Henry was using the *Prophetie* to threaten Becket. It is an odd fact that Merlin's prophecies encountered most resistance from English writers, who were much less likely than continental chroniclers to incorporate the prophecies into their work; see Crick, 364. Yet in England, too, there was considerable use of the *Prophetie*; Gerald of Wales was one writer who made use of them (Crick, 366).

[30] See Caroline D. Eckhardt, *The Prophetia Merlini of Geoffrey of Monmouth: A Fifteenth-century Commentary* (Cambridge, Mass.: The Medieval Academy of America, 1982), and "Another Manuscript of the Commentary on *Prophetia Merlini* Attributed to Alain de Lille," *Manuscripta* 29 (1985), 143–47.

[31] R.W. Southern, "Aspects of the European Tradition of Historical Writing: 3," 160. See also Marjorie Reeves, "History and Prophecy in Medieval Thought," *Medievalia et Humanistica* 5 (1974), 51–75.

[32] Julia C. Crick, *The "Historia regum Britannie" of Geoffrey of Monmouth, IV: Dissemination and Reception in the Later Middle Ages* (Cambridge: D.S. Brewer, 1991), pp. 218–20, 222. Crick also argues here, as in the article cited above, that the association of the *Historia* with wisdom literature, prophetic and apocalyptic texts may suggest a readership among educated clerics and political propagandists.

*Arthuri,* an apparent continuation of the *Historia* which develops the mystery of Arthur's end. The second is an overtly political deployment of the material, Etienne de Rouen's curious letter exchange between King Arthur and Henry II in the course of the latter's campaign in Britanny in 1167. The court features of wit, propaganda, and exemplification through the negative portrait of a king are features in this work. In the *Draco,* Arthur is the *tyrannus* we will also meet in the Welsh saints' lives, dealt with separately in chapter 6. The third is William of Rennes's verse adaptation of the chronicle tradition of British history; by this time we have moved out of the seminal period for the Arthurian story and into the period of its greatest elaboration, the thirteenth century. Each of these works shows an impulse similar to some of Geoffrey's own, in the pushing of the chronicle form towards other generic boundaries, whether of fantastic narrative, polemic, or nationalist epic.

The curious Latin text called the *Vera historia de morte Arthuri*[33] may represent an early rebellion against the bleakness of the ending to the Arthuriad in Geoffrey's *Historia,* and thus suggests one direction in which Geoffrey's material could be developed, with a concentration on the proto-romantic possibilities of the content to the (deliberate?) exclusion of the implications of the form. The details in the episode, and most particularly the reference to the Messianic hope regarding Arthur, would seem to place this work outside the chronicle tradition, especially when we keep in mind the strictures of William of Malmesbury, Gerald of Wales, and William of Newburgh on that particular subject. Nevertheless, there is manuscript evidence that it was sometimes attached to Geoffrey's *Historia* as an intended supplement.[34] In this short prose text, probably of the late twelfth century,[35] Arthur's deathbed scene is described:

---

[33] Edited by Michael Lapidge, "An Edition of the *Vera Historia de Morte Arthuri,*" *Arthurian Literature* 1 (1981), 79–93.

[34] In Paris, Bibliothèque de l'Arsenal, MS 982, the *Vera Historia* is inserted between two chapters of the *Historia,* and in Paris, Bibliothèque Nationale, MS Lat. 6401D, it is quoted as if it were by Geoffrey; see Richard Barber, "The Manuscripts of the *Vera Historia de Morte Arthuri,*" *Arthurian Literature* 6 (1986), 163–64.

[35] When Lapidge edited the text, he knew of only one complete manuscript, London, Gray's Inn, MS 7; he also made use of an abbreviated version in London, British Library, MS Cotton Cleopatra D.III. Since that time, several other manuscripts have come to light: London, British Library, MS Cotton Titus A.XIX; Paris, Bibliothèque de l'Arsenal, MS 982; Paris, Bibliothèque Nationale MS lat. 6401D, and Oxford, Bodleian Library MS Digby 186. See Michael Lapidge, "Additional Manuscript Evidence for the *Vera Historia de Morte Arthuri,*" *Arthurian Literature* 2 (1982), 163–68, and Barber, "The Manuscripts of the *Vera Historia de Morte Arthuri,*" 163–64. The Gray's Inn manuscript is dated to the beginning of

*VERA HISTORIA DE MORTE ARTHURI*: SYNOPSIS

Wounded after Camlann, Arthur is resting when a mysterious, handsome youth appears and wounds the king with a spear made of elm, dipped in adder's venom. It is this wound which proves fatal. Arthur gives orders to be taken to the isle of Avalon, where he hopes to find relief from his wounds. The physicians of the isle labor over him, but in vain. Arthur therefore calls for the archbishop of London, who comes to him along with the bishops of Bangor and Glamorgan. In their presence, Arthur confesses, rewards his followers, and settles the rule of his kingdom on Constantine son of Cador. He takes the sacrament, stretches himself out on a hair-shirt, and dies. His body is embalmed, taken to a chapel dedicated to the Virgin, and left outside while the funeral rites are conducted. During the rites, a violent storm begins, followed by a mist which lasts all day, and constant thunder. When the mist clears, the body is gone, and only the sealed tomb, which gives the appearance of a solid block of stone, remains. To this day, no one knows what became of Arthur's body. It is said by some that he is still alive.

There are clearly many elements drawn from the fantastic strain of Celtic narrative in this account. The youth and his weapon are described at some length, in terms that have magical overtones:

> When the king had been disarmed, lo a youth – beautiful in appearance, tall in stature, showing the virtue of great strength in the shape of his limbs – seized the path, sitting on horseback, and armed in his right hand with a shaft of elm. This rod was stiff, neither twisted nor knotted but straight, and with a point sharpened like that of a lance, although it was sharper for wounding than any lance, for indeed in former times it had been hardened in the fire by the efforts of artifice, and its hardness had been tempered with equal care in water, and it had been infected with viper's venom so that whatever harm was lacking in the strength which cast it would be made up for by the strength of the poison.[36]

---

the fourteenth century (see Lapidge, "An Edition," 79). Lapidge first dated the text to before 1203, because a reference to an archbishop of St. David's may suggest the revival of the controversy over St. David's status by Gerald of Wales ("An Edition," p. 81); no emendation of this date has been suggested. The text does not mention the discovery of Arthur's tomb at Glastonbury in 1190 or 1191; it seems likely, then, that it was written before the final decade of the twelfth century.

[36] "*Vera Historia*," 84:
> Rege quidem exarmato, ecce quidam adolescens – pulcher aspectu, statura procerus, forma membrorum magnarum uirium preferens uirtutem – carpebat iter, equi tergo insidens, dextram uirga hulmea habens munitam. Que rigida erat, non torta neque

The youth's sudden advent, his remarkable appearance and stature, and the history of his weapon, forged of magical wood and going back to "former times," all suggest the world of Celtic narrative. The mist and the disappearance of the king's body, too, belong to this world:

> In the meantime, while the bishops are celebrating the final rites, the air thunders, the earth shakes, tempests pour down from the heavens, lightning flashes, and the various winds blow from their various quarters. Then, after the shortest time, a mist followed which, absorbing the brightness of the lightning, wrapped the guards of the king's body in such blindness that they saw nothing, although their eyes were open. This mist persists from terce to nones; the air never grows quiet from the crashing thunder as the time goes by. And finally, when the mist is gone and calm restored, they find no part of the royal body.[37]

Analogues for the storm range from the biblical description of the crucifixion, to the mist which shrouds Dyfed in *Manawydan uab Llŷr*.[38] The attachment of a Messianic hope to Arthur is, as we have already seen, an old Welsh one.[39] Indeed, were it not for its status as a continuation of Geoffrey's Arthuriad, the *Vera historia* would be found here in the chapters on Celtic Latin Arthurian narrative. It may be that in this text we observe the beginnings of the movement of

---

nodosa sed plana, et cuspide acuta ad modum lancee (sed quauis lancea ad nocendum acutior) – siquidem preterito tempore artificis industria ad ignem rigida effecta (rigorque non dispari studio aquarum temperatus humore), et uipereo infecta ueneno ut quod forte iaculata minus noceret pro iaculantis defectu uirium uirus suppleret.

Richard Barber points to the similarity between this poisoned spear and that with which Goronwy kills Lleu in *Math uab Mathonwy*, the fourth branch of the *Mabinogi*; see "The *Vera Historia de Morte Arthuri* and its Place in Arthurian Tradition," *Arthurian Literature* 1 (1981), 73.

[37] "*Vera Historia*," 90:

Interim, episcopis exequias celebrantibus, aer tonat, terra nutat, desuper crebro irruunt tempestates, fulgura choruscant, aureque diuerse uariis se alternant uicibus. Demum, interposita breuissimi temporis morula, aeris subsecuta est caligo que fulgurum absorta est claritatem et tanta cecitate regii corporis obuoluit custodes, ut apertis oculis nihil uiderent. Hec ab hora tertia usque ad nonam perdurat assidue; aer nullo tempore celebris horarum uicibus a tonitrui quiescit tumultu. At deinde, cum caligo subducitur et serenitas restituitur, corporis regii nullas repperunt reliquias.

[38] Barber suggests a later moment in the same narrative, when Pryderi and Rhiannon are struck motionless when they touch a golden bowl and disappear in thunder and mist ("*Vera Historia*," 72); the opening sequence seems to me to be closer, but in any case it is clear that the mysterious mist has Celtic roots: one might also think of the hedge of mist in Chrétien's *Erec*.

[39] See Constance Bullock-Davies, "'Exspectare Arturum': Arthur and the Messianic Hope," *Bulletin of the Board of Celtic Studies* 29 (1981/82), 432–40. Bullock-Davies argues that political Messianism was a persistent factor in Wales from the third century.

Arthurian history into fantasy romance. But because the *Vera historia* seems to have been perceived as a continuation of Geoffrey's *Historia*,[40] it also belongs here. It is a witness to the unwillingness of many medieval writers to entertain the abrupt departure of Arthur in Geoffrey's work. It also fulfills the taste, at the courts of the twelfth century, for marvels.

At the same time, it is possible that the *Vera historia* is itself a continuation of certain (subversive or playful) tendencies in the *Historia*. Despite its additional detail, this "true" history of Arthur is no clearer as to his end than is Geoffrey.[41] The references to Avalon, following as they do the episode with the mysterious youth, seem designed to raise expectations which are then left unfulfilled, as Arthur is not in fact cured there:

> Then the king, somewhat restored by an improvement in his condition, orders that he should be taken to Gwynedd, because he proposes to pass some time in the isle of Avalon because of the amenities of that delightful place (and for the sake of peace and for the easing of the pain of his wounds). When he had come there, the doctors busied themselves with all the skill of their art over his wounds, but the king experienced no efficacious cure from their efforts.[42]

This is neither the debunking of Avalon that we have seen in some of the responses to the Breton/ Briton hope, nor the wholesale adoption of the notion that we will see below in the *Draco Normannicus*. There may be something tongue-in-cheek in the providing of extra details about which wounds were fatal, juxtaposed with an ending far more mysterious than the slightly ambiguous one in Geoffrey. That is, this Latin text is no corrective to Geoffrey's excesses, but rather seems to share at least his playfulness. One also wonders about the posture of

---

[40] Suggested by Barber, "The *Vera Historia de Morte Arthuri*," 72. In "The Manuscripts of the *Vera Historia de Morte Arthuri*," Barber notes that his original argument gains support from the fact that two of the newly-discovered manuscripts of the text were found in manuscripts of, or based on, Geoffrey's *Historia* (163).

[41] The Gray's Inn manuscript begins "hec est uera historia de Morte Arthuri"; there is no title in the Cotton Cleopatra manuscript (see Lapidge, "*Vera Historia de Morte Arthuri*," 84, n. 1). The list of variants in "Additional Manuscript Evidence for the *Vera Historia de Morte Arthuri*" gives no indications as to title in those manuscripts.

[42] "*Vera Historia*," 86:
> Denique rex, parumper melioracioni restitutus, iubet se transuehi ad Venodociam, quia in Auallonis insula delectabili propter loci amenitatem perendinari proposuerat (et quietis gracia causaque uulnerum suorum mitigandi dolorem). Ad quam ubi peruentus est, medici pro sue artis industria pro regis sunt solliciti uulneribus; sed rex eorum sollicitudinibus nullam salubrem persensit efficaciam.

the text when it is said that the archbishop of St. David's did not accompany the others to the king's deathbed because he was prevented by illness;[43] the remark probably serves to embed contemporary squabbles over episcopal supremacy in the work, thus at least temporarily intruding the contemporary reality into the Arthurian past.

The *Vera historia* also entertains, at least in passing, the political aspect of Geoffrey's project. Embedded in the fantastic account of the king's end is a further demonstration of Arthur's exemplary status. His followers mourn his approaching death, because "they despaired that anyone could safeguard the liberty of Britain as he did."[44] The local and patriotic concern is extended with a generalization on the fluctuations of rule: "for if indeed, as the proverb says, 'it is rare for a better man to succeed a good one,' then it is much rarer that an excellent man should succeed an excellent one."[45] Geoffrey's *Historia* surely illustrated this proposition, and the author of the *Vera historia* would seem to indicate that he understands *optimus* much as Geoffrey would have: Arthur meets his death by accepting the sacraments, rewarding his followers, providing for the rule of his kingdom, and surrendering his soul in a supremely penitential exercise. The narrative voice pauses at this point to return to the theme of kingship, asserting that on the day of Arthur's death, justice and the rule of law died too.[46] Whatever *facetiae* may be present in the details of the death, whatever fanciful, Celtically-inspired touches accompany the death, Arthur remains, in the *Vera historia* account, the best of kings, to be mourned on his own account and also because of the unlikelihood that his like will be seen again.

For Geoffrey, for the anonymous author of the *Vera historia*, and even for those historians who would debunk the more exotic aspects of his story, Arthur remains the good king, the example of what is best in a ruler. I have suggested in the Introduction a link to the preoccupations of the emerging genre of the mirror for princes. We turn now to the other side of the courtly coin; if one seeks to educate

---

[43] *"Vera Historia,"* 86: "... graui corporis incommodio irretitus fuisset..."
[44] *"Vera Historia,"* 86: "... quia eius simili Britannie desperant tueri libertatem."
[45] *"Vera Historia,"* 86: "... siquidem, si iuxta uulgare prouerbium 'Raro bono succedit melior,' multo rarius optimo succedit optimus."
[46] *"Vera Historia,"* 88: "... in ista enim die in Britannia iusticie tepuit disciplina, legum raruit obseruancia, pacis turbata est tranquillitas, libertatis est captiuata nobilitas..." ("On this day in Britain the rule of justice grew lax, the observance of laws grew rare, the tranquillity of peace was disturbed, the nobility of liberty was made captive...").

(or to praise or flatter) princes and nobles, one can do so through negative as well as through positive examples. And, perhaps surprisingly, Arthur sometimes serves in the negative role rather than in the positive one.

The *Draco Normannicus* is a chronicle written some time between 1167 and 1169 by Etienne de Rouen, a monk of Bec. Etienne is in the line of Latin chroniclers who adapted Geoffrey, but his work is not a straight retelling of Galfridian history. It is, rather, an odd mixture of Norman history, the lineage of Henry II, and contemporary events, the purpose of which is to glorify the king. One event dealt with is Henry's 1167 campaign to assert his claim over Brittany. Breton nationalism was linked, Mildred Day argues, with a sense of the Arthurian past, and the phrase "quondam et futurus was a battle cry."[47] Both the *Vera historia de morte Arthuri* and the comments made by William of Malmesbury confirm the early knowledge by Latin writers of the "once and future king." Day argues it was expedient for Etienne to mock the notion of the Arthurian return in his pro-Angevin chronicle,[48] something he proceeds to do in the curious exchange of letters which he presents as part of his account of the Breton campaign.

DRACO NORMANNICUS: A SYNOPSIS OF THE ARTHURIAN EPISODE

Henry marches against certain rebel lords in Brittany [September 1167]. One of these, count Roland, sends a letter to King Arthur, now ruling in the Antipodes, asking him either to come himself to the aid of the Bretons or to send an army. Arthur is enraged, and sends a reply to Roland in which he tells the count not to worry, for Henry is about to receive from Rouen the news of the death of his mother [the Empress Matilda]. Arthur also sends a letter to Henry himself, in which he rebukes Henry for attacking before declaring war. Arthur asserts his own glory in the most grandiloquent of language, calling himself the triple-crowned king and saying that he surpasses all other earthly conquerors. He says that he conquered the French, the English and the Britons. He recounts his war against the vast armies of the Roman Empire, led by the Emperor Lucius.

[47] Mildred Leake Day, "The Letter from King Arthur to Henry II: Political Use of the Arthurian Legend in Draco Normannicus," in *The Spirit of the Court*, ed. Glyn S. Burgess and Robert A. Taylor (Cambridge: D.S. Brewer, 1985), p. 153.

[48] In "Geoffrey and King Arthur in *Normannicus Draco*," *Modern Philology* 31 (1933), 1– 18, J.S.P. Tatlock goes rather further, calling Etienne "More obsequious than most"; and "a rather commonplace monk of the better sort," 2.

The preparation for battle is recounted in detail. Arthur tells how he defeated the Romans and sent Lucius's body to Rome as the demanded tribute. He then recounts the treachery of Mordred and his own final battle. He says that he was taken to the island of Avalon by his sister Morgan, a nymph, who used herbs to cure him of his wounds. He now rules in the lower part of the world, living eternally *lege fatorum* [by the law of the fates; perhaps the fays?]. He suggests that Henry should read Gildas [he means Nennius] and Geoffrey of Monmouth for further details; he threatens to return with his armies if Henry does not lift his siege of the Breton towns. Henry, unafraid, reads this letter to his nobles, and laughingly remarks that Arthur seems to him to be more like Darius than Alexander. He sends a reply to Arthur in which he asserts his own rights in Brittany. But Henry goes on to say that the death of his mother and his own respect for Arthur lead him to offer to hold Brittany under Arthur's law. The episode ends with an account of Matilda's death and the delivery of the news to Henry by a "certain monk of Bec."

There are two significant strands in this strange narrative. The first is Arthur's account of his departure for Avalon and his underworld/otherworld existence in the Antipodes. If Gerald, recording something as "factual" as the finding of Arthur's grave, cannot resist the lure of some (admittedly learned) discussion of Avalon, Etienne, with the license granted by invention, indulges in this delightful topic with great freedom. In his letter to Henry, Arthur recounts what happened to him after his final battle:

> Wounded, Arthur sought herbs thence from his sister, and the holy island of Avalon held these. Here Morgan, eternal nymph, received her brother, cured him and nourished him, and revived him and made him immortal. The Antipodes were given unto his rule; guided by destiny, the warrior stands unarmed and yet fears no battle. Thus he rules the lower hemisphere, he shines in arms, the other half of the world is his. No desire of Alexander or Caesar could make the land of the upper people endure their laws [as the lower realm endures Arthur's]. The Antipodes tremble at the fatal rule of this man; the lower world is subject to him. He soars to the upper world, and sometimes returns to the depths; as the laws of the Antipodes require, he rules everywhere, all powerful.[49]

[49] Etienne de Rouen, *Draco Normannicus,*ed. R. Howlett, *Chronicles of the Reigns of Stephen, Henry II, and Richard I* (RS 82, 1885), vol. 2, lines 1161–74:
Saucius Arturus petit herbas inde sororis,

This is the clearest early development of the idea of an otherworld existence for Arthur.[50] We have seen how some contemporaries would react to such embroidery, but Etienne's peculiar epistolary style in this section of the *Draco Normannicus* allows him to present this material while at the same time standing an appropriate distance from it. Arthur's speech is reported in the chronicle, as contained in the letter; and Arthur consistently refers to himself in the third person, with curiously depersonalizing and distancing effect.

Etienne gives his monarch some characteristics appropriate to his location; Arthur's first letter, to Roland, forecasts the death of Matilda in appropriately pagan and vatic terms:

> Henry's attack is known to me; fear nothing. He will hear sad news from Rouen: his mother dies. Clotho holds the spindle, Lachesis draws out the thread, and Attropos cuts it, and indeed she will leave this life. He will cease to harass the Bretons, but he will not cease to mourn, for no one is dearer to him in the world than she is.[51]

This is of course a true "prophecy,"[52] but Arthur's abilities in this regard, and his location, have very negative overtones in this work.

> Avallonis eas insula sacra tenet.
> Suscipit hic fratrem Morganis nympha perennis,
> Curat, alit, refovet, perpetuumque facit.
> Traditur antipodum sibi jus; fatatus, inermis,
> Belliger assistit, proelia nulla timet.
> Sic hemispherium regit inferius, nitet armis,
> Altera pars mundi dimidiata sibi.
> Hoc nec Alexandri potuit, nec Caesaris ardor,
> Ut superum tellus sic sua jura ferat.
> Antipodes hujus fatalia jura tremiscunt;
> Inferior mundus subditus extat ei.
> Evolat ad superos, quandoque recurrit ad ima;
> Ut sua jura petunt, degit ubique potens.

Day translates *fatatus* and *fatalia* as indications of fairy nature; Latham's earliest recorded use of the root (*fat-*) in that sense, however, is c. 1190. (R.E. Latham, *Revised Medieval Latin Word-List from British and Irish Sources* [London: Oxford University Press, 1965]). The older sense of fated, one under the rule of the fates, or destined, might also be appropriate for Arthur, so I have chosen that shade of meaning instead.

50 Day suggests that this is "apparently the earliest literary treatment of Arthur as immortal" ("The Letter from King Arthur," p. 155); Day and Tatlock suggest Geoffrey's *Vita Merlini* as a possible model for the Avalon section, but given the latter work's minimal circulation the argument seems to me unlikely.

51 *Draco Normannicus*, lines 957–62:
> Impetus Henrici mihi notus, nil timeatur;
> Audiet a Rodomo tristia: mater obit.
> Cloto colum, Lachesis filum tenet, attrahit, occat
> Atropos, et vitam deserit illa quidem.
> Desinet hic Britones, nec quibit ferre dolorem,
> Nam nihil in mundo carius extat ei.

52 As Tatlock notes, Etienne follows common practice by making extensive use of Geoffrey's

The passage above repeatedly draws attention to the *jura fatalia* which guarantee Arthur's existence, and the stress on the fact that his realm is lower, below, in the depths, has clearly hellish overtones. Elsewhere Arthur describes his army in supernatural terms: "For the fated army, unpierceable by arms, cuts down everything, makes all ways passable."[53] Arthur makes his status as ruler of the Antipodes part of his boast to Henry, but Etienne is of course not interested in portraying Arthur as being in the right in this case. Arthur's Antipodean existence allows Etienne to indulge in the sort of speculation which enraged the more sober of historians, while also portraying Arthur in an unflattering light. Tatlock suggests that the reference to the Antipodes had negative and grotesque overtones for Etienne's contemporaries, who would have associated the location at best with that region of the world which was the home of dog-headed men and other such monstrosities, and at the worst with the infernal regions.[54] The location, in combination with the insistence that Arthur rules *fatorum lege* and has been made *fatatus* (both words may carry implications of fairy nature) by his sister, the *nympha*, combine to suggest that if the Breton hope is indeed a fact, then it is an evil one. Day argues that Arthur's dubious immortality is a device by which Etienne contrasts Arthur "to King Henry as a Christian monarch."[55] For Etienne, the good king is the real monarch whose patronage he is courting.

The afterlife in the Antipodes, then, is one of the most striking aspects of Etienne's Arthurian episode. There is another significant feature of this account, one which is perhaps of even greater interest, given the focus of this study. Etienne's Arthur is tainted by the infernal associations of his realm; he is also a character much like the *tyrannus superbus* of the Welsh saints' lives. In the *Draco Normannicus*, Arthur recounts his exploits in the most bombastic language. Day points to the traditional structure of Arthur's challenge to

---

*Prophetie Merlini* throughout his chronicle; "Geoffrey and King Arthur in *Normannicus Draco*," 3.

[53] *Draco Normannicus*, lines 1198–1199:
   Nam fatata cohors, at impenetrabilis armis,
      Quaelibet obtruncat, pervia cuncta facit.

[54] Tatlock, "Geoffrey and King Arthur in *Normannicus Draco*," 12–18. Tatlock argues Etienne deliberately places Arthur's domain "in a region blighted by orthodox disapproval, by skepticism, ridicule, and grotesque description and portraiture . . . ," 17. For a different treatment of the island, compare William of Rennes's account of Avalon.

[55] Day, "The Letter from King Arthur," p. 154; Etienne builds up a contrast between Arthur, who rules *fatorum lege perenni*, and Henry, who will hold Brittany *sub Christi jure*, p. 157.

Henry,[56] but while a certain amount of boasting is part of the epic tradition, Arthur surely goes to extremes. Even before he speaks, he is characterized: "Arthur reads this; he gnashes his teeth, he rages, he boils with anger."[57] His reply to Roland opens with frequent references to the rising wind of his anger: "Arthur to Roland. A great wind is unleashed in the heavens, and refuses to hold back its gales for long."[58] Is this, given the nature of the portrait to come and the place from which these winds arise, so much hot air? Certainly Arthur presents himself as the greatest conqueror of all time:

> I have had many battles, and I have always and everywhere through military might carried off triumphant praises. I subdued the British by arms, and I conquered the English, and I tamed by the yoke the proud necks of the Franks. Thus I alone then wore the triple crowns of the triple kingdom, and there was no one in these lands equal to me. You boast of your wealth, your might and your arms in vain, for I excel, in power and in might, all that the world contains. The great Assyrian king who first subjected people to himself by the sword could not be ranked with me. Nor could the Chaldean, laying low the walls of Judea, able to drive such strong people from their seat. Nor the Macedonian, lord of the world, whom the sun and his sister [the moon] sing by the right of the tree suffused with light . . .[59]

---

[56] Day, "The Letter from King Arthur," p. 154.
[57] *Draco Normannicus*, line 953: "Haec legit Arturus, frendet, furit, aestuat ira"
[58] *Draco Normannicus*, lines 955–56:
  Arturus Rollando. Magnus ventus in auras
  Solvitur, et renuit tollere flabra diu.
[59] *Draco Normannicus*, lines 979–92:
  Conflictus varios habui, laudisque triumphos
    Viribus armatis semper ubique tuli.
  Substravi Britones armis, Anglosque subegi,
    Francorum domui turgida colla jugo.
  Sic triplicis regni diademata tunc tria gessi
    Solus, in his terris par mihi nemo fuit.
  Frustra te jactas opibus, virtute vel armis,
    Hos super excello, quos simul orbis habet.
  Non mihi magnus rex Assyrius aequiparetur,
    Primus qui populos subdidit ense sibi.
  Sed nec Chaldaicus Judaica moenia sternens,
    Plebes tam validas pellere sede valens.
  Nec Macedo, mundi dominus, quem solque sororque
    Arboris infusi lumine jure canunt.
The allusion to Alexander refers to a visit by Alexander to a grove of sacred trees, including a tree of the sun and a tree of the moon. When the light of the sun (or moon) strikes them, they begin to prophesy. One might also render the line "whom the sun and his sister rightly sing by the light of the suffused tree." Many thanks to A.G. Rigg and David Townsend for their suggestions with respect to this thorny passage.

The list of conquerors whom Arthur surpasses continues, but it is appropriate to stop with the reference to Alexander, for the rest of the episode develops the Alexander comparison.[60] We will see below that, when William of Rennes writes his version of Arthurian history, he draws parallels between Arthur and Alexander in part to illustrate the errors of unjust war. I have argued that Geoffrey of Monmouth takes considerable care to make Arthur's wars just ones, and that he stresses Arthur's peacetime role as lawgiver and restorer of territorial and religious rights. Writing in a different period, Etienne appears to be pursuing a course more like that which William would later follow. In fact, his Arthur seems to have spent his whole life engaged in conquest. Tellingly, all three of his "triple crowns" were achieved through war; there is no sense here that he had any birthright to the British crown. Later, in his account of the war against Rome, Arthur tells the story of the demand for tribute, but he characterizes it as an attempt by the Romans to induce him to return the land which he has seized;[61] that is, the request is tied to *his* previous conquests, and not to Rome's. And Henry's reply to Arthur stresses birthright and law:

> Neustria was Rollo's, as was all of Brittany; he has these through a peace agreement with the French. I am the heir of a double right. That which I rightly demand, descent and reason grant, the law sides with me, indeed orders [that they should be mine]. In a rage you order that I should leave the Bretons alone, but anger is a foolish passion, when reason is lacking.[62]

Like Geoffrey in his *Historia*, Etienne here employs the figure of the unjust king, ruled by passion rather than by reason or law. While Etienne clearly has a propagandistic purpose for this portrayal of Arthur, so opposite in every way to Henry II as Etienne describes

---

[60] Day suggests that the exchange of letters might have been modelled on the correspondence of Alexander in Julius Valerius's *Res Gestae Alexandri Macedonis*; see "Arthurian Romances in Latin: A Survey," in *King Arthur through the Ages*, ed. Valerie M. Lagorio and Mildred Leake Day (New York: Garland, 1990), vol. 1, p. 45. Tatlock notes that the books in the library at Bec would certainly have included a version of the Alexander story; see "Geoffrey and King Arthur in *Normannicus Draco*," 8.

[61] *Draco Normannicus*, line 1005: "Ut sibi restituam terras . . ."

[62] *Draco Normannicus*, lines 1263–68:
Neustria Rollonis fuit, atque Britannia tota;
  Has a Francigenis foedere pacis habet.
Heres juris ego gemini; quod jure reposco,
  Dat genus et ratio, lex favet, immo jubet.
Ut linquam Britones mandas iratus; at ira
  Fit furor insipiens, dum ratione caret.

him, it is not all that unusual for Latin texts to use the great King Arthur in this fashion. Readers accustomed to the vernacular traditions may have met with the ineffectual Arthur of later French romance, or with the "conqueror kyd," with all the good and bad that such an epithet can imply, of the *Alliterative Morte Arthure*; but this belligerent tyrant is perhaps less familiar. In the Latin texts in this study, however, the tyrant king is one possible refraction of the courtier's concern with kingship. While Geoffrey chose to make Arthur, Aurelius, and a few others exemplary in a positive sense, some Latin writers make of Britain's greatest king a negative exemplum. Arthur can be an anti-hero, in a genre which has at least as much in common with court satire and the associated mirrors for princes as it does with romance. Etienne's Arthurian episode is a particularly striking combination of these different narrative strains.

But the portrait of Arthur as conqueror is not used merely to show the evils of conquest or to flatter the Angevin king. The explicit references to Alexander are here used, not as William of Rennes would later use them to condemn Arthur because he is *like* Alexander, but rather, because he is *not* like Alexander. Henry's response to Arthur's claims is to ridicule them, at least to his own men; he laughs, saying that Arthur is more like Darius than Alexander.[63] William of Newburgh might or might not have read Etienne,[64] but he certainly seems to be making the same point through comparison to Alexander when he describes Geoffrey's account of Arthur's wars:

> Then that fable-maker, so that he could exalt Arthur to the heights, makes him declare war on the Romans . . . he makes the great kings of the world ally with the Romans against him, namely the kings of Greece, Africa, Spain, the Parthians, the Medes, the Ituraeans, Libya, Egypt, Babylon, Bithynia, Phrygia, Syria, Boeotia, and Crete; he says that they were all conquered by that man in a single battle, while Alexander the Great, renowned in every age, sweated through twelve years to overcome certain princes of such great kingdoms. He makes Arthur's little finger bigger than the back of Alexander the Great, particularly because before this victory over so

---

[63] *Draco Normannicus*, line 1235: "Arturi Darium praesens feritas imitatur . . ."

[64] Given the survival of the *Draco Normannicus* in a unique manuscript of the fifteenth century, Vatican Library MS Reg. 3081, it seems unlikely; see *Chronicles of the Reigns of Stephen, Henry II, and Richard I*, ed. R. Howlett, pp. xci–xcvii, for a description of the manuscript and for a discussion of two other manuscripts of the *Draco* which seem once to have existed. Both Williams of course depend on Geoffrey's *Historia*, the more probable explanation for the similarities.

many great kings he makes him remind his men in an assembly about the subjection of thirty kingdoms already achieved by himself and by them.[65]

William's obvious incredulity at the description of the Roman wars may allow us to read Etienne's description in a similar light; thus Arthur's list of the forces allied against him may be understood as another example of the king's overweening pride:

> Then all Rome gathers together with the lands subject to her, mindful of the arms of Caesar. The world follows, like a raging river crosses the Alps, a helmeted power seeks out Arthur. Greece, the power, wit, and all glory of philosophy, comes proud with its leaders, its legions. The mother of all tongues, the Babylonian power hastens, and does not know what that barbarian is pronouncing to himself. The Egyptians are there, once fount of astrology, nor do they see in the stars how sad the war would be for them. The Midians and the Persians do not consult the magical arts, so that they might discover in advance the various events [to come]. Africa, famous for the wars of Jugurtha, sends hither cunning Numidians, who have no equal in fraud. Libya with Syria, Spain, Parthia and Crete gather together, and they prepare arms with great strength. The strength of Bithynia, and likewise the whole of Boeotia, with the Phrygians, tries to hand over all things to death.[66]

[65] *History of English Affairs*, book I, *Prooemium*, p. 34:
Inde fabulator ille, ut suum Arturum ad summum evehat, facit eum Romanis bellum indicere . . . facit adversus eum convenire cum Romanis reges magnos orbis terrarum, scilicet Graeciae Africae Hispaniae Parthorum Medorum Ituraeorum Libyae Aegypti Babyloniae Bithyniae Phrygiae Syriae Boeotiae Cretae; omnesque refert uno proelio ab illo devictos, cum Alexander ille Magnus et omnibus seculis clarus per annos duodecim in quibusdam tantorum regnorum principibus superandis sudaverit. profecto minimum digitum sui Arturi grossiorem facit dorso Alexandri Magni, praesertim cum ante hanc victoriam de tot magnis regibus faciat eum commemorare suis in concione subactionem triginta regnorum a se et illis jam factam.

[66] *Draco Normannicus*, lines 1015–1022:
Cum sibi subjectis terris Romania tota
   Convenit, armorum Caesaris ipsa memor.
Hanc sequitur mundus, ceu torrens turbidus, Alpes
   Transvolat, Arturum vis galeata petit.
Graecia, vis, sensus, decus omne philosophiae,
   Cum ducibus, cuneis, tota superba venit.
Linguarum mater, properat Babylonica virtus,
   Nescit quid sibimet barbarus ille sonet.
Sic Aegyptus adest, olim fons astrologiae,
   Nec videt in stellis tristia bella sibi.
Media, cum Persis, magicas non consulit artes,
   Ut casus varios ante notare queat.
Africa, Jugurthae bellis famosa, dolosos
   Dirigit huc Numidas, nec sibi fraude pares.
Libya cum Syris, Hispania, Parthia, Creta

To be sure, the list of the assembled hosts follows Geoffrey closely; the embellishments may simply be the result of the poetic form. Taken in conjunction with other aspects of Arthur's personality in the *Draco*, however, this description's effect is not so much epic as bombastic. Henry's response to Arthur stresses the latter's reputation, but one senses that the young king is humoring the old one, "lest he feel himself insulted."[67] When Henry writes that "the great worth of Arthur is praised everywhere,"[68] a reader must agree that Arthur at least has so praised himself. When Henry withdraws from Britanny, offering to hold it under Arthur for the moment, there is no doubt who the true king is; the ruler of the Antipodes is a blowhard, and his greatest accomplishments seem as a result to be diminished. While Etienne recounts the battle between the Britons under Arthur and the Romans under Lucius with great detail and verve, the result is curiously flat.[69] The strangely impersonal third-person account, already enclosed in the epistolary frame, distances the narrative; as was the case with the Avalon material, the sense is that Etienne is both engrossed by but also removed from his subject.

Why did Etienne choose Arthur as Henry's correspondent? The political reality of the Breton hope and the campaign in Britanny may certainly have something to do with it. The popular appeal of the material is another factor; like Johannes de Hauvilla or the author of the *Awntyrs off Arthure*, discussed in chapter 5, Etienne is clothing his work in Arthurian dress when his primary concern is neither ancient British history nor romance narrative. But as we leave this use of the Arthurian story for others, apparently equally odd, I would stress that we will come to see Etienne's treatment as part of a consistent current of criticism in Latin Arthurian narrative. For Latin writers at least, Arthur is not always Geoffrey's perfect king; he *is* often an exemplary king, but the example can be foolish as well as praiseworthy.

William of Rennes's *Gesta regum Britanniae* dates to some time after 1236; it is thus somewhat outside the period of most of the Latin

---

Conveniunt, magnis viribus arma parant.
Bithyniae virtus, simul ipsa Boeotia tota
    Cum Phrygiis tentat tradere cuncta neci.

[67] *Draco Normannicus*, line 1249: "Ne se contemni reputet"
[68] *Draco Normannicus*, line 1255: "Nobilis Arturi probitas laudatur ubique"
[69] Day argues that the relation has "the immediacy of a first-person, eye-witness account" ("The Letter from King Arthur," p. 155), but I would argue that Arthur's referring to himself consistently in the third person creates distance rather than immediacy.

texts in this study, and belongs rather to the period of the vernacular elaborations of the Arthurian material in works like the Old French Vulgate cycle. Like other Latin (and vernacular) chroniclers, William decided to follow the whole of Geoffrey's sequence in his poetic version of the *Historia*. This decision, Rosemary Morris argues, is in part responsible for the tendency of modern Arthurian scholars to overlook his work, which appears to be just one more vaguely Galfridian chronicle.[70] William offers no additions like Wace's Round Table, although he does insert his own rhetorical decorations, dialogues, and a most curious description of Arthur's island paradise. But William casts Arthur in an explicitly epic mode, offering clear parallels between the British king and Alexander in, for example, the fact that Uther must remain with Igerna for three days in order to beget Arthur, and in the turn from just to unjust conquest. William, Morris argues, sets out to be "Virgil to Arthur's Aeneas,"[71] and from the same combination of poetic and patriotic motives. The presentation of Arthur as the culmination of British national identity, and the focus on the imperfections which motivate the tragic fall, seem to forecast the many vernacular *mortes*, some of which blame fate, and some the king, for the final outcome.

There are reasons to exclude William from this study. We do not know much about him, but his time and place demonstrate that he is not explicitly attached to the Angevin court or indeed perhaps to any court, although like most medieval writers he writes for a patron, in this case, as in many, a powerful churchman. Yet there are reasons to include him, too. One is his tendency to lay the blame on Arthur for his fall; along with a strong insistence on Arthur as the champion of the church and of law, this tendency allies William with the court writers discussed thus far and in the pages to follow. Another reason is William's imaginative response to Geoffrey's raw material; while William works hard to avoid the implications of Geoffrey's radical historiography, he follows him willingly in other ways, emphasizing in his addition of detail, in the heightening of certain fantastic moments, and in particular in his fondness for dialogue, the "story" in this history. And while William's poetic style rapidly becomes annoying, his fondness for verbal tricks demonstrates a playful attitude towards Latin which is characteristic of many of the writers

[70] Rosemary Morris, "The *Gesta Regum Britanniae* of William of Rennes: An Arthurian Epic?" *Arthurian Literature* 6 (1986), 61.
[71] Morris, "The *Gesta Regum Britanniae*," 97.

in this study. The truest reason for his presence here, however, is simply that he is an interesting Latin Arthurian writer, and it would seem unreasonable to exclude him on the grounds of his failure to fit a thesis which I have argued and will continue to argue is suggestive rather than complete or prescriptive.

It is not necessary to provide a summary of the *Gesta*, for William follows Geoffrey very closely. He adapts the whole of the *Historia*, not simply the Arthuriad, but he makes it clear from the outset that Arthur is the main focus of his work. The *Gesta* opens with an invocation of the Muse: "Tell, Caliope, so that I may tell again as you relate; whence the people of the Britons came, what the origin of their name was, whence noble Britain had its kings, who Arthur was, what his deeds were, what his end, and how an unlucky nation lost its kingdom."[72] Arthur is figured at the outset as the pinnacle of British history, but there is a sense of loss and doom here which is not present in Geoffrey at the opening, and is more commonly found in the vernacular *mortes* than in the Latin chronicle responses to Geoffrey. The next two lines are the more intriguing, then, for they offer the work to William's patron, the bishop of Vannes, as a *ludus* which may refresh him after reading the Scriptures.[73] It is hard at first to see any ludic qualities in the work, unless they are to be found in William's incessant word-play. Poetic history is here presented as a diversion appropriate enough for an educated churchman; perhaps we have returned to the world of court writing as it has been described above.

Each of William's ten books begins with a terse prose summary of its contents. The summary for book V, which includes the events from the reign of Constans on, reads: "A monk rules against the right, and a traitor succeeds him."[74] For William as for Geoffrey, the heart of this story is the unfitness of two of Britain's rulers. An excursus on Constans's name, however, reveals a concern which Geoffrey did not apparently share: "O inconstant son, falsely called

---

[72] William of Rennes, *Gesta Regum Britanniae*, in *The Historia Regum Britannie of Geoffrey of Monmouth V: Gesta regum Britannie* (Cambridge: D.S. Brewer, 1991), ed. and trans. Neil Wright; I.11–15:
> Caliope referas, ut te referente renarrem,
> Unde genus Britonum, que nominis huius origo,
> Unde suos habuit generosa Britannia reges,
> Quis fuit Arturus, que gesta, quis exitus eius,
> Qualiter amisit infelix nacio regnum.

[73] *Gesta Regum Britanniae*, I.16–17.

[74] *Gesta Regum Britanniae*, V.4–5: "Contra ius regnat monachus. Successit eidem/ Proditor."

Constant, you should go back to your cloister and resume your habit, and keep your holy vow! Put aside your regal ornaments, for rough garments suit you, not royal dignity."[75] This authorial intrusion is very unlike Geoffrey's style, and there is in general more use of direct dialogue, of the authorial voice or of the characters, than in Geoffrey. The most significant difference exemplified by this passage, however, has to do with the attitude towards religion. The focus is not on Constans's unfitness to rule, but rather on his breaking of his religious vows. Throughout the *Gesta*, William adds detail to stress the religious aspect of the work, one which we have already noted is more subdued than might be expected in Geoffrey. Compare, for example, the passages in which Hengist explains the religion of the Saxons. In Geoffrey, he says,

> We worship the gods of our fatherland, Saturn, Jove, and others who rule over this world: but especially we worship Mercury, whom we call Woden in our tongue. Our ancestors dedicated the fourth day of the week to him, which from that time to this is called Wednesday, derived from his name. After him we worship the goddess who is the most powerful of all goddesses, called Freia, to whom we have dedicated the sixth day of the week, which from her name is called Friday.[76]

Geoffrey's main interest here appears to be etymological or perhaps anthropological. In William's version of the same passage, on the other hand, the etymological detail is gone, to be replaced by an insistence on the pagan nature of the Saxons' belief: "We worship the powers of heaven, Juno with Jupiter, Mars with Pallas, and old

[75] *Gesta Regum Britanniae*, V.129–33:
> O puer inconstans, qui falso nomine Constans
> Diceris, ad claustrum redeas habitumque resumas
> Et sanctum uotum teneas. Regalia demas
> Ornamenta tibi; nam te decet hispida uestis,
> Non regale decus.

The plays on *Constans* and *regalia* are rather mild examples of what Morris calls "William's passion for *annominatio*," a passion to which he was a "hopeless addict"; see "The *Gesta Regum Britanniae*," 66–67. The addiction can be seen clearly a few lines later, as William refuses to abandon his point about Constans: "Rex igitur Constans, quem non constantia mentis/ Erigit in regem . . . ," V.139–40.

[76] *Historia regum Britannie*, c. 98:
> Deos patrios, Saturnum, Iouem atque ceteros qui mundum istum gubernant colimus: maxime autem Mercurium, quem Worden lingua nostra appellamus. Huic ueteres nostri dedicauerunt quartam feriam septimane, que usque in hodiernum diem nomen Wonnesdei de nomine ipsius sortita est. Post illum colimus deam inter ceteras potentissimam uocabulo <Fream, cui etiam dedicauerunt sextam> feriam quam ex nomine eius Fridei uocamus.

Saturn; satyrs, fauns and *lares*, and innumerable others; we prefer Mercury to all of these, he who directs us and our acts."[77] In part, William is simply showing off his classical learning; Morris argues that throughout the work he is competing explicitly with Walter of Châtillon's *Alexandreis*, a classicizing reworking of the Alexander story.[78] At the same time, the insistence on the ominous figure of "old Saturn," on the number of animistic deities worshipped by the Saxons, and on the controlling nature of Mercury, heightens the pagan nature of the invaders.

Kingship is still a major issue in William, but he focuses that issue through the lens of religion. William's Vortigern, like Geoffrey's, is tricked into marrying Renwein, but William sees a threat both to the kingdom and to Christianity. Another authorial intrusion exclaims,

> What are you doing, madman? What is this, most stupid of kings? Why have you been deluded by a face? Why are you entering into marriage against the precepts of God? for it is forbidden by divine law that a man and a woman of different creeds should become one. The German maiden is not marrying you, but your kingdom.[79]

For Gildas, the Britons are ravaged by the Saxons as a punishment for their own sinfulness. For Geoffrey, many British kings bring disaster to their people through their selfish following of their own (sinful) desires. William is clearly concerned with the political implications of Vortigern's actions, but the ethos is slightly different; the real problem is that the king should be the protector of both religion and his land, and a failure in one role is a failure in the other. The British people themselves express the linking of the concept of king as guarantor of justice and king as subject of God's law: "O king, it is amazing that you have joined yourself to a heathen maiden. There can be no contract between Belial and Christ; it is even more incredible

---

[77] *Gesta Regum Britanniae*, V.217–21:
   . . . Nos numina celi,
   Cum Ioue Iunonem, colimus, cum Pallade Martem
   Saturnumque senem, Satyros, Faunosque, Laresque
   Innumerosque alios; preponimus omnibus illis
   Mercurium qui nos et nostros dirigit actus.

[78] Morris, "The *Gesta Regum Britanniae*," 60; 62–78 offer a detailed comparison between William and Walter.

[79] *Gesta Regum Britanniae*, V.295–99:
   Quid facis, o demens? Quid id est, stultissime regum?
   Cur caperis facie? Quid inis connubia contra
   Preceptum Domini? Nam mas et femina cultus
   Disparis esse pares diuina lege uetantur.
   Non tibi sed regno uirgo Germanica nubit.

that you have given the reins of your kingdom into the hands of a people without law."[80] Perhaps this is a difference in emphasis rather than in kind; in the *Historia*, too, the British people argue against mixing with the pagans. William's shift from the third-person narrative to direct speech, however, gives such concerns greater urgency in the *Gesta*, and the links which are made specifically between the king's betrayal of religious law and the fate of his land are stressed. William consistently insists on the religiosity (or lack of it) of his kings. Geoffrey's Aurelius devoted his whole attention to restoring the realm, actions which naturally included the rebuilding of churches. William's Aurelius is called "servant of Christ, friend of piety, cultivator of faith, guardian of religion, lover of peace . . ."[81] In both versions Aurelius rebuilds the churches destroyed by the Saxons, but in William he also makes a point of destroying the pagan temples.[82] Uther is explicitly called *adulter* for his designs on Igerna,[83] and the young Arthur's virtues include that he is inured with grace in Christ.[84] One could multiply examples endlessly. The question is what to make of William's resolute devotion to the Christian element of the story.

Rosemary Morris suggests that part of what is going on has again to do with William's reaction to Walter's *Alexandreis*. In that work, Alexander is "the adumbration of an ideal Christian King, a proto-crusader," and she argues that the time of the Third Crusade, in which the *Alexandreis* was written, would have given the theme a "burning relevance."[85] Crusading may or may not have been in William's mind, but conventional historiography, I think, was. One of the most significant changes William makes to Geoffrey's structure is in his treatment of the *Prophetie Merlini*. His omission of the preface to Alexander, bishop of Lincoln, is completely understandable in this new context: he has his own ecclesiastical patron to think of. What is more remarkable is William's excision of most of the

---

[80] *Gesta Regum Britanniae*, V.330–33:
> O rex, mirandum est te coniunxisse puellam
> Sic tibi gentilem: nulla est conuencio Christi
> Ad Belial. Multo magis est mirabile regni
> Te dare frena tui populo sine lege regenda.

[81] *Gesta Regum Britanniae*, VI.109–11: ". . . Christi famulum, pietatis amicum,/ Cultorem fidei, custodem religionum,/ Pacis amatorem . . ."

[82] *Gesta Regum Britanniae*, VI.260–61.

[83] *Gesta Regum Britanniae*, VI.509.

[84] *Gesta Regum Britanniae*, VII.35–36: ". . . Christia/ gratia . . ."

[85] Morris, "The *Gesta Regum Britanniae*," 63.

prophecies themselves. William reproduces the first section, up to the descendants of the Boar (a section which, as it happens, includes remarks about the destruction of religion), and then abruptly stops with these words: "Afterwards Merlin prophesied these and many things which are difficult to commit to orderly meter . . ."[86] The narrative resumes with Vortigern's reaction.

What are we to make of William's omissions? On many grounds, the *Prophetie Merlini* would logically have been included. Prophecy, as discussed above, was part of serious history. Merlin's prophecies had an independent and lively existence. And William offers his work as a *ludus* to refresh a biblical scholar after the rigors of Scripture; Merlin's prophecies are both playful and designed to appeal to an educated audience's taste for exegesis and riddle-solving. Finally, if William's goal is as nationalistic as Morris argues it to be,[87] there are good ethnic reasons for keeping the prophecies, for the link between prophecy and national history is strong in the Celtic tradition.

It may be that William's classicizing approach encouraged him to abandon the more outrageously Celtic aspects of his source. On the other hand, he develops a life on Avalon for Arthur which, even if it can be likened to classical versions of the underworld, is nevertheless firmly fixed in his audience's mind as part of the Celtic tradition, the Breton/Briton hope mocked by Etienne de Rouen's Antipodean Arthur. Perhaps, then, William is merely responding to the obvious, which is that the *Prophetie Merlini* interrupt the narrative flow of Geoffrey's *Historia*. In the end, whatever the reason, William has excised that part of the *Historia* which contributes most significantly to that work's radical representation of human history. In place of Geoffrey's dissolution into meaningless apocalypse, there is a traditional story of kings and their relation to their people and to their God. And where does Arthur fit into this revised schema?

I have argued that the placement of the *Prophetie* in the *Historia* casts a shadow on Arthur's rule even before his birth, because of the negative implications, stemming from the final, apocalyptic moments of the *Prophetie*, of the celestial portents which foretell his birth. The irregular manner of his conception, too, was seen to be problematic, especially because of the close parallels between Uther's lust and

---

[86] *Gesta Regum Britanniae*, VI.69–70: "Postquam Merlinus hec pluraque uaticinauit,/ Quorum difficile est seriem committere metro . . ."

[87] Morris argues that "By adapting the Latin epic medium, William declares an intention to speak for Brittany on the international scene"; "The *Gesta Regum Britanniae*," 110.

Vortigern's. William reduces the banquet scene considerably, and as was the case with the excision of the *Prophetie*, the result is to move from a strange mixture of foreboding and hilarity to a much more conventional disapproval. Here is the scene in its entirety:

> The duke of Cornwall also comes with the companion of his bed, who surpasses all maidens as Cynthia does the stars or Phebus the moon. When the king sees the eyes and face of the duchess, then, he burns with love for her ... He sighs, tortured in mind, and, forgetful of the behavior that is appropriate for him, he wants to become Gorlois. Gorlois sees the error of the king, for which reason he secretly returns to his own country with his wife.[88]

Uther, elsewhere called *adulter*, is no potential figure of fun here, and if Geoffrey's strategy was to employ the recreational in order to catch the reader off guard, William's is simply to offer clear condemnation. There is a tension between William's paralleling of the conceptions of Arthur and Alexander – the conception of Arthur takes three nights, for "one night is not enough to engender so great a man"[89] – and the insistence on Uther's duplicity. Geoffrey too stressed the deception of Igerna by Uther, but what he left implicit seems to be explicit as William closes the scene with a reference not only to the glorious future but also to the overturning of good fortune by bad:

> The duke falls at the front of the battle. A messenger reports the death of the duke to his wife, but the sophistical form of the king contradicts him. With his false face set aside, the king resumes his true one. The woman whom he had taken as an adulterer, he now takes as a husband, and also conceives a child thence; noble Arthur and his sister Anna thus are born. From that time on, the happy island enjoys peace for a long time, but since often joys are mixed with sadness, the joy of the kingdom turns entirely to grief.[90]

[88] *Gesta Regum Britanniae*, VI.472–80:
  . . . Uenit et dux Cornubiensis
  Cum consorte thori, que quanto Cincia stellis
  Et Phebus lune tanto preest illa puellis.
  Rex igitur uisis oculis facieque ducisse
  Eius amore calet . . .
  . . . suspirat, torquetur mente, suique
  Oblitus decoris fieri Gorlosius optat.
  Percipit errorem regis Gorlosius; unde
  Clam redit ad patriam cum coniuge.

[89] *Gesta Regum Britanniae*, VI.498–99: ". . . non est nox unica tanti/ Ut tantus generetur homo . . ."

[90] *Gesta Regum Britanniae*, VI.505–14:
  . . . In primo marte peremptus
  Dux cadit. Occisi casum ducis intimat eius

The immediate context for this remark is the poisoning of Uther, and the remark itself is of course entirely conventional. In a sense this very conventionality is an antidote to Geoffrey's bleak vision; Uther has sinned, and in any case, joy customarily turns to sorrow. Yet while William may have removed the more extreme aspects of Geoffrey's historiography, particularly through his suppression of the *Prophetie Merlini*, he shares Geoffrey's sense of the intimate link between the fortunes of the king and the kingdom: it is the joy of the *regnum* that turns to grief.

The Arthuriad proper in William's treatment is in fact accorded some special "space," just as in Geoffrey, but its introduction is effected, not through the highly ambiguous means of the celestial chaos of Merlin's prophecies, but rather through a new, conventional, and classicizing invocation. The structure of the *Historia* makes of Arthur a bright figure who stands for a time against the chaos represented in the *Prophetie*; the invocation to the *Gesta* returns us to the model of Alexander through its invocation of classical heroes whom Arthur excels:

> Bright Caliope, come from Helicon, with the band of your sisters with you, and moisten my hollow, thirsty breast with your sacred spring; for I do not presume to describe the deeds of Arthur in verse without you, lest I should seem to demean them. Homer could not succeed without your willing it, nor Ovid, nor Virgil, nor Tullius himself, since Arthur surpasses Achilles in praise by as much as Achilles surpasses Thersites. The author of the *Aeneid* would have preferred the praises of Arthur to the story of old Anchises, [for those praises] are worthy of the Maeonian bard; grave Lucan would have fallen silent about the deeds of Caesar, and old Thebes would have lacked its eternal fame, had the deeds of Arthur preceded these poets. But lest so great a hero should perish without praise, I will try to lift up the praise of this invincible prince.[91]

Nuncius uxori, sed forma sophistica regis
Contradicit ei. Regis fallace remota
Uera redit facies. Quam rex cognouit adulter,
Cognoscit coniunx, prolem quoque suscipit inde;
Nobilis Arturus hinc nascitur et soror Anna.
Inde diu placida gauisa est insula pace.
Sed quia sepe solent misceri tristia letis,
Tocius in luctum uertuntur gaudia regni.

91  *Gesta Regum Britanniae*, VII.11–26:
Candida Caliope, cetu comitante sororum
Ex Elicone ueni pectusque arentis inane
Sacro fonte riga; neque enim describere gesta

These great deeds are on the pattern of those we have already discussed: Arthur's strength is associated with his piety, and William takes every opportunity to expand on Geoffrey's references to Arthur's restoration of church lands and rights. The description of the plenary feast is characteristic. Geoffrey's included a rhetorical set-piece, the description of Caerleon, which stressed its suitability for Arthur's royalty, and a very long list of the great kings, lords, and churchmen who answer Arthur's summons. The list ends by stressing Arthur's status as an over-king in the heroic mold: ". . . there is not a prince of any worth on this side of Spain who did not come at this edict. Nor is it any wonder, for the *largesse* of Arthur was known throughout the whole world, and bound everyone to love of him."[92] Arthur's *largitas*, his heroic generosity, is responsible for binding so dazzling a display of secular power to himself. In William's version, the names of the princes are not listed, nor the character of their retinues. Neither is Arthur's generosity the focus. Instead, William moves directly to the procession of "a hundred pontiffs, a thousand priests, sixteen kings, twenty consuls, along with counts and dukes and lords, whose numbers cannot be counted easily . . ."[93] which leads to the ceremonial crowning of Arthur.

William here reconfigures Arthur's royalty to focus on the support of the church; the hierarchy of the list, along with the decision not to name the princes,[94] underlines this new focus. Morris points out that William's vision of Arthur's court as one in which there was "nothing

> Arturi metrice ne detractare uiderer
> Presumo sine te. Nil hic prodesset Homerus,
> Nil Naso, nil Uirgilius, nil Tullius ipse
> Absque tuo nutu, quia quantis fortis Achilles
> Tersitem excedit, tantis prefertur Achilli
> Laudibus Arturus. Cuius preconia uatis
> Meonii condigna modis Eneidos auctor
> Hystorie ueteris Anchise preposuisset,
> Lucanusque grauis tacuisset Cesaris actus,
> Et ueteres Thebe caruissent perpete fama,
> Si precessissent Arturi gesta poetas.
> Sed ne depereat tantus sine laudibus heros
> Principis inuicti laudes extollere conor.

[92] *Historia regum Britannie*, c. 156: ". . . non remansit princeps alicuius precii citra Hispaniam quin ad istum edictum ueniret. Nec mirum: largitas nanque Arturi per totum mundum diuulgata cunctos in amorem ipsius allexerat."

[93] *Gesta Regum Britanniae*, VII.415–18:
> Centum pontifices, prelati mille, bis octo
> Reges, uiginti fasces, comitesque ducesque
> Et proceres, quorum numerum depromere non est
> In promptu . . .

[94] William is not simply avoiding too great a poetic challenge; as Morris notes, he is elsewhere

owned, but everything held in common,"[95] suggests a monastic community.[96] This reorientation of the Arthurian story makes the removal of the more radical elements of the *Historia*'s historiography quite understandable. It also removes William's work even more forcefully from the court context I have been developing for my other examples of Latin Arthurian writing, in that it reconfigures the court to match a religious rather than a secular ideal.

Perhaps William does not belong at all in the group of the other Latin writers of Arthurian narrative studied here. He seems much more the genuinely religious churchman than the clerically-educated courtier; more at home in the halls of a monastery than in the halls of the great. Indeed, it is important to stress throughout that there are differences, sometimes significant ones, between the Latin Arthurian texts here examined. Nevertheless, William sets himself the task of answering a question posed in various ways by all the writers in this study. What kind of king was Arthur, and how does the life of the king relate to the life of the *regnum*? William's answer is more straightforward than is Geoffrey's. Arthur is indeed the Alexander-like conqueror he only claims to be in Etienne de Rouen, and like Alexander, he falls because of a conqueror's sin, the lust for conquest. Arthur's bloodthirsty speech to his troops at Siesia provokes another of the narrative voice's outbursts: "What madness, oh brave men! Is that perpetual kingdom to be lost for an earthly one? You will lose on both sides through your excess. Britain should be content with its own borders. Rome, too, should not seek to exact tribute unjustly."[97] Another of William's additions, the speech of a Roman woman to her departing love, allows one to see Arthur as a harbinger of death:

> "I fear Arthur, who fought a duel with the tribune Frollo and killed him; Lot, Cador, Auguselus, Kay, Gawain, Hoel: the sound alone of those names terrifies me." No house is without wailing, no street without lamentation; female voices and plaints strike the sky, a

---

all too happy to render "Geoffrey's rebarbative nomenclature into hexameters"; "The *Gesta Regum Britanniae*," 65.

[95] *Gesta Regum Britanniae*,VII.320: "Nichil proprium, communia cuncta . . ."
[96] Morris, "The *Gesta Regum Britanniae*," 92.
[97] *Gesta Regum Britanniae*, VIII.474–78:
> Quis furor, o fortes, pro regno deperituro
> Perdere perpetuum regnum? Perdetis utrumque
> Excedendo modum: contenta Britannia fine
> Debuit esse suo; potuit quoque Roma tributum
> Quod petit iniuste non exegisse . . .

resounding echo repeats the horrendous uproar. The grieving wife performs the rites for her husband while yet he lives.[98]

Such evocations of the horrors of war need not necessarily, in a medieval text, imply disapproval of all conflict, but in William's treatment, the authorial interventions suggest that here at least one is intended to feel the pathos of the scene and to question the situation which has produced it. This passage is followed by the prophetic dream of the dragon and bear. The immediate reference is to Arthur's battle with the giant of St. Michael's Mount, but the placement of the dream serves also to underline the ambiguity involved in identifying the king with the "fearful dragon" which triumphs in the "mighty war" with the bear.[99] The dragon and the bear are both frightening and dangerous creatures, a sense that persists clearly in vernacular versions of the dream, such as that in the *Alliterative Morte Arthure*.

In his *Historia*, Geoffrey reports Modred's actions baldly and suddenly. William inserts a reference to God which would seem again to reassert conventional views of history. Arthur plans to march across the Alps to subdue Rome and place it under his rule,[100] "But God opposed these vows with his powers"; the betrayal by Modred is made known.[101] This passage and William's other changes to the story allow one to argue that this is God's punishment of Arthur for turning to unjust conquest.[102] But while William diverges from Geoffrey in assigning blame – and therefore explanation – for the destruction of Arthur's kingdom, he agrees with his source in showing the dire consequences of Arthur's fall. Indeed, if Arthur is partly responsible, that responsibility seems to disappear in the lengthy address by the narrative voice to Modred, an address which

---

[98] *Gesta Regum Britanniae*, VIII.166–73:
  "Arturum timeo, qui cum Frollone duellum
  Commisit mortique dedit rex ipse tribunum.
  Loth, Cador, Auguselus, Keius, Glaganus, Hoelus –
  Hec audita sono solo me nomina terrent."
  Nulla domus plangore caret, uia nulla querelis:
  Feminei planctus et uoces aera pulsant;
  Horrisonos tonitrus reboat resonabilis eucho;
  Exequias uiui facit uxor mesta mariti.

[99] *Gesta Regum Britanniae*, VIII.181, 182: ". . . draco dirus . . . ," ". . . bellum . . . ingens . . ."

[100] *Gesta Regum Britanniae*, IX.141–44:
  Ut niue cessante, cum prima uolarit hyrundo,
  Transuolet Alpinos cum multo milite montes
  Ytaliamque sibi Romamque dolente senatu
  Subdat et imperii moderetur frena subacti.

[101] *Gesta Regum Britanniae*, IX.145: "Sed Deus opposuit tantis sua numina uotis."

[102] See Morris, "The *Gesta Regum Britanniae*," 77.

enumerates Arthur's virtues and compares him to the cruel Saxons. The address includes a review of Arthur's victories, but the summary line, that Arthur is he "whom the whole world fears," is potentially double-edged, as the discussion above suggests.[103] When Arthur receives his fatal wound, then, perhaps God is directing the blow.

An odd footnote to William's adaptation of Geoffrey's Arthuriad is his description of Avalon. Geoffrey's vague reference to Arthur's death does little to leave hope in the bleak final pages of the *Historia*, and we have seen that later responses to the mysterious death range from potential parody to outright condemnation. Why does William, with his conventional conqueror meeting a conventional death, then create an afterlife for Arthur on an idyllic island with neither age nor sorrow, "full of every delight, nothing held individually, but all in common."?[104] In the Rodgers and Hammerstein musical *Camelot*, Arthur sings that in Camelot "it never rains 'til after sundown/ By eight the morning fog must disappear . . ." William, for his part, creates an island where there is "no snow, no winter's cold, nor does summer's heat rage immoderately."[105] The extraordinary description is followed by a very ambiguous conclusion: "Arthur, sorely wounded, goes to the court of the king of Avalon, where the royal maiden, treating his wound, takes his healed limbs to herself; and they live together, if one may believe it."[106] I confess that in attempting to account for this final flourish, I lose any sense of an overall purpose for William's Arthuriad. The rest of the text follows Geoffrey in the conventional decline into chaos for the Britons, and the final words of the poem assert again that it is no great work: "It is enough for me that I should be read to be pleasing in the mouth of children."[107] It is perhaps an admission of defeat to return here at the end to take refuge in William's stated intention to provide a *ludus* for his ecclesiastical patron, but the mixture of elements in William's adaptation of

---

[103] *Gesta Regum Britanniae*, IX.238: "Quem totus metuit mundus . . . ": Morris suggests that the list has ironic significance, because Arthur's apparent invincibility is of course an illusion; "The *Gesta Regum Britanniae*," 76.

[104] *Gesta Regum Britanniae*, IX.303–5: ". . . Nulla senectus,/ Nullaque uis morbi, nullus dolor: omnia plena/ Leticie. Proprium nichil hic, communia queque."

[105] *Gesta Regum Britanniae*, IX.298–99: ". . . non nix, non bruma, nec estas/ Immoderata furit . . ."

[106] *Gesta Regum Britanniae*, IX.314–17:
>Inmodice Iesus Arturus tendit ad aulam
>Regis Auallonis, ubi uirgo regia uulnus
>Illius tractans, sanati membra reseruat
>Ipsa sibi; uiuuntque simul, si credere fas est.

[107] *Gesta Regum Britanniae*, X.488–89: "satis est michi si puerorum/ Gratus in ore legar."

Geoffrey is an important corrective to the impression that Latin writing on Arthur is the consistent product of a particular education and background. William's obvious stress on religion and on conquest as the reason for Arthur's downfall divides him very much from Geoffrey's radical historiography, and while there is a strong political element in his depiction of the British (Breton) past, the contemporary political motives which one can discern in Etienne de Rouen are not to be seen here. Nevertheless, William shares with many of the writers in this study an interest in history, a sense of classical patterns and forms, and a concern for kingship; he also shows, in his set pieces, interpolated speeches, and in the description of Avalon, the instincts of a storyteller. Arthur is both a good king and a flawed conqueror, in a work whose themes recur in some form in many of the works in this study. The English Alexander is, like his Macedonian counterpart, an inexhaustible well of inspiration, example, and narrative.

# 3

## "Are you the only uncivilized knight produced by sweet Britain?": Arthurian episodes and knightly conduct

The full-blown romances discussed in the next few chapters are rarities, and I turn now to another set of rarities, those *disjecta membra* of the Arthurian tradition which, while they are not free-standing Arthurian stories, nevertheless differ from the direct responses of the historians to the question of Arthur's historicity; or indeed from the direct use of the Arthurian material for chronicle history. In the Arthurian episodes which follow, Latin writers play with Arthurian fictions in the service of works that are not primarily Arthurian in focus. Johannes de Hauvilla and Andreas Capellanus use Arthurian material to illustrate modes of conduct. Hauvilla's *Architrenius* includes a section in which Gawain leads the army of the just against the army of the covetous. The particular choice of characters here may be attributed to the world of courtly patronage, for in this episode Johannes gives his patron an Arthurian lineage and makes him one with Arthur and Gawain in terms of openhandedness. The Sparrowhawk episode from Andreas Capellanus's *De amore* uses Arthurian material to present the Rules of Love, and so comes closest of the works in this chapter to echoing the preoccupations of vernacular courtly romance. The final text, an episode from John of Glastonbury's fourteenth-century *Cronica sive Antiquitates Glastoniensis Ecclesie*, presents a squire who demonstrates how *not* to behave, as well as a most pious king. As the previous chapter ended with William of Rennes, a shadowy figure who seems in some ways unlike the courtier-clerics who dominate this study, here too we finish with a figure outside both the cultural and temporal scope of most of this study. John's Arthurian episode appears to be derived from a translation/adaptation into Latin of an episode from the vernacular *Perlesvaus*; his use of the episode remains interesting in the context of the broader purposes of his monastic chronicle. Here, as in the other two texts, the exemplary aspect is central, and the Arthurian setting incidental, except perhaps for its particular flavor.

Johannes de Hauvilla was a master in the cathedral school at Rouen at the end of the twelfth century. His only known work is his *Architrenius*, a narrative satire in Latin hexameters dedicated in 1184 to Walter of Coutances. Johannes, an intellectual writing for and about the "new men" of his age, is typical of the men discussed in the Introduction. Part of Johannes's social awareness, Winthrop Wetherbee argues, is to bring the resources of high poetry to focus on the conditions of his own place and time;[1] we can add that he uses the resources of Arthurian story to this end. Part – perhaps even the whole – of his purpose in the deployment of Arthurian story could be purely mercenary: Walter of Coutances was soon to become archbishop of Rouen, and Johannes's Arthurian episode includes an elaborate account of the Cornish-Arthurian descent of his patron. At the same time, there are similarities in spirit between this invention and similar passages in Geoffrey himself and in Walter Map.[2] This summary places the Arthurian portion of the poem in its context:

JOHANNES DE HAUVILLA'S *ARCHITRENIUS*: SYNOPSIS OF
THE ARTHURIAN SEGMENT
Architrenius sets off to ask Nature why all his thoughts tend to vice. Along the way he goes to the court of Venus, the house of Gluttony, the schools of Paris, the palace of Ambition, the mount of Presumption, and the site of a battle between the armies of the generous, led by Arthur and Gawain, and the forces of Avarice. Gawain speaks to Architrenius, identifying himself as being of Trojan descent, born in London and raised in Cornwall. He recounts the story of Corineus and the giants, and then retells the birth of Arthur. An elaborate excursus about the descent of Walter of Coutances's father follows. The army of Avarice is led by Crassus, Septimuleius, Cassius, and Ptolemy. Arthur, Gawain, and Ramofrigius (father to Walter of Coutances) go to war against Avarice, and the Arthurian portion of the *Architrenius* comes to an end. The narrative continues with Architrenius's journey to Thylos, a natural paradise where he encounters various ancient philosophers who lecture him on vice and virtue; the poem concludes with the arrival of Nature, who proposes to marry Architrenius to the maiden Moderation.

[1] *Johannes de Hauvilla: Architrenius*, ed. and trans. Wetherbee, p. xi.
[2] Similarities remarked on by Wetherbee, *Architrenius*, pp. xxvi–xxvii.

Gawain makes his appearance in book V. His first words stress the Cornish connection and thus provide an opportunity to flatter Walter of Coutances: "My people are Trojan, and London gave me birth. Cornwall, that gem discovered by the Phrygians after the cruel fate of Troy, was the nurse whose flowing breast sustained my upbringing."[3] Johannes makes use of Geoffrey's *Historia* in the material which follows about Corineus and the giants. When he reaches the birth of Arthur in V.17, he continues to tell the story as Geoffrey told it, but with his own moralization:

> The later progeny of Corineus spread the radiance of this triple sun over the world, and the bringing-to-birth of a fourth Phoebus produced Arthur, when the adulterer under a false appearance broke into Tintagel. For Pendragon could not overcome the strength of his love, and appealed to the versatile arts of Merlin. He assumed the appearance of the duke, and, hiding his kingly identity, assumed the outward appearance of the absent Gorlois.[4]

Geoffrey took considerable pains to assert Arthur's legitimacy while also allowing negative elements in the story of the conception. Here, Uther is portrayed as one who cannot control his passions, and he is openly called *adulter*. The stress on duplicity is also marked; Uther hides his kingly identity under a false face. The concern for duplicity in rulers, for appearances and reality, is one which motivates many court writers and which was clearly a thematic thread in Geoffrey's *Historia*. As was the case in the *Historia*, the *Architrenius* does not condemn Arthur directly – he is a consequence of this vice rather than a practitioner of it – but one can see how it is possible to move from the false, adulterous father to the negative portrait of the son in the romances discussed in the next two chapters.

But Johannes does not dwell on Uther or indeed on Arthur;

---

[3] *Architrenius*, V.384–86 (I quote Wetherbee's splendid translation, p. 137):
> Tros genus et gentem tribuit Lodonesia, nutrix
> Prebuit irriguam morum Cornubia mammam,
> Post odium fati Frigiis inventa smaragdus.

[4] *Architrenius*, V.436–42, trans. Wetherbee, p. 141:
> Hoc trifido sole Corinei postera mundum
> Preradiat pubes, quartique puerpera Phebi
> Pullulat Arturum, facie dum falsus adulter
> Tintaiol irrumpit nec amoris Pendragon estum
> Vincit et omnificas Merlini consulit artes
> Mentiturque ducis habitus et rege latenti
> Induit absentis presencia Gorlois ora.

instead, a description of Ramofrigius (Rainfroy, father of Walter of Coutances) follows:

> Such are the men the rich spring of this small place produced, the roses and lilies of humankind. Take it as a law: Cornwall can produce nothing rank. She gives birth to flawlessly fashioned creatures, and at her breast imbues her progeny with character, rendering them free of vicious habits and above all cleansing them of avarice . . . [5]

It is clear that one purpose of the Arthurian section in the *Architrenius* is to work in the Cornish aspects of the story and thus flattery of the patron and his generosity. There is however another function for this section and Gawain and Arthur's appearance in it. The episode ends with Gawain's description of the leaders of the armies of the generous:

> We are an army of another kind: Arthur, that new Achilles, the source and glory of the Round Table; Ramofrigius, not a stream but an ocean of largesse; and I myself, Gawain, who cannot recall consigning anything to my purse with stinting hand. The gleam in this right hand of mine is not gold, but a sword. It receives only what it deals out, and it strikes, not at purses, but at weapons. I am no base knight who hoards his wealth, no villain greedily acquiring money. [6]

The comparison of Arthur to Achilles is unusual, and it is unclear what its import might be, although it appears to stem from classicizing impulses like those of William of Rennes. The virtue attached to Britain's most famous monarch, generosity, is the same virtue Geoffrey of Monmouth says draws all the rulers from this side of Spain to Arthur's plenary court. This generosity is more than just the

---

[5] *Architrenius*, V.475–79, trans. Wetherbee, p. 143:
> Hic sinus hos, hominum rosulas et lilia, vernat.
> Regula: nil gignit olidum Cornubia. partus
> Expolit illimes et ab ubere pignora tersis
> Morigerat viciis et plus quam cetera scabram
> Limat avariciam . . .

[6] *Architrenius*, VI.1–8, trans. Wetherbee, p. 145:
> Ex alio belli cuneo sumus; alter Achilles,
> Arturus, teretis mense genitiva venustas,
> Et Ramofrigius, dandi non unda sed equor,
> Et Walganus ego, qui nil reminiscor avara
> Illoculasse manu. non hec mea fulgurat auro
> Sed gladio dextra; recepit, quod spargat, et enses
> Non loculos stringit. nec opes incarcero miles
> Degener et cupide cumulato rusticus ere.

openhandedness that any court writer would wish to encourage in his patron. It is also one of the cardinal virtues of a good king, one which extends into other aspects of rule. Rule is in fact a central concern of the *Architrenius*, and indeed the Arthurian reference can easily be understood in this broader context: Gawain and Arthur are famous names to attach to the argument for certain virtues of rule and self-rule.

After the encounter with Gawain, Architrenius moves on to the natural paradise of Thylos, where among the instruction he receives are these words from Pittacus on rule:

> That the mind's sweet enticements may be weakened, the vice of pride give way, the rough thickets of vice no longer present a menacing obstacle to your actions, and the obduracy of ill-considered severity grow mild, let clemency, inseparable companion of rulers, be at hand; let the boldness of the sword exercise control more gently and, so far as the force of law will allow, assert its authority sparingly. Let it be forbidden to punish with the lash crimes which strong words should be sufficient to prevent, and let the flow of blood be deemed abhorrent – though not the flow of tears, if poverty has ever had the power to extort tears from kings, or the plight of the cottager affected the throne; if ever compassion has caused the dry eyes of the mighty to well up with tender weeping, or a tyrant been eclipsed by tears that bedewed his scepter.[7]

This section is akin to many descriptions of the good king in the court texts discussed in the Introduction. The *Architrenius* is an odd mixture of material, but an important strand in the work is the concern with right rule – of self, of the ruler's self, and of the ruler's land – which motivates many of the court writers in this study. It would be wrong to make too much of Arthur and Gawain's brief

---

[7] *Architrenius*, VIII.23–34, trans. Wetherbee, pp. 199–201:
Mollescant animi dulces, viciumque tumoris
Cedat, et asperitas nullo silvescat in actu
Obicibus ledens, inconsultique rigoris
Robora lentescant, assit clemencia sceptris
Indivisa comes gladiique coherceat ausus
Micior et – iuris quantum permittit habena –
Imperio parcens, prohibens punire flagello
Deterrenda minis, fluvios exosa cruoris
Non lacrime, si quam regnis extorsit egestas
Et solium movere case, si quando potentum
Arentes oculos tenero compassio fletu
Impluit et latuit sceptro rorante tyrannis.

appearance in the *Architrenius*, but it would also be wrong to ignore the way that their appearance participates in a thread of coherence which links many Latin Arthurian works.

The *Architrenius* is central to the tradition of Latin satire but peripheral in the world of the Arthurian narrative. Because of his connection to the codes of love which so many vernacular romances appear to embody, Andreas Capellanus is, on the other hand, a central figure of Latin Angevin writing and of courtly romance. He is thought to have been associated with Marie de Champagne, daughter of Eleanor of Aquitaine, cited as a literary patroness by Andreas and by Chrétien de Troyes, among others. Marie presided over the court of Champagne from 1181 to 1187; Andreas may have been at court between 1182 and 1186.[8] If vernacular romances were indeed intended to "civilize" the inhabitants of court, then Andreas's *De amore*,[9] which embodies the rules of courtly behavior in specific relation to love, would seem to be a central text. The presence of nominally Arthurian material in this work is then less surprising than it might be in the *Draco Normannicus* or the *Architrenius*, but the Sparrowhawk episode poses significant interpretative problems of its own. The main difficulty has little to do with this embedded story, and much more to do with the overall thrust of the *De amore*. What "courtly love"[10] and Andreas's attitude towards the system his text apparently embodies might be, have long been subjects of dispute.

The *De amore* is divided into three sections which take up in turn how love may be obtained, how it may be kept, and why it should be rejected. The conventional antifeminist and antimatrimonial arguments of the third section have been the source of much debate over the total effect of the *De amore*. The Sparrowhawk episode is the final moment in the second book, and so it is clearly important to consider

---

[8] There is an André le Chapelain who appears as a witness to nine of Marie's charters between 1182 and 1186; the prominence of Marie de Champagne in the text encourages the idea that Andreas was connected with her. John W. Baldwin reviews the evidence for authorship in his *The Language of Sex: Five Voices from Northern France around 1200* (Chicago: University of Chicago Press, 1994), pp. 16–17.

[9] The title is in dispute; the commonest formulation in the manuscripts is *De amore*; see *Andreas Capellanus on Love*, ed. and trans. P.G. Walsh (London: Duckworth, 1982), p. 2. The text may be dated to some time in the 1180s: the reference to Hungary in the fifth dialogue may refer to the marriage of the daughter of Louis VII to Bela III of Hungary in 1186. Of the some forty surviving manuscripts, only three date to the thirteenth century; for a brief discussion of Andreas's earliest readers, see Baldwin, *The Language of Sex*, p. 19.

[10] The term is, of course, not medieval; it was coined by Gaston Paris in 1883.

the effect on it of what follows. If the *De amore* is an attempt to represent or create a "religion of love," as C.S. Lewis had it, then the Sparrowhawk story becomes a narrative example of and explanation for the kind of system being advocated, and the third book is difficult to explain except as Lewis did, as the retreat of a medieval man from the implications of this parallel religion.[11] For D.W. Robertson, this section is the key to the whole work, the rest of which is clearly ironic and intended to demonstrate the perversity of the recommended conduct.[12] If Andreas is conscious of the ironic stance of his model, Ovid, then the third book may be his real word on the subject, and one must consider the effect of that stance on the embedded romance: Walter Map's manipulation of the romance genre in the service of both the ludic aspect of *nugae* and the purposes of antifeminist satire is relevant here.[13] A reader like W.T.H. Jackson, on the other hand, argues that the *De amore* is "a simple manual for those who wanted to love *honeste*, that is, like gentlemen";[14] one need demand no more from it than that. Whatever the case, one can see, in the *De amore* as a whole and in the Sparrowhawk episode in particular, concerns which link Andreas to other court writers of Arthurian narrative.

One such link is in the concern manifested in *De amore* for proper speech. The bulk of the second book is made up of sample dialogues between members of various social classes, each with its appropriate level of appeal, of discourse. Toril Moi notes that all of Andreas's lovers use language to try to achieve their ends; ". . . the lover's

---

[11] C.S. Lewis, *The Allegory of Love: A Study in Medieval Tradition* (Oxford: Oxford University Press, 1936), pp. 41–43; Lewis's famous formulation is that Andreas, Chaucer at the end of Troilus, and Malory at the end of the *Morte*, all turn back in the end to God: "We hear the bell clang; and the children, suddenly hushed and grave, and a little frightened, troop back to their master," p. 43.

[12] D.W. Robertson, Jr., *A Preface to Chaucer: Studies in Medieval Perspectives* (Princeton: Princeton University Press, 1962), pp. 391–448.

[13] Lewis called Andreas an example of the formula "Ovid misunderstood"; "the very same conduct which Ovid ironically recommends [is] recommended seriously by the courtly tradition"; *Allegory of Love*, p. 7. Walsh argues that Andreas is "daringly and humorously discussing in stylised play ideas of love and marriage which have no status in the real world of twelfth-century society, but which challenge and criticise the prevailing mores of sex and mores imposed by feudal law and Christian precept"; *Andreas Capellanus on Love*, p. 6; he sees Andreas himself as derivative rather than original. A recent review of the state of the question is in Toril Moi, "Desire in Language: Andreas Capellanus and the Controversy of Courtly Love," in *Medieval Literature: Criticism, Ideology and History*, ed. David Aers (New York: St. Martin's, 1986), pp. 12–16.

[14] W.T.H. Jackson, "The *De Amore* of Andreas Capellanus and the Practice of Love at Court," in *The Challenge of the Medieval Text: Studies in Genre and Interpretation*, ed. Joan M. Ferrante and Robert W. Hanning (New York: Columbia University Press, 1985), p. 4 (reprint of *Romanic Review* 49 (1958), 243–51).

eloquence seems to give him pleasure for his own sake"; the discourse of love, grounded in the practices of scholastic rhetoric, both grants the lover mastery and enacts his entrapment within that discourse.[15] To put it in the terms of this study, Andreas shows that the lover achieves his goal through a sort of language restricted to those of particular accomplishments, and that without this specialized language, one cannot hope to succeed at the supremely courtly activity of love. Jaeger points out that Andreas stresses the need for the lover to employ *curialitas*;[16] the discourse of love and of the court are the same, and indeed, the persons who may properly engage in love include, for Andreas, clerics. The language of the *De amore* and its clear links to school discourses on love suggest a clerical audience.[17] But the *De amore* points to an audience beyond the courtier-clerics whom Andreas includes so clearly in his work. The centrality of the laity in the sample dialogues and the use of vernacular literary conventions suggest the upper nobility. Thus for John Baldwin, "Like his overarching theme, André's audience is ... equivocally located at the borders of two worlds, clerical and lay – where knights and clergy mingled freely."[18] We have returned to the world described in the Introduction, where worldly clerics and Latinate courtiers come together, where the former write both for themselves and for the latter.

Another link between the *De amore* and the Latin romances in this study is of course in the Arthurian narrative embedded in Andreas's text. The Sparrowhawk episode culminates in the Rules of Love, but there is much of interest in the narrative before that point:

THE KNIGHT OF THE SPARROWHAWK: SYNOPSIS
A British knight, on his way to Arthur's court, meets a beautiful maiden who tells him that he will not succeed in his desire, which is to win the love of a certain lady, unless he brings back the hawk which sits on a golden perch in Arthur's court. And he will never obtain the hawk until he proves in combat at the court that he has the love of a lady more beautiful than the lady of any man at

---

[15] Moi, "Desire in Language," p. 24. The connections between sex and language in the period are also discussed in R. Howard Bloch, *The Scandal of the Fabliaux* (Chicago: University of Chicago Press, 1986), and Alexandre Leupin, *Barbarolexis: Medieval Writing and Sexuality*, trans. Kate M. Cooper (Cambridge, Mass.: Harvard University Press, 1989).

[16] Jaeger, *The Origins of Courtliness*, p. 158.

[17] Baldwin discusses the popularity of Ovid in the clerical schools; see *The Language of Sex*, pp. 20–21.

[18] Baldwin, *The Language of Sex*, p. 20.

Arthur's court. And he will not be able to enter the court to prove his claim without the hawk's gauntlet, and he will not be able to get the hawk's gauntlet without defeating two strong knights. The knight puts himself in the maiden's hands, and she gives him her horse and warns him that, after he has defeated the knights, he must take the gauntlet off the pillar where it hangs himself rather than have it handed to him.

The horse takes the knight through a strange country, to a golden bridge whose center is partially submerged in a mighty river. The bridge is guarded by a knight who challenges the young British knight; the young knight defeats the bridge-keeper and begins to cross the bridge, despite the efforts of another man to shake him off the bridge into the water; when he reaches the other side, the young knight kills the other man. The British knight rides on through beautiful country until he comes to a marvelous circular palace, apparently lacking both doors and inhabitants. Silver tables are set up with all kinds of food in the meadow, however. As soon as the knight touches the food, a giant with a copper club appears through a hidden door and challenges the knight, who asserts his right to eat from the tables. They fight, and the knight defeats the giant by chopping off his club arm. The giant attempts to trick the knight by giving him the gauntlet but, forewarned, the knight takes the gauntlet from its pillar himself and rides off to cries of lamentation from invisible voices.

The knight arrives at Arthur's court, where he shows the gauntlet, enters the court and declares his intention. He is challenged to combat by a knight of the court, whom he defeats. He takes the hawk from its golden perch, taking as well the parchment which is attached to the perch by a little gold chain. The parchment, he is told, contains the Rules of Love established by the God of Love himself. The knight returns to the helpful lady of the forest; she sends him home fondly, and he reads and publishes the rules. The episode closes with the list of thirty rules, and these end book II of the *De Amore*.

Andreas has been accused of creating a pastiche whose various elements "lend the treatise a disconcertingly patchwork texture."[19] Of the whole, so too the parts: this embedded narrative contains numerous pieces of romance furniture which align it in general with the Celtic strain of romance narrative while also suggesting many echoes of work by writers such as Chrétien. The narrative insists on

---

[19] *Andreas Capellanus on Love*, ed. and trans. Walsh, p. 11.

the knight's nationality; the maiden addresses him as *Brito*, and at the end of the narrative sends him home with the words "sweet Britain seeks you."[20] It would seem that the knight is not in Britain during the events of the story, although the landscape through which he moves is littered with the marvels usually associated with Britain. The maiden in the forest may be of fairy nature: she is "of marvelous beauty" and knows all the details of what the knight has been told about his quest.[21] Her horse is magical. The knight rides through "a most wild and savage place" to a river "of deep waves, of marvelous width and depth;"[22] this is the classic frontier to adventure. The golden bridge, the guardians of the bridge, the silver tables, the giant with the copper club, and the hawk itself – these are all the stuff of fantastic romance. Indeed, King Arthur is here associated with the strange atmosphere of the tale, for it is in his palace that the hawk is to be found, and the odd set of conditions established for those who would wish to challenge for it suggests the Celtic preoccupation with *geasa* which surfaces also in the *De Ortu Waluuanii* and *Historia Meriadoci*. In part, then, Andreas would appear to be enjoying the marvelous in this tale, taking advantage of the link that exists at court between the codification of behavior in conduct texts and in courtly romance. At the same time, there are elements of the treatment which suggest concerns we have seen in the more "serious" strain of Arthurian Latin narrative.

The Rules of Love at the end of the tale are an obvious example of the way in which the tale presents a mode of conduct for inspection and (perhaps) emulation, but they are not the only example. The conditions which the knight must fulfill to challenge for and win the hawk belong to the realm of the inexplicable; the knight appears to us with these conditions established, and they are known to the lady by means unavailable to us. But when the knight eats from the silver table, his exchange with the giant moves us to a different world:

> He said to the youth, who was still reclining there, "What sort of presumptuous man are you, that you did not fear to come into this royal place and take the provisions of knights so audaciously and disrespectfully from the royal tables?"

---

[20] Andreas Capellanus, *De amore*, in *Andreas Capellanus on Love*, ed. and trans. P.G. Walsh, pp. 270, 280: ". . . dulcis te Britannia quaerit."

[21] *De amore*, p. 270: ". . . mira pulchritudine . . ."

[22] *De amore*, p. 272: "Per agrestia nimis atque ferocia loca . . . ad fluvium quendam devenit, qui mirae latitudinis atque altitudinis erat unda profundus . . ."

The Briton answered him: "The royal table ought to be spread out generously for all, nor is it fitting that the royal food and drink should be denied to anyone. Besides, it is appropriate for me to take the provisions prepared for knights, since the business of a knight alone occupies me, and knightly labor brings me into these parts. Therefore, it is doubly discourteous [*inurbane*] for you to try to deny me the royal table."

The gatekeeper responded to this: "Although this is the royal table, nevertheless no one may recline at it who is not one of those assigned to this palace, [and they] never let anyone pass unless he first enters into battle with the guardians of the palace and defeats them."[23]

There seem to be two competing systems of conduct here. The *ostiarius* behaves as one expects a vaguely supernatural gatekeeper in fantastic romance to do: he announces the set of conditions assigned to the table. But these conditions are presented by the British knight as being against *reason*, and reason is defined as what is properly due a knight. Furthermore, what is fitting and decent is conditioned by the fact that this is the king's table; thus the royal table becomes a figure for a certain sort of acceptable behavior. The knight, in other words, calls upon the world of courtly behavior, while the giant represents the world of fairy romance. Food is often associated in courtly romance with love;[24] one thinks of the great wedding feasts, or the encounters between knights and fairy women which often include rich foods, or even the Tent Maiden episode in the Perceval stories, where the uncouth Welsh knight helps himself to both food and kisses. Here the table is realigned as a symbol of courtly behavior wider than that associated with women; it is reexpressed in terms of the male-male relationship of king to knight.

---

[23] *De amore*, p. 276:

> qui etiam discumbenti iuveni dixit: "Quis tu tantae praesumptionis homo, qui ad haec regia veritus non es accedere loca, et in regia mensa militum tam audacter et irreverenter stipendia sumis?"
> Cui Brito respondit: "Cunctis abundanter regia debet esse exposita mensa, nec cibum regiumque potum decet alicui denegari. Nam et mihi licet de stipendiis, quae militibus sunt parata, praesumere, quia militaris sola me cura detentat, meque per has partes militaris labor exagitat. Duplici ergo ratione inurbane conaris regiam mihi contradicere mensam."
> His ostiarius ita respondit: "Licet ista sit regia mensa, non tamen in ea decet discumbere quemquam nisi illos qui huic sunt palatio deputati, qui etiam neminem ulterius transire permittunt, nisi primitus pugnam cum palatii custodibus committat et vincat."

[24] Baldwin suggests Andreas has surprisingly few references to food; *The Language of Sex*, pp. 181–82.

The exchange contains another example of this conflict of systems; the doorkeeper responds to the knight's assertion of his quest with threatening bombast which might remind one of Arthur's boasting in the *Draco Normannicus*. The knight, for his part, states another courtly principle:

> The doorkeeper said to him: "You fool! What kind of insanity motivates you, Briton? You would be able to rise from the dead ten times before you would get what you're asking for. And I, indeed, am the guardian of the palace, and I will trick you entirely out of your reputation and bereave Britain of your youth. My strength is so mighty that two hundred of Britain's best knights would scarcely be able to withstand my ire."

> The Briton answered him: "Although you claim great might and strength, nevertheless I desire to meet you in battle, so that you might know what kind of men Britain produces; but it is not fitting for a knight to fight with a man on foot."[25]

Predictably, the gatekeeper continues to assert his desire to best the knight, even with the knight on his horse, and the knight dismounts in order to even the odds. Translation flattens the insistence of the repetition of *licet* and *decet*: a world of rational codes and civilized manners is constantly opposed to the fantastic world of fairy romance, wherein the rules are perhaps even more absolute, but much less explicable and certainly much less urbane (the British knight calls the custom of the table *inurbane*).

Once the knight has defeated the giant, again the competing codes come into play; the giant begs for and receives mercy, addressing the knight in terms of the knight's code: "Are you the only uncivilized [*inurbanum*] knight produced by sweet Britain, that you seek to kill a conquered man with a sword?"[26] Yet even the urbane man needs the assistance of the fairy world sometimes, it seems, for it is only the

---

[25] *De amore*, p. 276:

> Ostiarius vero respondit: "O stulte! Quanta te ducit insania, Brito! Prius enim mortuus decies reviviscere posses quam ea quae asseris obtinere. Et ego quidem sum ille palatii custos, qui tua te faciam penitus opinione frustrari et tua iuventute Britanniam viduari. Tanta enim sum fortitudine potens quod vix ducenti meliores Britanniae milites possent irato mihi resistere."
> Cui Brito respondit: "Quamvis te asseras multa fortitudine potentem, tamen tecum cupio committere pugnam, ut cognoscere valeas quales producit Britannia viros; licet non congruat militem cum pedite proeliari."

[26] *De amore*, p. 278: "Numquid te solum inurbanum militem dulcis Britannia duxit, quoniam victum gladio perimere quaeris?"

mysterious maiden's warning that allows the knight to recognize the giant's attempt to trick him out of his prize.

The British knight's quest is carried out, then, in a manner which prepares a reader for this knight to receive the rules of courtly love conduct at the end of the tale. The knight has already been presented as a figure who operates, at least in part, in a sphere different from that represented by the outlandish figures he meets on his quest. We have also seen that the British knight has fairly clear ideas about what is appropriate for the *royal* table; it remains to examine Andreas's presentation of King Arthur and his court.

Arthur's court is presented in a manner which suggests the circular palace with the silver tables. Here too, there is an abundance of precious metals and gems:

> [He] came to a place of delight, where there were the most beautiful meadows adorned with every splendor, in which was built a golden palace, laid out in the best design. The palace was six hundred cubits long, and two hundred cubits wide. The roof and all the exterior parts of the palace were silver, but the whole of the interior was golden, and decorated with precious stones. And the palace was divided into many different rooms. In the most worthy part of the palace King Arthur sat on a golden throne, and around him there were the most beautiful women, their numbers beyond my ability to reckon, and many knights with noble countenances stood in his presence.[27]

While no absolute analogue to this palace immediately suggests itself, it is reminiscent of any number of marvelous palaces in Chrétien or, even more closely, the Welsh versions of the stories of Yvain or Erec. The important point is that these palaces are not usually associated with Arthur.[28] The presentation of the king here seems to align him

---

[27] *De amore*, p. 278:
> ... ad amoenitatis loca devenit, ubi alia erant prata pulcherrima omnique ornata decore, in quibus palatium aureum consistebat optima dispositione compositum. Erat enim palatii longitudo cubitorum sexcentorum, latitudo vero ducentorum. Tectum autem et exteriora cuncta palatii erant argentea, interiora vero aurea quidem omnia et pretiosis ornata lapidibus. Palatium etiam variis multum erat receptaculis distinctum. In digniori vero parte palatii in aurea throno rex sedebat Arturus, et circa eum residebant dominae pulchriores, quarum mihi non potuit esse numerus manifestus, et stabant coram eo milites multi et decori aspectus.

[28] In *Owain*, for example, Arthur's chamber is barely described, while Kynon's narrative includes a long description of a great fortress peopled by beautiful youths, a handsome man, and twenty-four lovely maidens; there is a table of silver, vessels of gold and silver, and splendid food. I suggest Welsh rather than French analogues because Chrétien's *Yvain* lacks the almost supernatural splendor and the retinue of maidens.

quite closely with the world represented by the giant. He is also completely silent, part of the tableau which the knight sees, displayed as the centerpiece of his retinue of maidens and knights. He is in no way involved in the completion of the knight's quest. In both episodes, in other words, the knight arrives at a marvelous palace, prevails in combat, and bears off a marvelous treasure which can be achieved only through a combination of martial valor and the meeting of certain conditions. There is a difference in the two episodes, in that the outcry which accompanies the knight's success with the gauntlet is absent when he wins the hawk, but otherwise, the Arthurian setting appears to function purely as decorative background to this part of the quest. The juxtaposition of the two value-systems in the episode with the giant, however, may echo here as well, in that Arthur's court is also ruled by a custom which belongs rather to the giant's world than to the knight's. Perhaps the knight's earlier assertion of what is appropriate for the *king's* table invites us to compare that code with Arthur's silent presence here. In any case, narrative *about* Arthur has once again been replaced by the use of the Arthurian setting as a backdrop for the assertion of a particular set of rules of behavior.

I have already suggested that the Rules of Love attached to the hawk's perch provide the most obvious example of how this narrative is used to convey instruction in behavior. The rules, and Andreas's intention in thus presenting them, have of course been an object of endless debate. Here I would make only two observations. The first is simply to register, with some surprise, the relative absence of words such as *licet* and *decet* in this list; only once is any of the rules presented in these terms.[29] Indeed, nowhere in the list is the behavior recommended described as *urbane*. Is it possible that the rules of love are in fact less important in this narrative than the rules of kingly and knightly behavior developed through the knight's encounter with the giant? Why else would the courtly vocabulary so evident in the knight's speech be absent from this list?

Arguing against this view is a second aspect of the presentation of the rules; that is, the insistence on their courtly setting. When the knight returns to Britain and gives the rules to the lady for whom he undertook his quest, she publishes them to the whole court:

---

[29] In Rule 11: "It is not decent to love women whom one would be ashamed to marry"; *De Amore* p. 282: "Non decet amare quarum pudor est nuptias affectare."

and when a court of ladies and lords had been called together, she revealed these aforementioned rules of love, and ordered that they should be strictly kept by all lovers, under threat of the God of Love. The whole court accepted them and promised to keep them forever, under the pain of love. And each person who had been called to court and had come together there, took back these rules in writing and published them throughout diverse parts of the world to all lovers.[30]

Here the insistence on the courtly setting is clear; one notes as well that the rules are written down and published abroad. We would appear to be back at Jaeger's view of the court as the source for the dissemination of new rules of civilized behavior. The shift in the vocabulary of behavior from the encounter with the giant to the text of the rules may result simply from Andreas's tendency to amalgamate all manner of current courtly material with little regard for the overall effect (the explanation often offered for the peculiar turn in the third book to antifeminist satire). That is, the Sparrowhawk episode crystallizes for us several different strains of court writing: the fantastic narrative that represents the court at play; the gentle advice to the monarch of the mirror for princes, here represented in the custom of the king's table; and the codification of the behavior of the courtly classes. The use of an Arthurian setting for these elements may be explained by the use of Arthurian narrative as a vehicle for each of these kinds of writing on its own. The firming of the association between the Arthurian court and courtly modes of conduct, in love and in war, will be the work of the vernacular, but Andreas's Sparrowhawk episode, shorn of its "marvels," returns us to the world of Arthur's plenary court as first described by Geoffrey, where the *facetia* of the inhabitants of Arthur's court, male and female, is an illustration of the court's excellence.

The final "embedded" Arthurian episode to be dealt with here once again moves us from the twelfth-century court context to a later, monastic manifestation of Arthurian Latin narrative. John of Glastonbury's mid-fourteenth-century account of the history of his abbey,

---

[30] *De amore*, p. 284:
> ... et curia dominarum plurimarum atque militum convocata regulas praedictas patefecit amoris et eas singulis amantibus sub regis amoris interminatione firmiter conservandas iniunxit. Quas quidem universae curiae plenitudo suscepit et sub amoris poena in perpetuum conservare promisit. Singuli etiam, qui ad curiam vocati convenerant, regulas iam dictas in scriptis reportaverunt et eas per diversas mundi partes cunctis amantibus ediderunt.

the *Cronica sive Antiquitates Glastoniensis Ecclesie*,[31] contains a number of references to King Arthur. Much of the material is drawn from John's chief source, William of Malmesbury's *De Antiquitate Glastonie Ecclesie*, and it is with that work that we should, however briefly, begin.

William arrived at Glastonbury in 1129, commissioned by the monks to write the lives of the Glastonbury saints, Dunstan, Patrick, Indract, and Benignus.[32] The *De Antiquitate* itself may not have been part of William's original assignment. A history of the abbey, it includes a careful focus on the abbey's charters, and may be understood as part of an effort to preserve the charter records of the English church.[33] Understanding William's purpose is complicated by the fact that his text does not survive in its original form, but rather with many later interpolations. Some sense of the "original" can be constructed through a comparison of the *De Antiquitate* with those parts of the text which William later inserted in his own *Gesta Regum*.[34] William's text is like many Latin works which make passing reference to Arthur in that there is no narrative to speak of in those references.[35] Arthur is, instead, annexed to the assertion of the abbey's antiquity and prestige, and that antiquity and prestige rely primarily, in William's account, on Glastonbury's claimed association with its various saints. The reliance upon hagiography for prestige continued after William.[36] The Glastonbury monks commissioned

---

[31] There are seven surviving manuscripts of the text; see John of Glastonbury, *The Chronicle of Glastonbury Abbey: An Edition, Translation and Study of John of Glastonbury's Cronica sive Antiquitates Glastoniensis Ecclesie* ed. James P. Carley, and trans. David Townsend (Woodbridge, Suffolk: The Boydell Press, 1985), pp. xi–xx.

[32] Only one life of Dunstan is now extant; see Antonia Gransden, "The Growth of Glastonbury Traditions and Legends in the Twelfth Century," *Journal of Ecclesiastical History* 27 (1976), 342–43.

[33] *The Early History of Glastonbury*, ed. John Scott, p. 12. Scott speculates that the monks may have expected more bolstering for their case from the saints' lives than William actually delivered, and that therefore the *De Antiquitate* might be the work of "the historian who needed to compensate the monks for his failure to fulfill all their expectations," p. 4. Gransden, "The Growth of Glastonbury Traditions," notes that after the Norman Conquest, many pre-Conquest houses suffered an "attrition of spiritual prestige" (338) because of the Norman suspicions about the traditions of the Saxon saints.

[34] See *The Early History of Glastonbury*, ed. Scott, for the transmission of the text, pp. 34–39.

[35] A paragraph in the section on Joseph of Arimathea which refers to Arthur, Lancelot, and the story of a miraculous fountain, along with Galahad and a miraculous shield, is a thirteenth-century marginal addition in one manuscript; *The Early History of Glastonbury*, ed. Scott, p. 186, n. 15. The passage recurs in John of Glastonbury. John also uses the story of Ider from the *De Antiquitate*; it too is an interpolation in that text, probably to be dated after the "discovery" of Arthur's tomb; p. 197, n. 77.

[36] Gransden notes that Caradoc amplified William's brief statement that Gildas spent many years at Glastonbury and died there; see "The Growth of Glastonbury Traditions," 346–47.

Caradoc of Llancarfan to write a life of Gildas for them, and Arthur's appearances in this and in other Welsh Latin saints' lives are discussed in chapter 6.

Arthur's burial place is barely mentioned in the *De Antiquitate*, in a passage which says that it would be tedious to name all the famous people buried at the abbey: "I pass over Arthur, famous king of the Britons, buried with his wife in the cemetery of the monks between two pyramids . . ."[37] There is nothing to compare to the elaborate account given by Gerald of Wales, discussed in chapter 2. Later, Arthur appears in the list of donors of land to the abbey. He is the first in an extremely long list, and there is nothing to differentiate him from the rulers, famous and unknown, who follow, except perhaps that he *is* first.[38] When one remembers William's strictures on the Messianic hope attached to Arthur, it is easy to see why he would not have developed any of these references into full-blown narrative. John of Glastonbury, however, happily includes in his chronicle material interpolated into William's *De Antiquitate*, along with other material drawn from vernacular romance, showing no such reticence towards that material.

The association of Glastonbury/Avalon with Joseph of Arimathea provides John with an opportunity to fashion a Latin narrative from romance sources. Chapter 18 of the *Cronica* is concerned with Joseph's travels. This narrative portion of the chronicle includes reference to "the book which is called the Holy Grail";[39] later chapters contain short excerpts dealing with Joseph from other books, both prose romances and the versified Bible. The sources for chapter 18 include the Gospel of Nicodemus, the interpolations in William of Malmesbury's *De Antiquitate*, discussed above, and the Vulgate *Queste*.[40] The later passages include among their sources the *Aurora*, or versified Bible, and the Vulgate *Queste*.[41] John's method, then, is one familiar from the methods of various redactors/ adaptors of vernacular romance, but despite the sources and the possibilities of the material, the Joseph of Arimathea sections of the *Cronica* are

[37] William of Malmesbury, *The Early History of Glastonbury*, c. 31: "Pretermitto de Arturo, inclito rege Britonum, in cimiterio monachorum inter duas piramides cum sua coniuge tumulato . . ."
[38] *The Early History of Glastonbury*, c. 69.
[39] *The Chronicle of Glastonbury*, c. 18: "ut legitur in libro qui Sanctum Graal appellatur."
[40] See *The Chronicle of Glastonbury*, pp. 278–79.
[41] See *The Chronicle of Glastonbury*, pp. 280–81.

harnessed, for the most part, to the project of developing the abbey's prestige. That is, the primary purpose of this narrative is propagandistic. The stress is on the abbey's rights to its property, rights which it dates to Joseph's building of the first church in the area. Valerie Lagorio argues that the monks incorporated Joseph into their history precisely because they wished to associate their founding with the prestige of apostolic conversion,[42] and John's account stresses Joseph's role as apostle to Britain. Arthur is linked to the apostle in two ways: chapter 21 includes an account of his descent from Joseph,[43] while chapter 20 includes a summary of some episodes from the Vulgate *Lancelot* and the *Queste* which deal with Joseph and Josephus.[44] These stories – concerning a miraculous fountain and a miraculous shield, and involving Gawain and Galahad – are not at all developed, serving again merely to corroborate the prestige of the abbey's claimed founder. Thus far, then, there is little Arthurian narrative in John.

Most of the more particularly Arthurian references in the *Cronica* seem similarly to be intended merely to add the luster of antiquity or association with a famous figure. For example, the abbey's Marian relics include a crystal cross given by the Virgin to King Arthur;[45] this relic does not occur in the abbey's relic list, but its antecedents are given in the narrative episode discussed below. The abbey's demesne, as in William's account, includes property given it by several ancient British kings, of whom Arthur is one.[46] Indeed the whole of this section is from William, although there are also later interpolations, with the effect that Arthur is no longer the first in the list of donors. Thus Arthur's importance seems, if anything, to be diminished in John's version.

The requisite account of the twelfth-century exhumation of Arthur's bones gives Arthur slightly more space than he receives in William's version, but again, John is quite restrained when we

---

[42] Valerie M. Lagorio, "The Evolving Legend of St Joseph of Glastonbury," *Speculum* 46 (1971), 213.

[43] Constructed using materials from the Vulgate *Estoire*; see *The Chronicle of Glastonbury*, p. 280.

[44] *The Chronicle of Glastonbury*, p. 279. This short section was interpolated in William's *De Antiquitate*.

[45] *The Chronicle of Glastonbury*, c. 9: "Item crux cristallina quam beata virgo contulit inclito regi Arthuro"; "Item, a crystal cross which the blessed Virgin brought to the renowned King Arthur."

[46] *The Chronicle of Glastonbury*, c. 16: Arthur is said to have given Brentmarsh and Pouldon, as in William.

consider other versions of this story. His account is much shorter than that of Gerald of Wales, and the stress is on the translation to the new tomb in the abbey: "The abbot and the convent, therefore, taking up their remains, translated them with joy to the great church and placed them in a tomb . . . in the choir before the high altar, where they rest magnificently unto this day."[47] John also recites the epitaph on the tomb, using the form recorded by Adam of Damerham, discussed in chapter 2. A second exhumation, carried out in sight of Edward I and his wife in 1278, is also described, and in the next chapter we are told that the king confirmed the liberties of the monastery and returned to it all the writs for its lands. Again, Arthur's function is to affirm and secure the abbey's prestige.[48]

References to Arthur in connection with Gildas, and to Arthur in connection to Ider, also serve to bolster the abbey's image. There is one Arthurian reference in the *Cronica*, however, which deserves closer attention, for it is more developed than any of those discussed thus far, and its content, while it certainly could be used to make claims for Glastonbury, is not obviously developed in that direction. The localization of the episode ties it firmly to Glastonbury, but the purpose seems to be to confirm Arthur's character as a Christian king, and thus repeats the focus of the other Latin works in this study on Arthur's exemplary nature.

THE "CHAPEL RIDE" EPISODE OF JOHN OF GLASTONBURY'S
*CRONICA*: SYNOPSIS

Arthur is sleeping at a convent at Wearyall on the island of Avalon, when an angel calls upon him to awake. The angel tells him to go at dawn to the hermitage of St. Mary Magdalene of Beckery. The next morning, Arthur tells his vision to Gawain, who tells him to ignore it. But the king has the vision again the following night. He determines to wait to see if the vision will recur for a third night, telling his squire to be ready to accompany him.

That night the squire has a dream in which he enters a chapel at the hermitage, where he sees a dead body upon a bier, surrounded by candles. The squire steals two golden candlesticks from the altar, but when he tries to leave the chapel, he is rebuked and wounded in

---

[47] *The Chronicle of Glastonbury*, c. 98: "Abbas igitur et conuentus suscipientes eorum exuuias cum gaudio in maiorem transtulerunt ecclesiam in mausoleo . . . scilicet in choro ante magnum altare, ubi usque in hodiernum diem magnifice requiescunt."

[48] Gransden suggests Edward I might have had political motives for his role in the exhumation; "The Growth of Glastonbury Traditions," 355.

the groin. The squire cries out, waking the king; the squire recounts the events and shows the king both the candlesticks and the knife in his groin. He dies and is buried at the convent.

The king goes to the chapel at dawn, where his way is blocked by swords waving across the door and striking fiery sparks. Arthur prays to be made worthy to enter this holy place, and begs forgiveness for his sins. The swords vanish, and Arthur enters the chapel to find an old man dressed in black. The old man begins to put on priestly garments, and the Virgin, with her son in her arms, appears. She offers her son to the priest during the mass, and the priest holds the boy up as the host. Arthur observes everything, and when the mass is done, Mary gives him the crystal cross which is now among Glastonbury's relics. Mary and her son vanish, and the old man explains to the king what he has seen. Arthur again repents his sins, affirms his faith, and changes his arms to honor what he has seen that night.

The original of this episode occurs in the French *Perlesvaus*; John's version is an adaptation which John seems to have drawn from another Latin translator of the French material.[49] The account which follows tends to conflate John's incorporation of the text with his Latin source, a procedure which I defend partly on pragmatic grounds (it is John's version which is readily available) and partly on the grounds that the two versions have a very similar dating and genesis.[50] Thus I consider the qualities of the Latin narrative in itself, and in John's redeployment of it. Even once we allow for John's various sources, it is possible to draw some conclusions about the use this fourteenth-century Latin chronicler makes of this material, observations which connect to this study as a whole.

The existence of this episode in two Latin versions testifies to the interpenetration of vernacular and Latin writing at this period. The Joseph of Arimathea material discussed earlier may have been prompted in part by a fourteenth-century vogue in the vernacular for

---

[49] In "A Glastonbury Translator at Work: *Quedam narracio de nobili rege Arthuro* and *De origine gigantum* in Their Earliest Manuscript Contexts," *Nottingham French Studies* 30 (1991), James Carley reverses his earlier position, that John himself translated and adapted the passage, to take account of new manuscript evidence which suggests that someone else, presumably also at Glastonbury, translated the episode from French into Latin, and that John simply used that translation in his own work; 7–8.

[50] According to Carley, the *Quedam narracio* version was probably produced at Glastonbury in the early part of the fourteenth century; John seems to have been writing about 1340; "A Glastonbury Translator," 8–9.

stories of the saint,[51] but we have seen that this material is often shorn of its narrative context and reduced to propagandistic use in John's *Cronica*. This episode, on the other hand, is fully developed as narrative, and thus testifies to the continuing appeal of Arthurian material as story to Latin writers. Even though John apparently already had a Latin adaptation of *Perlesvaus* to hand, his practice with respect to other sources and some changes of detail and phrasing that he makes here,[52] allow one to argue that the preservation of this story demonstrates its particular appeal to John. What, then, are the characteristics of the story?

The summary above makes it clear that the tale meets a continuing taste for the marvelous, here realigned as the miraculous. The squire is apparently really punished for an action which takes place in a dream; to will it would appear to be as bad as to do it, in other words. There is a quality of nightmare in this episode, in which the agent of retribution is only vaguely described: in John's version we read "But when he, wishing to leave, tried to go out of the chapel, there was someone close by who, speaking angrily, asked him why he had been the perpetrator of so sacrilegious a crime, and struck him in the groin."[53] When the king goes to the chapel, his way is barred by two disembodied hands waving swords;[54] again, there is the sense of unseen and unknowable forces at work. The mass, in which the priest actually eats the child offered by the Virgin, is particularly striking:

> And when he had come to the sacrifice of the host – that is, to the Lord's words, "This is my body" – he raised that same child in his hands. King Arthur, standing back, humbly adored the sacrament of the Lord, which was indeed, truly, the Lord Himself. When the child had been sacrificed, the old man put him back where he had been. But when he had come to the reception of the host, he took up that same child, the son of God, received him, and chewed him according to the institution of the Lord, who said "take and eat." When he had been received and the communion was finished, he appeared where he had first been, unharmed and whole, the paschal lamb without any spot.[55]

---

[51] See Lagorio, "The Evolving Legend of St Joseph of Glastonbury," 218; she cites *Joseph of Arimathie* and *Titus and Vespasian*, themselves drawn from French material.

[52] Detailed in Carley, "A Glastonbury Translator," 10.

[53] *The Chronicle of Glastonbury*, c. 34: "At ille uolens egredi capellam affuit quidam illum simmistam increpans, quare tanti facinoris et sacrilegii actor esset feriens eum in inguine."

[54] *The Chronicle of Glastonbury*, c. 34: "due manus."

[55] *The Chronicle of Glastonbury*, c. 34:
Cum autem peruenisset ad immolacionem hostie – id est ad uerba dominica: "Hoc est

This miracle is the climax of the episode in *Perlesvaus* as well, although in that text the connection is to the Grail quest, with Arthur's involvement necessitated in part by a spiritual languor which has overtaken him. With the larger context of the miracle suppressed, the miracle itself takes center stage, along with the king's reaction to it. And the adaptor's most notable change to the episode does indeed lie in Arthur's response to what he has seen:

> The king was suddenly struck with conscience and, contrite over his sins, vowed that he would believe firmly in the holy sacrament, and that whatever should be asked of him out of the love of God and of the glorious Virgin Mary and of her son our Lord Jesus Christ, he would agree to with good will. He also changed his arms in their honor. For before, from the time of the arrival of Brutus until, indeed, Arthur changed them, they were silver, with the red lions turning their heads backwards. In memory of the crystal cross which holy Mary had given him, he caused them to be green, with a silver cross, and on the right arm of the cross, in memory of the aforesaid miracle, he placed an image of blessed Mary, ever virgin, holding her son in her arms. And the king saying farewell to the old man, is greatly refreshed, made firm in the faith of the Lord, and passing from virtue to virtue.[56]

Arthur's contrition and avowed devotion to God present us once again with Arthur as Christian monarch, as crusader. The innovation in the design of his arms seems intended specifically to stress the ruler's dependence on God. The three lions – in the more traditional versions of Arthur's arms, three crowns – seem originally to have symbolized Arthur's superiority over other kings; they were later

enim corpus meum" – eleuauit eundem puerum in manibus suis. Rex Arthurus retro stans sacramentum illud dominicum immo uere ipsum Dominum suppliciter adorabat. Senex, immolato puero, posuit eum loco quo prius. Cum enim peruenisset ad hostie percepcionem eundem puerum, Dei filium, assumpsit, percepit, masticauit secundum eiusdem Domini institucionem dicentis: "accipite et manducate." Ipso percepto et communione facta, apparuit loco qui prius sedens illesus et integer ille agnus pascalis absque omni macula.

56 *The Chronicle of Glastonbury*, c. 34:

Repente rex compunctus et de delictis suis contritus se firmiter uelle credere in sanctum sacramentum uouit et quod quicquid ab eo peteretur propter amorem Domine et gloriose uirginis Marie et filii sui Domini nostri Ihesu Christi benigniter annueret. Arma quoque sua in eorum mutauit honorem. Nam que prius erant argentea cum tribus leonibus rubeis capita ad terga uertentibus, a tempore aduentus Bruti usque ad iam dictam mutacionem regis Arthuri, ob memoriam crucis cristalline sibi per beatam Mariam collate fecit esse uiridia cum cruce argentea et super dextrum brachium crucis ob memoriam predicti miraculi collocauit imaginem beate Marie semper virginis, filium suum in ulnis tenentis. Rex autem ualefaciens seni in fide Domini est solidatus et de uirtute in uirtutem proficiens multipliciter est exhilaratus.

understood to refer specifically to dominion over lands, and we have seen Etienne de Rouen's Arthur define himself as a triple king.[57] Here those symbols are replaced by images of devotion, and the narrative ends with Arthur's departure and increased faith. Thus once again we see an Arthurian story used to assert a moral imperative, here represented by Arthur's shift from conqueror, as implied by the three lions, to devotee of the Virgin. The shift in fact looks back to Arthur's original appearances in pre-Galfridian history as the king who bore the image of the Virgin on his shoulder/shield. The surfacing of this image after so many centuries in this odd Latin adaptation of what is itself an odd French romance, is testimony to the continuing ingenuity of Arthurian writers in molding the king to their own imperatives. While John may have chosen to include the narrative simply because it explained the crystal cross which, we have seen, he listed among the abbey's relics, his source's introduction of the new arms remains significant.

The chapter which follows the adaptation of the Chapel Ride episode in John is a summary account of Modred's treachery and Arthur's death. John seems comfortable with marvels only when they have an explicitly religious context, for while he sends his Arthur to Avalon, he does not develop an account of the island. He mentions Morgan only in passing, and he gives Arthur a most prosaic death: "But his disease worsened, and the medicines were only slightly helpful, and so he died, around the year of our Lord 542."[58] The narrative returns to the summary form characteristic of most of the Arthurian material in the chronicle. Etienne de Rouen and William of Rennes seem to have been willing to go much further, in their accounts of Avalon at least. Given Glastonbury's long-claimed association with Avalon, John's reticence is the more surprising, although one does not expect a monastic chronicle to dwell overmuch on the doings of a sorceress. Thus for John, Arthur's appeal, while it is felt sufficiently for him to keep the whole of the adapted Chapel Ride episode in his account, is always deployed in favor of Glastonbury or, as in this episode, in order to take advantage of the king's exemplary possibilities. The Avalon narrative is perhaps avoided *because* it is fantastic, and because it might suggest, as Etienne de Rouen enjoyed

---

[57] See Helmut Nickel, "Heraldry," in *The Arthurian Encyclopedia*, ed. Norris J. Lacy (New York: Peter Bedrick, 1987), p. 279.
[58] *The Chronicle of Glastonbury*, c. 35: "Set ingrauescente morbo, medicaminibus modicum proficientibus, anno Domini circiter quingentesimo quadragesimo secundo defungitur . . ."

suggesting, something rather dubious about the great king. I noted above that John records the epitaph on Arthur's tomb, in the form in which it appears in Adam of Damerham. The epitaph stresses Arthur's role as a most Christian king: "Here lies Arthur, flower of kings, glory of the kingdom,/ Whose character and probity commend him to eternal praise."[59] In John of Glastonbury, then, Arthurian narrative serves didactic, religious purposes.

Johannes de Hauvilla and John of Glastonbury both make use of Arthurian material in the service of larger programs. Johannes is writing moral satire, and John is writing monastic chronicle, for purposes both didactic and propagandistic. Even Andreas Capellanus, despite the overtly romantic flavor and "furniture" of his Sparrow-hawk episode, is making use of Arthurian narrative in the service of a larger goal, in his case to promote a form of courtly behavior. This behavior may or may not be included in the Rules of Love with which the Sparrowhawk episode concludes; I have argued that the discussion of what is appropriate for the king's table assumes a central role in the narrative. In the romances of the next two chapters, we will see an anonymous Latin author moving in a much more wholehearted way into the realm of romance narrative. Yet in his texts too, despite the marvels, the concentration on knights and their quests, and the ludic aspects of narrative play and subversion so characteristic of court writing, Arthur retains a central importance. The king may not always be the admirable Christian monarch he is in John's account, or the generous sovereign of Johannes de Hauvilla. Indeed, he is far more likely to remind one of the flawed rulers created by Etienne de Rouen, William of Rennes, and by many vernacular writers. But the use of Arthur as the focal point for a discussion of court themes such as right rule, both personal and political, keeps us in the didactic world to which John of Glastonbury so clearly belongs. There are marvels too, perhaps enjoyed more for their own sake than they seem to be in the episodes in this chapter. But as one might expect, even full-length Latin Arthurian romances like the *De Ortu Waluuanii* and the *Historia Meriadoci* show their serious concerns even as they feed the taste for the romantic and the exotic. Kings and courts continue to provide opportunities for both recreation and education.

---

[59] *The Chronicle of Glastonbury*, c. 98: "Hic iacet Arthurus, flos regum, gloria regni,/ Quem mors probitas commendat laude perhenni."

# 4

## "Understanding the thing as it is": *De Ortu Waluuanii* and the challenge of interpretation

The texts in chapters 4 and 5 share certain important elements and strategies with both Geoffrey's history and the more overtly "Celtic" works in chapter 6. Like Geoffrey's *Historia*, a text upon which they draw, both of these romances make considerable efforts, albeit sometimes sporadic ones, to offer an appearance of verisimilitude, to suggest that theirs is the truth of historical accuracy. Yet these efforts are part of a narrative mode which is also often overtly romantic, and much of the content of each narrative supports Southern's notion of the particular appeal of the marvelous in twelfth-century English writing. To be sure, one of the texts is more "historical," and the other more "romantic" or marvelous, at least in terms of content. Yet each shares Geoffrey's tendency to signal all manner of literary exploration through the manipulation of the narrative process. There are occasional experiments with generic markers, frequent moments of irony, parody, and even on occasion burlesque, and what sometimes seems to be a general, facetious irreverence towards the traditions of romance storytelling. The result, as was the case with Geoffrey's *Historia*, is that the audience is often left in doubt as to how to read the various signals, generic and otherwise, which the text is apparently sending. Indeed, concerns about perception, both within and beyond the world of the texts, are central to both these works, and dramatized on every level of their style and content. The concern for the realities underlying appearances may be linked to contemporary philosophical debates, as discussed below, but it is also a classic court theme, common in a world where power relationships dictate covert action and expression. And the Arthur of these works is also linked to the concerns of court satire and the mirror for princes; he is in the mold of the flawed king, admirable in some ways but dangerous in his power and in his occasional lack of self-regulation. Arthur is not central to these

131

works, which rather follow the pattern, in continental or Anglo-Norman romance, of concentration on the adventures of knights of the Arthurian court. He is nevertheless pivotal in their adventures. Stephen Jaeger argues that court narratives and courtly romances often draw a contrast between the inner life of the courtier and the outer, often perilous, life of and at the court.[1] In the texts that follow, the perils of that life are manifested in particular in a concern with the contrast between appearance and reality and the ambiguous relationship of signs, generic and linguistic, to "reality." *Facetia* dominates, with both ludic and serious implications.

The two Latin romances which are the focus of these next chapters, *De Ortu Waluuanii* and the *Historia Meriadoci*, are the work of the same author, and are probably to be dated to the first half of the twelfth century.[2] They may have been penned by Robert of Torigny, abbot of Mont-St.-Michel, and they belong squarely within the twelfth-century explosion of narrative which produced the works in this study. Robert was the librarian who showed Henry of Huntingdon an early copy of Geoffrey's *Historia*, and Mildred Leake Day, the most recent editor of these romances, points out that the catalogue of his known writings confirms the impression that he was a central contributor to the resurgence of all manner of writing, and particularly of historical writing, in the twelfth century.[3] His position and known writing connects him to the monastic chroniclers we have been examining, while his connections suggest the circle of courtly clerics likely to be the imagined audience for these romances. These

---

[1] Jaeger, *The Origins of Courtliness*, p. 241; Jaeger refers to the common motif of the "divided self" and its appearance in the romance motif of the fair unknown, pp. 237–38.

[2] *De Ortu Waluuanii* survives in one English manuscript, London, British Library, MS Cotton Faustina B.vi, of the early fourteenth century; *Meriadoc* occurs in this manuscript and also in Oxford, Bodleian Library MS Rawlinson B.149, of the late fourteenth or early fifteenth centuries. The work is no later than the beginning of the fourteenth century, then, while the fact that both romances make use of Geoffrey's *Historia* indicates that they must have been written after about 1136. In his edition, *Historia Meriadoci and De Ortu Waluuanii: Two Arthurian Romances of the XIIIth Century in Latin Prose* (Baltimore, Md.: Johns Hopkins, 1913), J. Douglas Bruce argued for a thirteenth-century dating, but Mildred Leake Day's arguments, based on details concerning armor, warfare, and legal custom, point to the early twelfth century; see "'The Rise of Gawain, Nephew of Arthur': Translation and Study of *De Ortu Waluuanii Nepotis Arturi*, a Medieval Latin Prose Romance," (Ph.D. thesis, University of Alabama, 1975); *The Rise of Gawain, Nephew of Arthur (De Ortu Waluuanii, Nepotis Arturi)* (New York: Garland, 1984); and *The Story of Meriadoc, King of Cambria (Historia Meridaoci [sic], regis Cambriae)* (New York: Garland, 1988). The texts of the romances will be drawn from Day's published editions. I favor a date towards the latter period of Henry II's reign, largely because of the legal context of the Black Knight episode in the *Historia Meriadoci*, discussed below in chapter 5.

[3] *De Ortu Waluuanii*, pp. xiv–xvii.

texts stand as central examples of the narrative experiments which seem to have absorbed the *litterati* of the twelfth century.

### *DE ORTU WALUUANII*: SYNOPSIS

Uther Pendragon, father of Arthur, followed the practice of holding noble hostages at his court; one of these is Loth, nephew of the king of Norway. Loth and Anna, Uther's daughter, fall in love and enter into an illicit relationship; when Anna becomes pregnant, she arranges to entrust the baby to the care of certain foreign merchants. She gives birth to a boy whom she names Gawain, and entrusts him, along with proof of his parentage, to the merchants, who set sail with the infant for Narbonne. The merchants go ashore to do their business, and the infant and his treasure are found by a poor man named Viamandus, who takes both treasure and child.

Viamandus raises the boy as his own, and when the child is seven years old, Viamandus journeys with him to Rome. Using the treasure to create an impression of wealth and power, Viamandus succeeds in winning land and a position of influence from the emperor. On his deathbed, Viamandus confesses to the emperor and Pope Sulpicius the origins of both his wealth and his "son"; he recommends that Gawain be kept in ignorance of his true parentage until such time as his natural parents should acknowledge him. The pope and the emperor agree.

The young Gawain is raised as a Roman knight, and distinguishes himself in trials of arms. Ignorant of his real name, he comes to be known by the sobriquet, "The Knight of the Surcoat." Wishing to prove himself in real warfare, he wins the right to enter into single combat on behalf of the Christians besieged in Jerusalem. He sets sail for the Holy Land with a large fleet, and, after twenty-five storm-tossed days, lands on an island controlled by Milocrates, a pagan king who has kidnapped the emperor's niece. Gawain and a companion enter the king's city and learn of his plans; Gawain enlists the help of a captive knight, Nabaor, to gain entrance to the emperor's niece. She assures Gawain of victory against Milocrates by giving to him the king's armor, concerning which it had been foretold that Milocrates should be killed by the first person other than the king to wear it. The two armies meet in battle, and Gawain does indeed kill Milocrates and free the emperor's niece.

Gawain and his army return to their voyage, only to meet the fleet of Egesarius, brother to Milocrates. A furious sea battle follows, featuring the pagans' use of the formidable Greek fire, a weapon whose preparation is described at great length. Gawain and his men prevail, and at last reach Jerusalem at the time appointed.

133

Gawain meets the pagan champion, a giant named Gormundus, in a duel which lasts three days; at the end of the third day, Gawain relieves the siege by killing Gormundus. The pagans are forced to flee, and Gawain returns to Rome in triumph.

Seeking new challenges, Gawain resolves to journey to the court of the famous king Arthur (who has now succeeded Uther). The emperor agrees to Gawain's departure, and sends with him the tokens of Gawain's true parentage, which the knight is instructed to present to King Arthur. Gawain sets off for Caerleon. Meanwhile Gwendoloena, Arthur's queen and a sorceress, tells Arthur of the approach of a knight who is stronger than he is. Arthur, seeking to test her prediction, sneaks out in the middle of the night and accosts Gawain rudely at a ford in the river; he is unceremoniously thrown from his horse, and returns, dripping, to his bed and the sarcasm of his queen. When Gawain arrives in court, Arthur refuses to accept his service, and Gawain, stung, vows to perform a deed which neither Arthur nor the whole of his army can. Arthur is then called upon to relieve the lady who rules the Castle of Maidens; he and his army are routed, but Gawain single-handedly rescues the lady and destroys the enemy army. Arthur, overjoyed, reveals to Gawain his true name and parentage, and the story closes with the court repeating "Gawain, nephew of Arthur."

*De Ortu Waluuanii*, like Geoffrey of Monmouth's account of Arthur, places this story of one of Arthur's knights in what was probably its appropriate historical period, the fifth century. What is unusual about the *De Ortu* is the detail provided to substantiate and actualize this historical setting, particularly the details of the young Gawain's life at Rome. Day suggests that the *De Ortu* displaces romance in the direction of reality;[4] while I will argue that the moments where the text strays into absolute fantasy are as important as its apparent moments of verisimilitude in its overall strategy, there is no doubt that the attempts at actualization of setting and explanation of motivation are one of the most striking features of this work. This appearance of sober veracity becomes crucial, paradoxically enough, when that appearance is undermined by other, nonconforming elements of the text. The resulting difficulty experienced by readers in interpreting the text and its disjunctions foregrounds the work's concerns with modes of knowing and of telling.

Identity is also an important theme in the *De Ortu*, one that is

---

[4] *De Ortu Waluuanii*, p. xxii.

connected to this concern for what we know and how we know it. On the surface, Gawain's story is presented as a version of the common Fair Unknown pattern; a young man, cut off from his birthright, seeks his fortune and finds his true identity. The details suggest the more specifically British reflexes of this motif, the Havelok/Horn stories.[5] Yet the author's interest in identifying Gawain, expressed in the constant attention which the text draws to his various epithets, is, I would argue, but one reflex of the central interest of this piece, and that is the question of appearance and reality, of how we judge and interpret what we see – or read. Both Day and Aubrey Galyon have noted this feature of the text,[6] but neither has, I think, focused on the issue of appearance and reality as a specifically literary and readerly one, the nexus of a concern with interpretation, with signs and signifiers on many levels, which extends beyond the world of the text.[7] A consistent use of the terminology of sign and thing indicates that this text participates in what Eugene Vance has called "the major thread of coherence in medieval culture"; that is, its persistent reflection "upon language as a semiotic system . . . upon the nature, the functions and the limitations of the verbal sign as a mediator of human understanding."[8] In the *De Ortu*, this concern meshes with the *facetia* characteristic of court discourse, producing a meditation on a central court theme, couched in and represented by the intricacies of court language. The clearest example of the confluence of these elements in the *De Ortu* is in the naval battle and the accompanying Greek fire digression.

When Gawain has defeated Milocrates and his army, he and his

---

[5] Day argues that the Havelok story lies behind the tale of Meriadoc (*Historia Meriadoci*, p. xxv). William Mullen argues that the *enfances* section of *Meriadoc* originated among the Scandinavians in England; he cites the Hroar-Helgi stories in *Hrolfssaga* and Saxo's *Gesta Danorum* VII ("A Critical Study of the 'Historia Meriadoci.'" Ph.D. thesis, Columbia University, 1951, pp. 8–18).

[6] Day in *De Ortu Waluuanii*, pp. xxiv–xxv; Aubrey Galyon in "*De Ortu Walwanii* and the Theory of Illumination," *Neophilologus* 62 (1978), 335–41. Galyon argues that the text exemplifies and responds to late thirteenth-century English philosophical debate about the doctrine of divine illumination. I think it is clear enough that the texts are to be dated to the mid-twelfth century rather than to the late thirteenth; but Galyon's comments point in the direction of Augustinian ideas about reality and perception which do, I believe, underlie this concern in the *De Ortu*.

[7] Day does argue, with reference to the Greek fire digression, that the alternation between appearance and reality in this passage is paralleled by decisions between "hearsay and technology" which the reader must make (*De Ortu Waluuanii*, p. xxv); her conclusion that a contrast between the romantic fantasy and the reality of twelfth-century warfare is being dramatized is acute, but only one facet of what are I think the text's broader literary concerns.

[8] Eugene Vance, *Mervelous Signals: Poetics and Sign Theory in the Middle Ages* (Lincoln: University of Nebraska, 1986), p. x.

companions set sail for Jerusalem, and on the way encounter the fleet of Milocrates's brother. The first sighting of the enemy fleet is, in Day's opinion, the most dramatic example of the discrepancy between appearance and reality in the text.[9] The centurion mistakes the boats with their banners for kingfishers, and adds a bit of popular lore: "For they say that when storms are coming, the birds, flying around ships in this manner, now in crowds, now separately, flock in a great flight, and by their actions predict a coming disaster."[10] This is not the first popular commonplace in the text. The relationship between Loth and Anna is described in common Ovidian terms, and the knight Nabaor, whose speech is a pastiche of aphorisms, gives the advice which allows Gawain to defeat Milocrates. Here, however, the popular wisdom represented by the centurion's observation is brought into question by the fact that what the centurion is seeing is not a flock of kingfishers at all, but rather the fleet of Buzafarnan/Egesarius.[11] Gawain points out the error, and describes the reality of the situation. Thus the traditional wisdom is undercut. Gawain, unlike the centurion, is said to understand the "thing as it is" – *rem ut erat intelligens*.[12] One might say that he apprehends the proper connection between sign and signifier, and yet the text does not, I think, present this as an uncomplicated relationship. Gawain's right reasoning is emphasized again when the enemy fleet appears ("and what he had worked out was not false supposition"),[13] yet the very language, with verbs such as *insinuo* and *opino*, is the language of subjectivity. Although Gawain has read the signs correctly, the presence of both this language and of the centurion's error underlines the opposite possibility.

What does it mean to "understand the thing as it is"? We might turn for a moment to consider the roots of Vance's "thread of coherence"; that is, St. Augustine's definition of signs and things in the course of his discussion of the interpretation of Scripture in *De*

---

[9] *De Ortu Waluuanii*, p. xxiv.

[10] *De Ortu Waluuanii*, p. 62:

> Ferunt quippe imminente procella aves huiusmodi tum gregatim, tum separatim circa remigantes, crebros girando exercere volatus, earumque gestus cladem portendere futuram.

[11] James Wieber, "A Translation and Literary Study of 'De Ortu Walwanii,' a Thirteenth-Century Romance" (Ph.D. thesis, Michigan State University, 1974), points out that the lore itself is mistaken and therefore comic; kingfishers were usually birds of good omen, and the centurion appears to be confusing them with vultures, p. 111.

[12] *De Ortu Waluuanii*, p. 62.

[13] *De Ortu Waluuanii*, p. 64: "Eumque insinuabat non falsum opinatum fuisse . . ."

*doctrina Christiana.* Of primary importance is the assertion that "things are learned by signs":

> All doctrine concerns either things or signs, but things are learned by signs. Strictly speaking, I have here called a "thing" that which is not used to signify something else, like wood, stone, cattle, and so on; but not that wood concerning which we read that Moses cast it into bitter waters that their bitterness might be dispelled, nor that stone which Jacob placed at his head, nor that beast which Abraham sacrificed in place of his son. For these are things in such a way that they are also signs of other things. There are other signs whose whole use is in signifying, like words. For no one uses words except for the purpose of signifying something. From this may be understood what we call "signs"; they are things used to signify something.[14]

Augustine draws a distinction here between simple things and things which point beyond themselves. The flock of kingfishers/ fleet of boats conforms to Augustine's reference to signs "which signify something else": "A sign is a thing which causes us to think of something beyond the impression the thing itself makes upon the senses. Thus if we see a track, we think of the animal that made the track; if we see smoke, we know that there is a fire which causes it . . ."[15] We immediately encounter a complication, however, in the nature of the interpretation given to this particular sign. To the centurion, the fleet is a flock of kingfishers; he moves from the mistaken sense-impression to the interpretation offered by folk-wisdom. That is, it is a matter of cultural agreement that kingfishers portend disaster. Augustine is very aware of the contractual nature of coventional signs, as he demonstrates in a discussion of omens and augury:

---

[14] St. Augustine, *De doctrina Christiana*, CCSL 32 (Turnhout, 1962), I.ii.2; the translation is *On Christian Doctrine*, trans. D.W. Robertson, Jr. (New York: Macmillan, 1958), pp. 8–9:
> Omnis doctrina uel rerum est uel signorum, sed res per signa discuntur. Proprie autem nunc res appellaui, quae non ad significandum aliquid adhibentur, sicuti est lignum lapis pecus atque huiusmodi cetera, sed non illud lignum, quod in aquas amaras Moysen misisse legimus, ut amaritudine carerent, neque ille lapis, quem Iacob sibi ad caput posuerat, neque illud pecus, quod pro filio immolauit Abraham. Hae namque ita res sunt, ut aliarum etiam signa sint rerum. Sunt autem alia signa, quorum omnis usus in significando est, sicuti sunt uerba. Nemo enim utitur uerbis, nisi aliquid significandi gratia. Ex quo intellegitur, quid appellem signa, res eas uidelicet, quae ad significandum aliquid adhibentur.

[15] *De doctrina Christiana* II.i.1: "Signum est enim res praeter speciem, quam ingerit sensibus, aliud aliquid ex se faciens in cogitationem uenire, sicut uestigio uiso transisse animal, cuius uestigium est, cogitamus et fumo uiso ignem subesse cognoscimus . . ."; Robertson, p. 34.

To use an analogy, one figure of a letter X set down in the form of a cross mark means one thing among the Latins, another among the Greeks, not because of its nature, but because of agreement and consent to its significance. And thus he who knows both languages does not use that sign with the same signification when he wishes to convey something in writing to a Greek that he implies when he writes to a man who speaks Latin . . . Therefore just as all of these significations move men's minds in accordance with the consent of their societies, and because this consent varies, they move them differently, nor do men agree upon them because of an innate value, but they have a value because they are agreed upon, in the same way those signs which form the basis for a pernicious alliance with demons are of value only in accordance with the observations of the individual.[16]

This emphasis on the contract of understanding, the recognition that "signs are not valid among men except by common consent,"[17] carries the implicit recognition of what Vance identifies as the "relational" aspect of man, and of the essential "fragility of language."[18] Court writers are vitally aware of both of these features of the human condition. For the courtly cleric writing romance, Latin or vernacular, language's role as the medium of instruction must be understood in terms of its risks as well as its potential benefits. Sight too is potentially deceptive, at least to the extent that the interpretation of signs, visual or verbal, is difficult. We may assume that the centurion's sight, his observation, is faulty, yet we must also consider the logic of the interpretation which follows from the first error; what is the status of the agreed-upon interpretation?

From another perspective, this awareness of the difficulties in and tenuous nature of signification may provide an opportunity for an exploration of what have been called "the creative possibilities inherent

---

[16] *De doctrina Christiana*, II.xxiv.37:
> Sicut enim uerbi gratia una figura litterae, quae decusatim notatur, aliud apud Graecos, aliud apud Latinos ualet, non natura, sed placito et consensione significandi, et ideo qui utramque linguam nouit, si homini Graeco uelit aliquid significare scribendo, non in ea significatione ponit hanc litteram, in qua eam ponit, cum homini scribit Latino; . . . – sicut ergo hae omnes significationes pro suae cuiusque societatis consensione animos mouent et, quia diuersa consensio est, diuerse mouent, nec ideo consenserunt in eas homines, quia iam ualebant ad significationem, sed ideo ualent, quia consenserunt in eas, sic etiam illa signa, quibus perniciosa daemonum societas comparatur, pro cuiusque obseruationibus ualent. Robertson, pp. 60–61.

[17] *De doctrina Christiana*, II.xxv.38: ". . . non constant talia signa inter homines, nisi consensus accedat." Robertson, p. 61.

[18] Vance, *Mervelous Signals*, p. 258.

in the multivalence of signs."[19] In the *De Ortu*, for example, while Gawain's judgment is true, so too, at another level of interpretation, is the centurion's, for although he was incorrect in assuming he was seeing kingfishers, he was correct in what the sight portended; there is battle, if not defeat (for the heroes) to come. An atmosphere of ambiguity with regard to accepted categories, both inside and outside the text, is thus established at an early stage.

Yet there is a caution to be observed here too. Augustine does indeed seem to revel in the richness of ambiguity in Scripture when he asks, "What could God have more generously and abundantly provided in the divine writings than that the same words might be understood in various ways . . . ?"[20] Yet Augustine continues "which other no less divine witnesses approve";[21] that is, "there is no danger if any of the meanings may be seen to be congruous with the truth taught in other passages of Holy Scripture."[22] Uncontrolled ambiguity is not necessarily desirable, and error is a real possibility. Augustine is discussing interpretation of Scripture and we are examining secular texts; perhaps it is rather a leap to move from Augustine on the interpretation of Scripture to a concern in courtly romance for the potential conflict between appearance and reality. Yet this leap is not so great if we remember the education of the probable readers and writers of these texts; once one recalls Clanchy's insistence on the fundamentally linguistic nature of the education of the schools, it is entirely clear why Vance's "thread" would be the reflection on the nature of language as a semiotic system. And whether specific scholastic discussions of signs are here implicated or not, the concerns for the difficult, tenuous, and possibly dangerous endeavor of reading, of signs and of texts, are clear. It is significant that this concentration of the language of signification occurs before the naval battle, and in that battle, the reader encounters what may be the most puzzling passage in the whole text.

This battle, like other battles in the text, is described in great detail, with a varied and fairly technical vocabulary, as well as with a regard

---

[19] Ross G. Arthur, *Medieval Sign Theory and Sir Gawain and the Green Knight* (Toronto: University of Toronto Press, 1987), p. 8.

[20] *De doctrina Christiana*, III.xxvii.38: "Nam quid in diuinis eloquiis largius et uberius potuit diuinitus prouideri, quam ut eadem uerba pluribus intellegantur modis . . . ?" Robertson, p. 102.

[21] *De doctrina Christiana*, III.xxvii.38: ". . . quos alia non minus diuina contestantia faciant adprobari." Robertson, p. 102.

[22] *De doctrina Christiana*, III.xxvii.38: ". . . nihil periculi est, si quodlibet eorum congruere ueritati ex aliis locis sanctarum scripturarum doceri potest." Robertson, pp. 101–2.

for what seem to be authentic battle tactics. There are battering rams, towers and catapults, and then, into this scene of authentic tactics, comes the notorious description of Greek fire. Greek fire was a real weapon, and it has been argued that the attention paid to it in the *De Ortu* tends to support a twelfth- rather than a thirteenth-century date for the text, because the weapon is clearly something both formidable and fabulous.[23] Occupying five pages in Day's edition, the description of Greek fire in the *De Ortu* is both wonderful and mystifying. Bruce's tone in treating the passage suggests disgust, but he does entertain the possibility that it may be "consciously burlesque."[24] Day argues that the passage is an example of *amplificatio*, used deliberately to heighten tension through delay at a crucial moment in the text;[25] she also considers the theme of appearance and reality, and the possibilities of parody (with something like the formula for Spanish gold in Theophilus's *De diversis artibus* as target) in the formula.[26] In the end, she considers the passage as an intrusion of the real world of technology into the world of Arthurian romance:

> The opponent armed with the new technology is both greater and less than the heroic ideal. With the new technology of warfare represented by Greek fire the world of the story is no longer quite the world of Arthur and his knights. It is already, even in the twelfth century, the modern world, where warfare is impersonal and death holds no glory.[27]

It is true, I think, that this passage is consciously burlesque. It is indeed an example of *amplificatio*, and it does have the effect of delaying the completion of a tense narrative situation. The passage also involves the audience in the game of appearance versus reality, as it tries to sort out whether the description is real, or fabulous, or both. The connection to the problems of signification in a literary text is clear. There may be a specific target for some of the parody – another indication of the piece's roots in the world of court writing. But the target is not so much a specific example of the kind of fabulous science embodied in the description; it is, rather, the audience's expectations regarding this story, and perhaps all stories.

---

[23] Day, "The Rise of Gawain," pp. lii–liii.

[24] *Two Arthurian Romances*, ed. Bruce, p. lxii. Galyon also sees the passage as burlesque (337), part of the narrative's exploration "of the failure of appearance to show reality" (336).

[25] Day, "The Rise of Gawain," p. cxlii.

[26] Day, *De Ortu Waluuanii*, p. xxv.

[27] Day, *De Ortu Waluuanii*, p. xxvii.

The signal for caution is the centurion's misinterpretation of the "sign" of the kingfishers; he was both wrong and right at the same time. To put it another way, he got the sign wrong, but the signification right. The audience, too, can never be sure what it is seeing or what the sight may mean – "apprehending the thing as it is" is no simple matter. The game of the text thus conveys a serious message about the reception and interpretation of truth as mediated through language and through narrative.

The wealth of detail in the description seems designed specifically to undercut the possibility of unambiguous understanding of "the thing as it is." It is not simply the presence of such clearly fabulous matter as the gall-bladder and testicles of a shape-shifting wolf, the blood of a dragon, and a three-headed, poisonous, flame-breathing asp. The whole *manner* of the description, its very structure, contributes to the general confusion. The extremely venomous quality of the asp, for example, is described at great length:

> For at its touch, the earth is robbed of vegetation and crops, the seas of fish, the trees of fruit; and even more marvelous, should the tiniest, merest drop infect a tree, no matter how large, [the drop will], corroding like a cancer, be absorbed into that tree through that spot and fell it to the earth. It is well established that no remedy can oppose this destruction; in fact, should men or beasts be touched at all on the surface of the skin, it penetrates in such a way as to kill them immediately . . . And from the venom flowing from its three mouths three extracts [lit. plants] are produced; that is, one from each mouth. Should anyone consume the first of these in food or drink, he will be driven mad, his mind unhinged; the second one brings death to the taster with a taste; and the juice of the third, whether eaten or administered as an ointment, infects with the king's evil.[28]

A formidable serpent indeed, and one which seems to have been much studied, and yet whose name, the author remarks coyly at the

---

[28] *De Ortu Waluuanii*, pp. 68–70:
Tellus namque eius ad tactum herba et segete, unda piscibus, arbores destituuntur fructibus; et unde magis mirandum est, si vel minutissima stilla arborem cuiuslibet grossitudinis sit infecerit, more cancri corrodens, quo loco cederit per medium consumpto humi sternit. Nullam huic cladi medelam obesse posse compertum est; quin homines et pecudes, si vel saltim cutis superficiem attigerit, in talia penetrans statim perimat . . . E sanie autem eius ab triplici rictu profluente tres herbe gignuntur scilicet ex singulis singule. Quarum primam siquis cibo vel potu sumpserit mente mutata in rabiem vertitur; secunda una cum gustu se necem infert gustanti; tercie vero succus, se potatum aut unctum, regio morbo inficit.

outset, escapes him.[29] This single absent detail glares out against the background profusion, and the case of the three-headed asp may be seen as a statement in microcosm of the problem of the Greek fire digression. An educated audience is here presented with a great deal of lore that adds up to very little.

If part of the purpose of the recipe for Greek fire is to mock contemporary "scientific" lore, then clearly we must assume an audience sufficiently knowledgeable to appreciate the parody. Geoffrey of Monmouth certainly imagines such an audience for his similar practice in the lore sections of the *Vita Merlini*, discussed in chapter 6. The author of the *De Ortu* sends signals to his own audience, not merely through the outrageous ingredients, but also through the genuine recipe for Greek fire, included at the end of the digression: "Also sulphur and pitch and resin, oil, tartar, and bitumen, are not withheld from the aforementioned [*predictis*] [ingredients]."[30] These are the real ingredients of Greek fire, and the manner of their introduction is laconic in the extreme compared to what is assumed under *predictis*. Even allowing a great deal of latitude for credulity and medieval belief, it is difficult to take all of this passage at face value. The authentic afterthought, juxtaposed with the incredible complexity of the list thus far, leads one to wonder if the author is not playing with his audience. One can even imagine a sort of social literary game, at court or in a certain kind of cloister, where the participants might try to outdo one another in the creation of such passages – one thinks here of the practice of creating parodies made up entirely of lines from the Bible or from classical texts.[31]

What might the goal of this play be? One thing which has been allowed to slip out of the scholarly discussion of this passage, perhaps because humor is a difficult thing to discuss, is that this passage is often funny. The effect is achieved, not by slapstick, but rather by quietly incongruous juxtapositions of the sort discussed above. Another case is the grisly description of the proper way to obtain the blood of a red-headed man. The description is both grotesque and, in the sobriety of its tone, funny. An unsettling tension between laughter and disgust is the result:

---

[29] *De Ortu Waluuanii*, p. 68: ". . . cuius nomen menti excidit . . ."
[30] *De Ortu Waluuanii*, p. 70: "Sulphur autem pix et resina, oleum, tartarum et bitumen, minime adimuntur predictis . . ."
[31] For a discussion of these and other Latin parodies, see Martha Bayless, *Parody in the Middle Ages: The Latin Tradition* (Ann Arbor: University of Michigan Press, 1996).

A youth whose beard and hair are red, whose face is sprinkled with pimples of the same color, is led into a beautiful bedchamber, and for the period of one month is fattened luxuriously on every kind of delicacy. Also, a fireplace is kindled before him every day, and he is made drunk with wine, to increase his blood, but he is diligently kept from feminine embraces. When the month has passed, burning coals are scattered here and there in the middle of the room on both sides alongside him. He is exposed among these when he is gorged with food and drink and his clothing has been laid aside, and like a roast on a spit, he is turned on each side in front of the fire. When he has been sufficiently warmed, and the veins all over his body are turgid, he is bled; that is, the veins of each arm are cut crosswise. Meanwhile, while the blood is diminishing, he receives wafers in wine to revive his spirit, lest through some weakness or trance, the desired liquid should clot. The blood is allowed to flow for a long time, until the loss of blood brings death and drives the soul from the body.[32]

There is nothing fabulous about this ingredient or the means for collecting it. One could indeed follow these instructions, however horrible; but whether one is meant to take these instructions at face value again becomes a question when the author moves on to the next ingredient, dragon's blood, as if he had almost forgotten about it: "And if it is asked how a dragon may be caught . . . "[33] The dragon receives far less attention than the red-headed youth; indeed, one is left with the impression that obtaining the blood of a dragon is a far less difficult matter than obtaining that of a red-headed man.

The Greek fire digression could end at many points; after the list of ingredients is complete, or after the red-headed man has been bled, or the dragon caught, or the fire prepared. Were this text to be read aloud, it is not difficult to imagine a skilled narrator pausing before

---

[32] *De Ortu Waluuanii*, p. 72:

> Juventus autem cui barba et cesaries ruffa fuerit eiusdem coloris impetigines faciem asperserint, pulcro inducitur thalamo, omniumque apparatu dapium, unius mensis delicate impinguatur spacio. Singulis quoque diebus foco ante eum accenso ad auctum sanguinem vino inebriatur, sed sedule a femineis servatur amplexibus. Mense vero expleto, in medio domus hinc et inde ad eius longitudinem igniti sternunter [sic] carbones, inter quos ipse cibo potuque inpurgitatus depositis indumentis exponitur; ac more veruum utroque in latere ad ignem versatur. Sufficienter autem calefactus, jamque venis toto turgentibus corpore fleobotomatur, scilicet, utriusque brachii fibris ex transverso incisis. Interim vero dum sanguinem minuit ad refocillandam mentem offas in vino accipit, ne, illa debilitata vel in extasi rapta, liquor concrescatur optatus. Tam diu autem sanguis effluere sinitur, donec eius defeccio mortem inducens animam corpore eiciat.

[33] *De Ortu Waluuanii*, p. 74: "Si autem queritur quomodo draco prendatur . . ."

each new section, leaving the audience to wonder when, if ever, the narrative proper would resume. For readers, too, the effect of the delay can be felt, as we are put through a bewildering array of possible reactions, including wonder, confusion, annoyance, horror, and boredom. The text itself is subverted, as the author makes use of the stylistic convention of *amplificatio*, and the narrative convention of fabulous detail, to undermine those same conventions, and to leave his audience with the task of sorting out the real from the spurious. If we assume an audience, at least part of which is up to this challenge, we may imagine the text being approached as an intriguing puzzle, a test for the wits of those reading it. Thus, instead of being swept away by the story, the text's readers or auditors stand back from it, and become aware of its conventions. This is exactly the situation necessary to produce parody: ". . . our awareness of this underlying schema disturbs our reading . . . ; expression becomes opaque, dense, and no longer a transparent vehicle of sense. It is this disturbance (or our own awareness of it) that moves the work into the category of parody."[34] This critical awareness is something which many of the works in this study seem to be trying to achieve; one is reminded again that irony is a dominant mode of court speech.

The Greek fire digression ends with a narrative recognition of its effect: "Therefore, as has been said above . . . "[35] And we are returned to the middle of the battle fray. A further incongruity arises at this point, for when finally the narrative of the naval battle resumes, Greek fire immediately becomes a serious and threatening weapon – the thing in itself, perhaps – and only Gawain is able to overcome it and rescue his comrades from certain death.

It seems, in fact, that one could argue that the narrative is structured around two modes, one seeming to encourage the audience to question what is real, and the other seeking to establish verisimilitude. Before this battle, for example, a certain realism is suggested by an interest in the representation of linear time in narrative. On the island where Gawain encounters Milocrates's foresters, word of the success of Gawain and his men reaches Milocrates through a single survivor who hides in the foliage until Gawain and his men return to their

---

[34] Joseph A. Dane, "Parody and Satire: A Theoretical Model," *Genre* 13 (1980), 152.

[35] *De Ortu Waluuanii*, p. 78: "Igitur ut superius dictum est . . ." In her translation, Day omits this phrase; yet it is not, I think, a merely mechanical flourish. Medieval rhetoricians cautioned against straying too far from the path of the story in the pursuit of *amplificatio*; this author has clearly done so, but, I think, to a purpose.

ships. The text then attempts to create a sense of simultaneity, despite the restrictions of linear narrative. The survivor reports to Milocrates, who rallies his allies; "meanwhile," the centurion is consulting with his men, and it is decided that Gawain and Odabel should go as spies to the city. The author is careful to make their success at mingling with Milocrates's men plausible: "For the huge crowd allowed them to proceed unnoticed, and the fact that they were not lacking in skill in the language of the country also contributed to their safety."[36] As Gawain reaches the city, the two strands of narrative which have been developing simultaneously meet; a last flash-back, in which we are informed that Milocrates had already sent for his brother Buzafarnan's aid, brings Milocrates's side of the story up to the minute, and it is a nice conceit that as we are acquiring this information, so too is Gawain, who, "remaining unknown among them, noted what each said with intent ear."[37] This experiment in simultaneous narrative is not as involved as the interlaced structure characteristic of French romances of the thirteenth century, but it does suggest an interest in methods of representing time in narrative.

The naval battle too, apart from the Greek fire digression, is carefully and accurately described. The battle descriptions once Gawain reaches Jerusalem and encounters Gormundus are also highly skilled, and although they display certain narrative tricks, their wealth of technical detail encourages a reader to take them at face value. Careful deployment of language dominates these passages. On the first day, for example,

> They strike and are stricken; they push forward and are repelled, and the wheel of Fortune turns between them with varying chance. No strength or fortitude is omitted, and the gaze of all is fixed on them. It is not known who is more ready to strike or who is braver to endure; such frequent strokes and such severe blows are exchanged ceaselessly between them, that it is difficult to tell who gives and who receives them. You cannot tell which of them is stronger; and the more they press the fight, the more they hunger for battle with stronger spirit. Now they mingle their blows with clever raillery, now they enrage each other with their cynical,

[36] *De Ortu Waluuanii*, p. 34: "Innumerosa namque turba eos qui essent non deprehensi sinebat dum eciam et hoc ad eorum accidisset tutelam quod illius patrie lingue periciam non ignorabant."

[37] *De Ortu Waluuanii*, p. 36: ". . . inter alios incognitus residens, singula que dicebantur intenta aure . . . notabat."

sarcastic remarks; now, breathless, they retreat, now, refreshed, they rush more bitterly together, their breath regained.[38]

The extensive use of the present tense makes the battle seem very immediate, and the author gives the impression that he, like the audience and the participants, is ignorant of the outcome. Indeed, the first day of the battle closes with no clues as to the eventual outcome: "in the morning they would fight again, and again the contest would begin anew."[39]

Another stylistic element which contributes to the sense of immediacy in the description is the direct address to the external audience. This address is in its turn paralleled by the indication that the eyes of the audience *within* the poem are also fixed on this battle. The language of the passage is carefully balanced; the now . . . now . . . structure, in particular, echoes the reference to the movement of the wheel of Fortune, creating a back-and-forth rhythm which serves to heighten the uncertainty about the outcome of the contest.

The description of the next day of battle further demonstrates the author's fondness for variation and decoration. The sun's rising is rendered in a classical turn of phrase, "at Aurora's rising."[40] There are more addresses to the audience, sound and visual effects, and backward and forward action paralleled by the syntax. The diction is consciously varied; for example, the shield-words include *clipeis, peltam, macheram, egide,* and *parma.*[41] The day concludes with another example of the desire to make the events plausible which is so at odds with the fantastic Greek fire passage; the author explains that a prearranged time had been set for the battle to stop, and that while the pagans were reluctant to abide by the terms of the agreement, they do in the end do so.

The third day proceeds much as the first two; there is an interesting

---

[38] *De Ortu Waluuanii*, p. 82:

> Feriunt et feriuntur, pellunt et propelluntur; rotaque fortune vario casu inter eos versatur. Nil quid virtutis et fortitudinis sit prossus relinquitur, cunctorumque obtutus in eos infinguntur. Quis promcior ad feriendum fortiorve ad paciundum ignoratur; inter quos tam crebri ictus, tamque graves sine temporis inter capedine dividebantur colaphi, ut quis daret vel acciperet, difficile posset adverti. Uter viribus pocior haberetur nescires; dum quo magis pungne insisterent eo valencioribus animis ad certamen inhiarent. Modo lepidis cavillacionibus suos ictus interserunt, modo cynedis salibus suorum vicissim mentes exasperant; modo haneli se retrahunt, modo aura concepta recreati acriores concurrent.

[39] *De Ortu Waluuanii*, p. 84: ". . . iterum in crastinum pungnaturi, iterumque luctamen ex integro iniciaturi."

[40] *De Ortu Waluuanii*, p. 86: "Aurora vero oriente . . ."

[41] *De Ortu Waluuanii*, pp. 82–90.

address to the audience: "If you had seen the spectacle of these two, the fight of the Lapiths would come into your mind; as often as they redoubled their blows, so often would you think of the anvils of the Cyclops being beaten with hammers."[42] References like this one, as well as the language of the text, confirm a learned audience such as we have been imagining at the Angevin court. Gawain's story is perhaps presented with all the historical details and rhetorical flourishes discussed in order to make it acceptable to such an audience; on the other hand, potentially burlesque passages like the Greek fire passage may be a joke between the educated author and audience at the fanciful nature of popular literature, or at the credulity of that literature's audience. They also represent the facetious touches which point to the court at play.

Thus far, then, we have seen the displacement towards the fantastic and perhaps parodic in the Greek fire digression, and the contrary movement towards the "realistic" in the treatment of battle in the text. The other elements of the narrative, too, may be organized around these two poles, and in fact the text itself divides into two parts – Gawain's Roman youth and his arrival at Arthur's court – whose broad outlines suggest one or the other emphasis. These are not, however, hard and fast divisions. The Greek fire digression, of course, occurs in the first part, and it is not in fact the first such passage in that section of the text.

The first example of the kind of description which one might more traditionally associate with romance, in this case a kind of travelogue of strange and unfamiliar places, occurs when Gawain and his men are washed up on the island:

> The inhabitants of this island were of such ferocity that they would spare no one, regardless of sex or age, but would inflict punishment on anyone, guilty or innocent, arriving from a foreign nation. . . . And they feed immoderately on the flesh of all cattle and fowl, and it is said that they are so dominated by passion that fathers do not know their own sons, nor indeed do the sons know by whom they were fathered. Their height does not exceed a measure of three cubits, and their lifespan is fifty years. Rarely does anyone die before the tenth year, nor live past the fiftieth year. They are prolix

---

[42] *De Ortu Waluuanii*, p. 92: "Horum si spectaculo assisteres, Laphitarum pungna tibi in mente occurreret, qui quociens ictus ingeminabant, tociens Ciclopum incudes malleis contundi crederes."

in the cultivation of food, accustomed to labor, abounding in wealth, and are known to be fertile in the propagation of children.[43]

There is a "wonders of the East" flavor to this passage, appropriate in the context of the hero's journey to Jerusalem. One also remembers Southern's comments on the appeal of the marvelous in twelfth-century England, or Bezzola on the courtly taste for the profane and the marvelous. It is difficult to decide whether the description of the sexual practices of the islanders is offered in the interests of information, disapprobation, or titillation; the use of similar passages in the *Vita Merlini*, to be discussed in chapter 6, comes to mind. In that text, such information contributes to the strains of parody and generic confusion in the work; because this is the first such passage in the *De Ortu*, one could be forgiven for restricting comment to remarking that it gives the impression that the author is seeking to vary his material to lend interest to his account.

Certainly much of the first part of the text suggests something other than romance, for even when romance motifs are invoked, it is in a rather restrained fashion. I have already mentioned the unusual amount of detail offered to fill out the account of Gawain's Roman boyhood in the first part of the text. The romance reflexes are less thoroughly worked out. The opening lines of the text are typical of the opening of Welsh king tales and romances; they function equally well in an historical or a romantic context, as a quick entry into the space and time of the text: "King Uther Pendragon, father of Arthur, subdued the kings of all of Britain's neighboring provinces to his rule."[44] The romance episode of the love between Loth and Anna receives relatively little attention, and the Ovidian commonplace which describes it – "For indeed, love is like a flame; the more it is hidden, the hotter it burns"[45] – is hardly remarkable. The motif of the unknown child of noble birth is surely the stuff of romance, but at

[43] *De Ortu Waluuanii*, pp. 24–26:

> Cuius incole tante feritatis existebant, ut nulli sexui, nulli pacerent [sic] etati, quin sontes et insontes ab extranea nacione venientes pari pena multarent . . . Nam et omnium pecudum ac volucrum carne vesci immodiceque dicuntur volumptati subditi, ut nec patres filios, nec filii a quibus sint geniti prossus agnoscant. Trium cubitorum statura mensuram non excedit, etasque ad quinquagesimum annum protenditur. Raro aliquis infra x vita diffungitur; nec quinquagesimum supervivens annum transgreditur. Cultu cibisque diffusi, laboribus assueti, diviciis affluentes in propagacione sobolis noscuntur fecundi.

[44] *De Ortu Waluuanii*, p. 2: "Uterpendragon Rex, pater Arturi, omnium Britannie confinium provinciarum sue dicioni reges subegerat."

[45] *De Ortu Waluuanii*, p. 2: "Verum quia ad instar flamme amor quo magis tegitur: eo magis accenditur indeque capit augmentum, unde minui festinatur."

this point the text's interest seems directed more at the details of that child's life in Rome.

Viamandus establishes himself in the style of a wealthy Roman, and Gawain is raised as a Roman youth, acquiring his military training and earning his reputation in the circus at the *equiriis*, the annual horse races held on February 27 and March 14, in honor of Mars. Like most young romance heroes, he desires to set out on an adventure to prove himself, but the adventure he wins, to act as the Roman champion against Gormundus at Jerusalem, is decided after lengthy deliberations in the Roman senate; readers hoping for Arthur and his court will thus far have been disappointed. On the other hand, the concern for appearance and reality, for signs and signifiers, is central here. The *enfances* of Gawain – a favorite British hero – are presented in such a way as to stress this theme of signification. Viamandus, for example, is described as a man "poor in goods but of respectable stock and character."[46] The text does not condemn him, noting only that "opportunity of place and time make a thief";[47] his circumstances have placed him in the way of temptation, but his conduct towards the boy is exemplary, demonstrating that despite his reduced circumstances and the outward evidence of the theft, he is indeed a good man. His impersonation of a nobleman is in fact less of an imposture than it seems; the outward signs of his affluence mislead people about his origins, but not about his essential worth. The courtly concern for the masks which people wear is reflected here, along with the related interest in the relationship between those outward appearances and inner realities. When one remembers the social origins of many of the members of the Angevin court, it is not difficult to imagine the appeal of a character such as Viamandus for that audience.

Gawain is also not what he seems. He appears throughout the story under various epithets, and is not named until the end of the work. Gawain's quest for his true identity recalls the adventures of any number of romance heroes, and seems particularly to suggest the pattern of the Fair Unknown. Gawain's difficulties with the Arthurian court are not unusual in such narratives: Perceval, for example, is mocked when he first appears at Arthur's court. If the Fair Unknown romances pattern themselves in part, as Jaeger suggests, on the rise of an unknown in courtier narrative, then the

---

[46] *De Ortu Waluuanii*, p. 6: ". . . rebus quidem pauper sed genere et moribus honestus . . ."
[47] *De Ortu Waluuanii*, p. 6: ". . . oportunitas loci et temporis reddit latronem . . ."

conflict is not surprising; the new favorite must deal with the hostility of those he displaces. In this text, however, the hostility emanates chiefly from Arthur, and the king's odd behavior suggests instead the court theme of kingship and the conduct of the ruler. But this theme appears chiefly at the end of the work. More important in Gawain's experiences is the quest for self. It is a fundamental irony of Gawain's situation that while he is unknown to himself, he is always accompanied by signs which point to his identity, and that information is known to others, if not to him.

When Viamandus dies, he commits Gawain, his story, and his royal tokens to the emperor and to Pope Sulpicius. Thus does Gawain come to be known as "the boy without a name."[48] The irony of the situation functions at two levels, because both the audience of the text and figures within the text itself are aware of the real identity of the Fair Unknown. Later, at the *equiriis*, Gawain dons a crimson tunic over his armor, and is acclaimed by the crowd as "the knight with the surcoat."[49] This is the name which is to remain with him throughout the rest of the text. Thus an outward sign is substituted for the true identity of the hero; the sign is a covering, a literal veil beneath which his true self is figuratively hidden. This familiar exegetical trope could appeal to an audience more clerical than courtly, while the emphasis on dress may be of particular resonance to an audience for whom, perhaps, clothes do make the man.

Nabaor is another character in the first part of the text who exemplifies the central concern with what people look like, and who they are. Nabaor appears to be of the enemy, yet he is a faithful friend to Gawain. This friendship might suggest that he is deficient in loyalty to his own lord, but it is later made clear that Nabaor is himself a knight of the emperor, made captive with the niece. As for the niece, she is an unusual prisoner. She is well treated by Milocrates, and is, indeed, the queen of the land, but her captivity irks her to the extent that she would rather be free and poor than a captive, no matter how wealthy or powerful. The complex loyalties of the characters underline the uncertainties of the world in which they move. The text would appear to be moving towards a position where outward appearances, particularly in matters of human character, are to be regarded as deceptive, and any judgment based on such perceptions as flawed.

---

[48] *De Ortu Waluuanii*, p. 16: ". . . puer sine nomine . . ."
[49] *De Ortu Waluuanii*, p. 18: ". . . Miles cum tunica armature."

The action of this section of the text also tends towards the central thematic concern with perception. The princess seals Gawain's hopes of victory by giving to him Milocrates's own armor and sword, "concerning which it was fated that the king would be stripped of his royal crown by him who should first wear it, apart from the king."[50] The fate on the sword may be one of the Celtic aspects of the narrative, an example of *geasa*, or prohibitions or injunctions forbidding or enjoining someone to do something. *Geasa* could apply to persons, places, or things; several of the texts to be discussed in this study include curses or oaths which are akin to forms of *geis*. This supernatural detail contrasts with Nabaor's shrewd assessment of the psychological impact upon Milocrates's army when they see the city burning: ". . . and, set on fire, it will be a horrible spectacle for the king and his men, and it will offer the means of victory to them [Gawain's men]."[51] Both Milocrates and his men will be presented with visible symbols of their defeat, before that defeat has in fact happened. The text offers both romantic and more hard-headed reasons to expect the hero's victory; is the verisimilitude of the latter intended to undermine the former?

The second movement of the text occurs when the victorious Gawain, seeking more adventure, journeys to the court of Arthur. If the general thrust of the first section of the text has been in the direction of an historicized narrative, then this (much shorter) portion of the work is far more clearly fixed in the world of romance. The king's court becomes central to the hero's experiences, and the concern for appearance and reality is refocused here in the court setting. Here this concern crystallizes exclusively around Gawain's identity, and again, the concern is not what Gawain does *not* know, but rather, what everyone else does know. Knowledge in this part of the text is located in the realm of the supernatural, for Gwendoloena, Arthur's queen, is said to be a sorceress.[52] Her revelation of her dream to Arthur abounds in references to perception.

Gwendoloena begins by challenging Arthur's self-image: "'Lord,'

---

[50] *De Ortu Waluuanii*, p. 48: ". . . de quibus fatatum erat quod ab eo devictus rex regali spoliaretur apice, qui preter ipsum ea primitus induisset." For a complete discussion of *geis* and its survival in medieval romance, see John Revell Reinhard, *The Survival of Geis in Mediaeval Romance* (Halle: Max Niemeyer, 1933).

[51] *De Ortu Waluuanii*, p. 46: ". . . igne incensa regi suisque horrendum spectaculum; illis autem victorie causam prebeat."

[52] Wieber argues that the unusual name, and the statement that the queen is a sorceress, are deliberate errors made in the interests of humor ("A Translation," p. 75).

she said, 'you boast about your worth and praise it excessively, and you think that no one is your equal in strength.' "[53] Arthur responds by asking her if her *animus* does not also "sense" the same thing.[54] In other words, we are dealing here with a perception about Arthur's essential being. Yet when Arthur decides to test Gwendoloena's prophecy, the challenge to his self-perception moves out of the realm of philosophy and into that of physical comedy, with the great king himself as its target. Arthur's punishment for lack of self-knowledge and an unwillingness to accept counsel shows the importance of this virtue for a king, even as it distances the lesson and makes it amusing.

Before the opening encounter between Gawain and Arthur, Gwendoloena promises Arthur a sign that will prove the truth of her assertion: "And lest you should judge that I am declaring frivolous things, take this as a sign of the matter: I foretell to you that he will send me a gold ring and three thousand-pieces with two horses by late morning."[55] It seems clear that the audience is being encouraged to question Arthur's wisdom in seeking the encounter at all. His decision shows a regard for custom which overrides his knowledge of the worth of his wife's predictions: "Now Arthur, knowing that she had never deceived him with this sort of prediction, nevertheless decided to test the matter without her knowledge. For he had a custom, that immediately that he heard that any strong man had come there, he would go to meet him, so that their combat would show who was the stronger."[56] Perhaps pride is leading the king, quite literally, to a fall. The foolish vow suggests the situation in *Arthur and Gorlagon*, discussed in chapter 6, as well as the more familiar analogue in *Sir Gawain and the Green Knight*. In that text, Arthur's refusal to eat before he has seen a wonder is followed by the arrival and challenge of the Green Knight. That the challenge is not immediately answered is a humiliation for the "childgered" Arthur and his court. In the *De Ortu*, as in *Sir Gawain* and indeed most of the texts to be discussed in the next chapters, Arthur is less than

---

[53] *De Ortu Waluuanii*, p. 100: "'Domine,' ait, 'tu te de tua probitate nimium gloriaris et extollis, neminemque tibi viribus parem existimas.'"

[54] *De Ortu Waluuanii*, p. 102.

[55] *De Ortu Waluuanii*, p. 102: "Et ne me frivola arbitreris asserere, signum rei habeto quod anulum aureum et iii myriadas cum equis duobus eum mihi summo mane missurum tibi prenuncio."

[56] *De Ortu Waluuanii*, p. 102: "Arturus autem eam se nunquam in huiusmodi presagiis fefellisse recogitans rem probare ea tamen ignorante statuit. Consuetudinis enim habebat quod statim ubi aliquem strenuum virum advenire audisset; se illi obvium daret, ut mutuus congressus validiorem ostenderet."

perfect. It may be that there is a whole tradition of the negative representation of Arthur in British romance, of which *Sir Gawain* and the *De Ortu* are only two examples.

It is also important here that the king is shown to be ignoring advice, even though he knows that this advice is entirely reliable. The sorceress-queen of the *De Ortu* has the potential to be an ambiguous figure, for sorceresses often feature in antifeminist writing. Yet she seems to function here more as a romantic stand-in for the counselor figure one would expect to appeal to an audience of courtly clerics. She is perhaps sanitized by biblical analogues such as Pilate's wife; in any case, the point of the episode, underneath the romance coloring, is that a king is shown to make a perverse decision to ignore counsel in favor of an arbitrary custom. That behavior is something a courtier may be reluctant to reprove in real life, but a courtly writer can use narrative to suggest some of the possible outcomes of such a decision.

In the *De Ortu*, Arthur's pride results in his own humiliation. He is deliberately rude upon encountering Gawain: "Are you a fugitive, a thief or a spy?"[57] Gawain's reply is a model of moderation (Gawain is traditionally fair-tongued): "I am wandering because I do not know the roads; but the flight of an exile does not drive me, nor does the pillage of a robber goad me, nor does deceit cover any treachery."[58] Arthur compounds his rudeness, a fact which is particularly striking when the reader knows that Arthur has already been alerted to Gawain's worth. Here, then, is a character who knows the reality of a situation, and yet deliberately ignores that reality. It is notable, too, that Gawain stresses that he is practicing no deception; he is what he seems to be, and yet we know that in another sense, he is ignorant of himself.

Arthur suffers for his actions, as he is promptly unhorsed into the river. Kay, seeking to avenge his lord, ends up on top of him in a bit of contemptuous slapstick: "but just in the same way, he was thrown prostrate on top of Arthur in a single heap with the first blow."[59] Arthur then attempts to sneak back into bed, and his feeble excuses clearly do not fool Gwendoloena, who unlike Arthur recognizes signs when she sees them:

---

[57] *De Ortu Waluuanii*, p. 102: "Exulne es, predo an insidiator?"
[58] *De Ortu Waluuanii*, p. 104: "Erro quidem ut viarum inscius; sed nec exulis me fuga agitat, nec predonis rapina instigat, nec fraus insidiantis occultat."
[59] *De Ortu Waluuanii*, p. 104: ". . . sed eodem pacto et ipse super Arturum in una congerie primo ictu prosternitur."

Arthur climbed back into bed. Queen Gwendoloena asked him, stiff as he was with cold and drenched, not only by the rain, but also by the water of the river, where he had tarried for so long and why he was so wet. Arthur said, "I heard some sort of noise in the court, as if of my men fighting. I went out to them, and it took me a while to settle them down, and it happened that I got drenched in the rain." The queen said, "Whatever you say."[60]

This foolish king, treated with unspoken contempt by his wife, does not behave as one expects of that Arthur who is, the text elsewhere assures us, "renowned for his deeds throughout the whole world."[61] He is far more like Etienne's blowhard, and he has his vernacular analogues too. The role of his wife in his humiliation may suggest that Arthur who is the butt of the joke in Robert Biket's *Lai du cor*, where the cuckolded Arthur predictably is drenched by the magical drinking horn, only to be led into misreading this obvious sign by the wiles of his wife.

This section of the text, in fact, seems to be divided between those who interpret signs correctly and those who do not. Gwendoloena's prescience allows her to interpret signs correctly; we are told that she stood the next day on the battlements, awaiting a sign, and upon seeing the messenger with the horses, she "understood the matter" (*rem intellexit*).[62] Yet it should be noted that prescience is not *required* for understanding; Arthur has information, but refuses to act on it, for reasons which are less than flattering. Pride and a concern for custom led to the encounter at the ford; once Gawain has arrived at court and presented his credentials, Arthur's reaction continues to be at odds with the obvious evidence of Gawain's worth. His decision to reject Gawain's petition and keep him in the dark about his identity, until Gawain has performed some spectacular feat in Arthur's own presence, seems bizarre. One cannot help wondering why the unhorsing of Arthur was not enough, and Arthur's continuing rudeness in calling Gawain "lazy and cowardly"[63] is juxta-

---

[60] *De Ortu Waluuanii*, p. 106:
> Arturus vero cubile repetiit. Quem regina Gwendoloena frigore rigidum, et totum tum imbre, tum rivi undis madefactum quo tam diu moratus complutusque fuisset interrogat. Arturus, "Afforis in curia tumultum ac si certancium percepi ad quos egressus; in eos pacando moram feci, nimboque ingruente me contigit complui." Regina, "Sit ut dicis."

[61] *De Ortu Waluuanii*, p. 98: ". . . insignia rerum gesta que jam toto orbe . . ."

[62] *De Ortu Waluuanii*, p. 108.

[63] *De Ortu Waluuanii*, p. 112: ". . . inertemque et timidum . . ." Raymond H. Thompson, "Gawain Against Arthur: The Impact of a Mythological Pattern upon Arthurian Tradition in

posed with Gawain's continuing assertion that, while he has deserved no such insults, he still desires to serve Arthur.

Gawain's success at the Castle of the Maidens is presented precisely as a challenge to Arthur's self-image; from his vantage point above the battle, Gawain taunts Arthur and his knights – " 'Oh king,' he said, 'are you chasing deer or rabbits, that you go scattered all over the place along these byways?' "[64] He presents the head of the pagan king to Arthur with these words: " 'Now where, o king,' he exclaimed, 'are your famous champions, of whom until now you have boasted that no one is their equal in strength? . . . now do you deem me worthy to be your knight?' "[65] One is reminded again of the challenge of the Green Knight, a challenge to the self-perceptions of Arthur and the Arthurians. Gawain's question is rhetorical; the audience and Gawain (and Gwendoloena) already know that Gawain is worthy to be one of Arthur's knights, and Arthur's final act will merely be a confirmation of that essential reality.

If Arthur has hitherto been the subject of criticism for his willful refusal to recognize things for what they are, he becomes, at the end of the text, the voice of signification. He tells Gawain of his identity in terms of perception and reality: "You are clearly mistaken, and your assessment lacks truth; and you will learn, in short, that you have been deceived in this opinion . . . I will show . . . you your lineage, and knowledge of this thing will be your reward."[66] At last the themes of appearance and reality and the search for identity converge, as Gawain learns that he is not the "boy without a name" or the "knight with the surcoat," but Gawain, Arthur's nephew. The earlier epithets are presented as successive signs which have ceded the one to the other, until this moment of ultimate revelation:

> "When you were a child, you were 'Boy without a name,' and from that beginning up to the present, you have been called 'the Knight with the Surcoat'; and now you will be valued as 'Gawain,' your

---

Accounts of the Birth of Gawain," *Folklore* 85 (1974), 113–21, sees this scene as a remnant of the hostility, in myth, between hero and substitute father-figure. Arthur's rudeness is unusual, but it is easily explained as part of the effort to produce a subversive portrait of the king.

[64] *De Ortu Waluuanii*, p. 116: " 'Numquid,' ait, 'O rex, cervos an lepores agitis, qui sic passim dispersi per avia tenditis?' "

[65] *De Ortu Waluuanii*, p. 120: " 'Quonam sunt,' exclamat, 'O Rex, tui famosi athlete, de quibus te adeo jactabas neminem eorum parem virtuti? . . . Tuumne adhuc me militem dignaris?' "

[66] *De Ortu Waluuanii*, p. 120: "Plane falleris, fideque caret tua estimacio; et te hac opinione prossus deceptum noveris . . . Ostendam . . . tibi tue propaginis seriem, cuius rei cognicio tui laboris erit remuneracio."

own name." And when Arthur had said this, three and four times from the whole court, "Gawain, nephew of King Arthur" was redoubled and repeated.[67]

The repetition of the name by king and court seems to provide a firm assertion that any problems which might be involved in the assigning and interpreting of signs have been resolved. Yet Arthur's earlier, unaccountable behavior may render his role as the one who confers identity problematic. He is clearly right this time, in this case, but the larger questions of interpretation raised through Gawain's quest remain. The court context is central to the resolution of Gawain's identity quest, but it is also potentially part of the problem, for the court which conveys identity could presumably also withhold it, as Arthur's own arbitrary actions have suggested. And while "Gawain" may be the knight's "own name," the presence in the conclusion to the tale of his other masks reminds one of the potential division between the inner and the outer man. Gawain's story began with the clandestine love between his father and mother; Jaeger remarks that in courtier narratives, the supreme example of the inner life – that life which is not constrained by the artificiality of the court – is the clandestine love affair.[68] The *De Ortu* ends with the court claiming the fruit of that union and placing him in a network of identity and kinship; but the text's concerns with the difficulty of signification suggest that in this naming, too, there is the potential for further conflict.

There is a coda to the text, one which serves to reiterate the essentially literary nature of its endeavors:

> Whoever wants to know what other virtuous exploits Gawain performs should ask them by request or payment from one who knows. Knowing that as it is more dangerous to take part in a battle than to report one, so is it more difficult to write down a history with eloquent style than to tell it in the words of common speech.[69]

---

[67] *De Ortu Waluuanii*, p. 122:
"In puerili quidem etate, 'Puer sine nomine,' a tirocinio autem usque ad presens, 'Miles' es vocatus 'cum tunica armature'; jam a modo 'Waluuanius' proprio censeberis notamine." Hec Arturo dicente, terque, quarterque ab omni cetu, "Waluuanius nepos regis Arturi!" ingeminatum et inculcatem [sic] est.

[68] Jaeger, *The Origins of Courtliness*, p. 241.

[69] *De Ortu Waluuanii*, p. 122:
Cetera que virtutum Waluuanii secuntur insignia qui scire desiderat a sciente prece vel precio exigat. Sciens quod sicut discriminosius est bellum inire quam bellum referre, sic operosius sit composito eloquencie stilo historiam exarare quam vulgari propalare sermone.

This epilogue suggests that the author is aware of popular, vernacular tradition concerning Gawain and, further, that he regards his effort as different from vernacular stories.[70] The invocation of the rhetorical tradition of (Latin) writing in this epilogue serves to distance this text from such popular traditions. In the Introduction I discussed the possibility of competition between vernacular storytellers and Latinate courtier-clerics (who were, it must be remembered, producing *both* Latin and vernacular written texts), and it may be that the difference this author remarks on could be as simple as the fact that his version is written with an eye to Latin rhetorical style. If his only goal is to produce an amplified narrative, in keeping with the demands of medieval rhetoric, then the description of the Barbarous Isle, the Greek fire digression, and all the lively battle passages may simply be means to that end, with no particularly significant comment to make on the whole question of Arthurian narrative in Britain. Yet the insistence at the end of this text seems to confirm the argument I have been developing throughout this chapter; that is, that there is an enormous literary self-consciousness here, one which is found in both the Latin and the vernacular products of court writers. One thinks of Chrétien de Troyes's contempt for popular storytellers who "tear apart and corrupt" their story material.[71] Both Chrétien and the author of the *De Ortu* see themselves as different from those storytellers; in what does this difference consist?

The author of the *De Ortu* experiments with the portrayal of time. He explores the gap between what things seem to be and what they in fact are, and he provides in the final scenes between Arthur and Gawain a portrayal of the king which deflates the king's heroism and which delivers a message on the importance of attending to good counsel. It is possible to argue, then, that the difference between this "history" and the sort of tale one could get from a professional vernacular teller of oral story is, in the mind of the author of the *De Ortu*, also a matter of a more complex approach to the accepted material and the accepted methods of conveying that material. It is tempting to conclude that the text must, at least in part, be intended to explode the conventional form and characterization of popular

---

[70] Rigg, *History of Anglo-Latin Literature*, suggests that this passage may indicate that the very use of the Latin language "may have raised cultural expectations above the level of pure entertainment"; p. 48.

[71] Chrétien de Troyes, *Erec et Enide*, ed. Mario Roques (Paris: Champion, 1981), l. 21: ". . . depecier et corronpre."

storytelling in order to highlight the problems of signification and the consequent difficulty of interpretation, of literature or of life.

On one level, the *De Ortu* is a perfectly entertaining story, even if, because of its language, it could not be called popular. Walter Map called his tales *nugae*; William of Rennes called his chronicle a *ludus* – here too one senses the court at play. But we have seen with Map that an author may in fact be proud of his *nugae*, and William's *ludus* has been shown to contain serious moral messages. The *De Ortu*, too, is offered as a different, more skillful kind of story, and here our efforts at interpretation might have to stop, were it not for the fact that the *De Ortu* does not stand alone. Tendencies hinted at in the *De Ortu* – concerns for the tenuousness of interpretation, a playful delight in the undermining of expectation, and a legalistic concern for the conduct of the monarch – come out into the open once and for all in the author's other work, the *Historia Meriadoci*.

# 5

# "*Dies fantastica*": the *Historia Meriadoci* and the adventure of the text

The *Historia Meriadoci* is at first glance a work quite different from the *De Ortu*. Like the *De Ortu*, it focuses on a knightly protagonist, rather than on Arthur, but its abundance of folklore and romance motifs and its quick succession of adventures evoke the atmosphere of a typical *roman d'aventure* in a way that the previous text did not. The central concern for signs and their interpretation around which the whole of the *De Ortu* pivots is absent, and yet there is much in this work to confirm the impression that the author of both texts is vitally interested in the process of the creation of literary meaning. Occasional moments of burlesque or parody in the *De Ortu* become a central principle in the *Historia Meriadoci*, and the abundance of romance markers in the text encourages one to see the genre itself as the focus of interest here. Once again, the issue is how we are to interpret the signs we are given, but here the signs are the conventional ones of a literary genre which is thus subverted. A genre can be understood as a contract between author and audience, creating what Jauss has called a "horizon of expectations";[1] the author's subversion of the terms of the contract becomes another means by which to highlight the fragility of all such significative and hermeneutic systems. It is significant that the difficulty develops within a political frame of reference; Meriadoc must deal, again and again, with the duplicity of kings and their counselors. The knight must learn to negotiate both real forests and the metaphorical thickets of courtly speech, in order to survive and take his rightful place in the political realm.

## HISTORIA MERIADOCI: SYNOPSIS

The king of Cambria, Caradoc by name, rules for a time in peace and prosperity, but as he ages, he passes most of the actual control

---

[1] Hans Robert Jauss, "Literary History as a Challenge to Literary Theory," *New Literary History* 2 (1970–71), 13.

of the kingdom to his brother Griffin, retaining for himself only the name of sovereignty and passing his days in hunting and other pleasures. For a time, Griffin acts honorably as his brother's regent, but eventually, wicked counselors succeed in convincing him that he must rid himself of his brother and take the name of ruler for himself. Caradoc dreams of his brother's treachery, but refuses to heed the dream or his wife's correct interpretation of it, and is slain in the forest by two of Griffin's men. His wife dies of grief and the children, Meriadoc and Orwen, are left in the care of Ivor, the royal huntsman, and his wife Morwen.

Despite Griffin's feigned grief and his treacherous execution of his own associates for the murder of Caradoc, the nobles of the realm are convinced of Griffin's guilt. They demand custody of the royal children, hoping to protect them and arrange advantageous marriages for them. Griffin pretends to accede to their wishes, and has the children brought to court, but instead of turning them over to the nobles, he orders twelve men to take them into the forest and hang them. Ivor, learning of the plot, rescues the children through an elaborate stratagem. He and his wife and dog flee to another part of the forest with the children, and there they all remain concealed for five years.

One day, Kay and King Urien of Scotland are riding in the forest. Urien comes upon Orwen and her nurse; overcome with passion, he seizes the girl and makes off with her. Meanwhile, Kay has encountered Meriadoc and Ivor; admiring the youth greatly, he seizes him and rides off with him. Ivor and Morwen are paralyzed by grief for two years.

When two years have passed, Ivor and Morwen resolve to go looking for their charges. Morwen heads for Scotland, arriving on the day that Orwen is to marry Urien. There is a joyful reunion. Meanwhile, Ivor has made his way to Arthur's court, where he and Meriadoc, too, are reunited. With the journey of Kay, Ivor and Meriadoc to Scotland, the reunions are complete.

Meriadoc makes the case against Griffin to King Arthur, who orders Griffin to appear to answer the charges. Griffin, however, retreats to his fastness on Snowdon, where he resists Arthur's siege for three years. At last hunger compels his surrender, and he is executed. Meriadoc is offered the kingship of Cambria, but chooses instead to improve his prowess as a knight, leaving the kingdom to Urien, his brother-in-law. This resolution ends the first movement of the text.

One day, a knight arrives at Arthur's court, the Black Knight of the Black Forest, to press a case against Arthur for the ownership of the Black Forest, which both men claim. The Black Knight defeats thirty-seven of Arthur's knights, but is in turn himself defeated by Meriadoc, who accepts his fealty and restores the forest to him. Meriadoc responds in a similar way to the subsequent appearances of the Red Knight of the Red Forest, and the White Knight of the White Forest.

Meriadoc journeys with his new companions to the court of the emperor of the Alemanni, who is at war with Gundebald, the king of the "land from which no man returns"; Gundebald has kidnapped the emperor's daughter. Meriadoc enrolls as one of the emperor's mercenaries, and is soon leading his men into battle against Saguntius, the chief knight of King Gundebald. After a victorious battle, Meriadoc and some of his men pursue the fleeing Saguntius into a wild forest. Soon night and day seem to be confused, and Meriadoc and his men come upon a splendid castle where none had been before. Entering the castle, they are entertained by a beautiful maiden, but insulted in a bizarre fashion by her steward; they leave the castle in confusion. A great storm then arises, and Meriadoc and his men are forced to take shelter in a strange castle from which, one of their number says, no man returns without shame. They are overcome by a strange fear; Meriadoc alone has the nerve to explore the castle, but he is soon embroiled in a battle in the castle's kitchen with two churls. There is great confusion, and Meriadoc eventually ends up alone in the forest. Gradually, he comes upon various of his men, until the restored band reaches the scene of the battle between the troops of the emperor and those of Gundebald. Meriadoc and his men turn the tide and assure the imperial troops of victory.

Meriadoc now turns to the task of rescuing the emperor's daughter. He arrives at Gundebald's city, pretending to be a knight seeking service. Aided by the gift of a marvelous horse from the emperor's daughter, he defeats Gundebald in single combat and receives the homage of his nobles, in the name of the emperor. The emperor, however, has decided to marry his daughter, promised to Meriadoc should he achieve her rescue, to the king of Gaul, as an attempt to secure peace with that monarch. He pretends to welcome Meriadoc back and to praise his triumphs, but then arraigns him on charges of having raped and impregnated the princess. The strategy backfires, however, because the king of Gaul refuses to take a "whore" in marriage, and believes that the whole affair has been contrived to shame him. He renews his attacks on the emperor. Meanwhile, Meriadoc escapes and joins the ranks of the Gauls. He kills the emperor in battle. The king of Gaul, recognizing who he is, rewards him with the hand of the princess and with all of the territory that he had conquered on the emperor's behalf. Meriadoc founds a royal line, and lives in honor all the days of his life.

While we had to wait for the end of the *De Ortu* for the author to make any statement about his intentions or methods in writing that work, *Meriadoc* opens with such a statement:

> I have thought it fitting to write down a story worthy of remembrance, whose text is decorated with records of such great prowess and attractiveness that, were I to run through each episode in turn, I would turn the sweetness of honey into disgust. Therefore, considering the benefit to my readers, I have set out to restrict it with a concise style, knowing that a brief oration with meaning is more worthy than a prolix, meaningless narration.[2]

The author describes his procedure the same way as he did in the *De Ortu*; he is writing down a *historia*. Here, however, he gives the reader a few more clues as to how and why. The story is worthy to be recalled, and he has set himself the task of recalling it in a form which will be both agreeable and of worth, not plodding through every episode, but selecting and arranging his material with these considerations in mind. The prologue suggests similar vernacular prologues, and again one thinks of *Erec et Enide*, where the poet explains that he has given a *bele conjointure* to his material.[3] The conflict between courtly writers and the popular, oral tellers of vernacular story may lie behind this very rhetorical opening. This sort of prologue is also part of the academic tradition, and the focus on *utilitas* may recall the *accessus ad auctores*, sections of which outline the purpose and qualities of a work. Walter Map's image of the industrious bee-reader is also suggested here. The *Historia Meriadoci* is, then, situated from the start as a work with pretensions to both *doctrina* and *utilitas*, and the evocation of the academic context in the rhetorical set-piece of the

---

[2] *Historia Meriadoci*, ed. Day, p. 2:
  Memoratu dignam dignum duxi exarare historiam, cuius textus tantarum probitatum tantique leporis decoratur titulis, ut, si singula seriatim percurrerem, favi dulcorem in fastidium verterem. Legencium igitur consulens utilitati illam compendioso perstringere stilo statui, sciens quod maioris sit precii brevis cum sensu oracio quam multiflua racione vacans locucio.

[3] Chrétien says that his work "draws a very elegant narrative composition from a tale of adventure" ("tret d'un conte d'avanture/ une molt bele conjointure") (*Erec et Enide*, lines 13–14). The *conjointure* is what distinguishes Chrétien's production from that of popular storytellers.

prologue further suggests the Latinate culture we have been examining.

In the *De Ortu*, a central and serious theme was the question of interpretation, of reading signs correctly. While this question features in the *Historia Meriadoci* as well, albeit approached from a different angle, this work has also a more conventional and easily identified nexus of concerns, focusing on the connected issues of good kingship and law which so interested Geoffrey. It is evident from the plot summary that Meriadoc spends most of his life in the company of less than perfect rulers. Griffin and the emperor of the Alemanni, who bracket his story, are both treacherous and plot against him, and while Arthur acts as the agent of justice in righting Meriadoc's grievance against Griffin, he is himself, in the second movement of the story, shown to be less concerned with justice than one might expect. Indeed, the opening lines of the text, which situate the early part of the story in the time before Arthur's coming, make the tenuous nature of kingship, and perhaps the less than reliable nature of kings, clear: "Now before the time of King Arthur, who obtained the monarchy of all Britain, the island was divided into three parts; that is, Cambria, Albany and Logres. It was subject to the reigns of many kings, and many acquired the rule of the island at the same time as Fortune provided."[4] Like the opening of the *De Ortu*, this passage situates the reader in the place and time of the text. In addition, a note sounds here which echoes throughout *Meriadoc*; that is, the recognition of the role of Fortune in the affairs of men. The recognition is of course a commonplace, but there are reasons for seeing its inclusion at the opening of *Meriadoc* as particularly significant. To open the work with an acknowledgment that this was a time when Fortune controlled the rule of Britain is to create an atmosphere of uncertainty. Such an atmosphere heightens suspense, particularly in the early part of the story; it also, and perhaps more importantly, creates a more general atmosphere of uncertainty which may have implications for the progress of the narrative and the reader's experience of that narrative. This is a text which often seeks to unbalance the reader; the conventional opening, in retrospect at least, paradoxically also warns of the vagaries to come.

---

[4] *Historia Meriadoci*, p. 2: "Igitur ante tempora regis Arturi, qui totius Britannie monarchiam obtinuit, insula tres in partes digesta, Kambriam videlicet Albaniam et Loegriam, plurimorum regum subiacebat imperiis, eiusque quam plures, prout Fortuna rem ministrabat, uno in tempore gubernacula sorciebantur."

Whatever the seeds planted by the opening of the text, *Meriadoc* unfolds briskly and, at first, as a clear condemnation of greed, ambition and evil counsel. Although one could well question Caradoc's decision to resign his kingdom while retaining the style of king – something which failed miserably for Leir, for example – he has been stricken by a mysterious illness, and Meriadoc's later decision to resign his newly regained kingdom to his brother-in-law is not condemned. The focus of this first episode is rather the transformation of Griffin from loyal brother and conscientious regent to treacherous usurper. What is most important is that the "infection of evil"[5] which turns Griffin's thoughts to the crown is fanned into a flame by wicked and ambitious counselors. Court satire often focuses on the ambitions and deceits of courtiers, and the clear message to the ruler in the mirrors for princes is to seek good counsel and eschew bad. Caradoc has made one disastrous decision; Griffin's susceptibility to the arguments of the flatterers of the court will lead to another.

The courtiers are masters of words. As in many of the other works in this study, the concern for appearance and reality, and more particularly for the gap between language and truth, is staged for us in this episode, here specifically in the court context. One can imagine an audience of courtier-clerics both relishing the display of the courtiers' verbal skills, while also perhaps taking home a lesson about the rhetor's responsibility in the public sphere. The author expends his own considerable rhetorical skills in reproducing the courtiers' arguments; this lengthy passage is a brilliant indictment of the manipulation of princes and policy through the manipulation of words:

> [Y]ou should know that the decrepit old man who is your superior is certainly unworthy to lead us, for it is now agreed by almost everyone that he has lost the use of his wits. Indeed, it should be seen as the greatest shame to you that you should be behind him in dignity, you who are distinguished by the same noble lineage and who are known to be the greater in bodily strength and wisdom. Indeed, we have learned, as is already popular rumor, that he has sent for a certain prince of a foreign people to marry his daughter, and he wishes to commit to him the governance of this kingdom committed to you. And should it happen that he enters into this offered marriage, you may take it as certain that he will despoil you

[5] *Historia Meriadoci*, p. 6: ". . . nequicie pestis . . ."

of the honor owed you, and will certainly seize our ancestral estates
... Why then should you allow this foolish old man to live any
longer, when because of this matter we and the whole kingdom are
endangered? Indeed perhaps your mind has suggested to you that
the full right of the kingdom and thus the royal power should be
yours, now and for all time. But surely not unscathed? Is not
Caradoc raising a son who is already, at a tender age, showing
unquestionable signs of wonderful ability to come? Will he not,
when he attains a man's years, claim the paternal realm for himself?
If he cannot attain the crown with your consent, will he not strive
to extort your unwilling consent by force? Thus will follow civil
discord, internal war, slaughter of the citizens, and the desolation of
the country. Order us therefore to send to Tartarus a life which we
judge to be of such imminent danger to us. Behold, the whole
power of the nobility is obedient to you, the power of the whole
realm is ready to your will, if you would merely complete what we
have advised you to do ... give us your assent, and we will
undertake this matter with such cunning, that no suspicion can arise
against you about his death.[6]

The arguments of the counselors are convincingly portrayed. They
open with an appeal to their service to Griffin, and then start to
address his vanity and a sense of injury which he might or might not
yet possess. Caradoc is not named until late in the speech; up to that
point, he is described only in pejorative and depersonalizing epithets.
The counselors shift ground deftly; Caradoc is senile, Caradoc is
planning to seize the estates of Griffin and his nobles, Caradoc's son

---

[6] *Historia Meriadoci*, pp. 6–10:
> ... noveris, hunc decrepitum tibi preponi, quem omnium sensuum iam pene constat
officio privari. Maximo quippe dedecori tibi debet videri, illi te dignitate posteriorem
haberi, qui et eiusdem nobilitatis insigniris linea et cui maior cum virtute corporis
noscitur inesse sapiencia. Iam eciam fama vulgante, comperimus illum ad sue nate
coniugium quendam gentis extranee potentem accivisse regnique gubernacula tibi
commissa ei velle committere. Quem si contigerit sibi oblata inisse connubia, ratum
existimes quod et te debito honore destituet et nobis avita predia prorsus surripiet ...
Cur igitur illum infatuatum senem diucius sinis vivere, cuius causa et nos et tocius
regni statum patet periclitari? Verum tua tibi mens fortassis applaudit, omne ius
regium ac omne semper sicut nunc tibi regni cessurum negocium. Sed numquid
impune? Nonne Caradoco educatur filius quem eciam nunc etas tenella mire probitatis
futurum certis manifestat indiciis? Nonne, cum viriles annos attigerit, sibi paternum
vendicabit principatum? Cuius apicem si te consentaneo assequi non potuerit,
numquid tibi invito vi extorquere non laborabit? Hinc civilis discordia, intestinum
bellum, cedes civium, patrieque proveniet desolacio. Iube igitur ad Tartara dirigi cuius
vitam nobis tanto perpendimus imminere discrimini. Ecce universa manus procerum
tibi subditur, omnis regni potestas tue voluntati exponitur, si id dumtaxat perfeceris,
quod tibi a nobis consulitur ... tuum assensum tribue, et nos eo rem moliemur
ingenio, quo nulla tibi de eius nece possit oriri suspicio.

will claim the kingdom and provoke a civil war. The concerns are familiar from Geoffrey's work; the counselors invoke the same need for a stable central government. There is, indeed, an apparent logic to the sequence of events, but only if one accepts the first, unacceptable premise; that Griffin should overthrow his brother. John of Salisbury allows for the deposition of a secular tyrant, but there is no indication, outside the words of the counselors, that Caradoc is such a tyrant. Deception occurs first in this text, then, not through a misinterpretation of conventional signs, but rather through a deliberate misappropriation of the language of counsel and of the structures of formal speech. The irresistible cadences, the rhetorical questions, the dramatic turn to the imagined civil discord, all make the counselors' case seem very compelling. The lengthy speech is followed by a terse "What more?";[7] the contrast between the elaboration of the persuasion and the completeness of the capitulation provides a stylistic underpinning of the central issue of the pernicious effect of bad counsel.

This section of the text also addresses the *De Ortu*'s concern with the correct interpretation of signs, and as was the case in that work, the king here refuses to believe the signs as they are correctly interpreted for him by his queen. While Griffin is accepting bad counsel, Caradoc is refusing good counsel. When Caradoc dreams that his brother is sharpening arrows in the forest, his queen has no difficulty reading the signs: "Indeed, arrows portend treachery."[8] Like Gwendoloena in the *De Ortu*, the queen is able to see what her husband cannot, and in both texts it appears that the king is almost willfully blind. Caradoc's refusal to heed his wife's warning delivers him to fate; he goes to hunt "as the fates were leading him";[9] and his murder is described in the phrase, "when king Caradoc had been given over to fate."[10] In the *De Ortu*, Arthur received no worse than a drenching for ignoring his wife's prophecy; here the unwillingness of a king to take good counsel has a fatal result, in two senses. Thus the opening episode of the *Meriadoc* introduces the audience to two ways in which one can be deceived; the first through a manipulation of language (which is itself a system of signs) and the second through a refusal to read signs which are obvious to others. In both cases, the

---

[7] *Historia Meriadoci*, p. 10: "Quid multa?"
[8] *Historia Meriadoci*, p. 12: "Insidias quippe portendunt sagitte."
[9] *Historia Meriadoci*, p. 12: ". . . ut fata eum ducebant . . ."
[10] *Historia Meriadoci*, p. 18: "Rege igitur Caradoc fatis dato . . ."

deception is something in which the deceived cooperates. One is reminded of the collusion of British kings with fate in the *Historia*; in both works, pride or selfishness in a king – the fact that the self-deceived are rulers with power over others – has murderous rather than humorous consequences.

There are other elements of the first portion of the text which suggest that its main concerns are political, and indeed, there is much here to recall Geoffrey's concerns in the *Historia* – both the *De Ortu* and the *Historia Meriadoci* make some use of that text. Griffin's public grief recalls Vortigern's: "he feigned grief by tearing his clothes and ripping out his hair; he shed tears copiously, but it was joy rather than grief which brought forth those tears."[11] Griffin's coronation occurs "in the absence of and without the knowledge of the nobility,"[12] reminding one of Geoffrey's concern for right rule and emphasizing again that the evil counselors have presented themselves deceptively as the guardians of the rights of the nobility. The plans of the loyal nobility to protect Caradoc's children also stress right rule and domestic tranquillity: "Thus peace would be secured, and the future harmony of the country, and no noble would dare to take to himself the rule of the kingdom, while these [children] to whom the governance of the kingdom belonged remained in the public eye."[13] And when, at last, Meriadoc is restored to his rightful realm by King Arthur, the legality of the action is underscored by the text's emphasis on the consent, not just of the nobles of the realm, but of Arthur as well: "the dominion was passed to Meriadoc by the whole nobility of Cambria and with the assent of King Arthur."[14] Thus the legal and political concerns of this part of the text are carried through to its end. The concern for law and right rule is the frame within which the fantastic elements of the romance proper must be understood.

Griffin's usurpation is the first movement of the text; the second echoes many of the themes raised by the first. The emperor of the Alemanni receives less treatment than does Griffin, but he provides another example of the treachery of rulers and the manipulation of

[11] *Historia Meriadoci*, p. 16: ". . . scissa veste, abruptisque capillis, luctum simulavit, lacrimas ubertim effudit, set ipsas lacrimas pocius gaudium quam dolor extorquebat."
[12] *Historia Meriadoci*, p. 18: ". . . proceribus absentibus et nescientibus . . ."
[13] *Historia Meriadoci*, p. 24: "Sic pacem firmandam, patrie concordiam futuram, principum nullumque ius regni sibi vendicare ausurum, dum hii in medio consisterent, ad quos regni respiciebat gubernacio."
[14] *Historia Meriadoci*, p. 68: ". . . universe primatus Kambrie, rege Arturo annuente, Meriadoci cessit dominio."

speech, particularly public speech, to achieve dishonorable ends. Courtiers are not the only ones who are skilled with words; Henry II's delight in disputing with his advisors reminds us that a king can also be master of the art. Here, the emperor has entered into a contract with Meriadoc; Meriadoc has fulfilled his part of the contract, but the emperor hopes to renege on his part of the pact in the interests of political expediency. The text makes it clear that, while Meriadoc has entered into the agreement in good faith, the emperor has not: "for he had entered into this pact with him as if it were a joke."[15] The emperor's deceitful speech to his court, then, a speech which stresses mutual obligations and legal concerns, is particularly ironic. As he did with respect to Griffin's wicked counselors, the author uses this long speech to demonstrate the power of words to deceive and to obscure the right:

> This Meriadoc is the subject of my speech, and who he in fact is; he whom I have welcomed coming before me, whom I would have raised to a high level of honor should he have proved worthy enough. For first I accepted him as a paid soldier among the number of my household; thence I preferred him above all my warriors, soldiers and stipendiaries alike; I gave him my ear and my counsel; I also handed the most excellent provinces over to him to rule, the greater part of which I intended to confer on him, both for his virtue and for the redounding to my own glory, and indeed I admit that he has sweated strenuously over many tasks for me. Nevertheless I ask, whose strength won all this? Was it not mine? Is he not the victor through the strength of my army? Whose wealth supported the venture? Was it not from my treasury that wages were offered to his soldiers? Indeed, he conquered two kingdoms. But how? Through battle with my army. He also rescued my daughter from the hands of Gundebald. But how? Through the industry of that very daughter. Therefore, he has done nothing without my help. And nevertheless I would have shown my liberality and munificence to him . . . had not a crime of this man's intervened so that my intent was diverted . . . It shames me to make his shame known; nevertheless, unless it is made known to you, it cannot be known: without my knowledge, he has forced and raped my daughter, whom he knew was to have been betrothed by me in the royal manner and, as I think, as her swelling abdomen announces, he has left her pregnant. His crime exceeds my generosity, and he has prostituted her for himself, who ought herself to

---

[15] *Historia Meriadoci*, p. 184: "Ideoque pactum huiusmodi quasi pro ridiculo cum eo inierit."

have been betrothed untouched. I place my complaint before you, then, awaiting what your judgment, as justice dictates, shall decree in this matter.[16]

The legal language, as well as the carefully crafted rhetoric of the piece, would certainly appeal to an audience of courtier-bureaucrats. The speech culminates by stressing justice, and the placing of justice in the hands of the people. If these might be ideals for the audience of the work, then the fact that the speech is deceptive is all the more striking.

As did Griffin's counselors, the emperor builds an airtight case which depends on a single lie, or at least on a misrepresentation. The text does not say that the emperor's final charge is true, although it does indicate that Meriadoc, as the emperor had planned, has indeed embraced the willing princess in secret.[17] Day assumes that the princess is in fact pregnant;[18] I would argue that the ambiguity is both intentional and important here, as the emperor attempts to manipulate public opinion to achieve what the audience of the text knows in any case to be wrong. In the *De Ortu*, the counselors were manipulating someone who, we suspect, wished to be so manipulated – the self-deceived, as I have labelled Griffin also. Here, the emperor seeks to deceive a public judicial tribunal in order to achieve a perversion of

---

[16] *Historia Meriadoci*, pp. 198–200:

> Argumentum mee oracioni hic qui adest Meriadocus existit, quem quam favorabiliter ad me adventantem exceperim, ad quante dignitatis gradus sublimaverim satis habetur compertum. Primum namque ex stipendario in numero meorum familiarium eum accivi; deinde gregariis universis et stipendiariis militibus meis prefeci; auricularem et consiliarium meum constitui; preclaras illi quoque provincias ad regendum tradidi; hiisqui [sic] satis maiora ei conferre proposui, tum ob illius virtutem, tum quod id mee glorie rebar comparere, quidem strenuum eum fateor multisque pro me sudasse laboribus. Verumptamen queso cuius tociens triumphavit viribus? Nonne meis? Nonne robore mei exercitus victor exstitit? Cuius est suffultus diviciis? Nonne suis ex meo erario stipendia prebebantur militibus? Duo quidem regna subegit. Sed quomodo? Decertante meo exercitu. Natam quoque meam de manibus Gundebaldi excussit. Sed per quid? Per industriam mee ipsius filie. Nichil ergo absque meo egit amminiculo. Ut tamen meam in eo liberalitatem et munificenciam ostenderem . . . nisi scelus ipsius intervenisset quod me a meo divertit proposito . . . Pudet me meimet ipsius proferre verecundiam; nisi tamen proferatur a vobis, sciri non potest: filiam meam, quam me more regio desponsaturum noverat, me insciente, oppressit, violavit, et, ut puto, sicut venter tumescens innuit, gravidam reliquit. Meam munificenciam sua prevenit nequicia, illamque sibi prostituit que sibi illibata desponsare debuit. Apud vos igitur meam depono querelam, expectaturus quid vestra super hoc censura, equitate dictante, censeat.

[17] *Historia Meriadoci*, p. 196.

[18] Mildred Leake Day, "*Historia Meriadoci* and *Arthur and Gorlagon*: Two Arthurian Tales in a Unique Fifteenth-Century Collection of Latin Romances," *Fifteenth-Century Studies* 17 (1990), 69.

justice, and to sanction the breaking of a contract. The particular interest in contracts may have to do with the fact that the Angevin period sees a significant solidifying of English legal practices; I discuss below the possible reflection of specific legal reforms or innovations in a central episode of the *Historia Meriadoci*. What we see here, in the emperor's ready manipulation of speech and thus of his subjects, is perhaps one of the dangers inherent in the figure of the *rex litteratus*. An education is necessary for a king to read and understand the laws, but the education can be a dangerous weapon in the hands of king or courtier, when the will is evil.

The emperor stresses the need for reciprocity in contracts, yet he misrepresents Meriadoc's behavior; it is significant that this speech comes after an even more technical one in which Meriadoc refuses the rule of Gundebald's kingdom, offered him by Gundebald's nobility. He explains that he is the emperor's man, and indeed echoes the emperor's contention that what he has done, has been done at the emperor's instigation:

> . . . because he was a soldier of the emperor; because the enemy had been subdued by the emperor's order; because he had undertaken the labor in this matter so that he could free the daughter of the emperor from captivity; because whatever he had acquired in those regions he ascribed to the power and the name of the emperor; because the emperor was to give his daughter to him in matrimony, should he be able to seize her from the hands of Gundebald . . . [19]

Note that these are the emperor's arguments, with the crucial difference that Meriadoc is upholding his half of the bargain scrupulously. The emperor, on the other hand, bolsters his deception, not only with impressive rhetorical periods, but also with repeated reference to uncovering the truth of matters. He promises to reveal who Meriadoc "really is"; he reiterates the need to "make known" what Meriadoc has done; and he closes with reference to a piece of visual evidence which is never actually presented, the "announcement" made by the daughter's swelling womb. Again, the author works to demonstrate the manipulation of conventions of both language and law which leads to an incorrect interpretation of the

---

[19] *Historia Meriadoci*, p. 186:
> . . . quod miles sit imperatoris; quod ab eo ad subiugandos hostes directus; quod hiis rebus maxime suam operam adhibuerit, ut filiam imperatoris a captivitate excuteret; quod quicquid illis in regionibus adquisisset viribus et nomini imperatoris ascriberet; quod imperator sibi filiam se in matrimonio daturum, si eam e Gundebaldi posset manibus eripere, spoponderit . . .

thing as it is; of who Meriadoc really is, of what he has really done. It is nicely ironic that the emperor's success in this endeavor is also his downfall; the king of Gaul believes the story and refuses to go through with the marriage, and Meriadoc wins out in the end. Thus his career, or rather that portion of it which we are offered, is bracketed by exposure to the sophisticated manipulations in the political realm which he is himself destined to enter.

Confirmation of the text's central concern with rule and law is to be found in the Arthurian portion of the text; as was the case in the *De Ortu*, King Arthur is implicated in the exploration of this theme. Yet while in the *De Ortu* Arthur's willful refusal to read signs aright even when they are manifest to him led to humor, in *Meriadoc* the aligning of Arthur with Griffin and the emperor, at least in the matter of bad faith and the perversion of justice, seems to have more serious implications.

Meriadoc's conventional desire to seek his fortune at the court of the famous King Arthur soon has unexpected consequences, embroiling him in an affair which, despite a touch of strangeness, seems again designed to underline the text's central concern with law and with royal obligations and imperfections in that regard. The case presented by the Black Knight of the Black Forest for his rights in that forest certainly seems as tenable as do Arthur's counter arguments. Both cases are presented in legalistic terms; this is the case even for the Knight's final arguments, which offer an interesting juxtaposition of the doggedly literal and the quite fantastic:

> "Nevertheless, o king," he said, "if the settlement of this controversy depends on the outcome of these proceedings, it seems to me that the judgment of justice will assent more with me, for as a result of this same Black Forest I am tinged with ancestral blackness, and my name, the Black Knight of the Black Forest, is given to me from the name of the Black Forest."[20]

The fantastic elements of this situation will be discussed below; what is important here is the consequence of the presentation of the cases. The general concern for language, for its manipulation through rhetoric, and for the consequences of such manipulation on the rule

---

[20] *Historia Meriadoci*, p. 70:
"Verumptamen," ait, "O rex, si ex rerum eventu huius controversie consistat probacio, mihi nempe censura iusticie pocius assentire videbitur, qui et ex ipsius Nigri Saltus effectu avita suffundar nigredine et Niger Miles de Nigro Saltu ex ipsius Nigri Saltus mihi nomen dirivetur nomine."

of law, may have here as well a specific focus, suggesting not just an audience of courtier-clerics, but a specifically Angevin audience.

Henry II's policy of restoring the royal demesne upon his assumption of the crown is an historical fact which might lie behind this curious episode. The forest laws which Henry enacted in this pursuit were among the most controversial of his reign; it was under Henry that the royal forest reached its maximum extent.[21] A landowner, secular or religious, whose lands fell within the royal forest would find himself prohibited from hunting or cutting timber on what he thought of as his own lands, and Henry was not averse to using the forests to generate wealth; for example, he suspended the forest laws during the war of 1173–74, and, once the rebellion had been crushed, reversed his policy and collected huge fines. Richard Mortimer argues, in fact, that "it seems to have been the arbitrary nature of forest law as well as its ruthless application by foresters that made it particularly hated."[22] Certainly the Black Knight here invokes customary right against the innovation of Arthur's claim on the forest, and his response, when the king commits the quarrel to the judgment of the lords, suggests a cynical view of jury trial as mere window-dressing:

> Indeed, the Black Knight of the Black Forest, not doubting that they would reach a decision which would grant greater benefit to the king than to him, concluded that it would be more sensible and fitting to settle the case about which he had brought suit by his own strength than to commit it to the suspect judgment of others, when he knew that whatever judgment should be offered by the judges would be fixed and immutable. Therefore he jumped up in the middle of the council and said, "Since, O king, I see that you are acting against me in this case, I do not dare commit myself to the judgment of these men, whom I know without a doubt will decide rather for you than for me."[23]

---

[21] Charles R. Young, *The Royal Forests of Medieval England* (Philadelphia: University of Pennsylvania Press, 1979), p. 19. Young notes the many recorded complaints against Alan de Neville, the chief forester, and the many fines assessed by him, as evidence of the vigor of Henry's forest policy.

[22] Mortimer, *Angevin England*, p. 45.

[23] *Historia Meriadoci*, p. 72:

Verum Niger Miles de Nigro Saltu, illos quod magis regis gracie cederet quam quod ad suum profectum proveniret decreturos non dubitans, sanius et decencius esse duxit, id quod sui iuris calumpniabatur constare suis viribus disracionare quam suspecto aliorum arbitrio committere, dum ratum et inmutabilie [sic] sciebat futurum quicquid iudicii protulisset examen. Ergo coram omni concilio medius prosiliit et "Quia," ait, "O rex, te mihi ex adverso huic cause patrocinari conspicio, istorum me

From 1179, a defendant in a case of land right could opt for trial by jury, although the older system of trial by battle was still in place as well. In deciding to opt for a judicial duel, the Black Knight obviously expresses his lack of confidence in the judgment of men – is this distrust of a recent legal innovation? Henry had developed a procedure for disputes over land in which a jury based its verdict on local knowledge;[24] such knowledge ought, in the case of the Black Knight, to confirm his case, because his own argument rests on the hereditary right implied by his name and color. However, the Black Knight is in conflict with the king over a forest, and the Black Knight's words, along with Arthur's actions, remind us just how little constraint there is upon the king in such circumstances. W.L. Warren singles out the forest law as the problem around which the developing Angevin legal system was built:

> . . . the revelation that in court circles forest law was criticised, is a reminder that it was Henry's government itself which taught men to recognise the defects within it. The precision, sophistication, and impartiality of exchequer law and common law sharpened the contrast with the arbitrariness of forest law, and showed up in stark nakedness when the King acted at will to disseise, distrain upon, or imprison a man.[25]

It seems likely, then, that this contemporary concern is reflected in the portrayal of the Black Knight's claim, and the slightly fantastic element of the story may in part be a protective strategy intended to distance the implied criticism of royal abuse of power. The fact that the Black Knight finally, after thirty-seven victories against lesser knights, loses to Meriadoc might seem to suggest that the judgment of heaven favors the king after all, and that the Knight's strictures on royal justice need not be taken seriously. And yet Meriadoc delivers an astonishing rebuke to Arthur after his victory:

> He said, "You have vexed many of your men through this matter, which I have brought to an end by my service. Lo, you have what you desired, you possess what you falsely claimed, you have settled that concerning which you disputed. Therefore act liberally, as befits a liberal man towards a liberal man, so that by your grace to me the free possession of the Black Forest may be restored to him,

iudicio committere non audeo, quos procul dubio quod tibi pocius quam mihi succedat decreturos agnosco."

[24] Mortimer, *Angevin England*, p. 56.
[25] Warren, *Henry II*, p. 395.

who complains that he has lost it because of me. For in this matter, the whole sum of my request is that a noble man should not be deprived of his right, whose honor should rather be augmented than diminished."[26]

Meriadoc sets himself up as the one to restore the right, and Arthur continues to sink in the reader's estimation by comparison when he refuses to grant Meriadoc's request. It is only when Arthur's whole council urges him to accept Meriadoc's terms that he agrees. The court in fact pressures the king to do the right thing.

The incident with the Black Knight is similar to the episode which makes up the second half of the Middle English poem, the *Awntyrs off Arthure at the Terne Wathelyne*.[27] In that text, a Scottish knight named Galeron arrives at Arthur's court with a land claim against Arthur; Arthur has won lands from him in war with "wrang wile,"[28] and given them to Gawain. Gawain takes the offered duel and wins it, but agrees that the land in question should be restored to the Scottish knight. It seems that Gawain and Guenevere, who pleads with her husband to end the fight, are mindful of an encounter with the ghost of Guenevere's mother in the first part of the text. In that encounter, Guenevere's mother casts Arthur in the negative role of unjust conqueror, as this exchange demonstrates:

> "How shal we fare," quod þe freke, "þat fonden to fight,
> And þus defoulen þe folke on fele kinges londes,
> And riches ouer reymes withouten eny right,

---

[26] *Historia Meriadoci*, p. 94:

> "Multos tuorum," ait, "huius rei examinacione vexasti que mei est terminata obsequio. Ecce, habes quod optasti, possides quod calumpniabaris, decrevisti unde certabas. Age ergo liberaliter, ut liberalem decet in liberalem virum, ut mei gracia Nigri Saltus illi libera restituatur possessio, quam se mei causa desiderasse conqueritur. In hoc enim tota mee summa peticionis consistit, ne suo iure nobilem virum contingat destitui, cuius probitas pocius exigit augeri quam minui."

Day translates "calumnio" in a neutral sense, as "to institute action." The deponent verb is usually recorded only in the pejorative use (Lewis and Short), although there does seem to be a trend, in instances recorded in Latham, towards a neutral use of the nouns. It nevertheless seems to me that the negative context in which the verb occurs is intended to confirm that the case has been unjust all along.

[27] There are four surviving manuscripts of this poem; the Thornton MS (c. 1430–40), Douce 324 (c. 1460–80), the Ireland MS (in which the romances were added about 1450 or 1460), and Lambeth Palace MS 491 (first half of the fifteenth century). Helen Phillips has recently suggested that the three-fitt structure of the poem in the Ireland manuscript may in fact best reflect the central theme of the text; the central fitt in that structure concentrates on Arthur's use (and abuse) of power; see Helen Phillips, "*The Awntyrs off Arthure*: Structure and Meaning. A Reassessment," *Arthurian Literature* 12 (1993), 73–74.

[28] *The Awntyrs off Arthure at the Terne Wathelyne*, ed. Ralph Hanna III (Manchester: Manchester University Press, 1974), line 421.

Wynnen worshipp and wele þorgh wightnesse of hondes?"
"Your king is to couetous, I warne þe sir kniȝt.
May no man stere him with strength while þe whele stondes.
Whan he is in his magesté, moost in his miȝt,
He shal light ful lowe on þe sesondes.
And ȝour chiualrous king chef shall a chaunce:
False Fortune in fight,
That wonderfull whelewright,
Makes lordes lowe to liȝt."[29]

This rebuke makes Galeron's later assertion, that Arthur has won his lands through wrongful means, more convincing, and the text seems indeed to concern itself with the legal question of right to land, on both the local and the international scale. The doubt expressed in the *Historia Meriadoci* about the efficacy of trial by combat remains here. In both texts, one sees that power can, at least temporarily, thwart the right. However, just as William of Rennes asserts that God thwarted Arthur's grand plan to bring Rome under his own dominion, here too a warning is delivered: conquest is a dangerous and ephemeral business. Those who enter into this activity are putting themselves at the mercy of Fortune, who is notoriously capricious. She is also, perhaps, an instrument for punishing excess.

With the *Awntyrs*, we may have moved quite a distance from the world of courtly Latin writing, but the use of tale-telling for the delivery of complaint and admonition remains in this new linguistic and social context. And in some ways, this context might not be so very different from the twelfth-century one. Susan Crane has argued for close links between Anglo-Norman and Middle English romances, based in part on their common assertion of baronial rights to land and lineage. It is significant that these romances, unlike the chronicle tradition, concern themselves with the rights of barons rather than kings; Crane argues that "Whereas the chronicles justify the power of rulers in England openly, the romances argue for the rights of vassals covertly, under the cloak of imagination and invention."[30] While chronicle texts, both Latin and vernacular, can in fact offer criticism of the abuse of royal power, Crane's argument shows

---

[29] *The Awntyrs off Arthure*, lines 261–72.
[30] Crane, *Insular Romance*, pp. 15–16. Crane is here discussing Anglo-Norman texts, but will later argue that the concerns of Anglo-Norman and English barons are very similar, leading to a continuity between these groups of texts.

how it is that a Middle English text of the later fourteenth century could reflect the concerns of a Latin work of the twelfth.

The *Awntyrs* uses the props of romance – knights and ladies, scenes of aristocratic life, even a mysterious otherworldly encounter – to deliver, through the *memento mori* tone of the first half of the text, a moral message about just conduct in this world. The text is in part a sermon *exemplum* decked out in romance dress, presumably to make the whole more appealing.[31] It may also function, as I have argued many of my Latin texts do, as a mirror for princes, or at least, as a voice of complaint. And as is the case for *Meriadoc*, there might once more be a genuine legal issue behind the tale. The *quo warranto* proceedings of Edward I, more than a century after Henry II's exploitation of forest law, caused comparable concern among the nobles of the realm, as the king's lawyers required landowners to produce documentary evidence showing possession of their land. Whether this specific context would remain in mind by the time the *Awntyrs* was written is unclear,[32] although the story of the Earl Warenne's defiance of Edward's commissioners seems to have acquired the status of popular myth.[33] What is clear, is that both the *Awntyrs* and the *Historia Meriadoci* have as a central concern the behavior of a king and of his court, in a specifically legal context.

The Black Knight episode of *Meriadoc*, like the whole of the *Awntyrs*, has a moral and political message to deliver through a romantic episode.[34] The heroic king is shown in a decidedly bad light and the mechanisms of human justice are shown to be flawed, in that the Knight cannot trust a court case, and loses a judicial duel when he probably was in fact in the right.[35] The ways in which Arthur is undercut here – the slighting tone of Meriadoc's speech, Arthur's

---

[31] The ghost of Guenevere's mother, who appears in the first half of the poem, speaks in the aphorisms of sermon literature:

> For al þi fressh foroure,
> Muse on þi mirrour;
> For king and emperour,
> Thus diȝt shul ye be.

(*The Awntyrs off Arthure*, lines 166–69).

[32] The text is probably to be dated to the latter half of the fourteenth century.

[33] The story and its implications are discussed by Clanchy, *From Memory to Written Record*, pp. 35–43.

[34] Day notes the parallel with the *Awntyrs*, and suggests that perhaps *Meriadoc* was a source for the *Awntyrs*, noting that there was at least one manuscript of *Meriadoc* in England at the time the *Awntyrs* was written, and that the second was copied close to this period (*Historia Meriadoci*, p. xxxviii).

[35] Day cites the concern over the legitimacy of the judicial duel in *Meriadoc* as one of her arguments for dating. Opposition to the custom began as early as the eleventh century, and

error in refusing to believe the watchman and, in retrospect, the similarities between Arthur's conduct and that of Griffin and the emperor – suggest that at this point in the text, the intention is to subvert Arthur's heroic status, perhaps as a way of driving home the point about the imperfection of human and specifically regal institutions. Certainly were *Meriadoc* to close here, one might well conclude that kings in general, and perhaps even Arthur in particular, are the text's primary target.

There is, however, another level to the text which is equally, if not more, striking, and which complicates the question of the thrust of the text considerably. Just as the *De Ortu*, developing as an historical *enfances* of Gawain, manifested unexpected stylistic and philosophical challenges which resulted in difficulty in "naming" the text, so too does *Meriadoc* display features which serve to complicate rather than to simplify the task of interpretation. Romance elements – characters, settings, pattern of incidents – abound in *Meriadoc*, and in contexts which often lead one to suspect parody. As was the case in the *De Ortu*, while there are instances of this interest throughout the text, the first movement of the plot is rather more straightforward than the second, and in both cases it is during the Arthurian portion of the text that most of the oddities manifest themselves. Nevertheless, just as there was the Greek fire episode in the first movement of the *De Ortu*, perhaps to alert us to what was to come, there are strange moments in the first part of the *Meriadoc* too. The fact that there seem to be rather more of these is the result of *Meriadoc's* greater concentration on such moments and the problems they raise throughout.

A case in point is the account of the exile of Meriadoc, Orwen, Ivor and Morwen in the forest. The author notes that this exile lasts for five years, and, in what appears to be a desire to leave no loose end untied, he addresses the question of food:

> Ivor sought game through hunting, which conquered hunger, and a spring offered water. They were also able to find nuts and forest fruits and other plants which were edible; collected in autumn and stored, these provided food. Ivor and Meriadoc went hunting and birdcatching daily, while his wife Morwen, taking the girl Orwen with her, busied herself in collecting fruit and herbs.[36]

was common in the twelfth; the Lateran Council of 1215 banned the practice absolutely (*Historia Meriadoci*, pp. xiv–xv).
[36] *Historia Meriadoci*, p. 40:

There is nothing particularly remarkable about this passage, although the reader of romance might be surprised to find even this much attention to domestic arrangements. One does begin to wonder, however, if the desire to cover all the angles is not getting rather out of hand when the author remarks, "But it may be asked how they prepared meat for food for themselves, when they had neither fire nor pots in which it could be cooked."[37] Whether this would indeed be asked is itself a question; the ensuing explanation is not as long, complicated, or ridiculous as the Greek fire passage, but it certainly has the same effect of stopping the narrative cold. Why is it here?

On the one hand, this author seems always to want to explain things, to displace even this story, which is more overtly romantic than is the *De Ortu*, in the direction of realism. This tendency may be a response to anticipated criticism. At the same time, this sort of passage may represent an attempt to undercut traditional marvelous narrative, with its lack of concern for the details of real life. By reversing the normal narrative procedure, then, the author draws attention to that procedure. As in the *De Ortu*, the audience's awareness of conventions is thus invoked in order to produce a distance from the text, a distance in which a more critical attitude towards the genre and its assumptions may flourish. It is of course also possible that the author simply came across this information somewhere, as he did the ingredients in the Greek fire recipe, and desired to fit it in to his text. Detailed practical information occasionally occurs in romances; one thinks of the breaking of the deer in *Sir Gawain and the Green Knight,* or of the elaborate hunting scenes in that work and in the *Awntyrs off Arthure.* There is a difference, however, in that the hunting information concerns an aristocratic activity, whereas it could be argued that the cooking information belongs to a more lowly milieu, and thus deflates the aristocratic (and escapist) tone more typical of chivalric romance.[38] An accumulation of evidence, rather than any single instance, is however necessary if

---

Ferina caro quam venatu conquirebat cibum, latex haustum prebebat. Nuces quoque pomaque silvestria et ceteri fructus qui inibi inveniri poterant, autumpnali collecti tempore et reconditi, alimento serviebant. Ivorius cum Meriadoco venatum et aucupatum cotidie pergebat; Morwen vero, uxor eius, puella Orwen secum assumpta, in colligendo fructus vel herbas occupabatur.

[37] *Historia Meriadoci*, p. 40: "Set hic fortassis queritur quomodo sibi carnes ad esum paraverint, dum et ignis et vasa quibus elixari possent defuerint."

[38] If *Meriadoc* bears some relationship to the Havelok/Horn romances, then this sort of passage may be less surprising; the details of fishing and wrestling in those stories are certainly earthy. Yet the Havelok/Horn stories are in the vernacular, and have often been seen as

one is to argue convincingly for moments of deliberate subversion in either of these Latin romances. *Meriadoc* does indeed provide many more such moments.

The most notably bizarre episode in the first movement of the plot is Ivor's rescue of the children Meriadoc and Orwen from the execution which Griffin has ordered for them. Griffin orders twelve men to take the children into the forest of Arglud and hang them (with thin ropes), returning only when the bodies have fallen to the ground. The plan itself seems rather involved. The executioners take advantage of the odd requirements when, taking pity on the children, they decide to hang them with ropes so thin that they will break before the children are dead. Thus they can fulfill the letter of Griffin's orders without actually killing the children; the children are hanged, and the executioners stand aside, "staying to watch the children, as they had been ordered."[39] As for Ivor's plan of attack, it is positively baroque. Apparently unnoticed, he lays four large fires at the corners of the grove, throws meat into them, and climbs into a holly tree, with his wife and his dog, to wait. The smoke attracts wolves; soon there are some two thousand of them. The executioners, understandably, panic at this sight, and take refuge in the hollow bore of the oak tree. Ivor wounds some of the wolves, in order to whip them up into a frenzy. He then drives the wolves away with a blast from his hunting horn and builds a fire at the entrance to the tree. While all of this is happening, the text pauses twice for parenthetical remarks on the habits of wolves: "For it is their habit, always to fight where they see a fire, and with claws and teeth they dismember any one of their number who happens to be wounded. For wolves fear nothing as much as arrows and the sound of horns. For this reason they rarely or never wound hunters."[40] There is, then, an odd mix here of the factual and the strange, and indeed the factual is introduced as if to explain the strange, although the original configuration of Griffin's plan is never explained. Ivor's plan, for its part, becomes more and more involved.

---

among the simpler products of the vernacular; the language of *Meriadoc* alone requires a very different sort of audience.

[39] *Historia Meriadoci*, p. 30: ". . . ut sibi imperatum fuerat, observantes residebant."

[40] *Historia Meriadoci*, p. 34:
> Consuetudinis enim est illis, illo quo ignem perceperint semper contendere, eumque quem e sui numero sauciari contigerit unguibus et dentibus discerpere.
> Nichil enim adeo lupi quam sagittas et tubarum metuunt strepitum. Unde eciam raro aut numquam venatoribus lesionem inferunt.

The executioners, penned in the tree, finally ask for mercy, and Ivor allows them to emerge one by one through the low opening. As each one crawls out, Ivor cuts off his head in a scene of grisly humor:

> When he had stuck his neck out [of the hole], Ivor, standing to one side of the opening to the hollow, drew his sword and cut off his head. And pulling the headless body out, he cried, "Come out of there! Hurry up, come out! What's keeping you?" And one after another they all came out, and Ivor cut the head off each one as he came out.[41]

The elaborate strategy and the grim humor may suggest Celtic literature; in the second branch of the *Mabinogi*, for example, Efnisien crushes the heads of Irishmen concealed in ambush in bags of flour, quipping all the while. Certainly the Celtic flavor of some of *Meriadoc*'s fantastic elements has been remarked.[42]

The intricacy of the execution and Ivor's plan for foiling it seem unnecessary,[43] the latter especially when we have been told that the executioners have already decided that they do not want to kill the children. Ivor, of course, knows nothing of their intentions, but rather judges the scene on the basis of its appearance. Thus we return to the issue central to the *De Ortu*, and the author shows again the complexity of attempts at interpretation; here the executioners, who want to do the right thing while appearing to do the wrong thing, suffer as a result of the very appearance they present, and lose their lives. One can hardly blame Ivor for his interpretation of the scene; he, like the centurion in the *De Ortu*, is both wrong and right at the same time.

In addition to these two strange scenes, the opening section of *Meriadoc* also includes romantic reflexes which, while not remarkable

---

[41] *Historia Meriadoci*, pp. 36–38:
> Qui cum cervicem extulisset, Ivorius a foris e latere spelunce consistens, evaginato gladio, ei caput amputavit. Truncumque ad se cadaver extrahens, "Exite hinc! propere hinc," exclamat, "exite! Quid moramini?" Unus igitur post unum omnes egressi sunt, singulisque egredientibus Ivorius caput abscidit.

[42] By Ernst Brugger, for example, in his "Zu Historia Meriadoci und De Ortu Walwanii," *Zeitung für französische Sprache und Literatur* 46 (1923), 247–80, 406–40; he is in fact convinced that the author is a Welshman (435).

[43] Mullen notes similarities between this episode and the Hroar-Helgi story as told in Saxo; there, the children of slaves are killed and torn up to make it appear that wolves have eaten them, and the other children are hidden in a hollow tree, and food is brought to them every day on the pretense that they are dogs ("A Critical Study," p. 16). It is of course possible that there are roots to this episode which are no longer perfectly understood by the author; Day suggests that there may be elements of ritual sacrifice behind the death ordered for the children (*Historia Meriadoci*, p. xxvii).

in themselves, become so in their context. One may dismiss the passage on cooking in the wilderness, and perhaps even the complex rescue of the children, as examples of an almost obsessive authorial desire to neaten the plot; but what is one to make of the sudden abandonment of this method almost immediately after the careful description of survival in the forest? When Meriadoc and Orwen have been carried off by Kay and Urien respectively, Morwen and Ivor's reactions both illustrate and undermine romance commonplaces, through incongruous juxtaposition with the preceding passages and through manipulation of the time scheme. First, overcome with grief, they mourn for two years, barely eating or drinking. Then,

> Two years had passed, when one day, when they were going over what had happened with each other, Morwen said, "Why do we stay here alone? We fled here because of the children; so that we could save their lives, we have stayed here until now; since they have been taken away and we want to get them back, what's keeping us here?"[44]

This change of heart is, in its context, quite abrupt. It is of course necessary that the narrative move along to its next stage, but what follows serves to underline the odd juxtaposition of Ivor and Morwen's grief, their inaction, and their sudden call to action. Morwen vows to eschew pleasure or rest until she has found Orwen; a typical vow of its sort, but strange in coming after two years of inactivity. Furthermore, it becomes clear that she knows where to seek Orwen; she heard Kay call Urien by name and promise to meet him in Scotland. It soon transpires that Ivor, for his part, also knows where to find Meriadoc; he has recognized Kay from the time he has spent at Arthur's court. It is not unusual in romance narrative for one episode to follow another quite abruptly, or for a considerable passage of time to be contained within a few lines. Here, however, the shift from almost obsessive explanation to abrupt statement, as well as the intensity of the emotions described, draw attention to the incongruity of the narrative transition, so that the conventional becomes remarkable and thus suspect.

The narrative continues in its new, more romantic vein, and

---

[44] *Historia Meriadoci*, p. 46:
> Expleto vero biennio, dum una die se conquerentes invicem multa conferrent, "Quid," ait illa, "hic solitarii degimus? Causa puerorum huc confugimus, ut eos vite conservaremus, hic hactenus perstitimus; quibus ablatis et desideratis, quid hic nos ulterius detinet?"

subsequent events seem perhaps less strange than the sudden entry into this mode. A suggestion of interlaced narrative develops as the text follows first Morwen, then Ivor, and the way in which all the parties are brought together may remind the reader of the experiments in simultaneous narrative early in the *De Ortu*, when the action shifted from Gawain's camp to Milocrates's and back, with Gawain himself providing the link. Morwen reaches Scotland in a typical romance journey, vague with respect to both time and place: "Morwen took the way to Scotland, and arrived on the very day that King Urien married the girl Orwen."[45] The lack of detail about this trip has not, heretofore, been the normal procedure for this author. In the *De Ortu*, routes and stopping-places are by and large carefully described, and details such as provisioning and safe-conducts are often alluded to. In *Meriadoc*, the author may simply be following the more conventional romance procedure, or he may be calling attention to it by refraining, for a moment, from explaining everything and appearing to make every event seem plausible. The coincidence of Morwen's arrival on Orwen's wedding day is also not a typical strategy for this writer. In any case, the narrative reason for the two-year delay soon becomes clear; it has been necessary to allow Orwen to reach marriageable age. Orwen does not recognize her nurse at first, but the happy reunion soon follows.

The text then returns to Ivor, again without bothering about how he got where he was going: "Ivor, meanwhile, arrived at the court of King Arthur."[46] His entrance is spectacular:

> For he was a man of unusual height, with a fierce face, wild beard, and unkempt hair; he was clothed in woven reeds and fibres, with a sword at his side, a hunting-horn around his neck, a bow and arrows in his hand, and on his shoulders he carried a dead deer of great weight and immense size, which he had happened to kill on his way.[47]

This portrait combines suggestions of John the Baptist, the Celtic

---

[45] *Historia Meriadoci*, p. 48: "Morwen igitur ad Scociam iter arripuit; ipsaque die qua Urianus rex, puella Orwen sibi in uxore dotata . . . illo pervenit."
[46] *Historia Meriadoci*, p. 52: "Ivorius autem interea regis Arturi curiam adiit . . ."
[47] *Historia Meriadoci*, p. 52:
> Vir namque innormis proceritatis erat, torva facie, barba prolixa, incultis crinibus, scyrpis et papiris contextis amictus, ense latus cinctus, venatorium cornu collo, arcum cum sagittis manu, cervum vero exanimem magni ponderis inmenseque magnitudinis, quem sibi obvium casu venatu ceperat, humeris gestans.

wildman, and perhaps a figure like the Green Knight. But Ivor presents neither challenge nor threat to the Arthurian court, as this description might lead one to expect. Instead, he gives the deer to Kay, is recognized by Meriadoc, and another happy reunion follows. Is this a deliberate invocation of the wild challenger motif, undercut by the complete absence of any threat? Or is it simply a return to verisimilitude, with a recognition of just what Ivor would look like after seven years in the wilderness?

Certainly the author's compulsion for narrative neatness shows up again when it becomes time to reunite the children, and the two strands of the story. Morwen had heard Kay promising to meet Urien in Scotland; we are told that while his duties had hitherto prevented him from fulfilling that promise, he now intends to do so. Ivor and Meriadoc accompany him, and find Morwen and Orwen. The narrative strands are reunited, and the first section of the text is marked off with a set piece on the upward motion of Fortune's wheel:

> For what greater joy is there than for grieving parents and friends, separated for a long time, joyfully to find themselves together again, after great labor to find rest, and to exchange poverty and misery for riches and glory? The joy was shared by all, they continued in delights for many days through the great grace of Fortune, and past griefs were relieved by joy.[48]

One might note that this invocation of the joy after sorrow commonplace offers a return to the unremarkably conventional; it suggests a determination to conclude this portion of the text, however unsettling to expectation some of its moments might be, in a comfortable fashion.

As was the case in the *De Ortu*, however, the second, Arthurian portion of the narrative is even harder to locate firmly in generic or hermeneutic terms. The episode of the Black Knight manifests the text's concern for right rule, but it has another side. The Black Knight is only the first of three claimants. His appearance is itself presented as a marvel; this section of the text begins with the statement that Arthur is free for the moment from war and the need to travel, and when such is the case, something usually happens: "It usually befell

---

[48] *Historia Meriadoci*, p. 56:
> Que enim maior leticia quam parentes et amici tristes divcius divisi se tandem hillares reperire, post nimios labores potiri quiete, pauperiemque et miseriam divitiis et gloria commutare? Universos igitur commune gaudium optinet, plurimi in deliciis dies ob tantam Fortune graciam ab eis continuantur preteritique dolores relevantur gaudiis.

him that, whenever he happened to stay in the same place for some length of time, something of great moment would occur."[49] This romantic commonplace introduces the arrival, on three successive days, of three challengers; not only the Black Knight of the Black Forest, but also the Red Knight of the Red Forest, and the White Knight of the White Forest. Bruce remarked in disgust that "Nothing, perhaps, so insipid or absurd can be found even in Arthurian fiction . . . as these knights with their preposterous names."[50] The sequence does become preposterous; how does it achieve its effects, and why?

The opening episode, that of the Black Knight of the Black Forest, is not by itself clearly burlesque. We have seen that it fits well into a central thematic concern, both of this work and of the many courtly texts I have been examining. Even here, however, there are some odd features. First, the Black Knight's cumbersome name, as is the case with the names of the other two knights, is never shortened, and there are many places in the text where the repetition of the name, or later of all three of these names, is as funny as it is thorough. Second, there is the Knight's color. The withholding of the information that the Black Knight is literally black until the climax of his speech – it is his trump card in his case against Arthur – may remind one of the way in which similar information about the Green Knight is slipped into the description in *Sir Gawain and the Green Knight*: that "aghlich mayster" is not clearly said to be "oueral enker-grene"[51] until the last line of the stanza in which he appears. Until this point, the description moves back and forth between suggestions of the supernatural and the merely extraordinary. *Sir Gawain* is a poem openly concerned with and engaged in "game"; the Black Knight in *Meriadoc*, too, may well be a player in the Latin author's games with his audience. And given the possible reference to a heated contemporary controversy, it may be that here again we have a Latin court writer taking refuge under the cover of *facetia* in order to deliver his message.

The Black Knight episode takes up a good section of the narrative;

---

49 *Historia Meriadoci*, pp. 68–70: "Cui semper evenire solebat, ut, quociens eum aliquamdiu aliquorsum perhendinare contigisset, semper tociens alicuius magni negocii occurrebat eventus." The repetition of *aliqui-* in this passage is suggestive; the piling up of indefinite expressions is stressed in a way which seems almost parodic.

50 *Two Arthurian Romances*, ed. Bruce, p. xxxii. In his first edition, Bruce argued that this scene constituted intentional burlesque; he backs away from this opinion in his second edition, while noting that the sequence does disrupt a romantic narrative, in a fashion similar to the Greek fire episode in the *De Ortu* (pp. vii–viii).

51 *Sir Gawain and the Green Knight*, lines 137, 150.

the deliberations which precede the battles, and the battle with Meriadoc in particular are described at great length. Besides its legal overtones, the battle contains many romance elements; the battle at the ford, the description of the accouterments of the participants, and the respect and friendship which results between the two knights are all familiar. What makes these romance reflexes suspect is their multiplication, for when the matter of the Black Knight is finally settled, the Red Knight and then the White Knight appear.

The Red Knight of the Red Forest appears at court the day after the affair of the Black Knight, and he too presents a suit against Arthur, this one concerning the possession of the Red Forest. There is little debate this time – the legal point has been made. A duel is called for and Meriadoc fights it, defeating the Red Knight and making him his ally in a single line of text. Meriadoc is rewarded with the Red Forest, which he then gives to the Red Knight.

This episode is brief, and it could perhaps be argued that it exists to show that Arthur has learned his lesson. In the *Awntyrs off Arthure*, the Galeron episode functions in part to show that Gawain and Guenevere have absorbed the ghost's strictures. The cumbersome names of the knights, however, are beginning to become more noticeable. When, on the next day, the White Knight of the White Forest shows up with what is blandly described as "a not dissimilar lawsuit,"[52] the text takes on the appearance of burlesque. This episode is dismissed even more summarily than was the last, and the serious message of the Black Knight episode begins to yield to mockery of the conventions of the romance text. The reader is thus forced to notice the vessel, and is distanced from the story.

This whole final section of the text, in fact, seems primarily to be involved in undermining the normal settings and events of romance, perhaps with no more specific goal than the entertainment of the audience. Certainly the romance motifs come thick and fast from this point on, starting when Meriadoc, accompanied by his three new allies "namely, the Black Knight of the Black Forest, the Red Knight of the Red Forest, and the White Knight of the White Forest,"[53] sets off in search of adventures. The knights are not the only ones with odd names; Gundebald, the emperor's enemy, is "king of the land

---

[52] *Historia Meriadoci*, p. 98: "Huic Candidus Miles de Candido Saltu succedit, qui non dispari accione in ius ductus . . ."

[53] *Historia Meriadoci*, p. 100: ". . . scilicet Nigrum Militem de Nigro Saltu, Roseum Militem de Roseo Saltu, et Candidum Militem de Candido Saltu . . ."

from which no one returns."[54] Any suspicions that this name may in itself be something of a joke are sharpened by its occurring twice in the same sentence. And while Gundebald's title drops out of the text after this introduction, Meriadoc's companions continue to be given their full names throughout the narrative.

The core of the romance section of the text is, not surprisingly, to be found in the account of Meriadoc's adventures in the forest which he enters in pursuit of Gundebald's men after his first encounter with them. This is a typical romance forest; perhaps after skating so near to criticism of the all too real forests of Angevin England, the author feels the need for some such locale:

> Now that forest was so vast and wild, that no one had ever been able to measure its length or width, because of the ferocity of the monstrous beasts inhabiting it and because of the unnumbered and incredible apparitions which vexed and deluded travelers through the forest. For so many kinds of phantasms appeared in this forest, that no one crossing it escaped immune from their illusions. Also they make these men mad, depriving them of their human senses, whether through terror or through their own transformations, and they are snatched, mad, as if in a trance, into another world.[55]

This forest is presented as a gateway into another world, illusory to be sure, but no less effective in wreaking havoc upon perception for that. The deceptiveness of appearances is emphasized, a theme which is to continue through this section of the work. A fascinating signal that this is indeed a different realm comes in the many references to daylight. When Meriadoc and his men set up camp for the evening, they have no sooner settled down when it appears to be daylight again. Meriadoc's reaction is comical: "I had scarcely fallen asleep, and now it's daytime? So where is the night? I must surely need more sleep than usual, or the night is shorter than usual."[56] The humor here may support the idea that in this part of the text, the deceptions

---

[54] *Historia Meriadoci*, p. 100: ". . . regem terre ex qua nemo revertitur . . ."

[55] *Historia Meriadoci*, p. 114:
> Erat autem eadem silva vasta nimis et horrida, quam cuius esset latitudinis vel longitudinis nullus unquam rimari potuit; videlicet, ob feritatem inmanium belvarum eam inhabitancium et ob innumera et incredibilia fantasmata que per silvam viantes vexabant et deludebant. Tot quippe fastasiarum [sic] in ea apparebant species, ut nullus transeuncium ab earum illusionibus immunis effugeret. Quorundam quoque animos, humano sensu, tum terroribus, tum suis transformacionibus, privatos, quasi in extasim ad alia secula raptos dementes effecerant.

[56] *Historia Meriadoci*, p. 116: "Vix sompnum cepi, et nunc dies est? Ubi est ergo nox? Certe aut ego prolixiori solito sompno indigeo aut nox solito brevior est."

practiced on both protagonist and audience are intended simply to entertain, to engage all in the playful rather than the serious potential of the manipulation of words and situations.

This unusual day leads Meriadoc and his men to a castle, where Meriadoc believes no castle had been before. This magnificent structure and its beautiful mistress fit well into a romance forest. The elaborate description is certainly decorative; it does also tend to stress the visual, to report the effects that this splendid spectacle has on the viewers. Day's speculation that the lady of the castle suggests Fortuna – an idea supported by reference to her oriental dress, her location at the top of a flight of porphyry stairs, and so on – is certainly tenable, particularly in view of the invocation of Fortune at the outset of the text, but the focus throughout seems rather to be on the question of the interpretation by Meriadoc of this scene.[57] When the lady greets him by name, Meriadoc is utterly confounded, and her response to him is the firmest statement yet that the hero has moved into another world:

> "It is quite stupefying what I see and hear, for how do you know my face or name? or who has constructed such buildings so rapidly in this place, when not yet a month has passed since there was not a single stone erected here?" To which she said, "Do not be amazed, Meriadoc, if I call you by name, for it is a long time that you have been known to me by face and name. But you are very wrong about these buildings, which you say were constructed so suddenly, because this habitation has existed from earliest times. Nor is this place what you think it is, nor were you ever in this place except just now."[58]

The lady's speech makes it clear that Meriadoc has entered a world of confusion and illusion, and as the signals get more confused and confusing, it begins to appear that the reader is on an analogous journey through the text. What first presented itself as a tale of the

---

[57] *Historia Meriadoci*, p. xxxii. Day does suggest that Meriadoc's failure to read the iconography of Fortuna is ironic in the classic sense, because the audience surely would recognize the signs; such an irony may well be one of the ingredients in the overall effect of the passage.

[58] *Historia Meriadoci*, pp. 120–22:

> "Stupendum est non modice quod video et audio, vel quomodo mei faciem aut nomen cognoveris vel quis in hoc loco tantas structuras tam repente condiderit, cum necdum mensis transiit quod hic nec unus lapis edificii fuerit." Illa ad hec: "Ne mireris, Meriadoce, si te tuo vocaverim nomine, diu quippe est quod mihi et vultu et nomine haberis cognitus. Sed multum erras de hiis edificiis, que tam subito constructa asseris, quia et hec habitacula sunt a priscis temporibus. Nec hic locus est quem tu esse existimas nec umquam nisi modo in hoc loco fuisti."

Havelok-type, admittedly with a few strange features, has given way to a story with a serious message about the abuse of power (the Black Knight episode), then to a burlesque of the same story (the Red and White Knights), and has now moved firmly into the otherworld, where nothing is what it seems to be. As in the Greek fire passage in the *De Ortu*, the reader has to try to sort out the conflicting signals sent by the text; thus audience and protagonists are involved in similar efforts.

Meriadoc and his knights are invited to dinner, and they cannot help but notice that no one in the whole castle speaks at all. When Meriadoc inquires of the seneschal what is going on, the seneschal responds with an incredible display of rudeness. Meriadoc's bewilderment, contrasted with this bizarre behavior, makes the whole scene appear to be a comedy routine in which Meriadoc is the straight man:

> Meriadoc, thinking he was joking, asked him again courteously to answer his questions. But he, once more, panting like a dog, sticking his tongue out down to his chin, and cackling, derided Meriadoc. But Meriadoc, not understanding what he was doing even then and still thinking that the derision was a game, said, "Excellent sir, what are you doing? I have asked you things unknown to me but well known to you, and instead of an answer you offer the wrinkling of your nose and the twisting about of your mouth. Now I ask you finally to answer my questions." But the seneschal, saying nothing to him, for a third time leaned over, waving both hands with his fingers spread at his temples like the ears of an ass, eyes blazing, and mouth stretched open . . . [59]

Most of the instances of possible humor in the text discussed thus far have been a matter of rather subtle ironies, or subversions of narrative conventions, all open to other interpretations. The figure of the rude servitor is not uncommon in romance – one thinks, for example, of the character in Andreas's Sparrowhawk episode discussed in chapter 3 – but the exaggeration here is unusual. This scene is outright

---

[59] *Historia Meriadoci*, p. 124:

> At Meriadocus, eum hoc reputans ludendo fecisse, iterum eum ut quesita sibi intimaret blande rogavit. Ille vero iterato, more canis estuantis, linguam ab ore usque ad mentum deorsum exerens, subiuncto cachinno, Meriadocum deridebat. Meriadocus autem nec tunc quidem rem ut erat intelligens et derisionem adhuc lusum existimans, "Vir," ait, "eggregie, quid est quod agas? Ego que michi ignota et tibi bene sunt cognita a te quero et tu mihi reponsionis loco contraccionem narium et distorte bucce reddis valgium. Queso ut vel nunc demum interrogata mihi edicas." Verum dapifer, nichil ei locutus, tercio ad instar auricularium aselli ambas manus circa tempora sparsis digitis agitans, ardentibus oculis, patenti oris rictu, . . . incubuit . . .

slapstick, and colors the impression given by much of what follows. Meriadoc and his men are all overcome with fear, and run away from the table and the castle. They mount their horses and set off again, but suddenly the normal passage of time is again set aside as total darkness falls, and riders and horses alike bolt in every direction in a scene of mass confusion. When day dawns, Meriadoc and some companions find themselves in the middle of a river, with many of their comrades missing. Meriadoc identifies the cause of their distress: "a fantastic day has fed us on its delights."[60] This curious phrase acknowledges the incredible nature of the experience Meriadoc and his men have undergone, while at the same time suggesting that perhaps neither they, nor we, should take this part of the text too seriously.

It soon becomes clear that whoever is making sport of the hero, whether it be the otherworld in the text or the author, the game is not over yet. While Meriadoc and his men are attempting to escape from the forest, the text makes it clear that they are in fact moving deeper into this deceptive realm: "Although they hoped that they were on their way out of the forest, they tended always towards its depths."[61] The next episode is initiated by a sudden terrible storm, and there is another mysterious castle, this one a poor shelter because "no one who enters it has ever returned without shame."[62] Despite this warning, some of the knights decide to enter the castle, and they judge by its appearance that all is well. Eventually, of course, all who enter the castle, including Meriadoc, are overcome by a great fear. The only one still capable of action is Meriadoc, but his action is itself warped by the odd atmosphere of the place. Finding food in a chamber occupied by a beautiful maiden, he inexplicably grabs it and rushes out, without the courteous request, thanks, or even greeting that one might expect. He ends up in the kitchen, where he fights an opponent armed with a spit; he also disposes of a guard armed with a roof-beam.[63] This is a striking display of unknightly behavior, behavior which is in odd contrast to the Meriadoc who cemented the allegiance of the three colored knights through generosity and chivalric good manners. The hero has entered a world where all normal behavior is suspended, and it is noteworthy that what takes

---

[60] *Historia Meriadoci*, p. 128: " . . . dies fantastica nos deliciis pavit."
[61] *Historia Meriadoci*, p. 130: "Dumque se silvam egressuros sperarent, in interiora eius semper tendebant."
[62] *Historia Meriadoci*, p. 130: ". . . neminem umquam illud intrasse qui sine dedecore exierit."
[63] Day, *Historia Meriadoci*, p. xxxiv, suggests that these are originally the Vandal twins Raos and Raptos, but it seems to me that these derivations have little explanatory force in the text.

the place of good manners and prowess on the battlefield is fear, running around in the dark, rudeness to a woman, and a brawl in a kitchen. Perhaps knights are not all that they seem to be?

When Meriadoc and his men finally escape this second castle and the deceptive forest, their perceptions remain confused for a short time. Coming upon the sound of a battle, Meriadoc is moved to wonder whether the sound might be another illusion, but this time things really are as they appear to be; Meriadoc and his men have stumbled into a battle between the forces of the emperor and Gundebald. The author makes use of a conversation between the knights and a boy near the battlefield to bring the audience up to date on what has been happening in the real world. It appears that the author is keen to clear the sight of both protagonist and audience through this passage; yet as we have seen, this apparently more "real" world is also, in its way, as deceptive as is the fantastic forest. The issue of appearance and reality is in fact as difficult in the "real" world. John of Salisbury makes it clear that the philosopher's true task lies in perceiving the truly real and then conforming to it, a feat which is impossible if one remains in the world of appearances.[64] The world of kings and courts, I have been arguing, is shown in all of these texts to be a world of appearances as deceptive as is the fantastic forest. While Meriadoc shakes off his recent experience and takes up again the adventure of rescuing the emperor's daughter, the emperor's political machinations are about to make that fact clear.

The rescue of the emperor's daughter presents a curious mix of the two narrative strains we have been discussing. On the one hand, there are many resemblances between this section and the similar episode in the *De Ortu*; the emperor's daughter is a well-treated prisoner who has heard of the fame of her would-be rescuer, and desires to aid him in his plan. Like the princess in the *De Ortu*, she acknowledges that she has been treated well, but asserts the value of freedom above all. The conditions under which Gundebald meets his challengers, and the complex description of the land from which no man returns, are reminiscent of other bewildering complexities in the text, but the actual battle is rather anticlimactic, after all the preparations for it. Gundebald's death takes much less time to accomplish than did the description of the place where the encounter would occur. The author's desire to plug narrative loopholes emerges again when he

---

[64] Discussed by Türk, *Nugae curialium*, p. 70.

explains that Gundebald's men are restrained from taking revenge on Meriadoc because of a pact between Meriadoc and Gundebald. In this case the effort seems rather lame; there had been no indication up to this point that Meriadoc and Gundebald had ever met. It seems that the author's desire for realism on one level – he cannot help but think that in other circumstances, Gundebald's men would have killed Meriadoc – has led him to an unconvincing explanation at another level.

If we forget for a moment about the "mysterious forest" interlude in the *Historia Meriadoci*, the narrative falls neatly into three roughly parallel sections. In each, a ruler is shown to be unjust. In the first, Meriadoc suffers at Griffin's hands, and eventually wins revenge. In the second, Arthur is shown, through Meriadoc's actions, to be imperfect, although justice is finally served. And in the third, the emperor tries to betray Meriadoc, and Meriadoc must once again avenge himself on a ruler who wished to destroy him. Arthur is by no means as evil a figure as Griffin or the emperor, but he is imperfect, and the effect of placing him between these two examples of the abuse of power is to underline his deficiencies. The text would seem to be suggesting that no ruler can be perfect, because all are human; and this must include Britain's most famous king.

At the same time, the "mysterious forest" interlude, along with many of the other odd features discussed above, is an integral part of the narrative. If the portrayal of Arthur and the other kings provokes thought, it seems that many of these features can provoke only laughter or confusion. Many of the strange features of the text may provide the necessary, facetious covering of truth-telling. But just as the *Awntyrs* assume the dress of romance to sweeten the pill of the *exemplum*, so too does *Meriadoc* encourage its audience to laugh, in order that it will persevere and absorb the message of the text. The *Historia Meriadoci* offers us the court at work and at play; it is not surprising that kings should feature in both cases.

As in the *De Ortu*, there are times when the *Historia Meriadoci* appears to be toying with the audience's expectations. Taken together, the two texts display significant evidence of a deliberate manipulation of convention and expectation. The result is certainly entertaining, but I think that there is something more serious lying behind these games. In both texts, the ability to distinguish appearance from reality through the correct reading of signs both visual and linguistic is called into question. It is both important and difficult to read things correctly, to apprehend "the thing in itself." These difficulties are often encountered in the world of the court, and *Meriadoc* in particular highlights the dangers of the deceptive discourse practiced there. By shifting from one kind of story to another, by interrupting the narrative flow, by heightening and deflating narrative conventions, by seesawing back and forth between realism and fantasy, and even by encouraging laughter, *Meriadoc* confuses and confounds the audience's interpretive endeavors. And the game which results has a message. As we attempt to sort out what the text looks like, and what it is, we enter our own version of the mysterious forest. If we emerge into our "real" world with a greater awareness of the problem of interpretation, then here perhaps we have found the *utilitas* which the author stated at the outset as his concern. Or it may be that "a fantastic [text] has fed us its delights."

# 6

## "When I have done you will be little the wiser": *Arthur and Gorlagon, Vita Merlini,* and parody

The Latin narratives I have been exploring thus far treat Arthur in both historical and romantic modes; in each, the court themes of appearance and reality and right rule are present, along with the court fondness for facetious discourse. There is a third context in which Arthur appears in Latin literature, a context which for want of a better word I will designate Celtic. This vague term seeks to indicate a concern with narrative motifs, forms, and treatments which show the influence of Celtic, and more specifically, Welsh narrative. Wales had a well-established narrative tradition, one which remained vibrant throughout the whole of the Middle Ages. In addition, for much of the period with which this study is dealing, Wales had separate political and social structures from those of the Angevin world. But Wales and the Norman and Angevin worlds were in close contact, and the interactions between them, on the literary level at least, might have been encouraged by some shared interests. This chapter will show how native Welsh interest in kingship, along with a well-developed native tradition of parody, appear in Latin guise.

From the 1060s on, Norman conquest and settlement in Wales had brought the two cultures into close contact. The castles built along the border between England and Wales in the south were the most tangible expression of Norman ambitions in Wales.[1] The Anarchy, which seems to have filled Geoffrey of Monmouth with pessimism about the future, was a time of opportunity for the Welsh princes, who regained some of the land they had earlier lost to Henry I. Not surprisingly, Henry II attempted to reverse these losses, and to

---

[1] There are over 300 pre-1215 castle sites within Wales, particularly heavily concentrated in the south and in the central border region; see R.R. Davies, *Conquest, Coexistence, and Change: Wales 1063–1415* (Oxford: Clarendon Press, 1987), p. 90; there is a useful map of Norman penetration into Wales by 1200 on p. 38.

consolidate the sometimes tenuous Norman hold on Wales. But Henry met with determined resistance from both Owain Gwynedd in the north and Rhys ab Gruffydd in the south. The military and political successes of these two Welsh princes allowed parts of Wales to function quite apart from Angevin control for much of the twelfth century (Owain died in 1170, and Rhys in 1197). There was nevertheless considerable interaction between Wales and the Angevin world; indeed, after the 1160s, Henry was forced by circumstances elsewhere, especially in Ireland, to enter into an uneasy alliance with Rhys. This political interaction is echoed in the cultural cross-fertilization represented by figures like Gerald of Wales, Walter Map and Geoffrey of Monmouth. In fact, the literary exchange between Welsh and Anglo-Norman writers may be traced even further back, in such a way as to bring us to another court context, analogous to the milieu described in the Introduction.

The castles of the Norman marcher lords may have been a site for the earliest exchanges of story-motifs between Norman and Welsh storytellers.[2] There is evidence for the existence of a class of professional interpreters, the *latimarii*, from the time of the Conquest on. These were educated Welshmen fluent in their own tongue as well as in Latin and Norman, and they form a group analogous to the courtier-clerics of the Angevin court.[3] Traditional Welsh poets, whose role included the composition of praise-poetry for their princes, might also have been found on the marches. R.R. Davies suggests that attendance at courts of various kinds – of local Welsh princes, of Norman marcher lords, of the peripatetic diplomatic courts of the Angevin overlord – was an important element in bringing such people together.[4] Thus once more the court becomes the scene of cultural production; Constance Bullock-Davies describes the setting as one of cross-cultural and cross-linguistic influence: "*Cyfarwyddiad*, latimers, and French, Welsh, and English minstrels

---

[2] The question of directions of influence between French and Welsh romance is still hotly debated. Rachel Bromwich has contributed much to this debate; most recently, she argues that the large numbers of personal names of Brythonic origin in the work of French and Latin writers is "irrefutable evidence" for the transmission of Celtic stories to the Normans at an early date; nearly all place-names in these works are recognizable as Anglo-Norman forms of place-names in Britain or Brittany; "First Transmission to England and France," in *The Arthur of the Welsh*, ed. Bromwich *et al.*, p. 276.

[3] Constance Bullock-Davies, *Professional Interpreters and the Matter of Britain* (Cardiff: University of Wales Press, 1966), traces the presence of latimers in Wales and Ireland from before the Conquest, up to about 1230.

[4] Davies, *Conquest, Coexistence, and Change*, p. 103.

lived together in the same castles along the Welsh Marches from the time of the Conquest. They could not have failed to impart to one another something of each of their literatures."[5] While this description may give one a misleading impression of harmonious interaction between Normans and Welsh, it is the case that intermarriage and various other forms of alliances bred, in the marches at least, a unique society. Gerald of Wales was of both Anglo-Norman and Welsh origin; Davies argues that Gerald's frustration at being regarded as alien by each group "heralds the appearance of an Anglo-Norman Marcher society in Wales, distinct from the societies of England and of native Wales alike";[6] one recalls Clanchy's comments on border societies in twelfth-century Britain. It is not surprising, then, to find a body of Latin writing which shows clear markers of Welsh influence, while also demonstrating many of the court themes which run through the other Latin Arthurian narratives in this study. Such influence would have been likely in any case; given the characteristics of the Welsh tradition, it was almost certain.

I have been arguing throughout this study that it is a mistake to separate works in the vernacular from those in Latin; the same Latinate courtier-clerics who produced or were the audiences for the Latin Arthurian narratives in this study were among the founders and promulgators of the new vernacular genres. In the case of Welsh literature, too, the vernacular/ Latin split has more recently been corrected by a heightened awareness of the identity of the producers and consumers of vernacular and Latin texts alike. The earliest Welsh Arthurian poems, pre-Conquest texts of lore and prophecy, are nevertheless, according to Patrick Sims-Williams, to be understood in terms of Welsh Latin culture:

> We cannot and should not distinguish between a "historical" Latin tradition represented by Gildas's *De Excidio Britanniae*, the *Historia Brittonum*, and Geoffrey of Monmouth's *Historia Regum Britanniae* on the one hand and a "mythic" or "fictitious" vernacular tradition on the other. The Latin and Welsh texts share too many basic assumptions, such as the idea of the Island of Britain as a former and potential unity: from a functional point of view it mattered little whether this unity had been attacked by Anglo-Saxons or monsters, whether it had been defended by Aurelius Ambrosius or Arthur, or whether it would be restored by contem-

---

[5] Bullock-Davies, *Professional Interpreters*, p. 18.
[6] Davies, *Conquest, Coexistence, and Change*, p. 103.

porary Britons and Dubliners or by heroes returning from the past. The world-picture is the same in either case.[7]

In the cross-cultural milieu described above, the mingling of Latin and Welsh traditions would have been further encouraged by the fact that the native Welsh literary tradition shared certain themes and methods with those of Latin court writers (the Welsh or Breton heritage of some of these writers was also important). The works I have designated "Celtic" are linked to a narrative tradition which almost from the start has included comedy, parody, irony, irreverence, generic confusion – all the means of textual subversion discussed throughout this study's examination of Latin Arthurian texts. Geoffrey of Monmouth's *Vita Merlini* and the anonymous *Arthur and Gorlagon* are both highly accomplished flights of narrative fancy which clearly are laughing at us or with us, and we are more likely to "get" them if we are aware of some of the features which, I will argue, they are reflecting.

Welsh Arthurian narrative can be traced back before the Conquest, but even before these early appearances of Arthur, certain characteristically Welsh methods and themes had been established, in works like the *Four Branches of the Mabinogi*, which later recur in Arthurian guise.[8] The first branch of the *Mabinogi*, for example, gives us Pwyll, the rather dim king of Dyfed who starts his story by displaying both appalling rudeness and appalling ignorance in using his dogs to drive a pack of white hounds with red ears from a deer he has encountered in a clearing in the forest. This conduct suggests that Pwyll is unaware of what every reader of Celtic narrative knows; boundaries and places which stand out from the landscape – as this clearing in the forest does – are often signals that one is passing into the other world. Even were the audience to miss this clue, they could be expected to take note of the extraordinary dogs, whose colors clearly mark them out as otherworld beasts. Signification and the refusal of characters to read well-known signs are here, as in other texts examined thus far, used to satiric purpose. If the audience could not fail to recognize these signs,

---

[7] Patrick Sims-Williams, "The Early Welsh Arthurian Poems," in *The Arthur of the Welsh*, ed. Bromwich *et al.*, pp. 34–35.

[8] The *Four Branches* are probably to be dated to between 1050 and 1120, well before Chrétien's Arthurian romances, yet in a period which saw the beginning of a transition from Celtic to Norman modes of life and culture in Wales. They are thus ideally situated to allow us to extrapolate from them characteristics which reflect back on "pure" Welsh narrative, while also suggesting how that narrative might have begun to adapt itself to later influences.

what would they think of a protagonist who would first fail to recognize them and then act so rudely and rashly? Pwyll often behaves like a fool in the first branch, and his wife, Rhiannon, often castigates his foolishness. In particular, she reacts to a rash promise of Pwyll's with an acerbity which might remind one of the Guenevere of the *De Ortu*: " 'Alas,' said Rhiannon, 'why did you give such an answer? . . . there never was a man more slow-witted than you are.' "[9] The point of all of this is not that Pwyll is simply a buffoon, although there is a delicious irony in the contrast between his name, which means steadiness or discretion, and his conduct. This Welsh text presents an imperfect king, who must learn to overcome certain elements in his own character before he can become a good king. The irreverent treatment of Pwyll, then, is not merely an excuse for a little comic relief. The laughter at Pwyll's expense emphasizes the fact that he does have shortcomings; the potentially serious situations which result in the story make clear the impact which human imperfection can have upon the affairs of the kingdom. Nevertheless in this text, everything works out for the best. The foolish king learns from his mistake – humor rather than satire is the operative narrative mode, and humor, as D.H. Green suggests in his study of irony in the medieval romance, "grants a value to what it laughs at and shows a sympathetic understanding of human imperfection."[10] The mode here may be rather different from rebukes in Latin court satire and from the sparkling covering of wit over truth-telling in the Latin texts explored thus far, but the motive – to make use of narrative to teach a lesson about right rule – is the same.

The concern with the education of a ruler continues throughout the other branches of the *Mabinogi*, as well as in other Welsh and Welsh Latin texts. In the latter category are the Welsh saints' lives, products of the twelfth-century renaissance; the six Welsh lives in which Arthur appears represent "the most extensive body of surviving Arthurian texts written before, or at about the same time as, Geoffrey of Monmouth's *Historia* . . ."[11] These lives, to be sure, have their own agendas; promoting the primacy of particular monasteries,

---

[9] *Pwyll Pendeuic Dyuet*, ed. R.L. Thomson (Dublin: Institute for Advanced Studies, 1980), p. 12: " 'Och,' heb y Riannon, 'paham y rody di attep y uelly? . . . ny bu uuscrellach gwr ar y ssynwyr e hun nog ry uuost ti.' "
[10] Green, *Irony in the Medieval Romance*, p. 10.
[11] By Jeff Rider, in his "Arthur and the Saints," in *King Arthur through the Ages*, ed. Valerie M. Lagorio and Mildred Leake Day (New York: Garland, 1990), vol. 1, p. 3.

perhaps, as well as revealing the holiness of their subjects.[12] Such agendas are not of course unique to the Welsh context; in chapter 3 I discussed similar efforts made by the monks of Glastonbury. These Welsh Latin lives are a mixture of Welsh and Latin hagiographical forms. Arthur appears in mere episodes in these works, and it has been suggested that his unsatisfactory or unsavory behavior in some of these episodes is simply the result of his assimilation to a stock hagiographical figure, the Recalcitrant King, whose purpose is simply to be chastised by the saint.[13] Yet Arthur is not always the saint's opponent. A review of his appearances in these works reveals a character with many facets.

Most of Arthur's appearances are brief. In the *Vita prima Sancti Carantoci*, he appears twice as the one who collects St. Carannog's magic altar for him; Carannog casts the altar into the waters when he wants to find out where God wishes him to go next. In the first episode, Arthur is engaged in hunting a "huge, terrible, most powerful serpent";[14] the saint, usurping Arthur's usual role as monster-killer, makes a pet of the beast and receives information about the whereabouts of his altar in return.

In the *Vita Sancti Iltuti*, Arthur simply provides the stage-setting for a conventional renunciation of the martial life: the young saint journeys to the court of Arthur, because "he desired to visit the court of so great a conqueror."[15] Illtud has a look at the court and moves on with no comment, and is converted by Cadog shortly thereafter. The court is implicitly rejected, as in court satire, but the focus is clearly on the progress of the saint. And in the *Vita Sancti Paterni*, Arthur is the stereotypical *tyrannus* who must be subdued by the saint.[16]

In all of these lives, Arthur seems a mere narrative convenience; not always the *tyrannus*, to be sure, but functioning in a similarly one-dimensional way in each case. More interesting, to a reader with

---

[12] These are the *Vita Cadoci* by Lifris; the *Vita Cadoci* by Caradog; his *Vita Iltuti* and *Vita Gildae*; and the *Vita Carantoci* and *Vita Paterni*; all found in London, British Library MS Cotton Vespasian A.xiv, copied at Monmouth c. 1200. Rider discusses the dates and possible purposes of these lives, pp. 3–8. For the text and a more complete discussion of the manuscript, see *Vitae sanctorum Britanniae et genealogiae*, ed. A.W. Wade-Evans (Cardiff: University of Wales Press, 1944). All citations from the lives are from this edition.

[13] See, for example, Geoffrey Ashe's entry on the saints' lives in *The Arthurian Encyclopedia*, ed. Norris J. Lacy (New York: Peter Bedrick, 1987), p. 470.

[14] *Vita prima Sancti Carantoci*, p. 144: ". . . serpentem ualidissimum, ingentem, terribilem . . ."

[15] *Vita Sancti Iltuti*, p. 196: ". . . cupiuit uisitare tanti uictoris curiam."

[16] *Vita Sancti Paterni*, p. 260.

Arthurian interests at least, is the *Vita Cadoci*. In this text, Arthur first appears sitting on a hillside, dicing with his companions Cei and Bedwyr, and observing Gwynllyw fleeing the enraged father of Gwladus, a girl he has kidnapped. Arthur's first reaction is lust – "he was enflamed with excessive passion for the girl and filled with evil thoughts" – but his companions hold him back: "But they, to prevent him, said, 'The performance of such wickedness should be far from you, for it is our custom to help the weak and the troubled.'"[17] Arthur gives aid, and St. Cadog is born as a result of the union of Gwynllyw and Gwladus.

The prime point of this episode is Cadog's birth story, but note how thoroughly the hagiographer invokes elements of traditional Welsh narrative. Arthur's hillside is very Celtic; major episodes in several of the *Four Branches* open with the king sitting on a high place, from which he sees something strange or miraculous – this is the significant geography so prevalent in Welsh narrative. Arthur's impetuous reaction is common enough for characters like Pwyll, and the control exercised over him by his retainers is another common feature of Welsh texts, where counselors are often more reliable than in a text like the *Historia Meriadoci*. In other words, this Welsh Latin hagiographical text has absorbed many of the characteristics of Welsh vernacular secular narrative. For our purposes, it is important that the relationship between king and counselors is part of that native tradition.

This process of narrative appropriation or interpenetration is even clearer in the second Arthurian episode of the *Vita Cadoci*. Arthur seeks vengeance on a man who has slain three of his knights. The man, Ligessauc, takes refuge with St. Cadog, and when Arthur comes after him, a court is held on the banks of the River Usk. Rivers, like hills and clearings, are common "significant" locations in Welsh texts. The nobles award Arthur cows as compensation, but "This having been accepted, Arthur scoffingly refused cows of one color, saying instead, with great subterfuge, that he would rather have particolored ones; that is, red in the back and white in the front."[18] This episode shows a king trying to subvert the decision of a tribunal. Arthur here

---

[17] *Vita Sancti Cadoci*, p. 26: ". . . libidine in amorem adolescentule nimium succensus, ac iniqua cogitatione plenus . . ." "At illi prohibentes eum dixerunt, 'Absit a te tantum scelus patrari, nos enim soliti sumus inopes anxiosque iuuare.'"

[18] *Vita Sancti Cadoci*, p. 70: "Hoc accepto, Arthurius insultans uni coloris uaccas renuit, uerum discolores accipere libuit, scilicet, in anteriori parte rubei, in posteriori uero candidi coloris distinctas plurima tergiuersatione gestiuit."

is unlike the Arthur of the *Historia Meriadoci*, in so far as he does have a right to compensation for the death of his men; but the concern over a king's attempt to rule *per voluntatem* instead of *per legem* is the same. In this tale, the otherworld animals requested by Arthur pose no difficulty for the saint, and when Cadog finishes by turning them into ferns as soon as Arthur's men seize them, the king acknowledges defeat and begs forgiveness. At this point he disappears from the narrative, and indeed, it would be a mistake to leave the impression that the *Vita Cadoci*, or any of these *vitae*, are even secondarily concerned with Arthur. What they do show, however, is that the figure of Arthur had what advertisers call name-recognition; he was, Rider says, "sufficiently prominent and impressive to be an adequate foil for the saints."[19] Rider goes on to argue that Arthur was also at this point, before Geoffrey had hardened his legend, "sufficiently indeterminate and flexible" to fit into whatever mold was required of him by the hagiographer.[20] Here, Arthur has been adapted by these writers to familiar Celtic patterns. The Welsh king may be foolish or wise, benign or harmful, a figure of fun, a hero – most important is that he is an acceptable focus of sometimes critical attention, a nexus around whom many social and literary issues cluster. But Welsh writers of both Latin and Welsh, like the other writers in this study, often make use of the coloring of the fantastic and the marvelous in the delivering of their admonitory message.

This approach to kings in general, and to Arthur in particular, is very clear in secular Welsh Arthurian narrative. I have already had occasion to refer to the treatment of Pwyll, king of Dyfed, in the first branch of the *Mabinogi*; it has indeed been argued that the work is a book on governance,[21] an argument which can easily be extended to the rest of the *Four Branches*. The second branch, *Branwen uerch Lyr*, draws a contrast between Bran, king of Wales, and Matholwch, king of Ireland. Bran acts in good faith to repair an insult delivered to Matholwch, while Matholwch – like Griffin in the *Historia Meriadoci* – allows himself to be persuaded by his counselors to take unjust action against Branwen, Bran's sister. In the third branch, *Manawydan uab Llyr*, Manawydan's quick wits lead to the lifting of a spell over Dyfed, while in the fourth branch, *Math uab Mathonwy*,

---

[19] Rider, "Arthur and the Saints," p. 17.
[20] Rider, "Arthur and the Saints," p. 17.
[21] By Elizabeth Hanson-Smith, "*Pwyll Prince of Dyfed*: The Narrative Structure," *Studia Celtica* 16/17 (1981/82), 127.

the foolishness of Pryderi, ruler of Dyfed, leads to his loss of the magical swine of Annwn. The ancient themes of friendship, marriage, and feud are set, in the *Four Branches*, against a constant concern for the ways in which a ruler relates to his kingdom. That is, the mirror for princes is not solely an innovation of Latin court writers of the twelfth century, at least not in terms of its themes and goals.

The responsibility for the composition of the *Four Branches* is sometimes assigned to that class of educated legal specialists responsible for writing down the Welsh laws. Rachel Bromwich writes,

> . . . it is relevant to consider the prose style of the Laws when we are led to speculate on the origin of one of the most significant features presented by the earliest extant examples of Welsh storytelling – the developed perfection of its narrative technique . . . The mutual contact between Law-man and storyteller is evinced alike in the number of legal and semi-legal terms frequent in the prose tales, and by a certain lightness of touch which characterizes the legal codes, when "cheerfulness breaks in" and the scribe's pen is captured by a whim of dry humour which recalls the vein of light satire underlying the *Four Branches*. At the same time, the clarity and simplicity of their style is a characteristic common to both which marks them off as offshoots of a common cultural tradition.[22]

When we remember the various legal and administrative roles of the Latin courtier-clerics at the Angevin courts, it becomes even easier to see how there could be a commonality of interest between these groups of men. In the Welsh context too, educated men in the ambit of princes move between modes of writing, between professional occupation and literary recreation, and the influence of business is felt even in the pursuit of leisure.

The criticism, overt or implied, of kings remains a feature of Welsh narrative after the *Four Branches*. Two Welsh Arthurian texts pick up these common attitudes towards kings while also parodying the central stylistic features of Welsh narrative; the parody in fact seems in these texts almost to displace the concern with kingship and rule. The features of the native tradition which are parodied include the Celtic fondness for repetition, particularly in sets of three; the frequent use of prominent places as borders in both a narrative and a physical sense; lists; elaborate descriptions and other sorts of narrative-slowing set pieces; and abrupt endings. There is not the space

---

[22] Rachel Bromwich, "The Character of the Early Welsh Tradition," in *Studies in Early British History*, ed. Nora K. Chadwick (Cambridge: Cambridge University Press, 1954), pp. 100–1.

here to examine *Culhwch ac Olwen* and the *Breudwyt Rhonabwy* at length; the sketch below will have to suffice to show how both set critical views of their protagonists in narratives which heighten the characteristics of Welsh narrative to a ridiculous degree.

*Culhwch ac Olwen*, the first example of a (fairly) connected Arthurian narrative in Welsh, may be dated in its present form to just after the Conquest.[23] The Arthurian frame is grafted on to a collection of well-known folktale elements, and the atmosphere, too, suggests the folktale. There is little that could be called courtly, and much of the humor is crude or even cruel. The episodic narrative is halted quite spectacularly twice; the first time by a list of Arthurian heroes, and the second by a list of tasks which Culhwch, the hero, must perform. The first list includes some clearly ridiculous names, and the second contains far more tasks than will actually be carried out. Both lists suggest, in the contrast between their rhetorical elaboration and their meager content or influence upon the narrative, a tongue-in-cheek approach to the oral/epic fondness for lists and lore in Welsh narrative. It is also important that Culhwch actually performs almost none of the tasks set him; despite his physical splendor, also described at length in the opening of the narrative, he is almost completely ineffectual.

This contrast between splendid appearance and reality, both in the protagonists and on the level of narrative, is also present in *Breudwyt Rhonabwy*, a thirteenth-century text[24] which is a full-blown, literary parody. It is no exaggeration to say that narrative plays little part here. Much of the text is taken up with lengthy and elaborate description of handsomely-clad troops preparing for the battle of Badon; the rest focuses on a game of *gwyddbwyll* which Owein and Arthur play while Owein's servants and Arthur's ravens fight to the death. Arthur's obliviousness towards the chaos all around him; Owein's caustic comments; the climactic decision to postpone the long-awaited battle – all of these define a text which is all style and no

---

[23] The final redaction is probably c. 1100; see Brynley F. Roberts, "Culhwch ac Olwen, the Triads, Saints' Lives," in *The Arthur of the Welsh*, ed. Bromich *et al.*, p. 73, and *Culhwch and Olwen: An Edition and Study of the Oldest Arthurian Tale*, ed. Rachel Bromwich and D. Simon Evans (Cardiff: University of Wales Press, 1992), pp. lxxvii–lxxxiii. Bromwich and Evans's additional notes about the archaic world of the tale suggest some support for those who see the tale as one largely uncontaminated by continental influences; see for example Gwyn Jones and Thomas Jones, who push the date well back into the early eleventh or even the later tenth century; *The Mabinogion* (London: Dent, 1949; rev. edn. 1974), p. ix.

[24] Madawg son of Maredudd, an authentic historical figure appearing in the text, died in 1159, and Iorweth his brother a few years later; see Jeffrey Gantz, trans., *The Mabinogion*, (Harmondsworth, Middlesex: Penguin, 1976), p. 177.

action. The ending of the piece, already mentioned in the discussion of Geoffrey's *Historia* in chapter 1, supports the suggestion that this is a work whose concerns are fundamentally with its surface: "This story is called the Dream of Rhonabwy, and here is the reason: no man, neither bard nor storyteller, knows the dream without a book, because there were so many colors on the horses, and such strange colors of arms and equipment and precious cloaks and powerful stones."[25]

For Ceridwen Lloyd-Morgan, the emphasis in the colophon on a book marks a new phase in Welsh literature, a turn to the concept of a single author in control of his material.[26] This control is, I think, manifested through the elaborate surface of the text, a surface which conceals – or rather reveals – deeper thematic concerns. As the battle between the servants and the ravens escalates, we must notice that it is an internal quarrel over a triviality – the game of *gwyddbwyll* – which has provoked such apparently wholesale destruction. Arthur in particular seems capricious and largely ineffectual despite the splendid show of his men. The criticism of rulers often characteristic of Welsh narrative has here become pointed rather than indulgent. It has been argued that the text is intended, on one level, to explode the myths of the heroic Arthurian age;[27] if such deflation is part of the Welsh narrative method, it is hardly surprising that even Arthur should become a target. The treatment of Arthur here suggests that accorded the king in the Welsh saints' lives.[28]

The passage just quoted also demonstrates another level of the text's parody, directed in this case at the traditional form which carries the traditional matter. I have already referred to the splendid hosts, whose action is mostly off-camera, as it were, to the

---

[25] *Breudwyt Ronabwy*, p. 21: "A'r ystorya honn a elwir Breidwyt Ronabwy. (A llyma yr achaws na wyr neb y breidwyt, na bard na chyfarwyd, heb lyuyr, o achaws y geniuer lliw a oed ar y me[i]rch, a hynny o amrauael liw odidawc ac ar yr aruev ac eu kyweirdebeu ac ar y llenneu gwerthuawr a'r mein rinwedawl)." There is some question as to the responsibility for these lines. They may be an addition by a copyist, appended as an explanation of why this tale was never recited, but read; the need for such an explanation has been taken to indicate that the text is the work of an individual, conscious author (Thomas Parry, *A History of Welsh Literature*, trans. H. Idris Bell [Oxford: Oxford University Press, 1955], p. 82; see also Brynley F. Roberts, "Tales and Romances," in *A Guide to Welsh Literature*, vol. 1, ed. A.O.H. Jarman and Gwilym Rees Hughes, [Swansea: Chistopher Davies, 1976], p. 232).
[26] Ceridwen Lloyd-Morgan, "*Breuddwyd Rhonabwy* and Later Arthurian Literature," in *The Arthur of the Welsh*, ed. Bromwich *et al.*, p. 183.
[27] Brynley F. Roberts, "*The Dream of Rhonabwy*," in *The Arthurian Encyclopedia*, ed. Norris J. Lacy (New York: Peter Bedrick, 1987), p. 142.
[28] Lloyd-Morgan, "*Breuddwyd Rhonabwy*," p. 186.

*gwyddbwyll* game. The elaboration of the description interrupts the narrative movement as did the name- and task-lists in *Culhwch* or the Greek fire episode in the *De Ortu*; but here the disruption is all the more pointed because the narrative is essentially nonexistent. Six times an exhaustively-described messenger interrupts the game, and the contrast between the lengthy descriptions and the laconic responses of first Arthur and then Owein could not be more marked. The description suggests something *should* be about to happen – it *should* be intended to focus the audience's attention on a key moment – but the subsequent "action" is always anticlimactic. This procedure has the effect of frustrating audience expectations; the ending has the same effect, when it becomes clear that the whole elaborate edifice has apparently been constructed to support an executive decision to put the question off. In *Culhwch*, there is a quest which is carried to a successful conclusion, and the parodic elements add an element of fun and mischief to the tale, suggesting an awareness of narrative conventions and a willingness to poke fun at them, without perhaps adding up to thorough-going parody. *Breudwyt Rhonabwy*, on the other hand, includes parody of every aspect of traditional content and traditional form. This thoroughness is also displayed by the "Celtic" Latin texts to which we now turn, the anonymous *Arthur and Gorlagon* and Geoffrey of Monmouth's *Vita Merlini*.

*Arthur and Gorlagon* is the more obviously Arthurian of these two texts. This short Arthurian tale has been largely ignored, with the exception of a few arguments by folklorists in the first half of this century over the ultimate origins of the werewolf tale contained in the Arthurian frame.[29] Like *Culhwch*, the tale is an example of the fitting of folktale motifs into an Arthurian context; the whole is also presented in a fashion which strongly suggests Welsh narrative conventions, as well as the tendency to parody those same conventions. One is immediately confronted, then, with the problem of the origins of this text. There is little information by which to date it. It

---

[29] "*Arthur and Gorlagon*: Versions of the Werewolf's Tale," ed. G.L. Kittredge, *Harvard Studies and Notes in Philology and Literature* 8 (1903), 149–275; rpt. New York: Haskell House, 1966 (hereafter *Arthur and Gorlagon*). The work is discussed in R.E. Bennett, "*Arthur and Gorlagon*, the Dutch *Lancelot*, and St. Kentigern," *Speculum* 13 (1938), 68–75 and A. Haggerty Krappe, "Arthur and Gorlagon," *Speculum* 8 (1933), 209–22. There are brief notes in "The Latin Romances," in *Arthurian Literature in the Middle Ages: A Collaborative History*, ed. Roger Sherman Loomis (Oxford: Clarendon Press, 1959), pp. 472–79; and in Mildred Leake Day, "Arthurian Romances in Latin: A Survey," in *King Arthur through the Ages*, vol. 1, ed. Valerie M. Lagorio and Mildred Leake Day (New York: Garland, 1990), pp. 44–55.

survives in one, late fourteenth-century English manuscript, a manuscript which also contains *Meriadoc*.[30] Kittredge believed it to be a direct translation of a Welsh text,[31] and there is a great deal in the structure and strategies of the work to suggest at least a thorough familiarity with Welsh tales and techniques. As is true of Geoffrey, it hardly matters if the author was a Welshman, when it is so clear that he knew Welsh forms and methods. Whether it is a translation from the Welsh or the product of someone thoroughly familiar with Welsh literature, *Arthur and Gorlagon* remains a parody of conventional tale-telling in both form and content.

### ARTHUR AND GORLAGON: SYNOPSIS

Arthur is holding a Pentecost feast in the City of Legions. Arthur kisses Guenevere in public; she, annoyed, tells him he knows nothing about the nature of women. Arthur vows to abjure food until he has found out; he rides off with Cei and Gawain to the court of Gorgol, a king renowned for his wisdom. Gorgol persuades Arthur to dismount and eat with a promise to answer his question on the next day, but instead sends Arthur on the next day to his brother Torleil, where the scene is repeated. Arthur rides on, to the court of Gorlagon; here he refuses to dismount and refuses to be put off, and Gorlagon tells him a story.

There was once a good king who had in his garden a sapling with this quality, that whoever should cut it and strike the king with it would be able to turn him into a wolf. The king guarded the tree, and his secret, well, until his wife persuaded him to tell her about it. She, desiring to remove him and take a pagan lover, cut the sapling and struck the king with it, forgetting, however, that part of the spell which would bereave him of his human reason. The wolf fled to the forest, where for a time he expressed his rage through attacks on his wife's family, killing her brothers and her children by her new

[30] Bodley MS Rawlinson B. 149; see *Arthur and Gorlagon*, ed. Kittredge, p. 149. Other contents include the *Historia trium Magorum*, the story of Apollonius of Tyre, an Alexander the Great narrative, a treatise of Aristotle, and the *Historia Meriadoci*.

[31] *Arthur and Gorlagon*, ed. Kittredge, p. 199. Kittredge based his arguments on nomenclature and the preponderance of Celtic folk-motifs. He argues that the names with the prefix Gor- must be either Welsh or Armorican (p. 205), and chooses Welsh because he believes that the Latin was rendered from a prose text "similar in style and general character to the 'Four Branches'" (p. 205). Loomis, on the other hand, argues that the tale, Oriental in origin, was probably picked up by Breton *conteurs* during the First or Second Crusades, who then brought it back to be spread throughout Europe ("The Latin Romances," p. 478). Names cannot in themselves indicate translation; Rachel Bromwich, "Celtic Elements in Arthurian Romance: A General Survey," (*The Legend of Arthur in the Middle Ages*, ed. P.B. Grout *et al.* [Cambridge: D.S. Brewer, 1983], p. 42) argues that Celtic names and story themes for the most part penetrated continental romance independently of each other.

husband. Forced to flee his own country, he came to the country of another king, and hearing of that king's wisdom and kindness, threw himself at that king's feet. This king, recognizing something almost human in the wolf, decided to keep the wolf as a pet.

The good king had a wicked wife, who took the king's absence on business as an opportunity to commit adultery with the royal steward. The wolf, enraged on his master's behalf, mauled the steward. The queen told the king that the steward had been injured in an attempt to stop the wolf from killing her son; she had concealed the infant in the basement of the castle to lend credence to her story. The wolf, however, conducted his master to the place of the infant's concealment, and the king realized that the steward and the wife must be lying. The steward confessed, and was flayed alive for his crime, while the queen was torn limb from limb by horses and burned.

The king, suspecting that his wolf was in fact a man, decided to follow where the wolf would lead, and attempt to help him regain his human form. The wolf led the king back to his own country. The king fought successfully to win back the kingdom, and tortured the wicked queen until she returned the sapling to him; he then used the sapling to restore the wolf to his human form. The wolf-king executed his wife's lover but spared his wife, merely divorcing her. The good king returned to his own kingdom.

Here Gorlagon's story ends, but Arthur asks for a further clarification: there is a woman sitting with Gorlagon, holding a blood-stained head and kissing it. Gorlagon reveals that he was the wolf-king of the story, and that this woman is his first wife, and the head belongs to her lover. Arthur finally dismounts and eats, and sets out the next day for his homeward journey.

Even a plot summary suggests some of the features of this tale which lead one to suspect parody; these may be divided roughly into matters of form and content. The formal features which merit comment include the manner of opening and closing, the use of repetition, and the interaction between the frame and the werewolf narrative. It is as if the text sets out deliberately to create and then frustrate certain narrative expectations in its audience. The content of the story is manipulated in a similar fashion; the traditional oaths and quests of romance are turned on their head to make the king appear foolish, and as the quest is undermined, so too is the whole idea of quest-literature. In the end, nearly every detail of *Arthur and Gorlagon* contributes to the text's explosion of its narrative conventions.

The first note sounded is a conventional one, which immediately sets up certain expectations. The story begins with the rather abrupt opening typical of the Welsh king's-tale: "King Arthur was accustomed to hold a famous feast on the day of Pentecost at Caerleon, to which he invited the magnates and nobles of his whole realm, and when the rites had been celebrated as was customary, they went to the banquet which had been prepared with all that pertained thereto."[32] It is at this banquet that Guenevere accuses Arthur of not knowing anything about the heart and nature of women, thus initiating the narrative proper. The accusation is in response to Arthur's boisterous conduct: "Arthur, in an excess of joy, threw his arms around his queen, who was sitting next to him, and kissed her most thoroughly in front of everyone. And she was amazed and also covered in blushes . . ."[33] Guenevere responds to her embarrassment by telling Arthur he knows nothing about women. There are many romances where Guenevere's sharp tongue has something to do with initiating the action; one thinks, for example, of Chrétien's *Yvain*. The problem posed, too, is not unusual; it is the same as that reflected in the *Wife of Bath's Tale*. Thus far, romance expectations established by the conventional opening are met, and even Arthur's rather foolish behavior is not unexpected, given what we have already seen in both Celtic and Latin Arthurian literature. And if it is unusual, by the standards of continental romance, for Arthur himself to be the quester, the vow which he utters is exactly as such things should be: "I call all the powers of heaven as witness, if they [the heart and nature of women] have thus far been hidden from me, I will exert myself, neither sparing any effort nor taking any food until I have come to know the answer."[34] Yet it is this typical vow which gives the first hint that all is not as it appears to be in this story, for when Arthur rides right into the hall of Gorgol,[35] this is how he is greeted:

---

[32] *Arthur and Gorlagon*, p. 150: "Apud Vrbem Legionum celebre festum diei Pentecostes rex Arturus agebat, ad quod totius sue dicionis magnates et nobiles inuitabat, peractisque de more solemnijs, ad instructum cum omnibus pertinentibus conuiuium."

[33] *Arthur and Gorlagon*, p. 150: ". . . Arturus, in nimiam effusus leticiam, reginam sibi considentem iniectis brachijs amplexatus est, amplexusque cunctis intuentibus strictissime osculatus est. Ad hec autem illa obstupefacta simulque rubore suffusa . . ."

[34] *Arthur and Gorlagon*, p. 150: "Omnia celi obtestor numina, si me actenus latuere, dabo operam, nec labori indulgens nunquam cibo fruar donec ea me nosse contingat." Cf. *Sir Gawain and the Green Knight*, where it is Arthur's custom to refuse to eat until he has seen a wonder.

[35] Among many analogues, compare two Welsh ones: the arrival of Culhwch at Arthur's court in *Culhwch and Olwen*, and the arrival of Peredur in *Peredur*.

207

"Arthur, it is a great thing which you are asking, and there are few who know it; but listen to my advice, dismount and eat and rest yourself today, for I see that your journey and labor have tired you, and tomorrow I will tell you what I know about it."[36] It would be bad enough that Arthur is persuaded to break his oath here, but the scene is repeated almost verbatim the next day at the court of Torleil, who says: "Arthur, it is a great thing which you are asking, and there are few who know it. Thus, because there is not time to discuss these things now, dismount and eat, and rest yourself today, and tomorrow I will tell you what I know about it."[37] When Arthur again complies, only to find on the next day that Torleil, too, is unable or unwilling to answer his question, both oath and king look increasingly foolish and inept. Here the patterned repetition which is common in Welsh narrative is being used to subversive effect, underlining the unusual nature of the king's position as a quester and, apparently, not a very good one. And there is humor here too, when Arthur replies testily to Gorlagon's repetition of his brothers' words: "Tell me what you were going to tell me, and don't talk to me any more about eating."[38] It is at this point that Gorlagon embarks on the werewolf narrative. Arthur – and the reader – have been led to believe that this story will reveal something of the nature of women, but its relevance to Arthur's question is indeed, as Gorlagon has promised, not immediately clear. Even more to the point, the tale is not told without incident. A plot synopsis can reveal that there is much action and suspense in the story; what it cannot reveal is how often these features of the narrative are disrupted by Gorlagon's repeated efforts to get Arthur to break his oath. He frequently interrupts himself, usually at moments of high narrative tension, to repeat the "dismount and eat" formula. The repetition says little for Gorlagon's opinion of the king's credulity, and the repeated phrase – "when I have told you, you will be held little the wiser for it"[39] – keeps Arthur's limitations firmly before our eyes.

---

[36] *Arthur and Gorlagon*, p. 151: "Arture, magnum est quod queris, et perpauci sunt qui illud nouerunt; sed crede nunc consilio meo, descende et comede et hodie quiesce, quia itinere et labore te vexatum video, et cras quod inde sciero indicabo tibi."

[37] *Arthur and Gorlagon*, p. 152: "Arture, magnum est quod queris, et pauci sunt qui illud agnoscunt. Vnde, quia super hijs tempus nunc non est disserere, descende et comede, et hodie quiesce, et cras quod inde sciero indicabo tibi."

[38] *Arthur and Gorlagon*, p. 152: "Narra ut proposuisti, et de meo esu ne quidquam loquaris."

[39] *Arthur and Gorlagon*, p. 154: ". . . et cum inde tibi retulero parum inde doctior habeberis."

The repetition of the invitation to dismount throughout the werewolf story has another effect; the audience, both within and outside of the text, is constantly pulled away from the narrative. Arthur expresses his feelings clearly: "Even if all the gods were to cry out from heaven, 'Arthur, dismount and eat!' I would neither dismount nor eat until I knew what remains."[40] His exasperation mirrors the reader's, who must put up with the multiplication of these breaks in the narrative. And it seems that Arthur's frustration has as much to do with being left hanging as to the plot of the story, as it does with the frustration of the quest for knowledge which apparently brought him to Gorlagon in the first place. As the wolf stands with his protector on the seashore, about to embark on his revenge, Gorlagon breaks off again, and Arthur responds with what could be the reader's voice: "The wolf was standing on the seashore, wanting to get across. I'm afraid that if he's left alone, he will drown in the waves in his eagerness to get to the other side."[41] At this point Gorlagon's skills as storyteller are the focus, and in one particularly telling exchange, Arthur accuses him of spinning out his tale with useless interpolations, "just like a harper."[42] Tale-telling itself, as well as the outcome and purpose of the tale, has become the focus. Given the language of the text, one wonders if this particular observation is not evidence of the professional skirmishes between Latin and popular, vernacular storytellers.

The emphasis on food and feasts is itself suggestive of a court context, and one can imagine *Arthur and Gorlagon* quite precisely as a dinner entertainment, and a rather raucous one at that. The repeated attempts to get Arthur to eat might provoke gleeful repetition from an audience of the key lines. Furthermore, Arthur often replies to Gorlagon's pauses in such a way as to suggest that he feels that his host has something of an obsession with food:

> "If I wanted to eat, you wouldn't ask me to so often."

> "Please, order the table to be taken away, since those dishes in front of you keep interrupting our discussion."

---

[40] *Arthur and Gorlagon*, p. 156: "Etiam si omnes dij de celo clamarent: 'Arture descende et comede!' nec descendam nec comedam donec quod restat agnouero."

[41] *Arthur and Gorlagon*, p. 160: "Lupus transfretare cupiens astat in litore. Timeo ne si solus relinquatur desiderio transeundi vndis mergatur."

[42] *Arthur and Gorlagon*, p. 161: ". . . 'mos cithariste' . . ."

"If you were not anxious to eat [?], you wouldn't care that I am continuing my fast."[43]

Arthur's irritable replies to Gorlagon's repeated invitation set off that feature of the narrative, and eating becomes a recurring motif throughout the text. Arthur makes his oath at the Pentecost feast. He arrives at the courts of Gorgol, Torleil and Gorlagon during feasts. The wolf-king makes a point of visiting his sapling before taking food every day, "even when it meant fasting until evening,"[44] and it is this rather unusual behavior which alerts his wife to his secret. She discovers the powers of the sapling through refusing to eat until her husband tells her its secret; in fact, she makes a vow very similar to Arthur's: " 'I vow before all the gods of heaven,' she exclaimed, 'that I will not eat at all, until you tell me the cause [of your behavior].' "[45] She persists, and her vow works. And the eating motif continues. The second wicked queen accuses the wolf of eating her child, and the wolf does in fact maul her lover. The second king is unable to eat because of his doubts about his wife's story. And finally, the second king tortures the first wicked queen into handing over the magical sapling, by refusing her food and drink. These references would certainly make *Arthur and Gorlagon* a suitable after-dinner entertainment, but they also serve the larger project of the parody. The very conventional quality of Arthur's oath – I will not rest or eat until I have my answer – is thus undermined by the insinuation of details about eating in all parts of the story.

This overuse of the motif of eating to undermine the oath with which it is connected ultimately raises questions about the type of narrative for which such oaths are traditionally important.[46] The use of the patterned repetition characteristic of Celtic narrative to contain many of these instances further reinforces their impact, so that the text draws attention to itself, to *how* it is telling, or not telling, its

---

[43] *Arthur and Gorlagon*, pp. 157, 158, 159:
> "Si vellem comedere, vtique non me sepius ut comederem inuitares."
> "Jube, queso, mensam auferri, quia fercula tibi apposita tociens nostra interrumpunt colloquia."
> "Nisi te pigeret comedere, me parum curares diucius ieiunare."

[44] *Arthur and Gorlagon*, p. 153: ". . . licet usque ad vesperam ieiunasset . . ."

[45] *Arthur and Gorlagon*, p. 153: " 'Omnia,' exclamat, 'celi obtestor numina me nunquam amodo commesturam, donec mihi causam indicabis.' "

[46] In his *Survival of Geis*, Reinhard suggests that *geasa*, magical and apparently arbitrary conditions applied to heroes of old narrative, eventually became meaningless to some romancers, and so were omitted from their stories (p. 193); perhaps here, while the *geis* connected with eating has lost its original significance, it has been retained as a target for mockery.

story. The rhetorical interventions at the opening or closing of texts like the *Historia regum Britannie*, the *Historia Meriadoci*, the *De nugis curialium*, or indeed the *Breudwyt Rhonabwy*, draw attention to the written qualities of these texts, to their participation in literate culture; they are part of the authors' self-fashioning. Here too, the parodic attention drawn to the progress of the story implies a similar self-consciousness. I suggested above that in the Welsh world, as in the Angevin, the same writers, or the same sorts of writers, might be responsible for both Latin and vernacular literary production. The parody of traditional Welsh forms here need not undermine that assertion; parody is best practiced by those most thoroughly versed in its target. Linda Hutcheon suggests that parody is part of a literary artist's refashioning of inherited forms in the pursuit of self-assertion; one can see how a period such as the twelfth century would be particularly likely to encourage such a pursuit. It is also the case that parody need not be understood as wholly negative; *para*, Hutcheon points out, can mean "beside": "Parody, . . . in its ironic 'trans-contextualization' and inversion, is repetition with a difference. A critical distance is implied between the background text being parodied and the new incorporating work, a distance usually signalled by irony. But this irony can be playful as well as belittling; it can be critically constructive as well as destructive."[47] *Arthur and Gorlagon*, like many of the texts discussed throughout this study, is indeed playful. The play here involves the manipulation in Latin of traditional Welsh techniques, and it is characteristic of both Latin and Welsh parody that one also finds, beneath the playfulness, a message about rule, here in the form of the doubts expressed about Arthur's ability to learn.

The framed story in *Arthur and Gorlagon* is finally brought to a conclusion, despite all the interruptions, and one could argue that narrative closure is achieved. But there are a few final flourishes to consider. First on the level of form, a final Celtic characteristic – the abrupt ending – is invoked in a most startling fashion. Arthur continues to refuse to dismount even after Gorlagon has apparently completed his story, asking instead, "Now, just who is that sad-faced woman sitting opposite you, with a dish in front of her holding a human head sprinkled with blood, who's been crying whenever you've smiled, and who's been kissing that bloody head whenever

---

[47] Linda Hutcheon, *A Theory of Parody* (New York: Methuen, 1985), p. 32.

you've kissed your wife as you were telling your tale?"[48] The abrupt, unexpected introduction of this gruesome element after the rather leisurely progression of the framed tale once again brings the audience up short, following the apparent resolution of the framed tale with a new problem which completely overshadows that resolution. It is not uncommon to find brief, vivid scenes, often concerning the other-world, introduced suddenly and without explanation in Celtic narra-tive. In *Pwyll*, for example, there is a peculiar episode in which a monster hand attempts to steal a colt, and apparently leaves Pryderi, son of Pwyll, behind. While this episode used to be explained as a remnant of a no longer understood myth about the birth of a hero, it can be argued that the abrupt intrusion of the episode, and the resolute lack of explanation of it, are themselves narrative strategies designed to heighten the marvelous aspect of the tale. In the case of the ending of *Arthur and Gorlagon*, however, the reader's realization that Arthur must have been contemplating this strange spectacle throughout Gorlagon's tale tends to make what in another context might have had marvelous overtones seem simply bizarre. The explanation which follows serves to link tale and frame – this is the very wicked woman, and Gorlagon was the werewolf – but it is quite true, as Gorlagon has promised all along, that Arthur is little the wiser for the story. The effect on the audience, too, is the same as that of the repeated interruptions of the story; one is jolted into an awareness of narrative conventions, a situation which is hardly conducive to the suspension of disbelief which would be necessary in a straightforward narrative of this sort.

This neat tidying of loose ends is in itself another problem, since it seems to assert that, because the plot is finally worked out, the story has fulfilled its responsibilities. Yet neither Arthur, nor we, have learned the answer to the question posed at the outset. The tale closes with a final repetition of the invitation to eat, and the final lines must surely seem an understatement after the scene of the bloody head: "'Arthur, now dismount, if you want to dismount, since as far as I'm concerned you will stay there unasked from now on.' So Arthur dismounted and ate; and on the next day, marveling greatly over the things which he had heard, he began the nine days'

---

[48] *Arthur and Gorlagon*, p. 162: "Quenam est illa femina contra te opposita facie tristis, humanumque caput sanguine conspersum ante se in disco continens, que etiam tociens fleuit quociens risisti, tociens cruentum caput osculata est quociens tu tue coniugi, dum predicta referres, oscula impressisti?"

journey home."[49] But there is no answer here. Is such an answer to be found in the occasional misogynist asides sprinkled throughout the story? *Arthur and Gorlagon* seems an elaborate construction for the rather simple task, for a medieval author, of proving that women are untrustworthy. I am inclined to see those moments as an expected reflex in a Latin writer, whether of court or cloister; one thinks of Walter Map's parodic romance of *Sadius and Galo*, for example. There are other conclusions one can draw from the story which make a greater impression. Arthur's inability to keep his oath, and indeed his failure to learn anything of much use on his quest, tends to undermine his status. Yet as is the case with many of the works examined in this study, a critical treatment of the king is in one sense simply a pointer to a more radical conclusion. *Arthur and Gorlagon* is a text which deliberately exaggerates many of the features of traditional Welsh narrative, parodying both a traditional hero and the traditional type of narrative in which his stories are contained. To what end?

If *Arthur and Gorlagon* is a straight translation from the Welsh, then we have another Welsh parody to put alongside *Culhwch ac Olwen* and *Breudwyt Rhonabwy*. *Arthur and Gorlagon* is more closely aligned with the latter than the former, in that it involves a comprehensive mockery of both the form and the content of traditional narrative. Arthur is the rather dim king in the tradition of Pwyll; the repetition of Gorlagon's doubts about Arthur's ability to learn from the tale may suggest that he is even worse than Pwyll, who does learn from his errors and experiences. The quest fizzles out, thus undermining the whole idea of quest; the final marvel is introduced in such a way as to provoke startled laughter, thus undermining the whole idea of the marvelous. *Arthur and Gorlagon* presents such a negative portrait of both Arthur and Arthurian story that it may in fact be called an anti-romance; that is, while the familiar court themes of kings and counsel are here, the focus has shifted to the generic features of the text. Kittredge tended to attribute the Arthurian frame to the Latin translator/author.[50] If he was correct in so doing, then the specifically Arthurian butt of the satire is the creation of a Latin writer and may perhaps be explained by the kind of professional

---

[49] *Arthur and Gorlagon*, p. 162: "'Arture, nunc descende, si descendere volueris, quia ibi pro me amodo imprecatus remanebis.' Descendit igitur Arturus et comedit; dieque sequenti, super hijs que audiuerat valde miratus, domum itinere dierum nouem redijt."
[50] *Arthur and Gorlagon*, ed. Kittredge, p. 209.

rivalries I have described in the Introduction; these rivalries are not between Latin and vernacular forms so much as they are between written and more oral, popular, forms. On the other hand, the text shows a clear familiarity with Welsh traditions. We may be dealing, then, with a learned writer familiar enough with Welsh techniques to make them the focus of parody; the playfulness in parody stressed by Hutcheon seems clearly to be at work in *Arthur and Gorlagon*, which is nothing if not funny. Finally, it may be that the original Welsh text was itself a parody along the lines of *Culhwch* or *Rhonabwy*. It does not seem to me to be possible to decide where the parody started; suffice it to say that it is clearly present in the text as we have it. Even if this text is an exact translation of a Welsh one, it is significant that this should be one of the very few Arthurian texts chosen for preservation in Latin. The Welsh narrative tradition, and the possibilities for parody inherent in that tradition, made some impression on at least one learned Briton. The text refuses to offer enlightenment – neither Arthur nor the audience departs from it any the wiser. Thus we return again to the question of interpretation. For this Latin author, as for the others in this study, the subversion of the text represents, not necessarily a rejection of narrative, but rather an engagement with the fundamental questions of narrative; what, and how, does it mean?

*Arthur and Gorlagon* casts its narrative experiments in a familiar mold; both the conventional and the parodic aspects have analogues in traditional Welsh narrative. Geoffrey of Monmouth's *Vita Merlini*[51] is a more complicated case, because it is in many ways unprecedented, yet it is possible, reading the *Vita* against the background of the *Historia* and the Welsh and Welsh Latin tradition, to venture some suggestions as to what Geoffrey was up to. The *Vita* is a later work than the *Historia*,[52] and from a certain perspective can be seen as a heightening of the experimental tendencies already exhibited in the work. It is perhaps this peculiar character which is responsible for its obscurity; in marked contrast to the *Historia*, the *Vita* survives complete in only one manuscript.[53]

In the *Historia*, Geoffrey makes mention, not only of his "very

---

[51] Authorship was firmly established by John Jay Parry in his edition of *The Vita Merlini* (Urbana: University of Indiana Press, 1925), pp. 9–15.

[52] It may be dated some time between 1148 and 1151; for a review of attempts to fix a more precise date, see Curley, *Geoffrey of Monmouth*, pp. 110–11.

[53] London, British Library, MS Cotton Vespasian E.iv, from the later thirteenth century.

ancient book," but also of oral tradition; the deeds of the kings of the Britons "were reported joyfully and by memory by many people, as if they had been written down."[54] Whether Geoffrey was in fact a Welshman, or simply, as Brynley Roberts suggests, a sympathetic outsider, the *Vita Merlini* is further proof that he made much use of native tradition, written as well as oral;[55] in particular, the *Vita* shows the influence of the Welsh Myrddin material.[56] There are also non-Celtic, non-Arthurian sources; the natural science section of the work suggests firsthand knowledge of Isidore's *Etymologiae*, and perhaps also of Bede's *De natura rerum*.[57] Various folk-motifs, too, are woven through the text, most notably the wild man in the woods, the triple death, and the prophetic laughter. The *Vita*, then, which has been characterized as "a strange and horrifying fairy-story,"[58] is in fact a combination of a great deal of disparate material. The manner in which this material has been handled casts light, not only on the purpose of the *Vita*, but on the method of the *Historia* as well.

### VITA MERLINI: SYNOPSIS

Merlin, king and prophet to the South Welsh, is involved in a war against Guennolous, the king of Scotland. The loss of his friends in the battle drives Merlin mad, and he runs away to the forest of Caledon, where he lives as a "man of the woods." His sister Ganieda, wife to King Rodarch, sends messengers throughout the country in an effort to find her brother; one such messenger, coming upon the prophet in the forest, brings him back to his senses through music. Merlin joyfully accompanies the messenger to the court of Rodarch, but his reunion with his sister and with his wife

---

[54] *Historia regum Britannie*, p. 1: ". . . et a multis populis quasi inscripta iocunde et memoriter predicarent<ur>."

[55] A debated point: Tatlock notes that the *Vita* shows considerable use of Celtic material ("Geoffrey of Monmouth's *Vita Merlini*," *Speculum* 18 [1943], 269), but denies the possibility of previous tradition in Geoffrey's portrayal of Arthur in the *Historia*, arguing Arthur is not found in pre-Conquest Welsh literature. He did not take account of the very early Arthurian poems *Pa Gwr* and *Preiddeu Annwn* or of an early date for *Culhwch*. Gransden suggests Geoffrey's greatest debt was to his own imagination (*Historical Writing in England*, p. 204). Geoffrey's imagination was fertile, but the wealth of Welsh material in the *Vita* is ample evidence that Geoffrey knew and made use of many Welsh traditions throughout his work.

[56] Basil Clarke notes particularly the Myrddin-story as it appears in the Welsh poem "Afallennau"; this is the oldest Myrddin-material in Welsh, to be dated to anywhere between 850 and 1050; Geoffrey of Monmouth, *Life of Merlin: Vita Merlini* (hereafter *Vita Merlini*), ed. and trans. Basil Clarke (Cardiff: University of Wales Press, 1973), p. 1. For a complete list of possible Welsh source material, see Curley, *Geoffrey of Monmouth*, pp. 115–18.

[57] *Vita Merlini*, ed. and trans. Clarke, pp. 7–9.

[58] Brooke, "Geoffrey of Monmouth as a Historian," p. 86.

Guendoloena soon sours – the crowds at the court bring on a return of madness, and Merlin tries to run back to the forest. Rodarch has him chained to prevent his escape. When the formerly sullen Merlin laughs as Rodarch removes a leaf from Ganieda's hair, Rodarch offers the prophet his freedom in return for an explanation of his laughter. Merlin explains that Ganieda got the leaf in her hair as she was lying with her lover in the forest; he was laughing at the contrast between Rodarch's tenderness and Ganieda's unfaithfulness. Ganieda denies the accusation, and seeks to discredit Merlin by having him predict the death of "three" people – all are in fact a disguised servant of hers. Merlin predicts three separate deaths and is discredited in the eyes of Rodarch and the court, although we later learn that the boy does die a triple death as an adult.

Merlin returns to the forest of Caledon after apparently granting his wife Guendoloena permission to remarry, but when she does so, he returns from the forest riding on a stag, and kills her new husband with its horns. He is recaptured by Rodarch's men, and again falls silent. Rodarch has him taken to the marketplace in the hopes of cheering him up, and Merlin laughs twice, once at a begging servant, and next at a man buying patches for his new shoes. Again he refuses to explain until he is promised his freedom. Again Rodarch agrees, and Merlin explains that the poor servant stood unknowingly over buried riches, while the man with the new shoes had already drowned and would have no need for the patches.

Merlin returns to the forest, this time to a splendid house which he has Ganieda build for him there. He prophesies at length about the fate of the Britons. Ganieda returns to court to find Rodarch dead, and laments him. Meanwhile Taliesin has come to Merlin; the two discuss the weather, the waters, various kinds of fish, and famous islands, including the Isle of Avalon. Merlin is prompted to utter more prophecy. His men appear and tell him of a miraculous new spring; Merlin drinks of it and is restored to sanity. He and Taliesin discuss springs and lakes. The chieftains come to Merlin and ask him to be their king once more, but he refuses, citing his age, and enters into a discussion about birds. When he has finished, a madman, Maeldin by name, rushes up to them; Merlin recognizes him and gets him to drink from the miraculous spring. This madman, too, is cured. Merlin, Maeldin and Taliesin declare their intention to live in the forest in the service of God; Ganieda joins them. She offers the last prophecies of the poem.

The summary of the contents of the text reveals its strange nature; clearly this is a poem with a great deal of information and prophecy,

216

tinged with a certain amount of fatalism. Yet what becomes most obvious from the moment one first picks up the *Vita* is its insistence on laughter. Consider the first lines of the work. The *Vita* opens with a statement of the author's intention – "I prepare myself to sing the madness of Merlin, the prophetic bard, and the jocose muse"[59] – and in the first lines we find the first problem. What, exactly, is a *musa jocosa*? And whose muse is this? Both the prophet and the poet are moved by a muse, and often most peculiarly too. The phrase is odd, but it does occur in another, perhaps helpful, context. In book II of the *Tristia*, Ovid offers a defense of his own work:

> Believe me, my character is far from my songs:
> My life is virtuous, although my Muse is jocose.
> The greater part of my work is lying and fictive;
> It allows itself more latitude than does its author.
> Nor is the book an indication of the spirit, but an honest game;
> You will find in it many things suited to delight the audience.[60]

Ovid was, we assume, primarily engaged in a defense of himself from his banishment, yet the principle here – that writing has a character of its own and some sort of life of its own, that the responsibility is at least as much that of the audience as of the writer – is one which has been of interest to many of the writers studied thus far, and perhaps to none more than Geoffrey. The potentially playful – or tricky – nature of this writing is also emphasized. One thinks of Walter Map's complex presentation of his *nugae*, of John of Salisbury's assertion that, while all he writes might not be true, it is nevertheless useful; even William of Rennes's presentation of his *Gesta* as a *ludus* is suggested here. Notice too that Ovid's defense is specifically cast in terms of the gap between appearance and reality, here seen in the contrast between his virtuous life and his playful muse. It is certainly

---

[59] *Vita Merlini*, lines 1–2: "Fatidici vatis rabiem musamque jocosam/ Merlini cantare paro."

[60] Ovid, *Tristia* (*Tristium Liber Secundus*, ed. S.G. Owen [Amsterdam: Adolf M. Hakkert, 1967]), II.353–58:

> crede mihi, distant mores a carmine nostro
> (vita verecunda est, Musa iocosa mea)
> magnaque pars mendax operum est et ficta meorum:
> plus sibi permisit compositore suo.
> nec liber indicium est animi, sed honesta voluptas:
> plurima mulcendis auribus apta feres.

The "jocose muse" is also suggested by *Remedia Amoris*, lines 387–88: "si mea materiae respondet Musa iocosae,/ vicimus, et falsi criminis acta rea est."

possible that the resemblance to Ovid is merely coincidental,[61] but one can see how Ovid, like Geoffrey, would be keenly aware of what one can, and cannot, say in certain settings. In any case, the invocation of the *musa jocosa* at the opening of the *Vita Merlini* seems to show Geoffrey declaring that what follows is a game of sorts, something amusing, for a select group of listeners who will get the joke – Map's *arguti*, perhaps. *Jocus*, *subtilitas*, and *facetia*, it will be remembered, are all characteristics of life and speech at the Angevin courts. The manuscript history of the *Vita* certainly suggests extremely limited circulation, perhaps implying a select coterie of readers. This limited circulation may be surprising, given the vogue both for Galfridian history and for Merlin material, but it is perhaps less so if this work is a sort of after-dinner game for a small circle of courtier-clerics.[62] University-educated men were, as we have seen in chapters 1 and 2, among the most avid consumers of Merlin material.[63] But if this is a game or a joke, it is a joke of a very peculiar character, most peculiar in precisely those passages which have claims to inspiration by the *musa jocosa*.

A rough count reveals many words and phrases connected to the jocose muse sprinkled throughout the *Vita*: there are some six variants of *jocosus/ jocare*, four of *gaudere*, nine of *letus/ letare*, and nine of *risum/ ridere*, for example. But who is laughing, and at what? As the plot synopsis suggests, the narrative pivots on Merlin's laughter, and is intimately connected to both the madness and the prophetic ability which are the focal point of the poem. His laughter surfaces in

---

[61] But Curtius remarks in passing that this Ovidian Muse, whom he argues Ovid treats ironically, "is often invoked by the hedonistically-minded poets of the twelfth century" (Ernst Robert Curtius, *European Literature and the Latin Middle Ages*, trans. Willard R. Trask [Princeton, N.J.: Princeton University Press, 1953], p. 232).

[62] While there are more than two hundred manuscripts of the *Historia* (see Crick, *The Historia regum Britannie of Geoffrey of Monmouth III: A Summary Catalogue of the Manuscripts*), the *Vita* survives in only one complete manuscript (Cotton Vespasian E.iv); there are also four collections of extracts of about half the poem, and two manuscripts containing extracts from the prophetic and scientific sections (*Vita Merlini*, ed. Clarke, pp. 43–44). This manuscript history implies that the *Vita* was a much less popular work than the *Historia*, perhaps because it was intended for a narrower audience. Tatlock's argument for a vogue for the *Vita* rests on the use of a single passage concerning Avalon by such writers as Higden, John of Glastonbury, and John Leland ("*Vita Merlini*," 274–75); this seems to me insufficient evidence for any widespread knowledge of the poem, particularly given the use of Avalon in other works, discussed in chapter 2.

[63] In *The Historia regum Britannie of Geoffrey of Monmouth IV*, Julia Crick notes that prophetic and apocalyptic texts suggest a milieu of educated, well-situated clerical readers, pp. 221–22.

unexpected situations – let us first consider the enigmatic laughter which twice buys Merlin his freedom.

The first such laugh occurs when Rodarch draws a leaf from his wife's hair. Merlin wins his freedom when he explains that the leaf became tangled in Ganieda's hair while she was lying in the woods with her lover; the contrast between Rodarch's tenderness and Ganieda's faithlessness led Merlin to laugh. Merlin's laughter has been provoked by his recognition of the fallibility of human perception; the dramatic irony involved in his extra knowledge underlines the message that human beings can judge only according to a combination of appearances and preconceptions. As a result, such judgments are often mistaken, a point which the text seems eager to drive home through Ganieda's reaction to Merlin's revelation. She, naturally enough, seeks to discredit her brother, and her plot to trick him – presenting him with the same boy in three disguises – evokes the triple death prophecy. The last exchange, when the boy has been disguised as a girl, is marked by several references to joking and laughter:

> Then the boy left and immediately did what she had ordered, and returned in a feminine guise, dressed as a woman, and stood before the man, to whom the queen, jokingly, said "Now, brother, tell me about the death of this girl."
>
> "If this is a girl or not," her brother said to her, "she will die in a river," and his reasoning caused King Rodarch to laugh loudly, since he had been asked about the death of a single boy and had made three predictions.[64]

The triple death motif has many folklore reflexes.[65] Here, Geoffrey has used traditional material to underline the theme of appearance and reality, represented throughout this text in the irony of Merlin's prophetic knowledge. That knowledge provokes both the prophet's knowing laughter, and, in ironic contrast, the mistaken laughter of

---

[64] *Vita Merlini*, lines 334–41:
> Mox puer abcessit jussumque subinde peregit,
> et sub feminea rediit quasi femina veste
> et stetit ante virum, cui sic regina jocando,
> "Eya, frater," ait, "dic mortem virginis huius."
> "Hec virgo nec ne," dixit, "morietur in ampne,"
> frater ei, movitque sua ratione cachinnum
> regi Rodarcho, quoniam de morte rogatus
> unius pueri tres dixerat esse futuras.

[65] See *Vita Merlini*, ed. and trans. Clarke, pp. 12–14.

Rodarch. Rodarch's error soon becomes clear; after a brief interlude in which Merlin moves back to the forest, the poem moves into the future to show how the youth does indeed die all the deaths Merlin predicted for him. This knowledge is allowed only to the audience of the poem: none of the participants knows that Merlin is right. The prophet is discredited and the adulterous queen, as far as the court is concerned, vindicated. As was the case in the *De Ortu* and *Meriadoc*, the truth is available to all, but most misinterpret the signs which point to it. Is there perhaps something in the atmosphere of life at court which makes it particularly difficult for one to interpret correctly? John of Salisbury, it will be remembered, felt that it was impossible to be a philosopher at court, and Walter Map, in his own way, concurred. In the *Vita*, the audience is allowed to appreciate the irony in order that the author may further stress the blindness of the court, a blindness which the audience may recognize only too well. At the same time, there are implications beyond the court context, for one also senses through this incident the futility of prophetic insight, which sees the truth but is unable to make that truth felt, in the world of the poem at least.

The second incident of enigmatic laughter occurs when Merlin, who has been captured again by Rodarch's men, is taken to the marketplace. There he laughs twice, first at a poor beggar, and then at a young man buying patches for his new shoes. In the case of the leaf in Ganieda's hair, Merlin was laughing out of recognition of hidden vice; furthermore, the cuckolded husband is a stock figure of comedy, although the exemplary Rodarch seems rather ill-suited to this role. One may be uneasy, then, at Ganieda's behavior, but at least the situation is one which can lead to laughter. The cases of the beggar and the young man, on the other hand, are considerably different. The beggar stands, unknowing, over a hoard of coins; the young man has already drowned, and will have no need to patch his shoes. Here, then, Merlin is laughing at human blindness in the face of misery and death, and the message is different from the laughter at Ganieda's deception of her husband. Here fate is the agent of the situation which provokes Merlin's laughter.

The *Vita* is very concerned with fate – in itself an odd focus, one might think, for a work inspired by a "jocose Muse." The poem opens with the prophet railing at fate and apparently maddened by it; during the battle with Guennolous he laments, "O, the doubtful fates of men, with death ever near, always able to strike them with a hidden goad, and drive out the miserable life from the body!"[66] It is the recognition of fate which drives Merlin to the forest, and it is against fate that he rails when winter arrives: "Nineteen apple trees stood here, perpetually bearing fruit, and now they do not stand here. Who then has taken them away from me, where have they gone so suddenly? Now I see them, now I don't. So the fates support me and reject me too, both giving me sight and preventing me from seeing."[67] An apple tree features prominently in the Welsh Myrddin poem "Afallennau," but its role is quite different here. The Welsh poem contains a great deal of prophecy, as well as laments occasioned by the death in battle of the speaker's lord. As in the Welsh poem, the trees of the *Vita* become the focus for a lament of the *ubi sunt* sort, and indeed, there are many such laments throughout the work, almost as if Geoffrey were exaggerating this strain in his sources. There is much more at work in this passage, however. While a reader could be forgiven for wondering how such references and echoes are to be reconciled with the *musa jocosa*, there are several amusing aspects to this passage. Perhaps the trees have merely lost their fruit as apple trees do in the winter, but to the madman, who can no longer recognize them as apple trees without their fruit, they themselves have "disappeared." The madman's appraisal of the situation is both realistic and funny. In "Afallennau," however, the apple tree does seem to have a power of invisibility; thus to anyone familiar with that particular tradition, it is also possible that the trees have in fact disappeared, that malignant fates are playing a particularly cruel joke on the madman. This is humor of another sort, a cosmic laughter which is neither very warm nor very funny, at least in human terms. Finally, there is the reference to the double gift of the fates; Merlin has gained a new sort of sight through his madness, and yet normal sight seems to have been sacrificed. This duality acts as a figure for the whole poem, which continually challenges and baffles the audience's perceptions. The pleasure involved in the poem, then, must be that of

[66] *Vita Merlini*, lines 43–45:
  O dubios hominum casus mortemque propinquam
  que penes est illos semper stimuloque latenti
  percutit et miseram pellit de corpore vitam!
[67] *Vita Merlini*, lines 90–94:
  Tres quater et juges septene poma ferentes
  hic steterant mali, nunc non stant. Ergo quis illas
  quis michi surripuit, quo devenere repente?
  Nunc illas video, nunc non. Sic fata repugnant
  sic quoque concordant cum dant prohibentque videre.

a rather cerebral game, as the audience attempts to follow the changes being rung on the traditional material. Needless to say, many will be left behind. And the connection drawn between laughter, fate, and prophecy suggests that while laughter may be a response to the ironies of fate, it is not an uncomplicated one.

There are other places in the *Vita* where references to laughter and joking have less philosophical baggage attached to them; yet the peculiar mingling of the jocose with the unsettling persists. A key incident here occurs on the day of Guendoloena's remarriage. Taxed by his sister with his abandonment of his wife, Merlin had responded that she may marry again, but that her new husband should watch out for him.[68] This is a confusing message, and Merlin's reaction to Guendoloena's remarriage is equally mixed. Merlin decides to go to court and take to her "the gift [he] promised to her."[69] While his intentions are not yet absolutely clear, in retrospect his call to his former wife has a grotesque irony: "Guendoloena, Guendoloena, come out! Such presents are waiting for you!"[70] The bridegroom, on recognizing Merlin, laughs, and Merlin promptly kills him with the horns of a stag.[71] It is not clear if this had been Merlin's intention all along. The promised *munera* could be gifts, but also reward or payment; it might be argued that Merlin has been planning to pay Guendoloena back for her betrayal, even though he himself had rejected her, and indeed, had done so quite amiably apart from the warning. The jocose muse presides over this scene in several ways. There is the uncomplicated laughter generated by the wild appearance of the prophet, both in the bridegroom and in the audience. This laughter may give way to startled laughter at Merlin's actions. Finally, there is the pleasure involved in recognizing, in retrospect, the double possibilities in Merlin's words. The scene is nevertheless also rather grim and grotesque; again, laughter is woven through a scene whose

---

[68] *Vita Merlini*, lines 375–78:
> Huic igitur detur nubendi justa facultas
> arbitrioque suo quem gestit ducere ducat.
> Precaveat tamen ipse sibi qui duxerit illam
> obvius ut numquam michi sit nec cominus astet.

[69] *Vita Merlini*, line 450: ". . . munus ei promissum . . ."

[70] *Vita Merlini*, lines 457–58: ". . . Guendoloena,/ Guendoloena veni! Te talia munera spectant."

[71] Ziolkowski, "The Nature of Prophecy," suggests a connection between the incident and the shamanic, pre-Christian substratum of the Myrddin story: the shaman rides into the otherworld in the hide or on the antlers of a stag, pp. 155–56.

final meaning is ambiguous, so that one can never be sure if one's own laughter is the product of understanding or of ignorance.

Thus far we have been discussing the mingling of references to laughter with material which seems ill-suited to jocosity. Another jarring aspect of the *Vita* lies in a structural deployment of a similar technique; abrupt shifts in narrative material and tone are character-istic of the piece from the outset. Despite the jocose muse, the poem opens, as we have seen, with references to fate; a string of formal laments follows as Merlin flees to the woods. Merlin laments the arrival of winter, the disappearance of the apples, and his sorry state, while Ganieda's messenger, attempting to entice the madman to return to the city, expands at length on the sufferings of Ganieda and Guendoloena in the absence of their brother and husband. The laments are well done, and are very much in keeping with the Celtic atmosphere of the poem, but one could be forgiven for finding the messenger's offering a bit much, as the fourth such outpouring in the space of 150 lines. Merlin is indeed brought back to his senses, but the focus is on laughter rather than the expected empathy: "Suddenly the prophet jumped up and accosted the youth with jocose words and prayed him to sound the chords with his fingers and play again those elegiac verses."[72] It is poetry which restores the prophet's senses, but in a way we might not expect. The poem as a whole is similar; there is much to be learned, but matter and manner are not always congruent.

Like the laments, the prophecy passages of the poem offer stimu-lating difficulties. The prophecies suggest Welsh nationalistic prophecy, examples of which can be found in the Myrddin poems. A single theme emerges from the prophecies in the *Vita*, important in the *Historia* as well as here. Merlin sings of the fall of cities and kingdoms, the coming of Saxon, Danish and Norman invaders, and the alternation of brief periods of peace with wretched intervals of war. He directs his words at the "madness of the Britons";[73] both the *Vita* and the *Historia* show a great concern with the inability of the Britons to remain united among themselves and thus at peace. The disruptions of the Anarchy and the internecine feuding among the Welsh princes would each provide a suitable contemporary backdrop.

---

[72] *Vita Merlini*, lines 201–3:
    Ocius assurgit vates juvenemque jocosis
    affatur verbis iterumque movere precatur
    cum digitis cordas elegosque sonare priores.
[73] *Vita Merlini*, line 580: ". . . rabiem Britonum . . ."

The final part of this prophetic section of the *Vita* shows a complete inversion of all values, social, political, religious, and familial:

> Then peace and faith and virtue will all depart, and there will be civil war throughout the lands, and man will betray his fellow, and no friend will be found. The husband, despising his wife, will mate with whores, and the wife will join with whomever she desires, despising her husband. Honor for the churches will not remain, and the order will perish. Then bishops will bear arms, then they will follow the camps, they will place towers and walls on sacred ground and give to soldiers what they ought to give to the poor.[74]

Similar inversions feature, as we have seen, in the *Historia*; the connection is made explicit when Merlin says that he has already predicted this future at greater length to Vortigern when explaining the battle of the two dragons.[75]

Another connection with the *Historia* is made when Ganieda returns to court and discovers that Rodarch is dead. Her lament for him stresses his role as a guarantor of peace, justice, and religion:

> He was a lover of peace, for he gave law to a savage people in such a way that no one was harmed by anyone else. He treated the holy cleric with just control, and allowed both the powerful and the humble to be ruled by justice. He was generous and gave much away, and kept very little. He was all things to all men, doing whatever was fitting, the flower of knights, the glory of kings and the pillar of the kingdom.[76]

Descriptions of ideal kings in the *Historia* are very like this, and the ideal kings of Latin court writers are, as we have seen, those who rule

---

[74] *Vita Merlini*, lines 661–69:
> Tum pax atque fides et virtus omnis abibit,
> undique per patrias committent prelia cives
> virque virum prodet, non invenietur amicus.
> Conjuge despecta meretrices sponsus adibit
> sponsaque cui cupiet despecto conjuge nubet.
> Non honor ecclesiis servabitur, ordo peribit.
> Pontifices tunc arma ferent, tunc castra sequentur,
> in tellure sacra turres et menia ponent
> militibusque dabunt quod deberetur egenis.

[75] *Vita Merlini*, lines 681–83.

[76] *Vita Merlini*, lines 696–702:
> Pacis amator erat, populo nam jura feroci
> sic dabat ut nulli vis inferretur ab ullo.
> Tractabat sanctum justo moderamine clerum,
> jure regi populos summos humilesque sinebat.
> Largus erat nam multa dabat, vix quid retinebat.
> Omnibus omnis erat faciens quodcumque decebat,
> flos equitum regumque decor regnique columpna.

*per legem*. The negative tone of the prophecies in both the *Historia* and the *Vita*, however, reflects an awareness, perhaps based on experience, that such rulers are in fact few and far between. A lament for the transitory nature of human life follows Ganieda's lament. As in the *Historia*, the ideal is overshadowed because even an ideal king will die. Ganieda ends her lament by suggesting that the only refuge is in Christ, and announces her intention to leave the court and take up residence with Merlin. Her decision is a reflex of the *exeat aula* topos so common in court satire. One wonders, however, if the correctly Christian sentiments of this section are not undermined by the audience's knowledge that Ganieda had cuckolded her husband; again, the ironies of the *Vita* seem designed to undercut any conventional reading of the work.

The lament for Rodarch is in one sense another of the set pieces with which the *Vita* is peppered, giving it, at least superficially, the appearance of a collection of exercises, intended primarily to display the poet's virtuosity. The lament for a king is a popular form in Welsh poetry, something that a *cyfarwydd* or latimer at the court of an Anglo-Norman noble could doubtless have introduced to his baronial audience. But this lament, like the other set pieces in the poem, serves a larger thematic purpose. The prophecies in the *Vita* make it clear that kings like Rodarch are to be desired, but not often to be found. The lament adds the recognition that even when such kings exist, their periods of influence are all too brief. The forays into the genres of prophetic and elegiac poetry are thus placed in the service of a larger message, and do not exist merely to dazzle. In the first part of the poem, the talents of Merlin and the poet generated laughter of various sorts. Here, the emphasis is on the bitter futility of prophecy, which can see humanity's fate but play no part in altering it. The appeal to Christ may accord with the *Vita*'s "jocose" stance by offering a genuine refuge from the vagaries of life, but the fact that it is voiced by Ganieda may also make a mockery of this possibility. The *Historia*, for its part, lacks any such appeal, and may thus be seen either as that much bleaker than the *Vita*, or perhaps simply as that much more straightforward about its essential hopelessness.

Internal oddities are not difficult to find in the prophecies, and the deployment of the prophetic passages in the work as a whole adds to the sense of dislocation; prophecy, plot, and lore are all juxtaposed, in such a way as to require agile responses and a continual readjustment of reactions from the audience. The lament for Rodarch which follows the first section of prophecy gives way in its turn to the introduction of Taliesin, who has come to Merlin to answer his questions about winds and rain, something he does at great length. From Celtic myth and folktale, Geoffrey shifts ground to medieval encyclopedic and scientific works, specifically, Isidore's *Etymologiae* and Bede's *De natura rerum*.[77]

Basil Clarke argues that Geoffrey is "on the whole faithful in presenting such conventional material [from Bede and Isidore], turning it into pleasant verse without transforming it altogether."[78] In one sense, this passage returns to the virtuosic element of the *Vita*, in that it appears to be a display of learning and art with no apparent purpose except to impress. Geoffrey's rhetorical and poetic skills are on display here, married to the sort of marvels for which a twelfth-century court audience had a particular taste. The use of encyclopedic texts for some of the *Vita* may be intended to give legitimacy to some of the rest of the material, much as Geoffrey's imaginative history was woven through known history. Yet there is something more at work here. This section is oddly placed after the lament for Rodarch, and the strange juxtaposition alters radically the tone set by the prophecies and the lament, to the extent that a reader may be uncertain as to how to respond, either to this new material, or to what has gone before.

The issues are both thematic and stylistic. Recall for a moment the Greek fire digression in the *De Ortu*. That text not only interrupted its own narrative flow and tone with the "scientific" interjection; it also called the interjection itself into question through an exaggeration of the characteristics of such writing. In the *Vita*, the scientific information is presented with many qualifiers; people believe, or say, or hold that certain things are true, but there are few straightforward statements, particularly among the more outrageous sections of Taliesin's explanations. To be sure, Isidore, for example, will sometimes write that something "is said" to be so, but Geoffrey has vastly extended the use of this conventional manner of expression until it cannot help but draw attention to itself. Clarke feels that all these

---

[77] It is a nice conceit that Geoffrey should use a figure of Celtic myth to bring about the shift; the Welsh "Ymddiddan Myrddin a Thaliesin" ("Conversation of Merlin and Taliesin") has a similar conversation, including many passages of lore and prophecy. The Welsh poem is preserved in a manuscript of the second half of the thirteenth century, but whether the poem itself is older, and so may have suggested the appearance of Taliesin in the *Vita*, is unclear.

[78] *Vita Merlini*, ed. and trans. Clarke, p. 8.

qualifiers show caution on Geoffrey's part; Tatlock goes further and argues that they are so prevalent "as completely to shuffle off responsibility for truth, and to mark the aim as not instruction but entertainment."[79] I would argue that Geoffrey is demonstrating not simply caution, but almost contempt, for the types of lore which he presents. The qualifiers are not the only clue to his attitude. There is the odd placement of this section. There are also many places where the kind of information provided seems to have been selected from the available sources with an eye to the titillating. It is noted of the evil, sublunar demons that "they even undertake intercourse with women and make them pregnant, begetting in a profane way."[80] Sex is also an issue in the passages relating to the mullet and the murenas – the mullet inhibits the sexual urge, and one can go blind from eating too much of it.[81] This information is all in Geoffrey's sources, but does it all need to be in Taliesin's speech?[82] Perhaps this section is designed to appeal to the same audience which would have enjoyed the descriptions of aristocratic love-practices in Andreas's *De amore.*

Whatever the case may be, the poem's oscillations in tone continue, as Merlin slips into prophecy again when Taliesin mentions Avalon. The prophetic discourse and its implications are thus moved up to the time of Arthur, with an abbreviated version of the *Historia.* Yet the bleak tone set by the *morte* gives way in its turn to more lore, as Merlin's cure inspires Taliesin to provide a catalogue of unusual rivers, lakes and springs. Again with many qualifiers, we are treated to a wonders-of-the world excursion, whose connection to the previous passage seems tenuous at best. It is true that Merlin had asked Taliesin what could explain his sudden cure, but Taliesin's response, which includes lakes which make one tired of wine, stimulate or inhibit the sexual urge, and induce sterility or fertility, seems excessive.[83] If in *Arthur and Gorlagon* the reader departs from the text little the wiser

---

[79] *Vita Merlini*, ed. and trans. Clarke, p. 8, n. 3; Tatlock, "*Vita Merlini*," 279.

[80] *Vita Merlini*, lines 783–84: "Quin etiam coitu mulieres agrediuntur/ et faciunt gravidas generantes more prophano."

[81] *Vita Merlini*, lines 825–26; 830–35.

[82] Ziolkowski suggests that all of the natural history passages show Merlin learning to match his prophetic insight with an appreciation of the divine order through the study of nature ("The Nature of Prophecy," p. 161). But much of the lore occurs *after* Merlin has been cured of his madness, a fact difficult to explain if we accept the contention that his madness began because he could not deal with his prophetic gift without also having a sense of "overarching meaning" (p. 160), achieved through the study of nature.

[83] The lakes are Clitorius (line 1192), a lake in Boeotia (lines 1196–97), the spring of Cyzicus (line 1198), and two Sicilian springs (lines 1205–6).

for it, here he or she is almost smothered with information – yet the question of what to draw from that information remains.[84]

It is appropriate for Geoffrey to make Taliesin the mouthpiece for all this scientific knowledge. In Welsh tradition, the mythical Taliesin – to be distinguished from a possibly historical poet of the same name – is a figure of magical powers, whose shape-shifting ability has given him insight into much wisdom. One could argue that Geoffrey is simply transferring the motif into a more contemporary context, thus displaying his skill by modifying traditional Celtic material with the wisdom of another tradition. As I have suggested above, the intention might be to present the marvelous under a more respectable cloak. Nevertheless, the items selected for inclusion, the strange shifts in tone achieved by the various odd juxtapositions, and the stalling of what little narrative line there is in the poem by these repeated digressions, all suggest that Geoffrey is up to something more than a mere display of his skills and knowledge, however considerable those may be.

This impression is further strengthened by the next digression. The narrative line of the poem makes a brief reappearance with the arrival of the British chieftains. Merlin's first response to their request is a description of his old age, another sub-genre of Welsh lament poetry. He then returns to his familiar praise for the forest of Caledon. The attention of the chieftains may well be wandering: "While he was saying these things, the chieftains saw long lines of cranes in the sky, passing through the air in a curving flight."[85] Are their eyes caught by a strange development, or have they been gazing into space while waiting for the prophet to wind things up? This sight – or the chieftains' boredom – becomes the rather slim excuse for the next scientific interpolation. The chieftains ask Merlin what the cranes mean, and his response, as was the case with Taliesin's discussion of magical lakes, rivers, and springs, is surely more than is called for by the question at hand. After describing the nature of cranes, Merlin moves on to discuss many more birds, once again selected from Isidore. The information is interesting, but does not really provide

---

[84] Curley finds a Boethian flavor in the Taliesin sections. Taliesin's purpose is to show, through a discussion of the natural world, that "in spite of outward appearances to the contrary," the universe is ruled by a just God; *Geoffrey of Monmouth*, pp. 119–20. Perhaps Taliesin wants to have such an effect, but the structure of the poem seems to militate against any such comforting conclusion.

[85] *Vita Merlini*, lines 1292–93: "Hec dum dicebat proceres super ethera cernunt/agmina longa gruum flexo per inane volatu."

any insight into the strange behavior of these particular cranes. The reader may, however, be relieved to have another slew of lament and pastoral poetry cut short.

The connection between this section and the next is once more extremely abrupt: "When he had said these things, a certain madman suddenly came up to them, or perhaps chance had led him."[86] Chance is in one sense the hand of the storyteller, a sort of mocking *deus ex machina* which provides the only explanation for this otherwise jarring link. It is hard to see the point of the story of Maeldin, even as a companion for Merlin in his newfound desire to stay in the forest and serve God.

The final movement of the poem returns to prophecy and transfers the prophetic voice to Ganieda. The celestial imagery of Ganieda's prophecy is similar to that of Merlin's prophecies in the *Historia*; the final picture is a dark one, and although Ganieda ends with an appeal to Christ for aid, there is little sense in the poem that the grim outcome can be avoided. The poem ends with Merlin acknowledging that the gift of prophecy has passed to his sister, and one may wonder if we hear in his final words an echo of Geoffrey: "Is it you, sister, whom the spirit wishes to foretell future things, who has stilled my tongue and my book?"[87] After the *Historia* and the *Vita*, Geoffrey may have said all he intends to say.

Is it, in the end, possible to add up all the elements of the *Vita*? Some readers have certainly tried. Penelope Doob, for example, points to Merlin's refusal of Rodarch's gifts and pleas to remain at court; the mad prophet speaks here with the voice of court satire: "Let the lords whose poverty presses them have such things, those who are not content with a modicum but who seize the most they can. I prefer the woodland and spreading oak trees of Caledon to these things, and the high mountains with the green meadows beneath them."[88] Doob, who sees the *Vita* as a "profoundly religious poem," argues that this rejection shows that Merlin, even mad, is in some

---

[86] *Vita Merlini*, lines 1387–88: "His igitur dictis, quidam vesanus ad illos/ accessit subito, seu sors conduxerat illum."

[87] *Vita Merlini*, lines 1521–22: "Tene, soror, voluit res precantare futuras/ spiritus osque meum compescuit atque libellum?"

[88] *Vita Merlini*, lines 239–42:

> Ista duces habeant sua quos confundit egestas
> nec sunt contenti modico set maxima captant.
> Hiis nemus et patulas Calidonis prefero quercus
> et montes celsos subtus virentia prata.

ways morally superior to the court.[89] The fact that the mere sight of the court drives the prophet mad again certainly seems pointed, particularly in light of the tradition of court satire which I have discussed throughout this study. I have already suggested that Ganieda's withdrawal from the life of the court suggests the *exeat aula* topos; Curley follows Doob in seeing a more overtly religious element in this rejection, drawing a comparison between Ganieda and the twelfth-century recluse Christina of Markyate.[90] Cynicism about the halls of the great, perhaps induced by the Anarchy, could certainly mean that this rejection of the world at court would strike a chord for Geoffrey's audience, courtly or otherwise.

There are, however, other ways in which these lines may be interpreted, ways which return us to the *musa jocosa* and to courtly *facetia*. The Merlin who wishes to return to the forest is the same Merlin who shortly before spent some forty lines lamenting the arrival of winter, and railing at God because it is not always spring or summer. While appreciating the criticism of the court implied by Merlin's renewed madness and his rejection of Rodarch's offer, then, the reader might also chuckle at this sudden change of attitude in Merlin himself. Doob's study is intended in part as a counterbalance to Tatlock's opinion of the *Vita*, which is that it is not meant to be taken seriously;[91] yet one must not lose sight of the comic elements of the poem altogether, nor of the ability of wit and truth-telling to coexist in the Latin court writing of this period. The very strangeness of the poem's stylistic features suggests that they are as important to the generation of meaning in the work as are any more conventional possibilities.

But what was the intention behind the *Vita Merlini*? It is a very difficult work to categorize. Certainly there is something of the virtuosic exercise about it, particularly in the use of varying materials – Celtic and Latin – and varying forms – the Welsh lament, romantic narrative, religious poetry, wisdom literature, and nationalistic prophecy. Like Walter Map or Gerald of Wales, Geoffrey is showing off what he can do. Yet there are recurring themes or impulses weaving this material together. One such impulse, as the opening lines

---

[89] Penelope B.R. Doob, *Nebuchadnezzar's Children: Conventions of Madness in Middle English Literature* (New Haven, Conn.: Yale University Press, 1974), pp. 153, 155.

[90] Curley, *Geoffrey of Monmouth*, p. 121: Christina was Geoffrey's contemporary, and made her profession in the presence of Alexander, bishop of Lincoln.

[91] Tatlock, "*Vita Merlini*," 278.

made clear, is a certain facetious playfulness, manifested by the various kinds of laughter in the poem, the moments of comedy, the odd juxtapositions of the poem's various parts, and the almost gleeful manipulation of many types of writing. Some of the laughter in the poem is the poet's, as he deftly plays with and undercuts his audience's expectations about his work. This sort of generic playfulness is itself another major impulse or theme, the same which is at the heart of much of the *Historia* as well. Finally, the end of all this sleight of hand is suggested by the content and tone of the prophetic passages. It is clear that the author has in mind an ideal sort of rule – the strong, centralized rule of one good king – but also a rather bitter recognition that this state of affairs is extremely rare and transitory, in British history at least. The various references to fate, along with the almost unrelieved grimness of the prophecies, suggest that the role of fate in history is of major concern to the author. I argued in chapter 1 that in the *Historia*, Geoffrey is questioning the exemplary function of history: what good is an example if people either cannot read it, or will not heed it? The *Vita* is another work which, like all the works in this study, both invites and defies interpretation. The uncertainty of the form of the poem is in itself an echo of this central problem, a dramatization of the uncertainty of human perceptions and affairs. While there is much in the *Vita* to mitigate this rather grim picture – the entertaining nature of the scientific passages, the humorous elements of Merlin's story, and the laughter of the prophet himself – it would be a mistake to see the *Vita* solely as a sort of educated parlor-game, inspired by a jocose muse. The same techniques which can produce sophisticated enjoyment can also lead, as in the *Historia*, to an almost nihilistic appraisal of the abilities of man to understand or control his destiny, whether through action in history or through the organizing efforts of art. The forest may be an alternative to a court where no one listens to the prophet, but a recognition of one's helplessness is not necessarily a comfort.

# Conclusion: "A wise man may enjoy leisure" The place of Latin Arthurian literature

With Geoffrey of Monmouth's *Vita Merlini*, we have returned to the author with whom the Arthurian portion of this study began. The *Vita*, like the *Historia*, uses a mixture of literary forms and devices, a facetious style, here specifically invoked through the references to the *musa jocosa*, and a variety of sources, to create a work which is at once funny, fantastic, and profoundly unsettling. Its focus on kingship, fate, and their relationship reprises the themes of the *Historia*, while its narrative manipulations recall the earlier work's undermining of both the form and content of conventional historiography. It is appropriate that Geoffrey should thus "bookend" the Arthurian material in this study. He is the most influential of the writers here examined. He exemplifies many of the themes and approaches of court writing in its Arthurian guise. And in the *Vita*, he moves away from the specific focus on Arthur to return us to the larger world of rulers of whom Arthur is simply one (striking) example. At the end of this work, then, I move with Geoffrey, away from Arthur and back to the world of kings in general and the Angevin court in particular.

The first real story – he calls it a *fabula* – in Walter Map's *De nugis curialium* concerns Herla, an ancient king of the Britons. One day a pygmy king, a fabulous creature of outlandish appearance, comes to Herla's court: "This little man was mounted on a huge goat, according to the fable, a man who might be described as one could describe Pan – burning of face, with a great head, a wild red beard reaching a chest which was distinguished in its spotted hide. His stomach was hairy and his shins gave way to goats' feet."[1]

---

[1] *De nugis curialium*, I.xi: "Institit homuncio capro maximo secundum fabulam insidens, uir qualis describi posset Pan, ardenti facie, capite maximo, barba rubente prolixa pectus contingente, nebride preclarum stellata, cui uenter hispidus et crura pedes in caprinos degenerabant."

This king announces that he will be in attendance at Herla's wedding feast, and that in return, Herla must attend the pygmy king's wedding. The day of Herla's marriage arrives, and so too does a huge crowd of pygmies, with their own tents, precious eating vessels, splendid clothing, and rich food. The feast is splendid, and when the pygmy reappears a year later, calling on Herla to fulfill his end of the bargain, Herla agrees. The British party enters a cave under a high cliff, and comes to the pygmy's palace beneath the mountain. When the British leave after what they think has been an interval of three days, Herla is presented with a small dog, and told not to dismount until the dog does. The party emerges into the sunshine, only to discover that hundreds of years have passed, and that the Saxons have now overrun the kingdom. Members of the party who dismount immediately turn to dust; Herla orders that no one else is to dismount until the dog does, and it has not yet done so. The "punchline" of the story is this: in the first year of the reign of Henry II, Herla's hordes plunged into the River Wye, not to be seen again. The wily Map stops short of drawing the obvious conclusion, but it is clear that there is an even more peripatetic court which has taken the place of Herla and his retinue.

This story is typical of Map and of many of the court writers in this study. Under the cover of a marvelous tale of folk origin, a gentle dig at the perpetual wanderings of the Angevin court is administered. An admonition to rulers is also delivered through Herla, the duped king: like Pwyll, he fails to read the obvious signs, in the pygmy king's appearance, of an otherworld encounter, signs which could hardly be missed by the audience of the tale. Humor and the fantastic combine as a covering for a message, although in this case *jocus* may be the dominant tone. But in a fashion which reminds one of Geoffrey of Monmouth's use of incongruous juxtapositions in the *Vita*, Map moves from this *fabula* to the tale of the king of Portugal, a much less fantastic, and more gruesome, narrative.

This story, which Türk cites as an example of Map's non-Angevin satire,[2] recounts the rise through merit of a beautiful and noble youth at the court of the king of Portugal. He is the perfect courtier: "He was so outstanding in martial valor that his deeds did not seem possible for a single man alone. He reestablished peace, at the desire of the king and the kingdom, and entered through merit into the

---

[2] Türk, *Nugae curialium*, p. 171.

closest *familiaritatem* with his lord."³ Jealousy among the nobles of the court⁴ leads to the youth's downfall, however, as the envious courtiers manipulate their king, "whom they knew to be foolishly prone to the absurdity of jealousy,"⁵ into believing that the youth has committed adultery with the queen. The king orders the murder of the youth, and he himself beats and kicks his pregnant wife to death, boasting afterwards of his deed. Eventually, despite the flattering words of the wicked courtiers – "For they lavished him with praise, as if he were a man of spirit and strong action, so that he whom they had made a fool might endure in foolishness"⁶ – the king discovers the truth and is covered with remorse. The wicked courtiers are blinded and castrated. The king of Portugal lives still with the results of his crimes, having allowed clever courtiers to manipulate him through a knowledge of his own weaknesses, depriving him of good counsel, a good wife, his good name, and the love of his people.

From this story Map concludes that the court is a place of iniquity, and that he cannot easily "poetize" in these surroundings. But, he says, he will do as well as he can: "My purpose in this task is to forge nothing new, to bring forward no falsehood; but to tell, according to my powers, whatever I know, from seeing it, or whatever I believe, from hearing it."⁷

One knows what to make of such statements, particularly from so deceptive a writer as Map. The ironic covering provided by the modesty topos is important here, for I have chosen to end as I began, with a paradigmatic Angevin court writer, in order to highlight the themes of Latin court writing which I find in the Arthurian narratives I have explored in the course of these pages. Map's first story is a light-hearted, fantastic *fabula*, a tale of a feast which would well suit the dinner table. It is followed immediately by a grim court narrative removed from the Angevin context only by geography, whose focus on murder, the beating to death of a pregnant woman, and castration,

---

³ *De nugis curialium*, I.xii: ". . . virtute bellica tam preclarus apparuit, ut non viderentur eius opera possibilia uiro uni. Hic pacem desiderio regis et regni restituit, ingressusque merito in domini sui precipuam familiaritatem . . ."

⁴ They are called *curie magnates*; this story seems to reflect typical courtly complaints that low-born people are replacing the traditional hereditary aristocracy in their function of advising the king. But see the Introduction for an assessment of the validity of such complaints.

⁵ *De nugis curialium*, I.xii: "Sciunt eum zelotipie fatuum inepcia . . ."

⁶ *De nugis curialium*, I.xii: "Illi uero ipsum quasi uirum animosum et fortem attollunt multa laudum prosecucione, ut quem stultum fecerant perdurantem in stulticia teneant."

⁷ *De nugis curialium*, I.xii: "Meum autem inde propositum est nichil noui cudere, nichil falsitatis inferre; sed quecunque scio ex uisu uel credo ex auditu pro uiribus explicare."

would seem to make it ill-suited as post-prandial entertainment. Both kinds of stories apparently represent the writer providing what he knows or believes to be true. It is this question of what is true that is important. At loggerheads over so many other matters, Map and John of Salisbury might well agree on this one thing at least; that what is useful, *is* what is true. And Map's *nugae* about pygmy kings of the underworld *and* his contemporary tale of a foreign king and his court, are both useful in delivering messages about right and wrong rule. Kings should read the obvious signs, heed good counsel, recognize bad counsel, tame their own weaker impulses . . . While a court writer like John of Salisbury produces a sober work like the *Policraticus* to deliver such instruction, one of a more facetious spirit, like Map, produces the curious collection of tales which bounce happily back and forth between the funny, the fantastic, and the grave.

Why conclude as I began, with Map and not with King Arthur? I argued in the Introduction that the social and cultural context of the schools and the courts is the necessary background for an understanding of most – although not all – of the Latin Arthurian narratives in this study. Map, John of Salisbury, and Gerald of Wales share with Geoffrey of Monmouth, Etienne de Rouen, Andreas Capellanus, and probably the anonymous author of the romances in chapters 4 and 5, a common education and a common milieu. Whether they approve of the Angevin king or not, whether they see the court as a place of iniquity or advancement, they all exercise the opportunity, presented them by their education, to create narratives which contain messages appropriate for kings to hear. In addition, the atmosphere of the court, an atmosphere which encouraged a particular kind of facetious discourse, appears in the more fanciful and humorous aspects of some of the texts here studied. The taste for marvels, the interactions with the Celtic fringes of the Angevin world, also encouraged some of the fantastic elements which appear in these texts. But what I wish to suggest through the return to Map is that the real explanatory category here is Latin court writing, of which Latin Arthurian narrative is simply a manifestation.

This is not to say that King Arthur is unimportant, that Latin writers could just as easily have substituted some other hero for Britain's greatest king. Arthur is in many ways ideally suited to the court writer's many purposes. He is sufficiently remote in time to allow one to use him as an *exemplum*, while keeping a safe distance from any criticism that might be implied. He is also associated with the marvelous, so that the coloring of the fantastic can add another level of insulation and attraction. He has historicity, so that a school-educated cleric can present him as more acceptable, more real, than the fables of the oral storytellers with whom he might be in competition. And within that historicity there is also great fluidity, allowing one the room to invent and mold material at will. His British roots make him appealing both to conquerors seeking either to annex or to undermine his prestige, and to writers of British origin. Finally, Arthur has vernacular appeal, and if it is indeed the case that the same men who were writing for each other in Latin at court were also writing in the vernacular to educate and civilize their noble patrons, then it is entirely to be expected that Arthur should appear in many tongues, including the tongue of the Fathers.

What are we to do with the appearances of Arthur in Latin which suggest a monastic background and /or milieu rather than a courtly one? I have argued that a common education might sometimes impart a common approach to the intellectuals' *lingua franca*, but it is true that the manipulation of language which is revealed so clearly in the courtly taste for *jocus*, *facetia*, and *subtilitas* would be more likely to be nurtured and honed at court than in the cloister. Nevertheless, it is important to remember the communion between those worlds; if Robert of Torigny is the author of the *Historia Meriadoci* and the *De Ortu Waluuanii*, for example, one would have little trouble imagining such a man at the dinner table of the king, as well as in the refectory. John of Glastonbury is a different case, but then he is also removed from the main temporal focus of this study. I suggested at the outset that there were threads of coherence which linked the works in this study, threads to be traced ultimately to their common language and common subject, but it is important to conclude by noting that not all Arthurian Latin texts bear all the markers of court writing as clearly as do others. Yet in most of these texts, Arthur is a focus of attention in a way that he is not in the vernacular *roman d'aventure*. Even when the main narrative concerns the doings of a figure like Gawain or Meriadoc, Arthur is much more than a figurehead, more even than the point of departure and return he so often is in continental versions in particular. Even in Latin romance, Arthur retains his role from Latin – and vernacular – chronicle: the *rex* is the embodiment of the *regnum*. William of Rennes may not belong to the same world as does Geoffrey of Monmouth, but he too understands this link, even while he interprets its implications and what is required of the king some-what differently.

Finally, Map's first tale serves to underline a most important aspect of the Latin Arthurian narratives in this study. The world of fantasy is not to be found only in the vernacular. Many Latin writers feed their own and their audience's taste for the marvelous with far less reticence than one might expect, were one's sense of the reception of Geoffrey's *Historia*, for example, confined to the remarks of William of New-burgh. Even if the Greek fire interlude in the *De Ortu* has a point to make about the difficulties inherent in attempting to understand "the thing as it is"; even if Meriadoc's *dies fantastica* is linked thematically to the illustration of the deceptive nature of life at court; even if Gorlagon's repeated questions draw attention to deficiencies in the king; even so, *ludus, jocus,* and *facetia* often dominate in these narratives, sometimes to the point of submerging the message which they might contain.

John of Salisbury closes a typical condemnation of the frivolities of the court with a concession, writing that it is indeed sometimes acceptable for the wise man to indulge in leisure:

> But if moderation is displayed, I do not judge it to be indecorous for a wise man to busy himself from time to time with the pleasures of the senses: "moderation in all things," as it is often said. It is appropriate for a wise man to take his leisure occasionally, not so that the exercise of virtue may be forgotten, but rather that he may flourish and be somewhat reinvigorated.[8]

John is talking here specifically about music and dancing, but it seems to me that his remarks are helpful in understanding the role of Latin Arthurian literature as well. It may seem unnecessary to insist that Latin writers sometimes are simply having fun, and yet the *gravitas* which often attaches in our minds to Latin can make its playful manifestations something of a mystery to a modern reader. Facetious manipulation of language and form is one logical outcome of the kind of linguistic training received in the schools. A concern for legal matters and for kingship is also logical, given the sorts of employment which many schoolmen found. And the confluence of these things in

---

[8] *Policraticus*, VIII.xii:
Verum si moderatio adhibeatur, in his interdum sensuum voluptatem versari, sapienti non arbitror indecorum, ut saepenumero dictum est, nihil decorum est sine modo. Nam et otiari interdum sapienti familiare est, non tamen ut virtutis exercitium evanescat, sed quo magis vigeat, et quodammodo recreetur.

Arthurian literature in the Angevin world is also, I think, understandable, especially once one allows the possibility of recreation along with the more serious pursuits of the wise man.

A final question has to do with the relationship of this Latinate Arthur to his vernacular counterparts. That is, if the majority of the Latin Arthurian texts in this study belong in fact as much to the world of Latin court writing as they do to the worlds of Arthurian chronicle and romance, do they differ in any marked way from their vernacular analogues? Even when the same hands are penning Latin and vernacular versions, are these tailored differently, for different audiences? I have on occasion referred to Anglo-Norman, Middle Welsh, and Middle English texts which seem to me to throw some light on what is going on in the Latin texts, but my central purpose has been to highlight the unique character of the Latin rather than to fit them into a vernacular schema. Yet there is a final point which I would make about the relationship between Latin and the vernacular. As we have seen, Arthur is more often a flawed figure than a hero in Latin Arthurian narrative. After the perfect king of Geoffrey, we find the blowhard of Etienne de Rouen; the excessively ambitious conqueror of William of Rennes; the manipulator of law of the *Historia Meriadoci*; the *tyrannus* of the Welsh saints' lives; and the gullible fool of *Arthur and Gorlagon*. In her study of the development of Arthurian romance from Chrétien to Froissart, Beate Schmolke-Hasselmann notes that in the thirteenth-century texts in French, Arthur becomes a negative figure. Aggressiveness, lust for power, and injustice overcome his earlier, positive characteristics.[9] She sees this shift in the king's character as a manifestation of the dilution of the chivalric ideal after Chrétien; William of Rennes's treatment of Arthur in his *Gesta* fits well into this view of the development of French Arthurian literature. But Schmolke-Hasselmann also notes that there are hints of this critical attitude towards the king earlier than the thirteenth century, as for example in Robert Biket's *Lai du cor*, to which I referred during my discussion of the *De Ortu* in chapter 4. I would argue that the twelfth-century Latin texts in this study offer yet more evidence of the earlier appearance of that tendency. That is, what develops in the vernacular in the thirteenth century may have some roots in the Latin of the twelfth. The courtier-cleric's focus on

[9] Beate Schmolke-Hasselmann, *Der arthurische Versroman von Chrestien bis Froissart: Zur Geschichte einer Gattung* (Tübingen: Max Niemeyer, 1980), pp. 54–55.

the instruction of the king, perhaps combined with the willingness to poke fun at rulers in Welsh literature, lays the groundwork for a critical attitude to Arthur, *exemplum* of both good and bad alike.

Some of the Arthurian texts in this study show us Arthur as hero; more show us Arthur as a flawed human being. Sometimes the flaws are unimportant, and the *musa jocosa* reigns: if there is a lesson to be learned, it is learned as in Map's first tale, through laughter. Sometimes the flaws of the *rex* have dire consequences for the *regnum*, and the pessimism of Merlin in both of Geoffrey's works may reflect the pessimistic misanthropy of some of the more extreme examples of court satire. Yet on the whole, I find the spirit of the Latin Arthurian works in this study to be quite cheerful. William of Rennes called his poem a *ludus*, and while its ludic qualities may not be immediately evident, the playful qualities of texts like the *Draco Normannicus, Historia Meriadoci, De Ortu Waluuanii*, and *Arthur and Gorlagon* are clear, even as they deliver serious messages too. Other remnants of Arthurian story in Latin, from the Glastonbury accounts to the episodes penned by Johannes de Hauvilla and Andreas Capellanus, also show the richness of the Arthurian matter in the hands of Latin writers. The happy confluence of matter, method, and theme discussed in these pages has produced a group of works whose reception into the Arthurian canon can significantly broaden our understanding of the development of that canon. And as Meriadoc's response to his *dies fantastica* reminds us, there are many delights to be enjoyed along the way.

# Works cited

EDITIONS AND TRANSLATIONS

Andreas Capellanus. *Andreas Capellanus on Love*. Ed. and trans. P.G. Walsh. London: Duckworth, 1982.

"*Arthur and Gorlagon*: Versions of the Werewolf's Tale." Ed. G.L. Kittredge. *Harvard Studies and Notes in Philology and Literature* 8 (1903), 149–275. Rpt. New York: Haskell House, 1966.

Augustine. *De doctrina Christiana*. Corpus Christianorum, Series Latina 32. Turnhout, 1962.

On Christian Doctrine. Trans. D.W. Robertson, Jr. New York: Macmillan, 1958.

*The Awntyrs off Arthure at the Terne Wathelyne*. Ed. Ralph Hanna III. Manchester: Manchester University Press, 1974.

*Breudwyt Ronabwy, allan o'r Llyfr Coch o Hergest*. Ed. Melville Richards. Cardiff: University of Wales Press, 1948.

Chrétien de Troyes. *Erec et Enide*. Ed. Mario Roques. Paris: Champion, 1981.

*Culhwch ac Olwen: An Edition and Study of the Oldest Arthurian Tale*. Ed. Rachel Bromwich and D. Simon Evans. Cardiff: University of Wales Press, 1992.

Etienne de Rouen. *Draco Normannicus*. In *Chronicles of the Reigns of Stephen, Henry II, and Richard I*. Ed. Richard Howlett. Vol. 2. London: Rolls Series 82, 1885.

Geoffrey of Monmouth. *The Historia regum Britannie of Geoffrey of Monmouth I: Bern, Burgerbibliothek, MS. 568*. Ed. Neil Wright. Cambridge: D.S. Brewer, 1985.

*The Historia regum Britannie of Geoffrey of Monmouth II: The First Variant Version; a critical edition*. Ed. Neil Wright. Cambridge: D.S. Brewer, 1988.

Life of Merlin: Vita Merlini. Ed. and trans. Basil Clarke. Cardiff: University of Wales Press, 1973.

The Vita Merlini. Ed. and trans. John Jay Parry. Urbana: University of Indiana Press, 1925.

Gerald of Wales. *De Instructione Principum*. In *Giraldi Cambrensis Opera*. Ed. J.S. Brewer, J.F. Dimock, and G.F. Warner. Vol. 8. London: Rolls Series, 1861–1891.

Itinerarium Kambriae. Vol. 6 in Opera.

Speculum Ecclesiae. Vol. 4 in Opera.

Henry of Huntingdon. "Epistola ad Warinum." In *Chronicles of the Reigns of Stephen, Henry II and Richard I*. Ed. Richard Howlett. Vol. 4. London: Rolls Series 82, 1889.

# List of works cited

*Historia Meriadoci and De Ortu Waluuanii: Two Arthurian Romances of the XIIIth Century in Latin Prose.* Ed. J. Douglas Bruce. Baltimore, Md.: Johns Hopkins, 1913.

Johannes de Hauvilla. *Johannes de Hauvilla: Architrenius.* Ed. and trans. Winthrop Wetherbee. Cambridge: Cambridge University Press, 1994.

John of Glastonbury. *The Chronicle of Glastonbury Abbey: An Edition, Translation and Study of John of Glastonbury's Cronica sive Antiquitates Glastonienis Ecclesie.* Ed. James P. Carley. Trans. David Townsend. Woodbridge, Suffolk: The Boydell Press, 1985.

John of Salisbury. *Policraticus.* In *Joannis Saresberiensis Opera Omnia.* Ed. J.-P. Migne. *Patrologia Latina* 199 (1855).

Lapidge, Michael, ed. "An Edition of the *Vera Historia de Morte Arthuri.*" *Arthurian Literature* 1 (1981), 79–93.

Laȝamon. *Laȝamon's Arthur: The Arthurian Section of Laȝamon's Brut.* Ed. W.R.J. Barron and S.C. Weinberg. Harlow, Essex: Longman, 1989.

Map, Walter. *De nugis curialium: Courtiers' Trifles.* Ed. and trans. M.R. James. Rev. C.N.L. Brooke and R.A.B. Mynors. Oxford: Oxford University Press, 1983.

*La Mort le Roi Artu: Roman du XIIIe siècle.* Ed. Jean Frappier. Geneva: Droz, 1954.

*Le Morte Arthur.* Ed. J. Douglas Bruce. Early English Text Society, e.s. 88 (1903).

"Nennius." *Historia Brittonum.* In *Nennius: British History and The Welsh Annals.* Ed. and trans. John Morris. London: Phillimore, 1980.

Ordericus Vitalis. *Historia Ecclesiastica.* In E. K. Chambers, *Arthur of Britain* (London: Sidgwick and Jackson, 1927).

Ovid. *Tristium Liber Secundus.* Ed. S.G. Owen. Amsterdam: Adolf M. Hakkert, 1967.

*Pwyll Pendeuic Dyuet.* Ed. R.L. Thomson. Dublin: Institute for Advanced Studies, 1980.

*La Queste del Saint Graal: Roman du XIIIe siècle.* Ed. Albert Pauphilet. Paris: Champion, 1949.

Ralph of Coggeshall. *Radulphi of Coggeshall Chronicon Anglicanum.* Ed. Joseph Stevenson. London: Rolls Series 36, 1875.

*The Rise of Gawain, Nephew of Arthur (De Ortu Waluuanii, Nepotis Arturi).* Ed. and trans. Mildred Leake Day. New York: Garland, 1984.

Robert of Torigny. *Chronica.* In *Chronicles of the Reigns of Stephen, Henry II and Richard I.* Ed. Richard Howlett. Vol. 4. London: Rolls Series 82, 1889.

*Sir Gawain and the Green Knight.* Ed. J.R.R. Tolkien and E.V. Gordon. 2nd edn. Rev. Norman Davis. Oxford: Oxford University Press, 1967.

*The Story of Meriadoc, King of Cambria (Historia Meridaoci [sic] regis Cambriae).* Ed. and trans. Mildred Leake Day. New York: Garland, 1988.

Suger of St. Denis. *Gesta Ludovici Regis.* In E.K. Chambers, *Arthur of Britain* (London: Sidgwick and Jackson, 1927).

*Vitae sanctorum Britanniae et genealogiae.* Ed. A.W. Wade-Evans. Cardiff: University of Wales, 1944.

William of Malmesbury. *Gesta Regum Anglorum.* Ed. William Stubbs. Vol. 1. London: Rolls Series 90, 1887.

*The Early History of Glastonbury: An Edition, Translation and Study of William of Malmesbury's De Antiquitate Glastonie Ecclesie.* Ed. John Scott. Woodbridge, Suffolk: The Boydell Press, 1981.

# List of works cited

William of Newburgh. *Historia rerum Anglicarum*. In *Chronicles of the Reigns of Stephen, Henry II and Richard I*. Ed. Richard Howlett. Vol. 1. London: Rolls Series 82, 1884.

*The History of English Affairs*, Book I. Ed. and trans. P.G. Walsh and M.J. Kennedy. Warminster: Aris and Phillips, 1988.

William of Rennes. *The Historia regum Britannie of Geoffrey of Monmouth V: Gesta regum Britannie*. Ed. and trans. Neil Wright. Cambridge: D.S. Brewer, 1991.

## CRITICAL WORKS

Abram, Lesley, and James P. Carley, eds. *The Archaeology and History of Glastonbury Abbey: Essays in Honour of the Ninetieth Birthday of C.A. Ralegh Radford*. Woodbridge, Suffolk: The Boydell Press, 1991.

Alcock, Leslie. *Arthur's Britain*. Harmondsworth, Middlesex: Penguin, 1971.

Arthur, Ross G. *Medieval Sign Theory and Sir Gawain and the Green Knight*. Toronto: University of Toronto Press, 1987.

Ashe, Geoffrey. " 'A Certain Very Ancient Book': Traces of an Arthurian Source in Geoffrey of Monmouth's *History*." *Speculum* 56 (1981), 301–23.

"Saints' Lives, Arthur in." In *The Arthurian Encyclopedia*. Ed. Norris J. Lacy (New York: Peter Bedrick, 1987), pp. 469–71.

Bakhtin, M.M. *The Dialogic Imagination*. Ed. Michael Holquist. Trans. Caryl Emerson and Michael Holquist. Austin: University of Texas Press, 1981.

Baldwin, John W. *The Language of Sex: Five Voices from Northern France around 1200*. Chicago: University of Chicago Press, 1994.

"*Studium et regnum*: The Penetration of University Personnel into French and English Administration at the Turn of the Twelfth and Thirteenth Centuries." *Revue des Etudes Islamiques* 44 (1976), 199–215.

Barber, Richard. "The *Vera Historia de Morte Arthuri* and its Place in Arthurian Tradition." *Arthurian Literature* 1 (1981), 62–77.

"The Manuscripts of the *Vera Historia de Morte Arthuri*." *Arthurian Literature* 6 (1986), 163–64.

Bayless, Martha. *Parody in the Middle Ages: The Latin Tradition*. Ann Arbor: University of Michigan Press, 1996.

Bennett, R.E. "*Arthur and Gorlagon*, the Dutch *Lancelot*, and St. Kentigern." *Speculum* 13 (1938), 68–75.

Benson, Robert L., and Giles Constable, eds. *Renaissance and Renewal in the Twelfth Century*. Oxford: Clarendon Press, 1982.

Bezzola, Reto. *Les Origines et la formation de la littérature courtoise en occident (500–1200). Troisième partie: La société courtoise: Littérature de cour et littérature courtoise*. Paris: Champion, 1963.

Bloch, R. Howard. *The Scandal of the Fabliaux*. Chicago: University of Chicago Press, 1986.

Bromwich, Rachel. "The Character of the Early Welsh Tradition." In *Studies in Early British History*. Ed. Nora K. Chadwick (Cambridge: Cambridge University Press, 1954), pp. 83–136.

"Celtic Elements in Arthurian Romance: A General Survey." In *The Legend of*

242

*Arthur in the Middle Ages.* Ed. P.B. Grout *et al.* (Cambridge: D.S. Brewer, 1983), pp. 41–55.

"First Transmission to England and France." In *The Arthur of the Welsh: The Arthurian Legend in Medieval Welsh Literature.* Ed. Rachel A. Bromwich, A. O.H. Jarman, Brynley F. Roberts, and Daniel Huws (Cardiff: University of Wales Press, 1991), pp. 273–98.

*The Arthur of the Welsh: The Arthurian Legend in Medieval Welsh Literature.* Ed. Rachel A. Bromwich, A.O.H. Jarman, Brynley F. Roberts, and Daniel Huws. Cardiff: University of Wales Press, 1991.

Brooke, Christopher. "Geoffrey of Monmouth as a Historian." In *Church and Government in the Middle Ages: Essays Presented to C.R. Cheney on his 70th Birthday.* Ed. C.N.L. Brooke *et al.* (Cambridge: Cambridge University Press, 1976), pp. 77–91.

"Historical Writing in England Between 850 and 1150." *La storiografia altomedievale* 17, pt. 1 (Spoleto, 1970), 223–47.

*The Twelfth Century Renaissance.* London: Thames and Hudson, 1969.

Brown, Michelle P., and James P. Carley. "A Fifteenth-Century Revision of the Glastonbury Epitaph to King Arthur." *Arthurian Literature* 12 (1993), 179–92.

Brugger, Ernst. "Zu Historia Meriadoci und De Ortu Walwanii." *Zeitung für französische Sprache und Literatur* 46 (1923), 247–80, 406–40.

Bullock-Davies, Constance. "'Exspectare Arturum': Arthur and the Messianic Hope." *Bulletin of the Board of Celtic Studies* 29 (1981/82), 432–40.

*Professional Interpreters and the Matter of Britain.* Cardiff: University of Wales Press, 1966.

Bumke, Joachim. *Courtly Culture: Literature and Society in the High Middle Ages.* Trans. Thomas Dunlap. Berkeley: University of California Press, 1991.

Carley, James P. "A Glastonbury Translator at Work: *Quedam narracio de nobili rege Arthuro* and *De origine gigantum* in Their Earliest Manuscript Contexts." *Nottingham French Studies* 30 (1991), 5–12.

Chambers, E.K. *Arthur of Britain.* London: Sidgwick and Jackson, 1927.

Charles-Edwards, Thomas. "The Arthur of History." In *The Arthur of the Welsh,* ed. Bromwich *et al.,* pp. 15–32.

Clanchy, M.T. *From Memory to Written Record: England 1066–1307.* 2nd edn. Oxford: Blackwell, 1993.

"*Moderni* in Education and Government in England." *Speculum* 50 (1975), 671–88.

Crane, Susan. *Insular Romance: Politics, Faith, and Culture in Anglo-Norman and Middle English Literature.* Berkeley: University of California Press, 1986.

Crawford, T.D. "On the Linguistic Competence of Geoffrey of Monmouth." *Medium Aevum* 51 (1982), 152–62.

Crick, Julia. "Geoffrey of Monmouth, Prophecy and History," *Journal of Medieval History* 18 (1992), 357–71.

*The Historia regum Britannie of Geoffrey of Monmouth III: A Summary Catalogue of the Manuscripts.* Cambridge: D.S. Brewer, 1989.

*The Historia regum Britannie of Geoffrey of Monmouth IV: Dissemination and Reception in the Later Middle Ages.* Cambridge: D.S. Brewer, 1991.

"Two Newly Located Manuscripts of Geoffrey of Monmouth's *Historia regum Britannie.*" *Arthurian Literature* 13 (1995), 151–56.

Curley, Michael J. *Geoffrey of Monmouth*. New York: Twayne, 1994.

Curtius, Ernst Robert. *European Literature and the Latin Middle Ages*. Trans. Willard R. Trask. Princeton, N.J.: Princeton University Press, 1952.

Dane, Joseph A. "Parody and Satire: A Theoretical Model." *Genre* 13 (1980), 145–59.

Davies, R.R. *Conquest, Coexistence, and Change: Wales 1063–1415*. Oxford: Clarendon Press, 1987.

Day, Mildred Ann Leake. "Arthurian Romances in Latin: A Survey." In *King Arthur through the Ages*. Ed. Valerie M. Lagorio and Mildred Leake Day. Vol. 1 (New York: Garland, 1990), pp. 44–55.

"*Historia Meriadoci* and *Arthur and Gorlagon*: Two Arthurian Tales in a Unique Fifteenth-Century Collection of Latin Romances." *Fifteenth-Century Studies* 17 (1990), 67–71.

"The Letter from King Arthur to Henry II: Political Use of the Arthurian Legend in Draco Normannicus." In *The Spirit of the Court*. Ed. Glyn S. Burgess and Robert A. Taylor (Cambridge: D.S. Brewer, 1985), pp. 153–57.

"'The Rise of Gawain, Nephew of Arthur': Translation and Study of *De Ortu Waluuanii Nepotis Arturi*, a Medieval Latin Prose Romance." Ph.D. thesis, University of Alabama, 1975.

Doob, Penelope B.R.. *Nebuchadnezzar's Children: Conventions of Madness in Middle English Literature*. New Haven, Conn.: Yale University Press, 1974.

Echard, Siân. "Map's Metafiction: Author, Narrator, and Reader in *De nugis curialium*." *Exemplaria* 8 (1996), 287–314.

Eckhardt, Caroline D. "Another Manuscript of the Commentary on *Prophetia Merlini* Attributed to Alain de Lille." *Manuscripta* 29 (1985), 143–47.

*The Prophetia Merlini of Geoffrey of Monmouth: A Fifteenth-century Commentary*. Cambridge, Mass.: The Medieval Academy of America, 1982.

"The *Prophetia Merlini* of Geoffrey of Monmouth: Latin Manuscript Copies." *Manuscripta* 26 (1982), 167–76.

Fleischman, Suzanne. "On the Representation of History and Fiction in the Middle Ages." *History and Theory* 22 (1983), 278–310.

Fletcher, Robert Huntington. *The Arthurian Material in the Chronicles, especially those of Great Britain and France*. Cambridge, Mass.: Harvard University Press, 1906.

Flint, Valerie J. "The *Historia regum Britanniae* of Geoffrey of Monmouth: Parody and its Purpose. A Suggestion." *Speculum* 54 (1979), 447–68.

Galyon, Aubrey. "*De Ortu Walwanii* and the Theory of Illumination." *Neophilologus* 62 (1978), 335–41.

Gantz, Jeffrey, trans. Introductory notes in *The Mabinogion*. Harmondsworth, Middlesex: Penguin, 1976.

Gransden, Antonia. "The Growth of Glastonbury Traditions and Legends in the Twelfth Century." *Journal of Ecclesiastical History* 27 (1976), 337–58.

*Historical Writing in England c. 550 to c. 1307*. London: Routledge and Kegan Paul, 1974.

"Prologues in the Historiography of Twelfth-Century England." In *England in the Twelfth Century*. Ed. Daniel Williams (Woodbridge, Suffolk: Boydell, 1990), pp. 55–81.

Green, D.H. *Irony in the Medieval Romance*. Cambridge: Cambridge University Press, 1979.

# List of works cited

Hanning, Robert W. *The Vision of History in Early Britain: From Gildas to Geoffrey of Monmouth*. New York: Columbia University Press, 1966.

Hanson-Smith, Elizabeth. *"Pwyll Prince of Dyfed*: The Narrative Structure." *Studia Celtica* 16/17 (1981/82), 126–34.

Haskins, Charles Homer. *The Renaissance of the Twelfth Century*. Cambridge, Mass.: Harvard University Press, 1927.

Hutcheon, Linda. *A Theory of Parody*. New York: Methuen, 1985.

Jackson, W.T.H. "The *De Amore* of Andreas Capellanus and the Practice of Love at Court." In *The Challenge of the Medieval Text: Studies in Genre and Interpretation*. Ed. Joan M. Ferrante and Robert W. Hanning (New York: Columbia University Press, 1985), pp. 3–13. Reprint of *Romanic Review* 49 (1958), 243–51.

Jaeger, C. Stephen. *The Origins of Courtliness: Civilizing Trends and the Formation of Courtly Ideals 939–1210*. Philadelphia: University of Pennsylvania Press, 1985.

Jauss, Hans Robert. "Literary History as a Challenge to Literary Theory." *New Literary History* 2 (1970–71), 7–37.

Jolliffe, J.E.A. *Angevin Kingship*. London: Adam and Charles Black, 1955.

Jones, Gwyn, and Thomas Jones, trans. "Introduction" to *The Mabinogion*. London: Dent, 1949; rev. edn. 1974.

Keeler, Laura. *Geoffrey of Monmouth and the Late Latin Chroniclers 1300–1500*. Berkeley: University of California Press, 1946.

Krappe, A. Haggerty. "Arthur and Gorlagon." *Speculum* 8 (1933), 209–22.

Lagorio, Valerie M. "The Evolving Legend of St Joseph of Glastonbury." *Speculum* 46 (1971), 209–31.

Lapidge, Michael. "Additional Manuscript Evidence for the *Vera Historia de Morte Arthuri*," *Arthurian Literature* 2 (1982), 163–68.

Latham, R.E. *Revised Medieval Latin Word-List from British and Irish Sources*. London: Oxford University Press, 1965.

Leckie, R. William Jr. *The Passage of Dominion: Geoffrey of Monmouth and the Periodization of Insular History in the Twelfth Century*. Toronto: University of Toronto Press, 1981.

Leupin, Alexandre. *Barbarolexis: Medieval Writing and Sexuality*. Trans. Kate M. Cooper. Cambridge, Mass.: Harvard University Press, 1989.

Lewis, C. S. *The Allegory of Love: A Study in Medieval Tradition*. Oxford: Oxford University Press, 1936.

Lloyd-Morgan, Ceridwen. *"Breuddwyd Rhonabwy* and Later Arthurian Literature." In *The Arthur of the Welsh*, ed. Bromwich *et al.*, pp. 183–208.

Loomis, Roger Sherman. "The Latin Romances." In *Arthurian Literature in the Middle Ages: A Collaborative History*. Ed. Roger Sherman Loomis (Oxford: Clarendon Press), pp. 472–79.

Lovecy, Ian. *"Historia Peredur ab Efrawg."* In *The Arthur of the Welsh*, ed. Bromwich *et al.*, pp. 170–82.

Matthews, William. *The Tragedy of Arthur: A Study of the Alliterative 'Morte Arthure'*. Berkeley: University of California Press, 1960.

Middleton, Roger. *"Chwedl Geraint ab Erbin."* In *The Arthur of the Welsh*, ed. Bromwich *et al.*, pp. 147–57.

# List of works cited

Moi, Toril. "Desire in Language: Andreas Capellanus and the Controversy of Courtly Love." In *Medieval Literature: Criticism, Ideology and History*. Ed. David Aers (New York: St. Martin's, 1986), pp. 11–33.

Morris, Rosemary. "The *Gesta Regum Britanniae* of William of Rennes: An Arthurian Epic?" *Arthurian Literature* 6 (1986), 60–123.

Morse, Ruth. " 'This Vague Relation': Historical Fiction and Historical Veracity in the Later Middle Ages." *Leeds Studies in English* 13 (1982), 85–103.

Mortimer, Richard. *Angevin England 1154–1258*. Oxford: Blackwell, 1994.

Mullen, William B. "A Critical Study of the 'Historia Meriadoci.' " Ph.D. thesis, Columbia University, 1951.

Nederman, Cary J., ed. *Policraticus. Of the Frivolities of Courtiers and the Footprints of Philosophers*. Cambridge: Cambridge University Press, 1990.

Nelson, Lynn H. *The Normans in South Wales, 1070–1171*. Austin: University of Texas Press, 1966.

Nickel, Helmut. "Heraldry." In *The Arthurian Encyclopedia*. Ed. Norris J. Lacy (New York: Peter Bedrick, 1987), p. 279.

Packard, Sidney R. *12th Century Europe: An Interpretive Essay*. Amherst: University of Massachusetts Press, 1973.

Parry, Thomas. *A History of Welsh Literature*. Trans. H. Idris Bell. Oxford: Oxford University Press, 1955.

Partner, Nancy F. "The New Cornificius: Medieval History and the Artifice of Words." In *Classical Rhetoric and Medieval Historiography*. Ed. Ernst Breisach (Kalamazoo, Mich.: Medieval Institute, 1985), pp. 5–59.

*Serious Entertainments: The Writing of History in Twelfth-Century England*. Chicago and London: University of Chicago Press, 1977.

Phillips, Helen. "*The Awntyrs off Arthure*: Structure and Meaning. A Reassessment." *Arthurian Literature* 12 (1993), 63–90.

Porter, Elizabeth. "Chaucer's Knight, the Alliterative *Morte Arthure*, and Medieval Laws of War: A Reconsideration." *Nottingham Medieval Studies* 27 (1983), 56–78.

Radford, C.A. Ralegh, "Glastonbury Abbey." In *The Quest for Arthur's Britain*. Ed. G. Ashe (London: Pall Mall Press, 1968), pp. 119–38.

Reeves, Marjorie. "History and Prophecy in Medieval Thought." *Medievalia et Humanistica* 5 (1974), 51–75.

Reinhard, John Revell. *The Survival of Geis in Mediaeval Romance*. Halle: Max Niemeyer, 1933.

Rider, Jeff. "Arthur and the Saints." In *King Arthur through the Ages*. Ed. Valerie M. Lagorio and Mildred Leake Day. Vol. 1 (New York: Garland, 1990), pp. 3–21.

Rigg, A.G. *A History of Anglo-Latin Literature, 1066–1422*. Cambridge: Cambridge University Press, 1992.

Roberts, Brynley F. "Culhwch ac Olwen, the Triads, Saints' Lives." In *The Arthur of the Welsh*, ed. Bromwich *et al.*, pp. 73–95.

"Geoffrey of Monmouth and Welsh Historical Tradition." *Nottingham Medieval Studies* 20 (1976), 29–40.

"*The Dream of Rhonabwy*." In *The Arthurian Encyclopedia*. Ed. Norris J. Lacy (New York: Peter Bedrick), p. 142.

# List of works cited

"Geoffrey of Monmouth, *Historia Regum Britanniae* and *Brut y Brenhinedd*." In *The Arthur of the Welsh*, ed. Bromwich *et al.*, pp. 97–116.

"Tales and Romances." In *A Guide to Welsh Literature*. Vol. 1. Ed. A.O.H. Jarman and Gwilym Rees Hughes (Swansea: Christopher Davies, 1976), pp. 203–43.

Robertson, D.W. Jr. *A Preface to Chaucer: Studies in Medieval Perspectives.* Princeton, NJ: Princeton University Press, 1962.

Schirmer, Walter F. *Die frühen Darstellungen des Arthurstoffes.* Cologne: Westdeutscher Verlag, 1958.

Schmolke-Hasselmann, Beate. *Der arthurische Versroman von Chrestien bis Froissart: Zur Geschichte einer Gattung.* Tübingen: Max Niemeyer, 1980.

Shepherd, G.T. "The Emancipation of Story in the Twelfth Century." In *Medieval Narrative: A Symposium* (Odense, 1979), pp. 44–57.

Shichtman, Martin B., and Laurie A. Finke. "Profiting from the Past: History as Symbolic Capital in the *Historia Regum Britanniae*." *Arthurian Literature* 12 (1993), 1–35.

Sims-Williams, Patrick. "The Early Welsh Arthurian Poems." In *The Arthur of the Welsh*, ed. Bromwich *et al.*, pp. 33–72.

Southern, R.W. "Aspects of the European Tradition of Historical Writing: 3. History as Prophecy." *Transactions of the Royal Historical Society* 22 (1972), 159–80.

"The Place of England in the Twelfth-Century Renaissance." *History* 45 (1960), 201–16.

Spiegel, Gabrielle M. *Romancing the Past: The Rise of Vernacular Prose Historiography in Thirteenth-Century France.* Berkeley: University of California Press, 1993.

Stevens, Martin. "The Performing Self in Twelfth-Century Culture." *Viator* 9 (1978), 193–212.

Tatlock, J.S.P. "Geoffrey and King Arthur in Normannicus Draco." *Modern Philology* 31 (1933), 1–18.

"Geoffrey of Monmouth's *Vita Merlini*." *Speculum* 18 (1943), 265–87.

*The Legendary History of Britain: Geoffrey of Monmouth's Historia regum Britanniae and its Early Vernacular Versions.* Berkeley: University of California Press, 1950.

Thompson, Raymond H. "Gawain Against Arthur: The Impact of a Mythological Pattern upon Arthurian Tradition in Accounts of the Birth of Gawain." *Folklore* 85 (1974), 113–21.

Thomson, R.L. "*Owain: Chwedl Iarlles y Ffynnon*." In *The Arthur of the Welsh*, ed. Bromwich *et al.*, pp. 159–69.

Thorpe, Lewis, ed. *The Journey through Wales/The Description of Wales*. Harmondsworth, Middlesex: Penguin, 1978.

Türk, Egbert. *Nugae curialium: Le règne d'Henri II Plantagenêt (1145–1189) et l'éthique politique.* Geneva: Droz, 1977.

Turner, Ralph V. *Men Raised from the Dust: Administrative Service and Upward Mobility in Angevin England.* Philadelphia: University of Pennsylvania Press, 1988.

Uhlig, Claus. *Hofkritik in England des Mittelalters und der Renaissance. Studien zu einem Gemeinplatz der europäischen Moralistik.* Berlin: Walter de Gruyter, 1973.

Vance, Eugene. *Mervelous Signals: Poetics and Sign Theory in the Middle Ages.* Lincoln: University of Nebraska Press, 1986.

Warren, W.L. *Henry II.* London: Eyre Methuen, 1973.

White, Hayden. *Tropics of Discourse: Essays in Cultural Criticism.* Baltimore, Md.: Johns Hopkins, 1978.

"The Value of Narrativity in the Representation of Reality." *Critical Inquiry* 7 (1980), 5–27.

Wieber, James Leon. "A Translation and Literary Study of 'De Ortu Walwanii,' a Thirteenth-Century Romance." Ph.D. thesis, Michigan State University, 1974.

Williams, Daniel, ed. *England in the Twelfth Century.* Woodbridge, Suffolk: Boydell and Brewer, 1990.

Wright, Neil. "A New Arthurian Epitaph?" *Arthurian Literature* 13 (1995), 145–49.

Young, Charles R. *The Royal Forests of Medieval England.* Philadelphia: University of Pennsylvania Press, 1979.

Ziolkowski, Jan. "The Nature of Prophecy in Geoffrey of Monmouth's *Vita Merlini.*" In *Poetry and Prophecy: The Beginnings of a Literary Tradition.* Ed. James L. Kugel (Ithaca, New York: Cornell University Press, 1990), pp. 151–62.

# Index

# CAMBRIDGE STUDIES IN MEDIEVAL LITERATURE